Fifth Edition

Business Communication
for Managers

An Advanced Approach

John M. Penrose
San Diego State University

Robert W. Rasberry
Southern Methodist University

Robert J. Myers
Baruch College,
City University of New York

THOMSON

SOUTH-WESTERN

Australia · Canada · Mexico · Singapore · Spain · United Kingdom · United States

To Garnet and to Margaret—JMP
To Jenni, John Robert, and Paul Michael—RWR
To Clare and David—RJM

THOMSON
SOUTH-WESTERN

Business Communication for Managers: An Advanced Approach, 5e
John M. Penrose, Robert W. Rasberry, Robert J. Myers

Managing Editor:
Jack W. Calhoun

Editor-in-Chief:
George Werthman

Acquisitions Editor:
Jennifer L. Codner

Developmental Editor:
Taney H. Wilkins

Marketing Manager:
Larry Qualls

Production Editor:
Heather Mann

Manufacturing Coordinator:
Diane Lohman

Production House:
Lachina Publishing Services, Inc.

Printer:
Phoenix Color
Hagerstown, MD

Design Project Manager:
Bethany Casey

Cover and Internal Design:
Bethany Casey

Cover and Internal Photo:
Digital Vision, Ltd.

For more information
contact South-Western,
5191 Natorp Boulevard,
Mason, Ohio 45040.
Or you can visit our Internet site at:
http://www.swlearning.com

For permission to use material from this
text or product, contact us by
Tel (800) 730-2214
Fax (800) 730-2215
http://www.thomsonrights.com

Library of Congress Control Number:
2002116944

Preface

The appearance of this fifth edition marks several significant advances for both the text and for the study of business communication.

For the text, perhaps the most noticeable addition is the title change. After four editions dating back to 1989, we're transitioning the title—formerly *Advanced Business Communication*—and the content more to the needs of a business manager. Thus, the new title *Business Communication for Managers: An Advanced Approach* captures both the original focus on advanced topics for advanced readers, such as graduate students, junior and senior level undergraduate students, or business practitioners, and emphasizes the managerial locus of the material.

Over the years the way we communicate in business has changed. Today we rely on the Internet and associated technologies. We continue to move away from hard copy-based messages such as memos and letters, except for formal situations, and toward electronic messages systems, such as e-mail and instant messaging. While we still rely on appropriately formatted, hard copy reports, proposals, and instructions, the importance of the electronic medium is well established.

With our reliance on electronic media a new frustration has emerged—unwanted messages, or "spam"—which are slowing down our productivity and overwhelming our bandwidth. As we fight back with cable modems and faster computers, we also must juggle concerns for privacy and the ever-present need for virus and hacking protection.

The new technologies that affect how we communicate introduce new media and improve upon old ones. A few years ago fax machines, pagers/beepers and cell phones were at the beginning of their life cycle; now they are so commonplace we barely notice them. Cell phones are moving through many concurrent advances, such as integrated Internet connections, video capability, and text messaging. Personal digital assistants are no longer a gimmick but for many are now an essential business tool. Internet home pages are so common that businesses without one are something of a curiosity.

For all these changes to the way we communicate, the importance of communicating well has not diminished. Especially for managers, the value of a powerful PowerPoint® presentation, a well-phrased memorandum, a persuasive proposal, well-organized instructions, and a thorough, analytical report remains high. Research and anecdotal evidence continue to indicate that business people whose writing and speaking skills are weak are less likely to be hired initially, and do not rise as quickly or as high as those who do possess these skills. The intent of this text, then, is to help you improve these and other skills.

For the fifth edition, in addition to the title change, numerous other changes appear. Throughout the text are updates of the literature that support the foundational concepts; dozens of electronic sources supplement the classic literature and deliver the latest resources. All chapters received careful evaluation and modification, but several were dramatically updated or expanded. Chapter 9, Report Writing, has an amplified number of examples of report types and elements and Chapter 14, Media Management, has an expanded coverage of the oft-neglected interaction of a manger with the media. Chapter 13, Crisis Communication, has been largely revamped to include the crisis aspects of the September 11, 2001, disaster from a managerial perspective.

Found in this edition is a new chapter, Chapter 10, which instructs on the importance of writing effective instructions, documentation, and policies and procedures. Readers will quickly note the connection of these topics to the activities of managers.

We have moved the job search strategies section from the last editions, including resume and employment letters and the job interview chapters, to a separate companion text entitled *Employment Strategies for Career Success* (0-324-20005-6.)

Other changes abound throughout the text. For example, guidance on preparation of effective computerized slide shows, using software such as PowerPoint®, appear in multiple places. The end-of-chapter materials are totally revised. There are still Discussion Questions, but almost all are new to this edition. A new end-of-chapter pedagogical feature is the Communication in Action section that encourages readers to apply what they have learned in the chapter to business situations. Within Communication in Action is at least one Internet question that makes specific assignments that must involve the Internet. Finally, InfoTrac College Edition questions are integrated into the Communication in Action feature as well. This requires students to use this well-established and respected electronic research tool. Each new textbook includes a password for the student to use to access the InfoTrac as part of the class.

In keeping with our reliance on web pages and the Internet, a resource for this textbook to instructor and student alike is found on the book support website, http://penrose.swlearning.com. There you will find downloadable supplements for instructors (Instructor Manual and PowerPoint® slides) use as well as links and resources for students.

Other ancillaries include a printed Instructor's Manual with Transparency Masters (0-324-20052-8), an Instructor's Resource CD (0-324-20009-9) including the PowerPoint® presentation slides to assist with classroom presentation, the electronic Instructor's Manual with Transparency Masters, and an all-new Test Bank created specifically to assist in preparation of tests and quizzes. The Test Bank contains multiple-choice, short answer, and essay questions. Please contact the Academic Resource Center at 1-800-423-0563 or e-mail review@thomsonlearning.com to request these resources or to request a copy of *Employment Strategies for Career Success*.

The authors are pleased with this edition and hope you will agree with them on its value to students and business practitioners. Bringing this product to culmination has been the effort of a diverse and dedicated group of reviewers, support personnel, and editors.

One of the reviewers, Kathy Brzovic, of California State University at Fullerton, worked closely with the editors and authors. We especially appreciate her efforts and insight. We are also appreciative of the guidance from the other reviewers who guided us on making improvements to this edition. Those reviewers are:

Barbara E. Alpern
Walsh College

Dianna Briggs
University of Northern Iowa

Douglas A. Goings
Georgia College and State University

Sandra Ihle
University of Wisconsin

Linda M. LaDuc
University of Massachusetts, Amherst

Sally Lederer
University of Minnesota

Kenneth R. Mayer
Cleveland State University

Eltgad Roces
Pennsylvania State University, Hazelton

Paul R. Sawyer
Southeastern Louisiana University

Gretchen N. Vic
San Diego State University

Janet K. Winter
Central Missouri State University

Many thanks to Jennifer Codner, Acquisitions Editor; Taney Wilkins, Developmental Editor; and Heather Mann, Production Editor; and to all those at South-Western/Thomson Learning who worked to bring this product to you.

About the Authors

JOHN M. PENROSE is Professor of Business Communication and Chair of the Information and Decision Systems Department at San Diego State University. At SDSU he teaches graduate MBA and MS communication classes, as well as classes in the Executive MBA program. He taught at the University of Texas Graduate School of Business for 16 years. His research interests include computer graphics, nonverbal communication, and effective documentation. He has served as President of the Association for Business Communication and won its top awards. He serves on a number of editorial and review boards, is an active researcher, and is a consultant to business.

ROBERT W. RASBERRY, Ph.D. (University of Kansas) is a professor in the Management and Organizations Department in the Cox School of Business at Southern Methodist University. He teaches undergraduate, MBA, and Executive MBA courses in the areas of management, ethics, and leadership. He has authored journal and magazine articles, and has authored or co-authored several books. Two of his books are South-Western texts: *Employment Strategies for Career Success,* and *Effective Managerial Communication.* He regularly serves as a consultant and trainer to business.

ROBERT J. MYERS is Chair of the Department of Communication Studies and Director of the MA Program in Corporate Communication in the Weissman School of Arts and Sciences at Baruch College, CUNY. He is a member of the Public Relations Society of America (PRSA) and the New York Chapter of PRSA. He has co-authored two textbooks on business communication; contributed several chapters to a major handbook on executive communication; published original research on the public speaking of senior corporate leaders; and consulted in business, industry, and government for the past twenty years. He has also served on the editorial review boards of the *Journal of Business Communication* and the *Business Communication Quarterly* and is currently the managing editor of both publications. He served as founding director of the Bernard L. Schwartz Communication Institute at Baruch College (1997-1999), and since 1994 has been the Executive Director of the Association for Business Communication, an international professional society housed at Baruch College, with the mission of fostering excellence in business communication research, pedagogy and practice.

Brief Contents

Contents

Part One

Introduction to Business Communication for Managers

Chapter 1
Business Communication for Managers

Chapter 2
Information and Persuasion

Chapter 3
Advanced Visual Support for Managers

CHAPTER - 1

Business Communication for Managers

Welcome to the fast-paced world of advanced business communication—and to a paradox: for all the lip service given to the importance of communication, little is done to improve it. This paradox is especially noticeable in the business world, which focuses on bottom-line profits and performance. Managers proclaim the need for improved communication skills but often hesitate to invest in training their employees in communication skills. Managers see to it that those who are effective in communication are promoted and rewarded financially, but seldom do managers themselves have access to formal programs that are designed to improve these crucial skills.

Educational institutions—aware of the demand for communication skills—try to supply graduates with some degree of competence in communication. However, many demands compete for the students' attention; new topics work their way into the curriculum and new teaching methods are explored. One result is that for several decades the verbal skills of high school graduates have been slipping. Concern also exists about the skills of college graduates. A recent report from the Carnegie Foundation for the Advancement of Teaching takes a clear stand on communication: "The foundation for a successful undergraduate experience is proficiency in the written and spoken word."[1] Examining the undergraduate experience, the report clearly attacks the inadequate amount of instruction and the approaches used in the teaching of communication in the United States.

College programs that prepare students for business feel pressure on their curricula, too. For example, in the last 15 years the study and use of computers have grown, typically, from one undergraduate course to inclusion in almost every business course. Laptops are often required tools in advanced business courses. To allow examination of new topics, such as computer applications, colleges often sacrifice basic skills, such as writing and speaking. All too often, one business communication course and several English courses are expected to turn around 20 years of laxity in communication training and to produce a graduate possessing the written and oral communication skills demanded by business.

Unfortunately, graduate business programs often widen this gap between what is wanted and what is delivered. The graduating MBA or MS who has solid writing and speaking skills and an appreciation for when and how to use them is the exception. Those with communication skills usually have acquired it informally, over many years, from a maturity of vision few hold. Those who work and seek a graduate business degree at the same time may be better able than others to see the importance of effective communication in business and its lack of attention in the graduate curriculum.

Communication skills can be taught relatively quickly and are not particularly difficult to acquire, especially when a person has a solid foundation in the basics. When students are bright and motivated, and the skills being taught are tailored to them, the improvement can be dramatic.

Consider yourself lucky to be exposed to advanced business communication. The skills you acquire will assist you in studying, in acquiring a better job or more responsibility on your present job, and in doing that job more effectively than those who lack the skills. For a "fast-tracker"—the person with a mission, plans for how to achieve it, and the skills and knowledge that will be required—extraordinary communication skills are a necessity.

This book is written for use in an advanced business communication course, such as management, organizational communication, or business communication. The text is especially appropriate for advanced undergraduate studies and for graduate-level studies when these students have some knowledge of and experience in business. The text works well in business training seminars for the same reasons.

The goal of this chapter is to examine the crucial place and function of communication in business. To accomplish this goal, we look at the views of business leaders and scholarly literature as they relate to the importance of communication skills, to communication in business, to communication and management, to communication and ethics, to communication in cross-cultural messages, and to fears about communication. Finally, this chapter identifies how top businesspeople differ in their communication from others in business.

The Importance of Communication Skills

Communication does not exist in a vacuum; it is not something you do in the absence of other information. While you may practice accounting or finance in a mutually exclusive fashion, when you communicate, it is usually about something other than communication. Communication is a process that oils the gears that turn the machinery of business. Supporting this process are the skills of communication—skills that occupy as much as 90 percent of a top executive's working day.[2]

Research supports the view that communication skills are important in business. For example, in a study of 139 Texas business executives, knowledge of business communication was rated very important by 85 percent (far ahead of knowledge of principles of management, at 20 percent). The skills that require attention, according to 100 randomly selected Fortune 500 executives, are oral presentations, memo-writing, basic grammar, informational report-writing, and analytical report-writing. Another study of executives in Fortune 500 companies supports these findings but extends the important communication skills to include external communication and technical applications.[3]

In 1995, The National Business Education Association developed a set of standards for business school graduates. The standards were developed by business educators and then reviewed and approved by business professionals. The standards listed five communication skill areas: (1) Foundations of communication (written, oral, social and business listening, and informational reading); (2) Social communication; (3) Technological communication; (4) Employment communication; and (5) Organizational communications.[4] We will cover all of these areas, which we, too, believe are critical for the advanced business communication graduate.

Visual Skills

About 85 percent of our learning comes from visual stimuli; when spoken and visual stimuli are combined, enhanced learning can occur. Additional studies of comprehension endorse the value of visual support. For example, when participants only listened to a message, they remembered 70 percent of the message after three hours and only 10 percent after three days. Using only a visual message, recall was 72 percent after three hours and 35 percent after three days. These figures jumped dramatically, however, to 85 percent and 65 percent, respectively, when both spoken and visual communication were used. Other studies substantiate these results.[5]

Even though businesspeople have long been aware of the visual element of communication, they have been negligent in paying it much respect. Perhaps this lack of respect occurs because visual communication exists in a more artistic realm (as opposed to more central business issues, such as finance or management). However, numerous studies of the value of visual matter (particularly in supporting written and spoken communication) and of new technologies for preparing and sharing such visuals have increased the attention given to visual support.

The rationale for recall of pictures versus words lies in the speed advantage of learning from pictures. This speed is due at least partially to the ability of pictures to evoke mental images. Therefore, both written and spoken presentations benefit from visual support. Seeing words improves recall; seeing pictures provides even more benefits.

Balchin and Coleman extend the distinction between forms of visual communication to four basic intellectual skills: literacy, numeracy, articulacy, and graphicacy.[6] **Literacy** includes the basic skills of reading and writing. **Numeracy** expresses communication in numbers and mathematical notation. **Articulacy** brings in the art of spoken communication. **Graphicacy** connotes the visual communication of relationships not found in the other three skills. Integration of these four skills, the authors believe, leads to truly effective communication. As we settle into the twenty-first century, an additional literacy is emerging: **technical literacy**, which is the ability to appropriately use technological tools in an information society. Such tools include the Internet, e-mail, Web sites, and computers in general.[7] Certainly technical literacy is rapidly changing. Typing has given way to keyboarding; some rely on computer input by voice rather than through the fingers.[8] In many ways technical literacy will determine one's ability to communicate through the other four literacies.

By 2005, it is predicted that 75 percent of Americans will regularly access the Internet (50 percent in 2002). Streaming media will be a reality, with 50 percent of U.S. households having high-speed connections, although only 10 percent of the world's population will have Internet access. Cellular phones or other wireless devices will be used by 90 percent of Americans, with 50 percent accessing the Net with those devices. Over 31 percent of the world's population will be using wireless devices.[9]

The need to teach graphics (as well as speaking and writing) is supported by the research of Pollock and others. Their study of 150 executives listed in *Who's Who in Finance and Industry* recommends teaching graphic analysis to better prepare the advanced student.[10]

Chapter 3 of this text is devoted to understanding the role of visual support of written and spoken business communication. That chapter also explores various methods of preparing visual support.

Written Skills

Most studies—particularly the older ones—indicate that people see written communication as a neglected skill. Indeed, 79 percent of 218 executives in one study identified the ability to write as one of the most neglected business skills.[11] Within that same group, 44 percent said writing more clearly, in a better-organized way, was a major goal. Approximately the same percentage felt that better writing skills increased their productivity and was of high importance in their own career advancement.

When *Fortune* magazine reporters talked to successful corporate executives about business training, executive after executive said, in frustration, "Teach them to write better." The plea was not for the ability to do fancy writing but, rather, fundamental writing, "with clarity, precision, brevity, and force of logic." Hoyt Hudson, vice president of information systems at InterAccess, adds this: "One of the most surprising features of the information revolution is that the momentum has turned back to the written word. Someone who can come up with precise communication has a real advantage in today's environment."[12]

Young employees also understand their lack of effective writing skills. Hiemstra et al. discovered that 59 percent of CPAs believed that when they entered their profession their writing skills were not adequate for effective communication with other business professionals.[13] A similar study of CPAs found 80 percent "felt most deficient in the ability to organize ideas effectively and to write concisely."[14] Leaders in the accounting profession, including both practicing CPAs and educators, have indicated how important they believe written communication to be. In 1990 the Accounting Education Change Commission stated that accounting graduates *must possess* communication skills. This was followed in 1994 by a joint statement issued by the Institute of Management Accountants and the Financial Executive Institute, asking that college accounting programs increase the communication-skills emphasis. This resulted in the addition of a required communication course in many business schools. Also in 1994, the CPA exam began to be used in evaluating candidates' writing skills.[15] Another exam, the Graduate Management Admission Test (GMAT), has also added a writing component to its entrance examination.[16]

Companies appear to be increasing their emphasis on internal written communication skills and are therefore offering more training in this area. In some studies, the recommendation for areas needing improvement is quite specific; for example, one such study identifies long and short reports, progress reports, and analytical reports.[17]

The authors of this text consider the skill of writing to be so important that a total of seven chapters are devoted to the subject. These chapters are arranged in two sections: brief messages and expanded messages. The contents of the writing chapters cover all the writing needs expressed by employers that were noted in the studies mentioned above.

Spoken Skills

Not all the experts or surveys point to written communication as the most important skill area. Many suggest that spoken communication, which may take up more of an executive's time than written communication, is more important and demands more training.[18] Executives listed specific kinds of spoken communication: person-to-person, telephone, informal group discussions, formal group meetings, interviews, and formal presentations.[19]

Business professionals often remarked that oral skills are used more frequently than written skills at the beginning corporate levels.[20] Presentation skills have also been used by managers as a discriminator for employment performance.[21]

Educators and employers, however, do not always agree on the relative importance of the specific areas of business communication. In a survey of business communication educators and employers, employers placed much heavier emphasis on oral communication, interpersonal skills, and listening. Educators, on the other hand, advocated written communication and theoretical aspects of communication.[22]

Sometimes the effects of spoken communication in the workplace are subtle. Tannen, among others, chronicles differences in spoken communication in men versus women.[23] She believes lessons learned in childhood carry over to the workplace. Boys learn to play in larger groups, follow a leader's directives, and use language to call attention to themselves. Girls learn to play with a best friend, establish consensus, and ostracize those who seek to stand out. These behaviors that everyone must follow but few recognize may translate into females being disadvantaged in a male-dominated business world or even having problems with other females when they "break the rules." For suggestions on how to communicate across genders, see Table 1.1.

While many surveys underscore the importance of either written or spoken communication, others encourage a balance between the two. This combination of topics is strongly endorsed in the development of an MBA business communication course syllabus. Academic experts, managers, and MBA recipients agree on the essential nature of both written and spoken communication. Both, they believe, need to be addressed in MBA and advanced undergraduate-level business communication courses.[24]

Four different chapters of this text will emphasize the importance of spoken skills: Chapter 11 examines formal business presentations; Chapter 12 focuses on person-to-person and small-group meeting management; Chapter 14 introduces cutting-edge skills so you can effectively respond to interviews with reporters; and Chapter 16 describes how to make a classroom or office case presentation.

Listening Skills

With speaking comes its equally important counterpart: listening. Some estimates suggest we spend up to 70 percent of our workday communicating, with 45 percent of that time spent in listening activities. Interestingly, most research indicates we do not listen well.[25]

Table 1.1 **Strategies for Cross-Gender Oral Communication**

Some strategies for women dealing with men in business include the following.

1. Speak up! Don't allow yourself to be interrupted.
2. Avoid tag endings that may make you sound unsure of yourself, such as "isn't it?" "don't you think?" or "is that OK?"
3. Don't take male comments too personally. Remember that most men are direct and like to get straight to the point.
4. Focus on being logical and avoid giving unnecessary details (storytelling).
5. Avoid personal items. Stick to job-related issues and current affairs.

Some strategies for men dealing with women in business include the following.

1. Focus on being polite by using words such as "please" and "thank you."
2. Avoid monopolizing conversations, speaking for the woman, or interrupting her.
3. Don't call a woman names such as "honey," "dear," or "sweetheart."
4. Avoid barking commands to women. They prefer and respond much better to polite requests.
5. Pay attention when women speak. Use good eye contact, nod, and use "I'm listening" sounds such as "uh-huh."

Source: Adapted from C. Tymson, "Business Communication—Bridging the Gender Gap," retrieved November 11, 1999, at **http://www.tymson.com.au/articles.html**.

Listening is a critically needed skill in business.[26] A recent survey of executives revealed that 80 percent believed listening is the most important skill needed in American corporate offices. Its productive usage has been proven to enhance employee job performance and career advancement.[27] While communication skills are usually listed as a core managerial competence, the skill of listening often finds its way to the *top* of the communication skill list.[28]

Research by Maes et al. has found listening skills ranked second in importance, but first in frequency of use.[29] Brownell's research displayed that when managers actually see weak listening skills in employees, they attempt to present listening instruction that improves the needed skills.[30]

Wolvin and Coakley contributed significantly to the place of listening training by developing a listening taxonomy classification system. Their five levels of listening skills are used by managers to help employees understand how they receive and send information. At the first level, **discrimination**, a person cognitively interprets auditory and visual content received from others without additional behavior required. At the **comprehensive** level, a person sorts information for understanding and retention. Again, response is not required. All employees use the first two levels continually at every stage of business interaction. Level three, **therapeutic** listening, resembles the interactive process used by counselors. Here the employee's behavior creates a supportive climate where they empathetically hear and behaviorally respond with feedback to others. At the **critical** assessment level, a listener either accepts or rejects a speaker's verbal offering. Appropriate behavioral responses follow the listener's decision. If persuaded to agree they act in positive response. If they disagree they fail to take action. The final level, **appreciative**, is the everyday stage of basic interpersonal listening for enjoyment. Here we gravitate toward, and interact with, people who listen to us.[31]

At every level of the listening process a listener uses both verbal and nonverbal attending behavior that enhances the particular level. Nonverbal attending behavior includes factors like body movement, gestures, eye contact, and facial expressions. Verbal behavior includes making comments that encourage or discourage enhanced communication. Healthy organizational communication is promoted when listening behavior is both appropriate and effective.

Lewis and Reinsch labeled effective listening as when a listener follows directions, gives appropriate eye contact, and displays general attentiveness. Research indicates business managers do not listen well.[32] Hunt and Cusella surveyed training directors of Fortune 500 companies and found they rated their managers and subordinates between "fair" and "poor" on listening effectiveness.[33] Barker et al. found in their study of U.S. and Canadian managers, who were also leaders in their professional management associations, that almost 75 percent of the respondents classified their own listening behavior as passive or detached, "less-effective," listeners.[34]

Because employees communicate throughout the day, listening training focuses on helping them develop better listening skills, which enhances work performance and the quality of their personal lives. It is also a common denominator in being promoted. Sadly, though, listening effectiveness is often unchanged by corporate listening training programs. The Barker et al. study found this was because of the short duration of such training; "listening must be practiced, and practiced correctly, for one to retain or sharpen proficiency."[35] The research by Pearce et al. showed that university classrooms were ideal training grounds for improving listening skills, because of continual practice sessions.[36]

As advanced business students you have a wonderful opportunity to work on enhancing this important skill area in your numerous business classes. Case courses are especially good for this training. Chapter 15 presents several steps you can take to become a more effective listener. You can sharpen your listening effectiveness right away when you:

- Mentally and physically prepare for each dialogue;
- Use attending skills, like facial expressions or body language, to interact with each speaker;
- Ask clarifying questions at appropriate times, but do not interrupt a speaker;
- Know the other's point of view, but don't judge or jump to conclusions; and
- Provide feedback.

Reading Skills

While you probably agree that visual, written, spoken, and listening communication skills are critical factors in your future employment success, the area of reading skills may not rate as high for you. Most of us see the critical necessity of reading as a given. However, a recent report by the Conference Board of Canada, "Employability Skills 2000+," noted that the sum of a person's employability is the skills, attitudes, and behaviors needed to progress in today's work world. Predominant on the Canadian list of skills is "reading and understanding information, then sharing the information."[37]

Certainly not everyone reads in the same fashion, but because businesspeople spend so much time reading e-mail, reports, memos, or letters, some suggestions for improving your critical reading ability are in order:

1. Think about the title of the manuscript if it has one; what does it suggest regarding the content? Is it a comprehensive article ("A Thorough Discussion of . . ."), a historical or documentary review ("A Review of . . ."), an organization of existing information ("A Taxonomy of . . ."), a position statement ("The School Board's Failing Marks"), or persuasion to action ("A Proposal to . . .")?

2. Get a feel for the whole package. This might come from a table of contents, which should be scrutinized for major sections and amount of space devoted to each of them. If there is an abstract or executive summary, certainly read it and reread it. However, be aware that it may not fairly represent the article. Keep an open and critical mind. If you find no table of contents or abstract, page through the article and pay attention to sections, headings, and subheadings. Note also the relative space given to the sections.

3. Now—finally—read the text. First read it quickly for an overall feel for the content. You then will need to reread for deeper understanding of the content. Others prefer their first reading to be careful, slow, and methodical. With either technique, consider highlighting (to capture your reactions) or annotating (which combines underlining or highlighting but adds margin notes that interpret or react to the keyed phrases).

    Annotation is the more valuable approach if you need a thorough analysis of a complex message. You might want to generate your own system of highlighter colors or penciled circles, underlines, brackets, or arrows to represent places of confusion, disagreement, importance, or summary.

4. Examine tables, graphs, or other illustrations and think about how they complement or supplement the text. You might also challenge them to see if they misrepresent data, as discussed in Chapter 3.

5. Compare the message to other known information and challenge its assumptions and arguments. One approach for testing arguments is the "ABC Test" that asks: Is the information *a*ppropriate, is the support *b*elievable, and is the support *c*onsistent and *c*omplete?[38]

Following these steps should help you to read more critically and with greater understanding and comprehension. It may be more memorable as well. The strategic process of reading case situations will help you polish this skill area. In Chapter 15, we describe several steps to take in reading to analyze, remember, and solve problems through the use of basic business cases.

Communication in Business

While the results of research presented so far suggest that communication is important in business, the focus has been more on the importance of communication itself and less on its business application. This section presents the importance of communication in three main business dimensions: obtaining a job, doing a job, and maintaining and improving a career. You can find additional support in *Employment Strategies for Career Success*, a companion booklet to this text.

Communication and Obtaining a Job

Communication skills can help you acquire a first job or a better job. Surveys of business recruiters emphasize the esteem they have for communication skills. One hundred forty recruiters picked written and oral communication skills as the most important ability for applicants—over computer sciences, accounting, management, and six other business areas. Studies of personnel managers, upper-level managers, business managers, and businesspeople drew the same conclusion. Another study concluded, "The most common skill sought by MBA hiring organizations was communication (verbal and nonverbal), with 85 percent of respondents including this characteristic on the candidate-evaluation form."[39] A study of 500 managers determined oral communication was the highest-ranked competency in hiring decisions.[40] Additional testimonials from individual recruiters and in the popular press abound.[41]

Communication on the Job

On the job, poor communication skills can be harmful. A study of 443 companies asked whether they were happy with worker skills. Eighty percent said employees need improvement in their written communication skills.[42] A survey of business school deans and personnel directors of Fortune 500 companies clearly identified poor writing skills as the most common weakness of young executives. On the other hand, the survey identified the most successful executives as those who can communicate their own ideas to others. Not only are business practitioners more successful when they possess effective communication skills, but superior communication with subordinates also is considered the single most important factor in enhancing job satisfaction and group cohesiveness.[43]

Communication Related to Promotions

Just as communication skills are important in getting and doing a job, they also continue to support businesspeople throughout their business careers. Larry McConnell, director of information technology at the Massachusetts Registry of Motor Vehicles, says that unless you can communicate, your career will level off.[44] Other executives attest that ability to communicate facilitates promotions, upward mobility, and success.

In a study that examined 5,299 newly promoted executives, the authors found that these executives cited communication as playing the most significant role in their promotions.[45] Both oral and written communication were listed by nearly 80 percent of the executives as the single most important factor in the career preparation of a young person. Finance and accounting ranked second and third, respectively. Bennett and Olney's study of vice presidents at Fortune 500 companies determined that 97.7 percent of them believe communication skills had boosted their advancement to a top executive position.[46]

Communication and Management

Although some writers separate communication study from management study, the two are tightly interwoven. Management communication, as a discipline, has a longer tradition than business communication.

Most of the major writers on management philosophy stress the central role of communication in successful management. The trend of identifying this central role continues today. Table 1.2 presents a chronology of management views of communication from early in the 20th century.[47]

Also stressing the important joint role of communication and management, former *Harvard Business Review* editor David Ewing says, "Management communication is the number-one problem in business today. While the technology has advanced in leaps and bounds, managers' and academics' understanding of the substance of the process has not."[48]

Table 1.2   **Management's View of Communication**

Year	Person	Observation
1916	Fayol	Managerial work is a set of composite functions that includes communication.
1930s	Gulick	Management has seven functional areas, including directing and reporting (which include communication).
1938	Barnard	The first executive function is providing a system of communication.
1957	Simon	The administrative process cannot influence the decisions of the individual without communication.
1966	Katz & Kahn	The exchange of information and transmission of meaning are the very essence of an organization.
1973	Mintzberg	Managerial jobs have ten working roles; communication and interpersonal relations are found in three of the roles.
1974	Drucker	Communication is one of five basic management functions.
1982	Peters and Waterman	Open, informal communication is one of eight characteristics of the best-run American companies.
1983	Kanter	The most common roadblock for managers to overcome is poor communication.
1988	Iacocca	You can have brilliant ideas, but if you can't get them across, your ideas won't get you anywhere.
1991	Blanchard	Communication is a basic skill for the effective one-minute manager.
1995	Gates	Communication is the new revolution; the information superhighway is part of it.
1997	Kotter	Without credible communication, and a lot of it, employee hearts and minds are never captured.
2000	Amelio	Developing excellent communication skills is absolutely essential to effective leadership.

Communication and Ethics

A day seldom passes but that media present accounts of unethical or illegal behavior: improprieties at banks and brokerage houses, inappropriate political influence, and devious business dealings. Other types of unethical or illegal conduct reported daily include: conflict of interest, employee discrimination, undercutting product safety and quality, cybercrime, sexual harassment, rights violations, lying, theft, and the list goes on. In 2001 the business world was shaken as Enron, a Fortune Top Ten company, was charged with creative accounting, deceptive partnerships, manufactured earnings, and insider trading. Pulled in with Enron were financial giants such as J.P. Morgan Chase, Citigroup, Merrill Lynch, Bank of America, Barclays, and others. Big Five accounting firm Arthur Andersen, guilty of shredding documents and accused of participating in the Enron scheme, almost totally collapsed.[49] Communication played a critical role in Enron's fall. Internal documents such as e-mails, memoranda, and excerpts of minutes from meetings of Enron's board and the board's financial committee reveal the extent of unethical activity.[50] Clearly no single individual or organization was responsible for Enron's demise; rather a collective culture of indifference to ethical standards was communicated to all parties involved.

In order to better understand the ethical considerations confronting business today, this section will first examine the nature of business ethics, the impact of ethics on employees and the organization, and the critical way ethics drives communication issues. The second part of the section focuses on how technology has raised new concerns about communication ethics.

Business Ethics

Ethics are standards of behavior that tell us what we should do in a variety of situations. Some standards are codified in the form of government laws and regulations, others are set down as company policies, and still others are embodied in an individual's character, or what we often call integrity. As an advanced business communicator, you will need to determine your ethical responsibilities as an individual, as a member of an organization, and as a member of society. Read Figure 1.1 and see if you would say "yes" to the questions.

In the business discipline ethics is often examined from three concentric circles of responsibility. First, individual ethics focuses on the character and behavior of an individual. Second, organizational ethics examines the workplace behavior of individuals and of the group. Third, social ethics examines the systemic impact of business actions in the global arena.

Individual Ethics

Individual ethics can be seen in two ways: as ethical conduct, or the actions of people, and as ethical character, which tells us something about the nature of who individuals are as people.[51]

Behavior. Many philosophical theories are drawn upon to analyze the behavior of both people and organizations. Two primary theories consider the ends and the means of behavior. **Consequential behavior** is end-result oriented. If it is selfish in

A survey of 250 meeting planners and industry suppliers asked 12 questions and compared answers to an ethics experts panel's feelings. Selected results appear below.

	Percent saying "yes"		
Question	Meeting Planners	Suppliers	Ethics Rating*
Have you ever "borrowed" company office supplies for personal use?	64%	**	2.5
Have you ever "stretched the truth" on a résumé to make yourself look more appealing?	49%	**	9.5
Have you ever spent a good portion of a work day on personal business?	36%	**	7.5
Have you or has anyone in your organization ever accepted a personal vacation or similar "perk" from a supplier as a thank-you for booking business?	33%	63%	7.5
Have you ever padded an expense report?	37%	49%	6.5

* "1" is minor infraction, "10" major violation
** not reported

Source: Melinda Ligos, "True Confessions—Begging, Borrowing, and . . . Stealing?" *Successful Meetings*, November 1999, pp. 34–40.

nature, and focused strictly on individual gains, it is called **ethical egoism**. If the behavior is concerned with generating the best result, for the greatest number of people, or the greatest balance of good over harm, it is called **utilitarianism**.

Behavior that is **duty-based** concentrates on whether the action itself is good (truthful, promise-keeping, fair, respectful of others), and whether job responsibilities, ethical codes, or laws bind the businessperson to behave accordingly.[52] Within this concentration two other theories emerge. The **rights approach** examines the duty we have to protect and respect the moral rights of people. "This approach starts from the belief that humans have a dignity based on their ability to choose freely what they do with their lives, and have a right not to be treated as mere means to other ends."[53] Common rights that we should all enjoy are life, liberty, freedom to choose the life we want to lead, to be told the truth, not to be enslaved or injured, and so on.

Justice is another duty-based approach. Managers have a duty to treat employees fairly and equally, or to at least tell them why equality is not possible. Laws protecting civil rights are often the guides that we use in determining correct behavior in this category.

Character. Ethical activity can also be analyzed by focusing on the virtuous characteristics of the individual businessperson, such as courage, temperance, compassion, integrity, prudence, self-control, honesty, and fidelity.

Some ethicists separate out the virtue of compassion as an ethical standard. "This approach suggests that relationships are the basis of all human society and compassion and concern for others is essential to relationships and to the function of society. Therefore, ethical actions should always serve the interests of others with whom one deals and should serve to deepen the relationships one has with family, community, officemates, and even unfamiliar individuals we encounter."[54]

Organizational Ethics

When unethical events occur, a person's public image falls under attack. As a businessperson you sometimes do not have to be guilty of actual improprieties. If the organization, division, or office that you are managing is the place for the wrong behavior, you may be seen as guilty by association. Regardless of the specific behavior that occurred, CEOs of several large corporations have seen their golden image shattered within the past few years. Witness: "Andersen CEO Joseph Berardino . . . Richard McGinn at Lucent, Durk Jager at Procter & Gamble, Doug Ivestger at Coca-Cola, Jill Barad at Mattel, Richard Thoman at Xerox, Jacques Nasser at Ford Motor, Chuck Conaway at Kmart, Al Dunlap at Sunbeam, and Masatoshi Ono at Bridgestone/Firestone."[55]

Such examples represent strong organizations and individuals that suddenly experienced a crisis. Although crisis events do not necessarily signal illegal or unethical behavior, illegal and unethical behavior may have either caused the problem or else become a part of the process that individuals or companies follow in trying to solve crisis situations. Chapter 13 describes crisis events in detail, and the critical ethical action and communicative behavior individuals and organizations take in bringing such events to an end.

Within the business world our ethical conduct and character come into play through our personal and workplace behavior and communication. At Enron, executive presentations were under attack for being dishonest and deceptive. The CEO, Jeffrey Skilling, was not believed when he declared to the U.S. Senate investigating committees that he had absolutely no knowledge of any wrongdoing taking place in his company.

Coercion and manipulation are often used by businesspeople who lack character and virtue, elements that comprise the foundation of ethical communication. These elements distinguish normatively the roles and responsibilities of ethical communicators, and the boundaries within which they must act.

Many companies help employees stay legal and ethical by creating an ethical climate and developing a code of ethics (a set of rules to follow), or an ethical credo (values that the companies uphold). Organizational ethical codes and credos are not new. J.C. Penney began as the Golden Rule Company. Its code was written in 1913. The Johnson and Johnson credo was penned in 1941, and is credited with having helped J&J executives make critical decisions during its mid-1980s Tylenol product-tampering crisis.

In organizations that have a strong concern with all employees being ethical and doing the right thing, an ethics office usually exists. This is especially true following the 1991 establishment of the U.S. Sentencing Commission and the Federal Sentencing Guidelines (FSG). "In a response to deter white-collar crime, all business executives, for the first time, became responsible for the misdeeds of their companies and subordinates. In essence, with this law the government considers a corporation to be a moral agent, responsible for its employees' conduct. The FSG gave tremendous impetus to the establishment of hundreds of ethics offices, for it provided an incentive for organizations to develop and implement ethics and compliance programs."[56]

An ethics office makes it easier for an organization to communicate with its people about legal and ethical expectations and processes for doing the right thing. According to the Ethics Officer Association, a benchmarked ethics program includes the following 12 items:

1. An organizational vision statement,
2. A values statement that connects the vision and expected ethical behavior,
3. A company code of ethics,
4. An ethics officer who oversees the administration of the ethics program,
5. An ethics committee that reviews company policy and practices,
6. An ethics communication strategy,
7. A mandatory ethics training program for all organizational personnel,
8. An ethics help line where employees can call in suspicious behavior,
9. A measurement of how the program works and rewards for employees who do the right thing,
10. A monitoring and tracking system for how well policies are carried out correctly,
11. A periodic evaluation for the entire ethics program, and
12. Ethical leadership by top management.[57]

All individuals have ways of devising their own "quick tests" to tell when they are approaching the line between right and wrong. Rotarian Herbert J. Taylor designed one such test in 1932. Taylor was asked to take charge of a company facing bankruptcy. He created a 24-word code of ethics for his employees. Rotary International adopted the code in 1943. All Rotary Club members at weekly meetings recite it. It asks: "Of the things we think, say, or do:

Is it the truth?
Is it fair to all concerned?
Will it build goodwill and better friendships?
Will it be beneficial to all concerned?"[58]

Examine your own behavior. Figure 1.2 gives four sample questions like those used in organizational ethics training.

Social Ethics

The third of our three ethical arenas is the larger social and global marketplace. Both individual and organizational ethical behavior impact this third area. When one CEO proposes to a corporate board of directors that massive downsizing is in order to cut costs and boost yearly profits, and the organization follows through with the downsizing and fails to tell employees that money in their retirement plans was not protected, both of those actions tremendously impact society. As a result of the numerous unethical deeds of the early 2000s, society has called for new rules to govern organizations and their managers. These new rules are evolving from public-interest groups, the political parties, and leading corporations.

Figure 1.2	Legal or Ethical—How Do You Score?

Assume you work for one of the major brokerage houses as an analyst. Would the following behaviors be legal? Ethical?

1. You become aware that one of your clients has a new process that could lead to sizeable profits from a new product. The news is not public. Would it be legal to buy stock in the company? Ethical?

2. Based on #1 above, you chat with a friend about the situation and are overheard by a person nearby. Can that person buy stock before the public announcement? Would it be ethical?

3. Your boss offers to let you in on some insider trading that you both know is illegal as a favor for something you did for her. Ethical?

4. A broker friend at another firm recommends buying stock in an unknown organization and appears to have inside information. You don't ask any questions. Can you buy stock in the company?

Answers. Legal? 1, 3, and 4 are illegal. Ethical? As is so often the case, it depends on whom you ask and your own values and principles.

Source: Modified from Thor Valdmanis and Tom Lowry in "Wall Street's New Breed Revives Inside Trading," *USA Today,* November 4, 1999, p. B-1.

What are an organization's responsibilities? On one side there is a large group that takes a narrow, **stockholder** view of corporate responsibility. They believe, as Milton Friedman has long suggested, that an organization's primary responsibility is to maximize profits for its owners. This should happen within the boundaries of open and free competition and by obeying the laws that govern society. Friedman and others argue that managers are not trained in social work, and should not be pushed into compliance of spending stockholder's money on social causes—that is, refraining from price increases, spending money on equipment required by law but not wanted by the corporation, or hiring the hard-core unemployed.[59]

On the other side a segment of society takes a broader, **stakeholder** view of organizations. They see organizations as artificial persons, created by society, but made up of individuals who set goals and policies and perform actions that impact society as a whole. Out of this operation arises great social and economic power. That power must be channeled toward society in responsible ways. In fact the legitimacy of organizations is based on the presumption that they exist to serve a moral purpose in society by providing needed goods and services, rather than on the ability to maximize profits. Within the arena of stockholder-stakeholder responsibility the many social issues of the 2000s are being played out. These issues include corporate governance, equity and fairness, environmental and ecological concerns, employment and respect issues, and the public-private sector relationships.

Regardless of how the above issues will be resolved, corporations in the years to follow will find their practices and products being repeatedly subject to moral scrutiny. While examination of ethical issues is not the primary domain of communication studies, certainly the communication of messages in an ethical fashion is germane to the study of advanced business communication. Therefore, appearing throughout this text are comments, suggestions, and case studies recalling the need for ethical behavior.

Ethics and Technology

On August 25, 2000, Emulex, a fiber-optic communications equipment company, experienced a crisis. Bloomberg, a leading financial news service, reported the Emulex chief executive had resigned and the company had restated its earnings for the past two years. Within 15 minutes the price of Emulex shares dropped from $103 to $45 a share. Other news services quickly reported the story. The truth was, the story was a lie. Emulex was the victim of someone outside the organization issuing a fake press release.[60]

Technology has introduced new concerns about ethics and communication. To give you a flavor of how questions of ethics work their way into communication, consider how easily photographs that we see daily in the media can be digitally modified. Here are some incidents:

- When actor Dustin Hoffman was digitally given high heels and an evening gown in a *Los Angeles Magazine* story, he was awarded $3 million in a lawsuit over the image.
- *Time* magazine was criticized for altering a cover picture of O. J. Simpson to make him look more sinister.
- *Newsweek* upset the Society of Professional Journalists for touching up the teeth of Bobbi McCaughey, the woman who gave birth to septuplets.[61]
- A newspaper acquires a photograph of a prominent person who is visiting the city. The problem is that the person is obviously holding a cigarette. Because the newspaper does not want to promote smoking, an electronic darkroom is used to remove the offending cigarette.[62]

Photographs, drawings, and commercial designs can now be easily and quickly scanned with high resolution into a computer, modified slightly (to avoid copyright infringement), and issued as one's own work. Software is available with hundreds of images, but an inexpensive scanner can duplicate images from magazines or newspapers at no cost. Laws are relatively clear about taking someone else's copyrighted work, but the issue of how much electronic modification may legally occur is still being decided.

Another ethical and legal consideration that is emerging but not yet resolved relates to the ownership of another person's text or graphic image. The ease with which one can scan text from a publication; capture a graphic image, a digital music file, or source code from a Web page on the Internet; or locate and copy original text via electronic information databases is alarming.

Electronic Plagiarism

Electronic plagiarism is the term applied to this problem. Plagiarism is using another person's ideas or phrasing as your own work, without giving credit. E-plagiarism is the electronic process of doing the same. It is a growing problem on college campuses. Three events brought its seriousness to light. In May 2000, a science professor at the University of California-Berkeley found 45 out of 300 term papers had material that had been electronically lifted. In May 2001, a study disclosed that a Rutgers University professor had found 15 percent of the required term papers in his classes had been obtained from Web sites or term-paper "mills." Also in the study, 52 percent of the students had copied sentences from the Internet without crediting them. A University of Virginia physics professor found that out of 1,500 student papers, 122 had been plagiarized. In some instances passages were identical, while in others entire papers were the same.[63]

Colleges and professors are taking the offense on this issue. In each of the above violations the professor was using software created to detect e-plagiarism. When students submitted their papers by e-mail, or turned them in with a data disk, their files were converted into digital mathematical algorithms, which were then sent to virtually every Internet site. Feedback disclosed the copied material with as few as six words and the URL where it was located.[64]

Ethically, the use of plagiarized work is dishonest and wrong. It devalues another's work and it allows the offender to take unfair advantage of another person. To protect yourself, your colleagues, and your business, observe the following precautions.

Do Not:
- use a paper purchased, or obtained free, from an online research term-paper service or competitive intelligence company;
- use another colleague's work without that person's approval;
- use a paper written for you by a colleague or parent;
- use a paper or materials from an online source without proper acknowledgment;
- use electronic material (written, graphic, photo, etc.) and citing documentation, yet leaving out quotations; and
- use portions of electronic data without proper citation.[65]

Do:
- use your own ideas and words; and
- give credit for material you use.[66]

Cross-Cultural Communication

Cross-cultural communications support international business, and international business is the business of the 2000s and beyond. Between the 1980s and 2000, international trade increased three times faster than the world's gross domestic product. This produced great potential for both countries and multinational corporations.[67] Certain countries like Singapore, Taiwan, and Hong Kong in the Pacific Rim acquired attention for the strength of their economies, management styles, productivity, and innovativeness. Presently China, Vietnam, and Cambodia are making rapid strides to develop their economic infrastructure. The focus during the early part of the 2000s has shifted to the European Community. Dramatic changes have been made in Europe's formerly communist countries, and the shift in 2002 to the euro as a common currency has added economic strength to the European Union. Spain, Portugal, and Argentina likewise have taken advantage of this growing economic reality. With the passing of NAFTA in the mid 1990s, and the changing political climate, Mexico is becoming a recognized economic partner with America and Canada. But that union has also presented its cultural challenges to the United States as legal and illegal immigrants have flooded the southern states.

Who will emerge as the dynamic economic players in the first decade of this millennium? Perhaps it will be China or India, with their huge populations to increase their influence. Or maybe even Russia, as its economy stabilizes and its manufacturers begin to focus on quality products and customer satisfaction. The future is unclear.

As important as these countries and regions are in their influence on American business, equally important will be the ability of Americans to conduct business across cultures. Unfortunately, few Americans are prepared for such cross-cultural activity.

Many major American companies misjudge foreign business partners or distant markets. All too often, Americans seem to rush insensitively into unknown cultures only to make major business and social mistakes. An understanding of some of the dimensions of cross-cultural communication may better prepare Americans with the skills needed to conduct international business.

Chapel addressed this issue in his study of ways to improve international management communication. For those who want to be effective international communicators a three-prong cognitive process is required: (1) acquire cultural awareness and understanding; (2) develop both an abstract and usable knowledge of language (verbal and nonverbal); and (3) create a motivation to use cultural awareness for the development of global business relationships. This happens as managers become acculturated within their own native society, and as they seek to develop an awareness of the reality, validity, and distinctiveness of other cultural values and norms.[68]

Cultural Awareness

The work of Ronen and Victor argues that real failure in the international business arena frequently results from the inability of people to understand their lack of desire to interact with those in diverse cultures. This is more prevalent than the lack of technical or professional skills.[69]

In international business people of different cultures have difficulty communicating effectively without some caring and appreciation of each other's points of view, values, and goals. If individuals do not attempt to develop this awareness, stereotyping of people, information, and behavior takes place. This eventually can lead to systematic discrimination. Examples of this process became rapidly apparent following the September 11, 2001, terrorists' attacks on America. Peoples of Arab decent and Muslim faith were suddenly lumped together and stereotyped as "the enemy," which led to racial and ethnic profiling. Members of those groups were targeted even if they were U.S. citizens.

Associated with cross-cultural communication is the rapidly emerging role of cultural diversity awareness in the workplace. In 2000, white males moved closer to becoming a minority in the U.S. workplace; the customer base changed dramatically to incorporate people of all nationalities and ethnicities.[70] Rather than encouraging the cultural melting pot of just a few generations ago, in which workers tried to lose their accents, Americanized their names, or dressed like other Americans, today pride of background, language, and culture is respected. We are learning that differences are strengths. Extensive effort is under way researching and documenting ways to enhance the perception of cultural diversity, and developing training programs that promote it.[71] Figure 1.3 illustrates the dimensions of diversity.

Reading about and researching other cultures can enhance cultural awareness. But interactions among peoples of ethnic and social diversity in the domestic workforce produce a greater understanding. This awareness is especially apparent in communication transactions where the dynamic interrelatedness of culture, language, and cognition allow for better understanding and less ambiguity of meaning.[72]

All communication is either verbal or nonverbal. Verbal communication consists of sharing thoughts through the meanings of words, while nonverbal communication shares thoughts through all other means. Some nonverbal communication is associated with the delivery of words and some is not (see Figure 1.4). While the understanding of verbal and nonverbal communication and the interplay between them is essential among businesspeople who share the culture of the United States, it is even more important with cross-cultural communications because of the influences of religion, etiquette, customs, and politics. These four influences mediate communication far beyond mere language differences. Few topics can bring about such heated discussions as can religion; alienation can occur if the rules of etiquette are not observed; every person defends his or her own customs against all others;

| Figure 1.3 | **Dimensions of Diversity** |

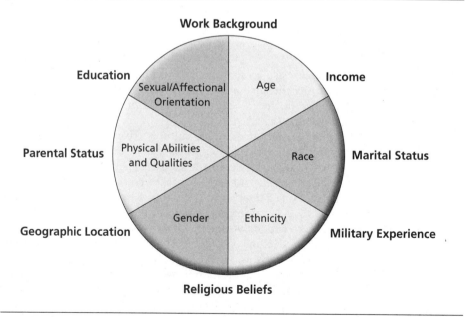

Source: Berkshire Associates, Inc. **http://www.berkshire-app.com/** (1995).

| Figure 1.4 | **Senses Appealed to by Nonverbal Communication** |

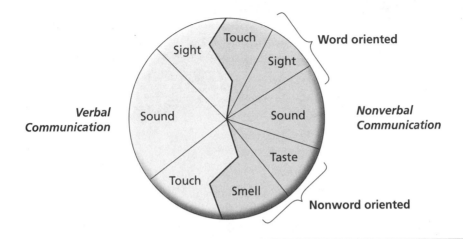

and disagreements over politics can start wars. These four influences surround and dictate the international business setting (see Figure 1.5).

While the extensive review of different countries' religions, etiquettes, customs, and politics is outside the purview of this text, examples of how they affect some of the major verbal and nonverbal communication activities illuminates how much preparation is required before entering into an international business transaction.

Verbal Communication

Within verbal communication, four areas deserve attention: jargon and slang, acronyms, humor, and vocabulary and grammar.[73] English is rich in colorful but American-based cultural phrases, such as "in the ballpark," "raining cats and dogs," and "put in your two cents' worth." Jargon has more of a business orientation, but still has phrases unique to American culture, such as "the bottom line" or delivering a "dog and pony show." Even though the words may translate directly into another language, the meanings often do not. Avoid jargon and slang.

Acronyms—the initial letters of a series of words—also should be avoided. People from other counties may be unfamiliar even with such common American acronyms as CEO, R&D, or VP. Use the full version the first time, and perhaps each time.

A third area of verbal difficulty is humor. Clearly, what is defined as humor varies dramatically across cultures. Americans often stereotype British humor as understated and dry or perceive Asians as sharing little humor. Conversely, many non-Americans view American humor as coarse and heavy-handed. Because of the serious threat of damaging an otherwise potentially viable business setting with inappropriate humor, the American businessperson is advised to avoid initiating humor.

Help your reader or listener by using your best grammar and by writing with accepted punctuation. English is often the language of business, but not all foreign businesspeople are adequately prepared to handle faulty communication. Since

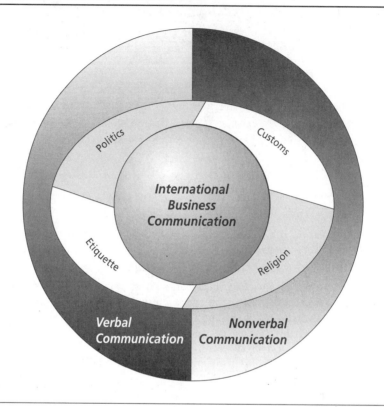

written punctuation carries rules for how to speak, you should speak your punctuation. Hesitate at commas, and speak in complete sentences. Select a tone that is not condescending, but rather appropriately businesslike.

Nonverbal Communication

Historically, we have emphasized the verbal aspects of intercultural communication, and have minimized the nonverbal components. Burgoon strongly argues the need to integrate verbal and nonverbal communication for more effective intercultural relationships.[74]

While some important elements of nonverbal communication—such as subtle voice intonations, slight facial expression changes, or flamboyant clothing—have relatively clear meanings to us, the meaning may be missed or misinterpreted in other countries. Some of the areas of nonverbal communication that can be misused are color, time, distance, voice, body movements, and clothing.

Many assume that the impression or image associated with certain colors crosses cultural boundaries. Actually, the interpretation of colors varies extensively. For example, while red means danger to us, it may be associated with festive occasions in China; mourning is symbolized by black in our culture but by yellow in the Philippines.

The American use of time is not universal either. We tend to set and respect deadlines and appointments. However, Latin Americans, for example, do not feel as compelled to stick to time schedules. Efforts to impose our standards of time on others can elicit opposition or anger.

The spatial relationships among people in the United States are approximately in the middle of a spectrum of behavior for other countries. For example, our speaking distance in business settings is typically about two feet; this distance would generally be too close for the British and too distant for those from the Middle East.

The voice—even as it delivers English that is to be translated into another language—carries meaning. From the viewpoint of those from many cultures, Americans tend to speak too loudly and too much. They often do not give adequate time for a reply and fill uncomfortable silences with words. In some cultures, such as the Japanese, silence is not negative, but rather may be a time for introspection. In some countries, the custom may allow men to speak loudly and in a gruff voice, and women—if they speak in business settings at all—are to sound quiet, reserved, and perhaps childlike. Indeed, attitudes toward women in business across cultures, for vocal and other reasons, can vary dramatically.[75]

The various body movements that are comfortable to us may be inappropriate in other settings. Normal social gestures in the United States, such as the way we cross our legs, may be offensive elsewhere. We tend to look a speaker in the eyes, perceiving the action to be one of openness and honesty. In another country, such conduct may be interpreted as far too aggressive.

American business attire is widely defined even in the United States, where we stereotype the appearance of such professionals as bankers, advertisers, accountants, or artists. Even those stereotypes may be hazardous when we encounter "business casual." When we wear our usual clothing in another country, we may find the colors too flamboyant, the weight uncomfortable for local conditions, or the length of a skirt or the absence of sleeves noticeably incorrect.

Given these pitfalls of cross-cultural communication, how can you prepare for international business? The answer lies in these steps:

- Undertake thorough and unhurried research and preparation;
- Maintain a nonjudgmental mind open to new ideas;
- Cultivate a desire to achieve maximum understanding and complete communication; and
- Avoid assuming that the U.S. culture is the only correct or dominant one.

Communication Apprehension

Many of us fear communicating and communication media. For example, some of us merely dislike or tolerate the task of writing; others hate or fear it. As the fear of communicating exceeds the perceived gain, individuals avoid communicating. Further, research suggests that those who are highly apprehensive about communication are likely to avoid jobs calling for high communication interaction or will be unhappy if forced into such jobs. Those with such fears appear to select communication channels perceived to be the least threatening.[76]

Public speaking can produce high anxiety. A recent study finds 96 percent of executives express some public speaking anxiety. "But among women, 35 percent report a 'high level' of anxiety . . . compared with 11 percent of men." The regularity of speaking is also a consideration. For those who only give occasional speeches: "42 percent of women report a 'high' level of anxiety, compared with only 15 percent of men."[77]

As the size of the audience grows, the fear may increase. Speaking in front of a group is our greatest fear, according to one survey—even outranking fears of height, insects, financial problems, and deep water.[78] As might be guessed, communication apprehension can adversely affect organizational efficiency and attainment of personal goals.

An area related to apprehension is electronically mediated communication. On encountering some of the complex, challenging communication technologies, such as computers or two-way video teleconferencing, some of us modify the message or our delivery or we seek alternative media. We may avoid new technologies because we are unfamiliar with them or because we are afraid of embarrassment over incorrect use. Indeed, some of us avoid such commonplace business media as telephones and answering machines. Others cringe at the idea of delivering a computerized slide show rich with builds, transitions, and audio and video clips.

Training and experience can help overcome the fear of speaking. Chapter 3 demonstrates the ease with which one can prepare computerized slide shows. Chapter 14 discusses ways of overcoming the fears that arise in various business situations, such as being your company's spokesperson to the press.

Advanced Communication

Thus far, you have seen evidence of the importance of communication in business. The research, for the most part, has focused on the advanced businessperson rather than the entry-level person. Going to work for a business organization with your advanced education, you may start as a mid-level manager. Your aspirations, no doubt, will be for advancement through the hierarchy. What communication skills will you need immediately and what skills will be needed later in your career? Figure 1.6 presents some answers to these two questions.

Hierarchical business communication has five stages. At the entry level, minimal skills beyond accepted grammar and punctuation are needed or expected; literacy is assumed. Communication is generally directed toward peers and upward, toward immediate supervisors. Messages may be complex and detailed but the audience, both immediate and ultimate, is small. In formal communications, the audience may be limited to a single supervisor.

The second level is the supervisory level, which requires entry-level skills plus the ability to organize sentences, paragraphs, and messages for coherence. Spoken communication, which may be relied upon heavily, is usually one-to-one or one-to-a-few. A substantial portion of the supervisor's formal communication is directed downward and is on relatively few topics.

Middle managers build on the communication skills that exist at the lower levels. For these middle managers, written communication may increase in importance, be

The Five Stages of Executive Communication

Stages	Characteristics	Importance of Language Rules	Message Complexity	Audience Size	Exposure to Subordinates	Breadth of Topics
5. Top Management	Communication at top levels with other executives; comfortable with large groups and media; compelling writer and speaker.					
4. Upper Management	Effective with outside exposure (i.e., luncheon talks, reports, company spokesperson) and internally (i.e., newsletters, union negotiations).					
3. Middle Management	Effective with common business media (i.e., letters, memos, staff meetings).					
2. Supervisors	Can organize sentences, paragraphs, and messages for coherence.					
1. Entry Level	Has basic spelling, grammar, and pronunciation skills.					

of a routine nature, and flow both upward and downward. Middle managers may experience more of a balance between what is sent and what is received than personnel at lower levels of the organization. Those at lower levels tend to receive more information than they initiate. Communication is important for middle managers because they must be quite adaptable. They must be capable of transmitting clear directions to supervisors, perhaps with a motivational or authoritarian tone, and also of responding concisely to messages from the upper levels. Yet another set of skills may be called on for communication with peers, with whom they share ideas, work, and social occasions. The audiences of middle managers range from a variety of superiors to peers and supervisors; these audiences receive a diversity of messages from middle managers.

For the upper manager, audience size increases. The upper manager is called on to represent the organization as a speaker at community group meetings and may be a leader in church or civic groups, such as the Rotary Club. Internally, the upper manager has control over the final appearance of many written documents, such as reports or newsletters, which often are largely prepared by subordinates. This manager edits weak communication and appreciates clear communication. Writing prepared at lower levels may feel the heavy pencil of the upper manager. Clarity and precision often characterize this manager's communication style. The upper manager may prepare communications for top management, such as written speeches or reports to a board of directors. Top management will assess the quality of the upper manager's communication abilities as it determines future assignments.

Top managers spend much of their time communicating with their peers. They often present terse, clear, goal-oriented messages to large audiences at one time, such as in annual reports, commencement addresses, or media interviews. Usually, the message is less complex than communications at lower levels in order to make the information more easily understood by many levels of the organization and by the public. Topics are broad and are often a synthesis of information that has moved up the organization or from outside. Communicators at this level tend to be more cautious about what they say because the message often affects many people. Top managers also will communicate to a substantial degree with subordinates, usually at a level or two below. The top manager's communication may be directive or persuasive. This manager often has extraordinary leadership skills, is charismatic, and engenders intense loyalty. See Figure 1.7 for a breakdown of how one study found chief executive officers (CEOs) spent their contact time.

The effective executive communicator (at middle, upper, or top management) is the product not only of business knowledge and skills, but also of communication knowledge and skills. These knowledge and skill areas work in concert for the truly effective communicator. Figure 1.8 outlines some of the more important knowledge and skill areas and illustrates the important interactions between general and specific business and communication abilities.

| Figure 1.7 | **How American CEOs Spend Their Time** |

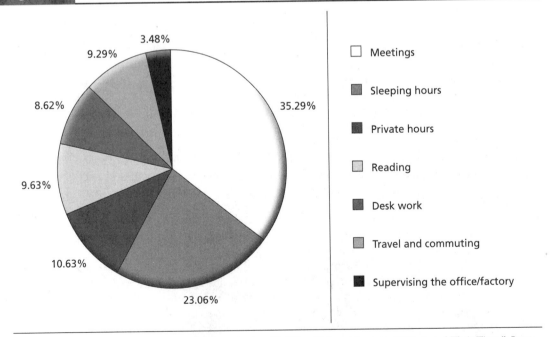

Source: Hideyuki Kudo, Takeo Tachikawa, and Noriniko Suzuki, "How U.S. and Japanese CEOs Spend Their Time," *Long Range Planning,* Vol. 21, November 6, 1988, pp. 72–82.

Figure 1.8   **Knowledge and Skill Areas**

THE EFFECTIVE
EXECUTIVE
COMMUNICATOR

BUSINESS KNOWLEDGE AND SKILLS

General
    Accounting
    Economics
    Finance
    Information Systems
    Marketing
    Computer science
    Management
        Decision sciences
        Organizational behavior
        Business policy
    Electronic commerce
Specific
    Knowledge and skills specific to the
      executive's industry and company
    Technical knowledge
        Trade practices
        Competitors and company
          personnel
    Corporate culture
    Decision-making skills
        Information-processing skills
        Insight
        Judgment
        Knowledge of external publics and
          environmental factors
    Leadership skills
        Organizing
        Planning
        Controlling
        Directing
        Leading
    International business skills
        Language fluency
        Cross-cultural training
        Diversity appreciation

**COMMUNICATION KNOWLEDGE
AND SKILLS**

General
    Listening
    Writing
    Reading
    Editing
    Speaking
    Nonverbal communication
    Technology skills
        Phone etiquette
        Word processing
        Spreadsheets
        Computerized slide presentations
        E-mail procedures
    Communication theory and processes
Specific
    Progress reporting
    Meeting coordination and leadership
    Industrial relations
    Supervisory relations
    Arbitration and negotiation
    Interviewing
    Persuasion
    Public speaking
    Media relations
    Social relations (as a company
      representative)
    Multidirectional communication skills
        Internal vs. external
        Personal vs. mass communication
        Peer vs. superior vs. subordinate
    Organizational communications
        Newsletters
        Mass meetings
        Management conferences
        Training sessions
    Company communications policies
        Formats
        Media choice
        Crisis-management policy
        Corporate identity

Summary

Just as middle, peer, and top managers use communication skills that are different from those of supervisors and entry-level employees, advanced students have different communication needs than lower-level students.

Effective communication is crucial in business. Those who are effective communicators rise quickly in their organizations. Those without such abilities—even if they are functional experts—often are held back. Numerous studies support conclusions that communication—written, spoken, listening, and visual—should be an integral part of the college curriculum, can get you a job or a better job or a promotion, and can make you a better manager.

A good manager also observes and communicates ethical standards of behavior to employees. Ethical content and conduct were examined in this chapter, as were ethics and technology. New technology has made the process of electronic plagiarism and document modification easier. While these means are available, ethical communicators avoid dishonesty and seek to protect the rights of others.

Many people are unprepared to communicate at the international level or fear some forms of communication, such as public speaking or being televised. Because audience size and topic importance are likely to grow as a manager rises in the organizational hierarchy, overcoming communication apprehension while improving skills is important.

The chapters that follow are directed toward helping you sharpen the communication skills you use as a manager. Included in these skills are the understanding of the importance of visual support, effective writing of various business messages, polished speaking skills in a diversity of settings, the ability to select from media options to best accomplish your goals, and the ways to frame and analyze a business case in both the classroom and office. Whatever your situation now—student or manager—these chapters will help you become an advanced communicator.

Discussion Questions

1. The opening pages of this chapter describe five communication skills that research indicates to be critical for managerial success. How do you rate yourself on each skill? In what ways can you work to bring improvement to each skill?
2. Why do you think good communication skills increase a person's chance of being hired for a job, and in receiving promotions later in that job?
3. Communication documents often leave a telltale sign of unethical behavior in organizations. Describe how managers you know, or have recently read about, use communication while in the middle of an ethical dilemma.
4. As you search the Internet for material to use in your class assignments, what guidelines do you employ to ensure that you use your findings in an accurate and honest way? What materials do you consider to be in the "public domain" and free to copy at will? What materials do you consider to be protected and needing permission or reference to use?

5. In examining cross-cultural communication do you believe it is more important to acquire cultural awareness and understanding, to develop a knowledge of and use of language, or travel extensively?

6. Communication apprehension is something that each speaker has probably experienced to some degree. Describe your own level of anxiety as you prepare for individual and group presentations and written projects. How do you personally manage your apprehension? How have you observed others managing theirs?

Communication in Action

1. Your communication instructor recently stated that the business school dean at your college is leaning toward increasing the number of communication courses to be offered in your business school. It seems the dean is being "encouraged" by local community business folk and recent school alumni. Before any decision is made the dean also wants to hear from current students. Your instructor has asked you to send a memo to the dean. Prepare a short memo to the dean describing your belief that additional courses (and resources for those courses) are needed or are not needed. Be sure to support whichever stand you take with good rationale. If you do support an additional communication course, indicate the impact communication skills have on getting a job and being promoted in those jobs.

@ Internet

2. You have recently been hired into a new sales position with a medium-size company. Your first few weeks are being spent at the company's main office. There you are learning about the company's divisions, the products you will sell, and the territory you will cover. While the company has a great sales course, management has found it beneficial to outsource basic communication-skills training. The company will pay for one communication-skills seminar. This can be in the area of speaking, writing, or listening (or a combination of two or more). Your immediate manager asks you to do a Web search and to isolate several training companies that seem to have outstanding communication skills.

   Your assignment. Using an Internet search engine, locate several Web sites of companies that offer communication-skills training. Compare the different sites according to three criteria: learning objectives, length of training time, and cost. Assemble your findings according to the criteria. Make a decision on the training program that excites you most. Send your manager (your instructor) an e-mail message that describes your findings and supports the program you would like to attend. Take the rest of your findings with you to class for discussion.

3. You work for a local trade association, which is a nonprofit organization. Your office is planning the large annual convention. Members will assemble from almost every state in the nation and about ten foreign countries.

Feedback from past conventions has faulted the association staff with nonverbally communicating messages that are contrary to what people are saying verbally. Your boss asks you to do some research on nonverbal communication and share it at the next staff meeting.

Your assignment. Do an Internet search on the topic of nonverbal communication. Put together an outline of your findings with at least six to eight major areas that you would want to cover in your staff presentation. One interesting nonprofit site has been prepared by Carter McNamara, **http://www.mapnp.org/library/**. When you arrive at the site, scroll through the "Free Management Library" listings. You will find a link to "Communications (Interpersonal)." In that file you will find links to search the pages that follow for information on nonverbal communication.

4. Your instructor has given a very serious lecture on e-plagiarism, and how it will not be tolerated in course assignments. To emphasize the seriousness of the issue the instructor gives an Internet assignment to research the issue. You have heard about a popular Web site, **http://www.magportal.com/**, which contains lots of magazine articles. You decide to sample it and look under the "business" area for articles on e-plagiarism. Examine several of the articles that are highlighted. Make a list of at least ten critical things that you will take back to class for a discussion on the topic, along with a bibliography listing the articles.

InfoTrac

5. American companies that are found guilty of breaking the law often pay large settlements. This occurred with Prudential Insurance Company a few years ago, when they agreed to pay a fine of $35 million for misleading sales practices.

Your assignment. Use InfoTrac to locate an article on the Prudential case. The article, "Persuasion, Probity, and Paltering: The Prudential Crisis," by Betsy Stevens, was in *The Journal of Business Communication*, October 1999, Article No. A58082897. Read the article and answer the following questions:

a. What role did communication play in the Prudential case?

b. Were the ethical problems related to conduct or character issues? Were the ethical problems related to individual, organizational, or social ethics?

c. Did Prudential address ethical behavior in any of its company documents?

d. How did Prudential change its communication practices?

Notes

1. Boyer, E. L. (1987). *College: The undergraduate experience in America* (pp. 59–85). New York: Harper & Row.
2. Hulbert, J. E. (1979, May). Facilitating intelligent business dialogue. *Business Education Forum, 33*(8), 10–15.

3. Olney, R. J. (1984, March 2). Executives' perceptions of business communication. Paper presented at Southwest Conference of the Association for Business Communication, San Antonio, TX; and Swenson, D. H. (1980). Relative importance of business communication skills for the next ten years. *The Journal of Business Communication, 17*(2), 41–49.

4. Lee, D. W. (1999, November/December). Perspectives of "Fortune 500" executives on the competency requirements for accounting. *Journal of Education for Business, 75*(2), 104–108.

5. Pride, S. S. (1967). *Business ideas: How to create and present them* (p. 172). New York: Harper & Row; Carlson, C. (1967, April 19). Best memories by eye and the ear. *Kansas City Times*, sec. A, p. 13; Timm, P. R. (1981). *Functional business presentations: Getting across.* (pp. 130–150). Englewood Cliffs, NJ: Prentice-Hall; Berelson, B., & Steiner, G. (1978). *Human behavior: An inventory of scientific findings,* 2nd ed. New York: Harcourt, Brace & World; Koehler, J. W., & Sisco, J. (1981). *Public communication in business and the professions.* St. Paul, Minnesota: West Publishing Co.; Raudsepp, E. (1979). Present your ideas effectively. *IEEE transactions on professional communication, 22,* 204–210.

6. Balchin, W. G. V., & Coleman, A. M. (1966). Graphicacy should be the fourth ace in the pack. *The Cartographer, 3,* 23–28.

7. Evans, R. (1999, October). Serving modern students in a modern society at the community college: Incorporating basic technological literary. *T.H.E. Journal,* 102–108.

8. Bork, A. As quoted in S. Charp. (1999, October). Technical literacy—Where are we? *T.H.E. Journal,* 6–8.

9. Lake, D. (2001, March 26). The 5-year forecast: Where's the information revolution going? *The Industry Standard.* Retrieved October 8, 2002, from **http://www .thestandard.com/article/display/0,1151,22847,00.html**.

10. Childers, T. L., & Houston, M. J. (1983). Imagery paradigms for consumer research: Alternative perspectives from cognitive psychology. *Advances in Consumer Research, 10,* 59–64. Valdosta, GA: Association for Consumer Research; Balchin, W. G. V., & Coleman, A. M. (1972). Graphicacy should be the fourth ace in the pack; Balchin, W. G. V. (n.d.). Graphicacy. *Geography, 57,* 185–195; Schmid, C. F. (1983). *Statistical graphics: design principles and practices* (pp. 11–12). New York: John Wiley & Sons; Pollock, J. A., et al. (1983, Spring). Executives' perceptions of future MBA programs. *Collegiate News and Views,* 23–25.

11. U.S. execs rate business writing. (1984, December). *Training and Development Journal.*

12. Hudson, H. As quoted in Jacobs, P. (1998, July 6). Strong writing skills essential for success, even in IT. *Infoworld,* 86.

13. Hiemstra, K., Schmidt, J., & Madison, R. (1985, December). Certified management accountants: Perception of the need for communication skills in accounting. *The Bulletin of the Association for Business Communication, 48*(4), 5–9.

14. Garver, L. W., Hiltebeitel, K., & Barsky, N. (2000, July 1). Get it write: Build skills to enhance your career. *Pennsylvania CPA Journal,* 16–23.

15. Writing skills: What they're looking for (1991, October). *Journal of Accountancy,* 39.

16. 1999 Graduate management admission test GMAT bulletin and registration form. (1995). Princeton, NJ: Graduate Management Admission Council, 28–29; Blum, J. D., & Ferrara, C. F. (1994, September). Writing skills: Another hurdle for CPA candidates. *New Accountant,* 16–17.

17. Roman, K., & Raphaelson, J. (1981). *Writing that works* (p. 1). New York: Harper & Row; Simonds, R. H. (1960, November). Skills businessmen use most. *Nation's Business,* 88; Cox, H. (1968, Fall). Opinions of selected business managers about some aspects of communication on the job. *The Journal of Business Communication, 6*(1), 3–12; Glassman, M., & Farley, E. (1979). AACSB accredited schools' approach

to business communication courses. *The Journal of Business Communication, 16*(3), 41–48; Flatley, M. (1982). A comparative analysis of the written communication of managers at various organizational levels in the private business sector. *The Journal of Business Communication, 19*(2), 48; Lahiff, J. M., & Hatfield, J. D. (1978). The winds of change and managerial communication practices. *The Journal of Business Communication, 15*(4), 19–28; Belden, M. (1976, September). Effective systems reports. *Journal of Systems Management, 23*(9), 18–20.

18. Rader, M., & Wunsch, A. (1980). A survey of communication practices of business school graduates by job category and undergraduate major. *The Journal of Business Communication, 17*(4), 33–41.

19. Moss, M. (1995). Perceptions of communication in the corporate community. *Journal of Business and Technical Communication, 9*(1), 63–77.

20. Huegli, J. M., & Tschirgi, H. D. (1974, Fall). Communication skills at the entry job level. *The Journal of Business Communication, 12*(1), 24–29.

21. Scudder, J. N., & Guinan, P. J. (1989, Summer). Communication competencies as discriminators of superiors' ratings of employee performance. *The Journal of Business Communication, 26*(3), 217–229.

22. Clipson, T. W., & Young, M. C. (1985, March 7–9). A comparative study of business employers and educators concerning most significant business communication topics (pp. 55–65). Proceedings, Association for Business Communication, Southwest, New Orleans, LA.

23. Tannen, D. (1995, September–October). The power of talk: who gets heard and why. *Harvard Business Review*, 138–148.

24. How undergraduate business communication programs can meet the communication needs of business: Report of the undergraduate studies committee (June 1973). *ABCA Bulletin, 36*(2), 5–7; Penrose, J. M. (1976, Winter). A survey of the perceived importance of business communication and other business-related fields. *The Journal of Business Communication, 13*(2), 17–25; Rader & Wunsch, A survey (pp. 33–41); Golen, S., et al. (1988–1989). Empirically tested cognitive communication skills for the MBA, with implications for the AACSB. *The Organizational Behavior Teaching Review, 13*(3), 45–58.

25. Pearce, C. G., Johnson, I. W., & Barker, R. T. (1995, December 1). Enhancing the student listening skills and environment. *Business Communication Quarterly, 58*(4), 28–39.

26. Salopek, J. J. (1999, September). Is anyone listening? *Training and Development, 53*(9), 58–60.

27. Cohen, A. (1993). The right stuff. *Sales and Marketing Management, 151*, 15; Curtis, D. B., Winsor, J. L., & Stephens, R. D. (1989). National preferences in business and communication education. *Communication Education, 38*, 6–15; Messmer, M. (1999). Skills for a new millennium. *Strategic Finance, 81*, 10–12; Roebuck, D. B., Sightler, K. W., & Brush, C. C. (1995). Organizational size, company type, and position effects on the perceived importance of oral and written communication skills. *Journal of Managerial Issues, 7*, 99–115.

28. Zabava Ford, W. S., Wolvin, A. D., & Chung, S. (2000). Students' self-perceived listening competencies in the basic speech communication course. *International Journal of Listening, 14*, 1–13; Scudder, J. N., & Guinan, P. J. (1989, Summer). Communication competencies as discriminators of superiors' ratings of employee performance. *The Journal of Business Communication, 26*(3), 217–229; Cooper, L. O. (1997, December). Listening competency in the workplace: A model for training. *Business Communication Quarterly, 60*(4), 75–85.

29. Maes, J., Weldy, T. G., & Icenogle, M. L. (1997). A managerial perspective: Oral communication competency is most important for business students in the workplace. *The Journal of Business Communication, 37*(1), 67–81.

30. Brownell, J. (1990, Fall). Perceptions of effective listeners: A management study. *The Journal of Business Communication, 27*(4), 401–415.

31. Wolvin, A. D., & Coakley, C. G. (n.d.). A listening taxonomy. In Wolvin, A. D., & Coakley, C. G., eds., *Perspectives on listening* (pp. 15–22). Norwood, NJ: Ablex.

32. Lewis, M. H. & Reinsch, N. L., Jr. (1988). Listening in organizational environments. *The Journal of Business Communication, 25*(3), 49–67.

33. Hunt, G. T., & Cusella, A. P. (1983). A field study of listening needs in organizations. *Communication Education, 32*, 393–401.

34. Barker, R. T., Pearce, C. G., & Johnson, I. W. (1992). An investigation of perceived managerial listening ability. *Journal of Business and Technical Communication, 6*, 438–475.

35. *Ibid.*

36. Pearce, C. G., Johnson, I. W., & Barker, R. T. (1995, December). Enhancing the student listening skills and environment. *Business Communication Quarterly, 58*(4), 28–39.

37. Thomas, M. (2001, March 11). Let's talk skills/Communicating effectively key in business. *The Calgary Sun*, p. 14.

38. Axelrod, R. B., & Cooper, C. R. (1997). *The St. Martin's guide to writing,* 5th ed. (p. 459). New York: St. Martin's Press.

39. Dowd, K. O., & Liedtka, J. (1994, Winter). What corporations seek in MBA hires: A survey. *Selections—The Magazine of the Graduate Management Admission Council*, 34–39.

40. Maes, J. D., Weldy, T. G., & Icenogle, M. L. (1997, January). A managerial perspective: Oral communication competency is most important for business students in the workplace. *The Journal of Business Communication, 34*(1), 67–80.

41. Hyslop, D. J., & Faris, K. (1984, April/May). Integrate communication skills into all business classes. *Business Education Forum*, 51–57; Penrose, J. M. (1984, Summer). A discrepancy analysis of the job-getting process and a study of resume techniques. *The Journal of Business Communication, 21*(3), 5–15; Edge, A., & Greenwood, R. (1974, October). How managers rank knowledge, skills, and attributes possessed by business administration graduates. *AACSB Bulletin, 11*, 30–34; Simonds, Skills businessmen use most, p. 88; Cox, Opinions of selected business managers, 3–12; Jobs of the future. (1986, November–December). *Getting Jobs, 1*(1), 1.

42. Stinson, L. M. (1995, October). Communication in the workplace: Implications for business teachers. *Business Education Forum, 50*(1), 28–30.

43. Beax, H. H. (1981, Spring). Good writing: An under-rated executive skill. *Human Resource Management*, 2; Stine, D. & Sharzenski, D. (1979). Priorities for the business communication classroom: A survey of business and academe. *The Journal of Business Communication, 16*(3), 15–30; Baird, J. E., & Bradley, P. H. (1978). Communication correlates of employee morale. *The Journal of Business Communication, 15*(3), 47–55.

44. McConnell, L. As quoted in Jacobs, P. (1998, July 6). Strong writing skills essential for success, even in IT. *Infoworld, 20*(27), 86.

45. Bond, F. A., Hildebrandt, H. W., & Miller, E. L. (1981). *The newly promoted executive: A study in corporate leadership* (pp. 1–23). Ann Arbor, MI: University of Michigan Graduate School of Business Administration.

46. Bennett, J. C., & Olney, R. J. (1986). Executive priorities for effective communication in an information society. *The Journal of Business Communication, 23*(2), 14.

47. Fayol, H. (1949). *General and industrial management,* translated from the original French, 1916, reprint. London: Pittman & Sons; George, C. S., Jr. (1972). *The history of management thought.* Englewood Cliffs, NJ: Prentice-Hall; Barnard, C. I. (1938). *The functions of the executive.* Cambridge, MA: Harvard University Press; Simon, H. A. (1957). *The models of man.* New York: John Wiley & Sons; Katz, D.,

& Kahn, R. L. (1966). *The social psychology of organizations*. New York: John Wiley & Sons; Mintzberg, H. (1973). *The nature of managerial work*. New York: Harper & Row; Drucker, P. (1974). *Management: Tasks, responsibilities, practices*. New York: Harper & Row; Peters, T. J., & Waterman, R. H. (1982). *In search of excellence*. New York: Harper & Row; Kanter, R. M. (1983). *The change masters*. New York: Simon & Schuster; Iacocca, L. (1986). *Iacocca*. New York: Bantam; Gates, B. (1995). *The road ahead*. New York: Viking. As excerpted by *Newsweek*, November 1995, 60; Kotter, J. (1996). *Leading change*. Boston: Harvard Business School Press; Amelio, G., & Simon, W. L. (1999). *On the firing line*. New York: Harper Business.

48. Ewing, D. (1987). In brochure announcing introduction of *Management communication quarterly*. Thousand Oaks, CA: Sage Publications.

49. Byrne, J. A., France, M., & Zellner, W. (2002, February 25). The environment was ripe for abuse. *Business Week*, 118–120.

50. Enron papers describe deals. (2002, January 2). *The Dallas Morning News*, p. 2D.

51. Northouse, P. G. (2001). Chap. 12: Leadership ethics. In *Leadership: Theory and practice*, 2nd ed. (pp. 249–276). Thousand Oaks, CA: Sage Publications.

52. *Ibid*.

53. A framework for thinking ethically. (2001). Markkula Center for Applied Ethics, Santa Clara University, 1.

54. *Ibid*., 2.

55. Jones, D. (2002, April 8). Scandals, setbacks topple CEO's formerly golden image. *USA Today*, p. B1.

56. Rasberry, R. W. (2000, May/June). The conscience of an organization: The ethics office. *Strategy and Leadership*, 18.

57. *Ibid*., 20.

58. The 4-way test. (n.d.) Rotary International. Retrieved on April 15, 2002, from **http:// www.rotary.org/aboutrotary/4way.html**.

59. Friedman, M. (1970, September 13). The social responsibility of business is to increase its profits. *The New York Times Magazine*, 33.

60. Berenson, A. (2002, August 26). Fake report on net sends stock into dive. *The Dallas Morning News*, p. 24A.

61. Ballint, K. (1999, October 26). Photo magic. *ComputerLink* magazine in the *San Diego Union-Tribune*, pp. 6–7.

62. Hundertmark, J. (1991, October). When enhancement is deception. *Publish!*, *6*(10), 51–55.

63. As others see it: E-plagiarism. (2001, May 14). *Pittsburgh Post-Gazette*, p. 17A; McCabe, C. (2001, October 14). Old plague of plagiarism infected by new sources on internet. *The Boston Globe*, p. 1; Marklein, M. B. (2000, January 5). Revealing the answer to cheating: The return of the college honor code could halt the erosion of ethics. *USA Today*, p. 9D.

64. Green, M. (2000, April 1). "TurnItIn" snares online cheaters. *NEA Today*, 22–23.

65. Hinchliffe, L. (1998, May). Cut-and-paste plagiarism: Preventing, detecting and tracking online plagiarism (3 pp.). Retrieved February 19, 2002, from **http://alexia .lis.uiuc.edu/~janicke/plagiary.htm**.

66. Avoiding plagiarism (5 pp.). University of California Davis, Student Judicial Affairs. Retrieved February 19, 2002, from **http://sja.ucdavis.edu/avoid.htm**.

67. Cushman, D. P., & King, S. S. (1994). Communication in multinational organizations in the United States and western Europe. In *Communicating in multinational organizations* (pp. 94–114), Wiseman, R. L., & Shuter, R., eds. Thousand Oaks, CA: Sage Publications.

68. Chapel, W. B. (1997, July). Developing international management communication competence. *Journal of Business and Technical Communication*, *11*(3), 281–297.

69. Ronen, S. (1986). *Comparative and multinational management*. New York: John Wiley & Sons; Victor, D. A. (1992). *International business communication*. New York: HarperCollins.

70. Baytos, L. M. (1995). *Designing and implementing successful diversity programs* (p. xxiv). Englewood Cliffs, NJ: Prentice-Hall.

71. A five-person panel examined "Challenges to Communicating Multicultural Values: A Workplace Assessment," at the Association for Business Communication International Convention, Orlando, FL, November 1–4, 1995.

72. Chapel, W. B. (1992, November 6) Integrating verbal and nonverbal messages for international business communication competence. Midwest Conference of the Association of Business Communication, New Orleans, LA.

73. Axtell, R. E., ed. (1985). *Do's and taboos around the world* (pp. 140–159). New York: John Wiley & Sons.

74. Burgoon, J. K. (1985). Nonverbal signals. In M. L. Knapp & G. R. Miller (Eds.), *Handbook of interpersonal communication* (pp. 344–390). Beverly Hills, CA: Sage Publications.

75. Chaney, L. H., & Martin, J. S. (2000). *International business communication*, 2nd ed. (pp. 47–49). Upper Saddle River, NJ: Prentice-Hall.

76. U.S. execs rate business writing (1984, December). *Training and Development Journal*; McCroskey, J. C. (1970). Measures of communication-bound anxiety. *Speech Monographs 37*, 269–277; Falcone, F. I., Daly, J. A., & McCroskey, J. C. (1977). Job satisfaction as a function of employees' communication apprehension, self-esteem, and perceptions of their immediate supervisor. *Communication Yearbook*, 4th ed. (pp. 263–276), International Communication Association. New Brunswick, NJ: B. D. Ruben; Reinsch, N. L., Jr., & Lewis, P. L. (1984, Summer 1984). Communication apprehension as a determinant of channel preferences. *The Journal of Business Communication 21*(3), 53–61; Borzi, M. G., & Mills, T. H. (2001, March 1). Communication apprehension in upper level accounting students: An assessment of skill development. *Journal of Education for Business, 76*(4), 193–200.

77. Does giving a speech spook women more? (2002, April 8). *Business Week*, 12.

78. Wallechinsky, D., & Wallace, I. (1977). *The book of lists*. New York: William Morrow.

CHAPTER - 2

Information and Persuasion

The goal of this chapter is to lightly touch on themes that will be developed more fully in later chapters. First, some general principles for presenting information effectively will be outlined. Second, some of the basic issues related to the process of persuasion will be considered.

Presenting Information Effectively

We observed in the previous edition of this book that "We are drowning in a sea of e-mail, voice mail, cell phone calls, and letters, memos, reports, printouts, and faxes." We still are.

Moreover, several developments have exacerbated the problem.

The first development is that the volume of e-mail received by businesspeople, especially senior management, continues to increase. As Del Jones reported recently in an investigation of how CEOs cope with the steep rise in e-mail: "In the three seconds it takes to read this sentence, more than a half-million e-mails will land in in-boxes. By 2005, nearly that many will land each second." Terms like "e-mail avalanche" and even "e-mail tsunami" are used in the Jones article to convey the magnitude of the problem.[1]

The second development, related to the first, might be referred to as "A funny thing happened on the way to the paperless office." Despite predictions that e-mail would reduce the amount of paper in the office, the opposite has happened. As the sheer volume of messages has increased, given the ease of message production afforded by e-mail, so too have sales of paper to offices, as employees at all levels of the organization print out copies of e-mail messages primarily for backup and ease of reading.

Quantity of information is not the only problem faced by executives. In fact, what makes this "information overload" all the more vexing is that so many of the messages present information ineffectively, and by doing so waste time and create confusion. Consider how often we find ourselves muttering: "What is the point of this memo (or e-mail)?" "What does this letter mean?" "Couldn't he say this in fewer words?" "Why is this report organized like this?" and so forth. The problem of too much information, therefore, is coupled with the problem of information that is presented ineffectively. Although ambiguity is sometimes intentional in business communication (see the discussion of "Strategic Ambiguity" below), more often writers and speakers intend their readers or listeners to understand and retain information. To these two ends—understanding and retention—these six general principles of presenting information apply: directness, conciseness, organization, clarity, redundancy, and multisensory messages. It is our conviction that the application of these principles will help your readers and listeners to manage the "message mania" in their professional lives.[2]

Directness

Put simply, the strategy here is to get to the point. Routine memos and letters, as well as positive or good-news messages, can be organized according to the direct plan. As Chapter 5 will explain and illustrate, the direct plan takes its name from the placement of the main point of the message, usually in the first sentence.

A wise approach to presenting information is to think of the direct plan as the rule and any departure from the direct plan as an exception. Most executives should be able to employ the direct plan in 75 percent of their writing and, in doing so, make their writing easier to understand and retain.

What are the exceptions to presenting information by the direct plan? The two major categories are negative or bad-news messages and persuasive messages. These two types of messages usually require an indirect plan. Chapter 6 will explain and illustrate indirect-plan messages in depth. At this point, let it suffice to say that in the indirect plan, the beginning of a message is the position of most emphasis, the end is the position of the second-most emphasis, and the middle is the position of least emphasis. In routine and positive messages the main point should be given the position of most emphasis: the beginning. In a persuasive message, the main point should be delayed because resistance from the reader is expected. The main point is accorded the position of second-most emphasis and preceded by a series of steps designed to motivate or induce the reader to accept the writer's point of view (more on persuasion later in this chapter). In negative messages, the main point should usually be de-emphasized by placing it in the middle of the message and preceding it by an explanation preparing the reader for the bad news.

In short, while situations will occur in which you will want to de-emphasize the point, employing the direct plan to get to the point will be appropriate in most of your writing. In doing so you will create a more efficient document—that is, less effort (input) will be required by your readers to understand your memos or letters (output).

Conciseness

Conciseness may be expressed in two ways: use as many words as you need or use as few words as necessary. In either case, conciseness will improve the presentation of information.

Chapter 4 will offer some specific suggestions for making your writing more concise. The purpose in this chapter is to make an important distinction between conciseness and brevity, and in doing so to clarify the notion of conciseness.

Conciseness does not mean brevity. Brevity simply means using few words. We would all agree that a memo consisting of a two-sentence paragraph is brief. But it is not necessarily concise. Conciseness requires that the message contain an adequate number of words to achieve the writer's purpose. If, for example, the two-sentence memo leaves the reader puzzled, it has sacrificed both conciseness and the reader's understanding for the sake of brevity.

Some organizations have missed this important distinction with their insistence on one-page memos and other such requirements. If, after eliminating any unnecessary words and phrases (see Chapter 4 for examples), a writer still requires a page and a half to make a point clearly, explain a problem adequately, or offer a few recommendations, then it makes sense to use the extra space. Use as many words as you need to adequately convey information to your readers. Be concise.

Organization

The understanding and retention of information is enhanced when the appropriate mode of organization for a message is employed. Here are nine basic patterns of organization to consider while planning messages. They may be employed singly to organize an entire message or in combination to organize sections within a message or even paragraphs within sections. The nine basic patterns are direct, indirect, order of importance, chronology, problem–solution, causal, spatial, structure/function, and topical.

1. **Direct Plan.** As noted above, this is the pattern of choice when planning the organization of an entire message, particularly messages that are routine, neutral, and pleasant. The basic outline for the direct plan is

   Main point
   Support for, or explanation of, main point
   Restatement of the main point (optional)

   The paragraphs in support for or explanation of the main point may be organized according to the patterns described below. (See Chapter 5 for illustrations of messages organized according to the direct plan.)

2. **Indirect Plan.** The second major pattern to consider when planning an entire message is the indirect plan. Again, the indirect plan of organization is most appropriate for messages that the reader may find unpleasant and that may meet resistance from the reader. The basic outline for a negative message is

   Buffer (delayed opening)
   Reasons for negative message
   Negative message
   Positive ending

   Persuasive messages, organized according to the indirect plan, often have their steps labeled differently by different writers. We outline the steps of a persuasive message as

   Attention
   Interest

Desire

Conviction

Action

(See Chapter 6 for illustrations of messages organized according to the indirect plan for negative or persuasive messages.)

3. **Order of Importance.** Suppose you have outlined a direct-plan memo with the main point being a recommendation to promote an employee to a supervisory position. You have three reasons to support your recommendation.

A sensible way to organize the presentation of the reasons is by decreasing order of importance—that is, state the most important reason first, then follow with the next-most important and the least-important reasons. Here is an example of how an actual outline of such a memo might look.

Recommend Denise Brown for supervisor (main point)

She has great interpersonal skills (most important reason)

She possesses excellent technical knowledge (next-most important reason)

She has the most seniority among staff (least important reason)

This is an effective and efficient way to organize a message.

4. **Chronology.** The organizing criterion in this case is time. A clear example of this type of organization is seen on the typical résumé. The chronological résumé format is so named because the work experience section of the résumé is organized in reverse chronological order.

Chronology is a useful organizing principle for other types of messages as well. For instance, accident reports are usually written using the chronological approach. Also, sections of memos or longer reports that provide background on a problem under study are often organized chronologically. Here is an outline illustrating how a section of a report might be organized chronologically.

1995   LDDS Changes Name to WorldCom

1998   WorldCom Acquires MCI

2000   Justice Department Blocks Bid by WorldCom to Merge with Sprint

2002   WorldCom Declares Chapter 11 Bankruptcy

Another important use of the chronological pattern of organization is the writing of instructions and directions. The steps or stages are explained and presented in chronological order. Here is a partial outline of instructions prepared for a customer service representative answering a telephone.

Greet caller.

Identify yourself.

Ask for the customer's account number.

Ask how you may assist the customer.

This is a natural and useful way to organize information for readers.

5. **Problem–Solution.** Readers and listeners are very comfortable with this pattern of organization because it is used so frequently. In short messages, the first part of a message describes a problem, and the second part proposes a solution. Here is an example of a problem–solution outline.

> Employees accepting gifts from contractors (problem)
> > Christmas gifts
> > Other gifts
>
> Communicate corporate policy prohibiting gifts (solution)
> > Memo to employees
> > Letter to contractors

Such a familiar pattern as this facilitates a reader's understanding and retention.

6. **Causal.** You have two options here: moving from cause to effect and from effect to cause. With the cause-to-effect pattern, you begin by identifying a present cause and then describe a probable effect—you reason forward in time. With effect to cause, you begin by describing an observed effect and then propose to explain the probable causes—that is, you reason backward in time. Both are common ways to organize messages or parts of messages. Here are examples of both patterns.

> Cause to Effect
> > The high school population in the city has declined by 20 percent (cause).
> > Therefore, companies face a shortage of clerical help (effect).
>
> Effect to Cause
> > The high school population has declined by 20 percent (effect).
> > The declining middle-class birth rate is the likely cause (cause).

7. **Spatial.** Also called the geographic pattern, this is another common pattern of organization. The basis for this pattern is spatial relationship, or geography. Where physical objects or their locations are described, this pattern may be appropriate. An example of a spatial pattern of organization is

> Sales forecast by region (2003):
> > Northeast region
> > Southeast region
> > Midwest region
> > Northwest region
> > Western region

For such a topic, the spatial pattern seems most appropriate.

8. **Structure/Function.** Typically, this is a two-part pattern: The first part describes the structure of something; the second part describes the functions of the structural parts. Another variation of this theme is to describe

the structure and function of each part in turn. An illustration of the latter version is

> Employee Relations Division
> > Affirmative Action (structure and function)
> > Compensation and Benefits (structure and function)
> > Personnel Operations (structure and function)
> > Labor Relations (structure and function)
> > Training and Development (structure and function)

9. **Topical.** Sometimes called the categorical pattern of organization, this is often used to organize messages, particularly when the patterns described above seem inappropriate. With this pattern, topics or subjects are broken down into subtopics or categories. Here is an illustration of the topical pattern.

> Employee behavior subject to disciplinary action
> > Unsatisfactory work performance
> > Insubordination
> > Violation of safety rules
> > Falsification of company records
> > Destruction of company property
> > Absence from work
> > Theft
> > Use of controlled or intoxicating substance

These nine ways to organize messages, used alone or in combination, present information in a way that enhances reader understanding and retention of information.

Clarity

Ensuring that information is clear to readers and listeners requires careful consideration of your audience and the application of these four techniques: define or eliminate unclear words; compare or contrast unfamiliar information with information that is familiar; exemplify; and quantify meaningfully.

1. **Define or Eliminate Unclear Words.** If you believe that your reader or listener might not understand a word, either define it or substitute another word more likely to be understood. This is particularly important when making oral presentations. Although a reader can reach for a dictionary, the listener is condemned to sit there puzzled or confused.

    Be especially careful about professional jargon when writing or speaking to people outside the profession. Many words and expressions you use daily may be baffling to an audience unschooled in the lingo of your profession. Even when writing to someone within the same organization, be careful to avoid this barrier to clarity—for example, a data-processing specialist writing to a marketing manager, or a benefits manager speaking to a group of management interns, must tailor the speech to the audience.

2. **Compare or Contrast the Unfamiliar with the Familiar.** One of the best-known techniques for ensuring that information is clear to an audience is to compare or contrast information that may be unfamiliar with information that is known to the reader or listener. Economist Paul Krug, writing for *The New York Times*, illustrates the principle beautifully in a column in which he describes the business scandals associated with Enron, Dynergy, Adelphia, and WorldCom in terms of the behavior of a manager of an ice cream parlor, who is trying to get rich with a not-very-profitable business.[3]

3. **Exemplify.** Information is usually clarified when a writer or speaker offers an example, real or hypothetical, brief or extended. A benefits manager explains how a major medical insurance policy supplements the basic plan by offering a hypothetical example of an employee filing a claim after a hospital stay. A sales manager, writing a directive for the sales force, offers examples of correct and incorrect uses of an expense account.

4. **Quantify Meaningfully.** Business writing and speaking usually contain numbers or statistics that often require a context to be meaningful. For example, "We are proposing a modest budget increase of 6 percent" is not as meaningful as "We are proposing to increase the budget $7,800,000, or 6 percent, over last year's budget of $130,000,000." Or, compare "Net income for common stock in 2000 was $4.26 per share on an average of 123 million shares outstanding" with "Net income for common stock in 2002 was $4.26 per share on an average of 123 million shares outstanding. This is down from last year's record of $4.48 per share on an average of 130 million shares outstanding, but better than 2000 when we earned $4.16 per share on an average of 129 million shares outstanding." The comparison of financial results over three years places the 2002 results in a more meaningful context.

An interesting exception to such strategies employed by business communicators to ensure clarity is the practice of strategic ambiguity. As Eric Eisenberg explains, some communicators achieve their goals by creating messages that are deliberately and strategically unclear. The strategy works because of the inherent ambiguity of language, which allows people to assign different meanings to the same message. Examples are a strategically ambiguous corporate mission statement that allows members of the same company to assign different meanings yet subscribe to the same statement (Ford's "Quality Is Job One"), or a strategically ambiguous statement to the public by a corporate spokesperson during a time of crisis which later allows for more specificity, or even deniability, as more information on the crisis becomes available to the corporation.[4]

Redundancy

Writers and speakers enhance the understanding and retention of information when they design their messages to include a degree of redundancy. This is especially important for oral messages because listeners, unlike readers, do not have the message in front of them to consult or reread.

Repetition and Restatement

Repetition (repeating the same words) and restatement (expressing the same message in different words) ensure that writers and speakers emphasize key points and ideas. For example, in criticizing a newspaper article about her firm, a speaker, over the course of her presentation, could refer to it as "inaccurate, incorrect, faulty, fallacious, unreliable, imprecise, inexact, wide of the mark, mistaken," and "off-target." Get the impression that she didn't care much for the article? Her audience could hardly miss her point. Note, too, that as a matter of style, it can be more effective to restate and rephrase the same point ten times than to simply repeat the word "inaccurate" ten times.

Internal Summaries

Long written or oral messages benefit greatly from internal summaries. Such summaries permit a writer or speaker to remind the reader or listener of what main points have been made before moving on to the next. For example:

> So far, I have offered two reasons as to why we should move the firm to New Jersey: a 30-percent reduction in the cost of utilities, and substantially lower state and local taxes. Add to these two reasons a third: quality-of-life considerations.

If this were the last reason, the summary at the end of the message could recapitulate all three reasons.

Multisensory Messages

One more technique to consider as an aid to understanding and retaining information is the use of multisensory messages—that is, the combination of oral, visual, written, and graphic messages. As we noted in Chapter 1, research suggests that oral and visual messages together increase recall over just oral or visual messages alone. We devote an entire chapter, Chapter 3, to visual support.

In sum, the effective communication of information can be enhanced by attention to these six principles: directness, conciseness, organization, clarity, redundancy, and multisensory messages.

The Persuasive Process

Sometimes, even when information is presented according to these six principles, the message still will be ineffective. Usually, these cases involve writers or speakers asking readers or listeners to do something that they do not want to do—that is, the readers or listeners resist the purpose of the message.

As noted earlier in this chapter, the likelihood of resistance on the part of readers or listeners is one rationale for employing the indirect plan of organization. With this plan of organization, the request or call for action is delayed until the end of the message. By delaying the call for action, the beginning of the message is used to secure the attention of the reader or listener, and the middle of the message is used to motivate the reader or listener to accept the purpose. Because resistance is expected, we do not risk a reader rejecting the request at the beginning of a memo and reading no further; we do not risk an audience tuning out our oral presentation at the very beginning. As we employ the term, persuasion is a process by which we motivate readers and listeners to (1) change existing attitudes and behavior or (2) adopt new attitudes and behavior or (3) do both.

Changing Existing Attitudes and Behavior

Often our persuasive goal is to change attitudes and behavior that already exist. For instance, your company might discover that employees view pilferage (taking home pens, pencils, pads of paper, and so forth) as a kind of fringe benefit. You are asked to write a memo that will persuade them that it is more like petty theft and that they should desist. Or a survey by the Human Resource department might find that most employees view the forthcoming merger of your organization with another larger firm as something very negative. You must draft a letter from the president of the firm, to be sent to the home of all employees, that seeks to persuade them that the merger will be beneficial and positive.

In both cases, the assumption underlying the decision to employ persuasion is that simply requesting employees to stop pilfering company supplies, or telling them that the merger is a good thing, will not work. They know that the company does not approve of pilferage; yet they still do it. They have been told that the merger will benefit them; they do not believe it. Persuasion is needed.

Adopting New Attitudes and Behavior

At other times, the persuasive purpose is to motivate readers or listeners to adopt new attitudes or behavior. For instance, you might write a proposal to persuade management to adopt a centralized database management system for your company. Or a department store might decide to persuade customers who use American Express and VISA cards to accept and use the store's own credit card. For this, the persuasive letter is designed.

Just like the examples of changing existing attitudes and behavior, both of these examples assume resistance by readers and listeners. For instance, simply proposing and describing a central database management system to a group of senior executives is unlikely to motivate them to approve the expenditure. They need to be persuaded. Similarly, writing to customers who use VISA or American Express and offering the department store's credit card is likely to be ignored or rejected. Why should they bother? They need to be persuaded, too.

Changing and Adopting Attitudes and Behavior

At times, you may need to pursue both of the goals simultaneously. That is, you need to change attitudes or behavior and induce the adoption of new attitudes or behavior. The design of your message will reflect this more-complex purpose.

The most obvious case of such a dual purpose is the task often faced by salespeople: they must change the attitude of a potential customer toward the product that they are using and motivate the customer to buy a new product or service. In another example, to motivate an executive to replace the firm's photocopying equipment with a competitor's brand may require persuading him or her that (1) the equipment in use is not as good as thought, and (2) the firm should choose the competitor's particular brand of new equipment. Failure to achieve the first purpose may make the second purpose superfluous. The executive may respond, "Yes, your photocopier is impressive, but our present equipment seems just as good. Why should I change?"

Summary

Effective managers present information that can be understood and retained. To this end, we have considered the principles of directness, conciseness, organization, clarity, redundancy, and multisensory messages.

Effective managers also design persuasive messages to change existing attitudes and behavior and to motivate others to adopt new attitudes and behavior.

The themes presented in this chapter about the communication of information and the process of persuasion will be developed more fully and illustrated with concrete examples of business communication in the chapters that follow.

Discussion Questions

1. Nikolai Bezroukov observes: "In Greek mythology, Sisyphus, an evil king, was condemned to Hades to forever roll a big rock to the top of a mountain, and then the rock always rolled back down again. A similar version of Hell is suffered every day by people with forever full e-mail boxes."[5] How bad is your e-mail in-box? How do you manage your messages?

2. What is the distinction between brevity and conciseness? How might an emphasis on brevity reduce the effectiveness of business communication?

3. Take a random sample of memos and letters received over the course of a week at work. Assess the directness, conciseness, organization, and clarity messages in the sample. Based on that assessment, if you were asked to recommend a training session on business writing for your department or company, what emphasis would you recommend?

4. Consider the following scenarios. Which of the nine patterns of organization would be appropriate for each?

    a. You need to write a memo in which you document how an employee's performance has declined significantly over a period of several months.

    b. You need to prepare an oral presentation in which you explain how territories for sales representatives in the Northeast have been reorganized.

    c. You need to write a memo in which you identify serious lapses in security at corporate headquarters and propose measures to improve security.

5. Think of a time when you failed to be persuasive at work, at the university, or in your personal life. Why do you think you failed? Think of a time when you succeeded at being persuasive at work, at the university, or in your personal life. Why do you think you succeeded?

Communication in Action

@ Internet

1. First, read Eric Eisenberg's article on strategic ambiguity (see note). Next visit a half-dozen Web sites of Fortune 500 corporations and read some recent press releases. What examples of strategic ambiguity are you able to identify in the press releases?

2. Visit Kaitlin Duck Sherwood's Web site, **http://overcomeemailoverload .com**, and read her "Top Tips for Overcoming Email Overload." Visit the *USA Today* Web site and retrieve two articles by Del Jones published in the Money Section on January 3, 2002: "E-mail avalanche even buries CEOs" and "Speed-read and don't spare the key." How much advice from Sherwood or the CEOs interviewed by Jones do you already follow and how much do you plan to adopt?

InfoTrac

3. Retrieve Jim Paul and Christy A. Strbiak's article, "The ethics of strategic ambiguity" (A19527181).[6] What are some of the important ethical issues raised by the authors regarding strategic ambiguity?

4. Retrieve both W. H. Weiss's article "Writing clearly and forcefully" (A80853855), and Jennifer Laabs's article "Make It Your Business to Write Clearly" (A65650795).[7] Each year numerous articles are published for business professionals about how to improve writing in the workplace. These two articles you have retrieved are fairly typical. Write a summary of the advice offered in the two articles on presenting information and then compare it with the advice in Chapter 2.

Notes

1. Jones, D. (2002, January 4). E-mail avalanche even buries CEOs. *USA Today*, p. A1; Jones, D. (2002, January 4). Speed-read and don't spare the delete key. *USA Today*, p. A2.
2. Memo 4/9/97, FYI: Messages Inundate Offices. (1997, April 8). *Wall Street Journal*, p. B1.
3. Krugman, P. (2002, June 28). Flavors of fraud. *New York Times*, p. A27.
4. Eisenberg, E. M. (1984). Ambiguity as strategy in organizational communication. *Communication Monographs, 51*, 227–242. (See Eisenberg, E. M., and H. L. Goodall. (2001). *Organizational Communication*, Third Edition. Boston: Bedford/St. Martin, pp. 24–25 and 30–31.

5. Bezroukov, N. (n.d.). Information/work overload annotated webliography. Retrieved October 8, 2002, at **http://www.softpanorama.org/Social/overload.shtml# E-mail**.

6. Paul, J., & Strbiak, C. A. (1997). The ethics of strategic ambiguity. *The Journal of Business Communication, 34*(2).

7. Weiss, W. H. (2001, September). Writing clearly and forcefully, *Supervision, 62,* 14; Laabs, J. (n.d.). Make it your business to write clearly. *Workforce, 79,* 22.

CHAPTER - 3

Advanced Visual Support for Managers

In many ways, the visual support that accompanies your written or spoken words has the most powerful impact because it clarifies, enhances, and emphasizes the message content. Research indicates that visual data are usually retained longer and more accurately than text or oral presentations alone. This is especially true when the information is complex, difficult, or new. Further, the way you deliver your visual support can have a direct influence on your professional image, particularly during corporate presentations. According to Walter Kiechel III, formerly of *Fortune's* board of editors,

> Let us in no way minimize the opportunity, or the danger, involved. The thirty minutes an executive spends on his feet formally presenting his latest project to corporate superiors are simply and absolutely the most important thirty minutes of that or any other managerial season.[1]

This chapter discusses how to extend the impact of written and oral communication through visual support, which can enhance such business media as reports, presentations, and training sessions. Five main topics are presented: principles of graphic excellence; types of visuals; when to use visual support; media selection, preparation, and usage; and planning and execution hints.

Principles of Graphic Excellence

Too many of the visual aids that businesspeople use are poorly thought out, incorrectly prepared, and misleading. Unfortunately, many are also either drab and lifeless or so cluttered that they are incomprehensible. Others demonstrate high-quality presentation yet fail to present the data in a comprehensible manner. All of these visuals fall outside the principles of graphic excellence.

Successful visuals integrate substance, statistics, and design to achieve four principles: clarity, precision, efficiency, and integrity.[2] The best visuals give the viewer the greatest number of ideas as quickly as possible in the least amount of space. Clarity, precision, and efficiency come with effort and reflect understanding of some general design concepts: emphasis, unity, balance, space, scale, shade and color, texture, and pattern.[3] Let us look at each of these design concepts in detail.

Emphasis makes an item stand out from others through special treatment, such as typeface or pattern. Overuse of emphasis, such as too much of a bright color, just causes confusion.

Unity is the relationship among parts that makes them function as one. Figure 3.1 shows, in the top example, a lack of unity—there appear to be eight separate bars. In the unified revision below it, one sees four pairs of bars.

Balance refers to the placement of elements in pleasing ways. One type, formal balance, has shapes arranged symmetrically. The other type, informal balance, can combine multiple smaller objects on one side against a sole larger object on the other. An example of informal balance would be a large photograph balanced by two small graphs.

Space is either positive or negative. An image such as a bar is positive and is surrounded by empty, negative space. Place positive elements in negative space so that the bars or other images seem to be resting upon the negative space. One way to accomplish the desired effect is to make sure that for bar graphs, the bars are wider than the space between them.

Applying **scale** involves presenting data so that it is not disproportionate; for instance, a small x-axis compared to a much larger y-axis is a scale problem. Figure 3.2 illustrates a scale problem with the y-axis on a graph. By varying the scale, the same data give a much different impression. To avoid giving a biased presentation, most statisticians follow the convention that the height of the y-axis should be about three-fourths the length of the x-axis and then make the appropriate adjustment to the scale increments.

Shades and colors should be planned as well. Light and bright colors jump forward and should be used for emphasis, while darker and more muted colors recede. If you use multiple colors that are not trying to emphasize specific elements, arrange the colors from dark to light. Many colors carry specific connotations—some of which are positive (green signals growth) and some of which are negative (red shows danger). Additional comments about color appear near the end of this chapter.

| Figure 3.1 | Lack of Unity Versus Use of Unity |

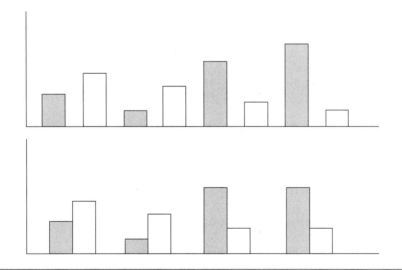

Figure 3.2   **Variation in Impact Because of Scale Change**

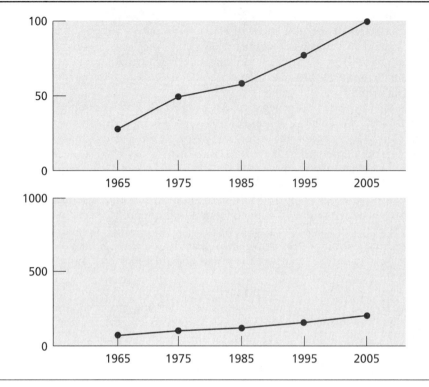

In using **texture and pattern**, avoid visual distortion by not putting patterns that interact visually, such as diagonal lines in opposite directions, next to each other. Bear in mind that vertical lines make items appear taller whereas horizontal lines make them look shorter.

The goal is to represent data accurately; that is, to achieve graphic integrity. To measure graphical integrity, Tufte uses his lie factor.[4]

$$\text{Lie factor} = \frac{\text{Size of effect shown in graphic}}{\text{Size of effect in data}}$$

For example, if a graph is drawn to exaggerate a bank's financial resources by 50 percent more than the data support (by using a bar that is too large, or a three-dimensional object rather than a two-dimensional object), the lie factor is 1.5. A 1.0 factor reflects accurate representation.

The debate between the artistic delivery of data regardless of the cost in accuracy versus avoiding a high lie factor at all costs brings out interesting philosophical and artistic questions and arguments.[5] Being aware of these potential pitfalls in both directions is a partial safeguard against major blunders in either direction. Careful observation of graphics in many prominent newspapers, magazines, and television advertisements will identify lie factors well above 1.0. Sometimes the designer of the graphic did not intentionally mislead but was overwhelmed by the data or became too involved in its presentation.

Keep these four principles—clarity, precision, efficiency, and integrity—in mind as you read the balance of this chapter and as you prepare your illustrations.

Types of Visuals

Most business visuals fall into one or more of the following categories: tables; graphs; charts, drawings, and diagrams; maps; photographs; and text. This section describes these visuals and suggests how they should be designed.

Tables

Tables present data in words, numbers, or both, usually in columns and rows. While tables are often the least enticing technique visually, they can be the most accurate method. As with most visuals, there are rules or standardized approaches to preparing tables, not all of which are always followed, but of which you should be aware.

- Keep tables as simple as possible. As a table becomes too complicated, consider breaking it into two or more tables.
- If you wish to follow common practice for printed or typed tables, enumerate tables by inserting Arabic numerals above each one.
- Place a descriptive phrase after the table number, such as "Relationship of Income to Expenditures, 2003 to Present." For a table that accompanies an oral presentation, you may wish to simplify the phrase.
- Place units of time (if included) in a row rather than a column.
- Try to present the data in logical fashion (increasing years, alphabetically, and so on) where the logic is immediately apparent.
- Employ good design techniques, such as ample white space, judicious use of boldface, and appropriate use of shading when designing tables.
- Use the word "Source" and follow it with a bibliographical citation if the data in the table come from a source other than your own primary research. In an oral presentation, you can speak your citation.

See Table 3.1 for a sample table, which shows the standard table format and identifies the parts of a table.

With the widespread use of computerized spreadsheets and printers capable of a variety of visual treatments, many of the long-standing rules for tables prepared with typewriters are fading. Tables now often incorporate different weights of lines (called rules), shading, italic and boldface type, color, and different sizes of type. Table 3.2 duplicates the data in Table 3.1 to show some of these treatments.

Graphs

Graphs, probably the most widely used visual support, come in many forms. Among the most popular are the line, bar, pictograph, geographic, pie, 3-D, high–low–close, Gantt, and scatter graphs. Usually graphs include data plotted on axes.

Table 3.1   **Sample Table**

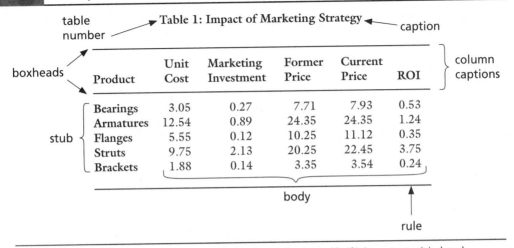

Table 1: Impact of Marketing Strategy					
Product	*Unit Cost*	*Marketing Investment*	*Former Price*	*Current Price*	*ROI*
Bearings	3.05	0.27	7.71	7.93	0.53
Armatures	12.54	0.89	24.35	24.35	1.24
Flanges	5.55	0.12	10.25	11.12	0.35
Struts	9.75	2.13	20.25	22.45	3.75
Brackets	1.88	0.14	3.35	3.54	0.24

The following design considerations apply to most graphs:

- Place time units on the horizontal axis.
- Start the vertical axis with zero and increase in units, without a break, to the top to adhere to graphical integrity.
- Place an Arabic number under the graph and include a title for the graph, also called a figure or illustration. For example, you might label a graph "Figure 3: Mid-level Management Turnover by Year, 2003 to Present."

- Keep all text in the same plane so that the page does not have to be rotated to be read. That is, avoid text printed diagonally or angled 90 degrees from the main text.

- Label both the x- and y-axes to identify the individual items on the axis. Thus, the label "Years" would be used for 2001, 2002, 2003, and 2004.

- Make sure to include a legend (or key) when necessary, but keep it unobtrusive. The legend is there to assist in understanding the graph, not to steal attention.

- If you decide to box the graph, do not allow the box to clutter the impression. Use boxes on other graphs in the same presentation for consistency if you place a box on the first graph.

- When selecting a typeface for a graph, try to match the typeface of the text of the report. Keep type sizes consistent—or at least complementary—if possible.

- Create a hierarchy of text treatments. For example, for inclusion in a written report, a graph might use a 12-point type for items on axes, such as 0, 1, 2 or 2003, 2004, 2005, and for text in the legend and source. Labels for the axes might be elevated with a 14-point treatment, and the title could be 14-point uppercase and boldfaced.

Line Graphs

Line graphs plot data on a two-dimensional axis. When a single line is plotted, a trend is shown. Most trends are plotted over time. When more than one line is plotted, comparisons of the trends can be made. Use line graphs to reflect frequencies, percentages, and distributions, and to compare multiple trends.

In designing line graphs, keep these thoughts in mind:

- Differentiate between multiple lines by using different techniques, such as solid, dashed, or dotted lines. Use solid lines for the primary data and dashes for secondary data, projections, or extensions. If no obvious primary (or first or most recent) line emerges, make the lowest line the heaviest or the solid line.

- Be wary of having more than four lines; readers become confused with too many lines, especially if they overlap.

- Make sure the plotted line is the heaviest line; the x-axis (horizontal) and the y-axis (vertical) should be medium-weight lines; the grid lines, if used, should be the lightest. If using colors for data lines, employ darker colors near the bottom of the graph and use progressively lighter colors on up the graph. Heavier and darker treatments at the bottom help achieve a feeling of low center of gravity, which aids aesthetics.

See Figure 3.3 for an example of a multiple-line graph.

Bar Graphs

Bar graphs are popular because they can present a variety of information. Their main application is in showing comparisons. A bar typically is two-dimensional, and may be filled with shading or color, and the number the bar represents may be placed on or above the bar. You should be able to move from the top of the bar

Figure 3.3 | **Multiple-Line Graph**

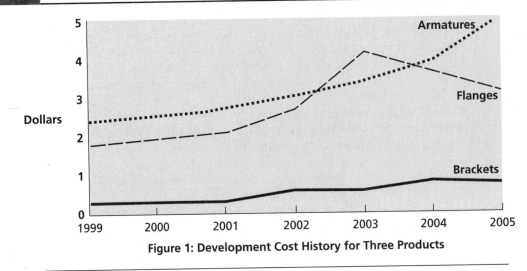

Figure 1: Development Cost History for Three Products

to the appropriate axis to determine the value that the box represents. A bar that meets these criteria is clear and is not as subject to misrepresentation as three-dimensional bars often are.

As you draw bars, keep these guidelines in mind:

- Draw bars so they are wider than the space between them.
- Prepare gridlines so they disappear behind the bars.
- Hold the maximum number of bars to 12—preferably far fewer.
- Draw bars of the same width.
- Arrange the items so that the bars appear in increasing, or perhaps decreasing, order if the x-axis does not show a time element and there is no other logical order to the x-axis items. Be aware, however, of other graphs in the same presentation with the same x-axis items. It is better to have a consistent arrangement of x-axis items across graphs than to modify the x-axis items for each graph to accomplish increasing or decreasing bars.
- When using segmented bar graphs (graphs that divide individual bars into parts), place the largest portion of the bar at the bottom to give a feeling of a low center of gravity. Use dark colors or treatments on low portions for the same reason. Then work in the next largest portion. Avoid conflicting adjacent patterns for the segments.
- Do not use part of the y-axis to form the leftmost bar; there should be some space between the y-axis and the first bar. This space typically is one-half the amount of space between the other bars.

- Make bar graphs more precise by placing numerical values on or above the bars. The numbers should not be obtrusive. If the numbers are to be printed on bars that are black or patterned, they should be positioned within white boxes so that they can be legible.

The bars in bar graphs may be vertical or horizontal: Decide which direction to place the bars by first placing the time units on the horizontal axis and then deciding whether you wish to portray a comparison by time (a vertical bar graph) or by another variable (a horizontal bar graph). If there is no time dimension, use a graph that employs vertical bars. Figures 3.4 and 3.5 illustrate vertical and horizontal bar graphs. The bars in each are "staircased" since there is no inherent order.

When you break a single bar into components (which usually total 100 percent), it becomes a segmented bar graph. For example, a whole bar could represent income for 2004, but its segments could break income into taxable and nontaxable income. The bar for each year then would have two parts, each drawn to scale. Usually the parts are treated in some fashion to differentiate them from each other, such as using color or shading. The segmented bars may be vertical or horizontal. See Figure 3.6 for a segmented bar graph.

You may wish to group some bars together, especially when they do not add up to 100 percent of something as a group. For example, you may wish to compare three of five regions for net profit by year. Thus, you would cluster Regions 1, 2, and 3 as bars on each year. In drawing a clustered bar graph, the clustered bars

| Figure 3.4 | **Vertical Bar Graph** |

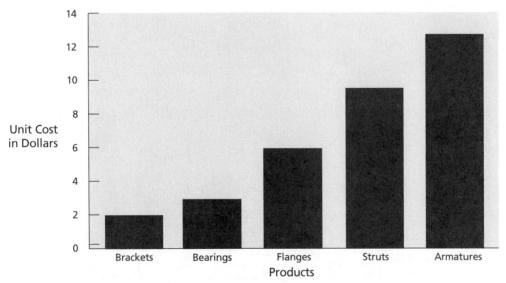

Figure 1: Unit Cost of Five Products

Figure 3.5 | Horizontal Bar Graph

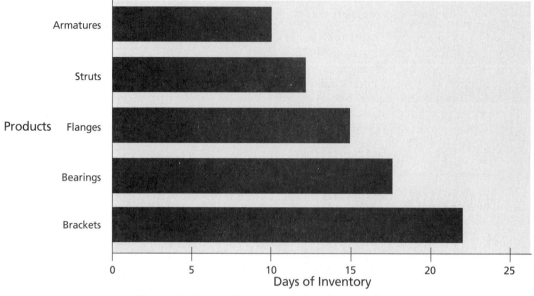

Figure 1: Days of Inventory for Five Products

Figure 3.6 | Segmented Bar Graph

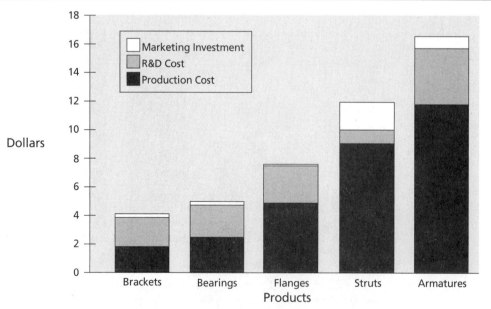

Figure 1: Price Components by Product

should touch each other and there should be an equal amount of space between clusters. See Figure 3.7 for an example of this type of bar graph. Compare Figures 3.6 and 3.7. Each bar in Figure 3.6 correctly adds up to 100 percent (marketing investment, R&D cost, and production cost). In Figure 3.7 there are five clusters of three bars each. If the goal is to compare the five products by the three types of costs, this approach is best, because all bars share a common zero point.

When confronted with data that could be either a segmented or a clustered bar graph, determine the main purpose of the graph. If it is comparing the sum of the parts, select the segmented bar graph. If, however, comparison of the parts is the primary intent, pick the clustered bar graph. Each type of graph allows the secondary purpose of the alternative analysis.

Most graphs are drawn in the upper-right quadrant (Quadrant 1) of the intersection of a vertical and a horizontal axis. This quadrant represents the positive half of the vertical line and the positive half of the horizontal line. Sometimes you wish to show negative numbers as well as positive ones, which means you must use more than one quadrant. A bar graph that uses two quadrants, such as the example in Figure 3.8, is a bilateral bar graph.

The reason most bilateral bar graphs use the upper-right and lower-right quadrants is that time is usually a variable, and thus plotted on the x-axis. Therefore, the other variable is the one with positive and negative values.

If there is no inherent order to the sequence of the bars (such as years), apply some order that enhances comparison, such as highest positive to lowest negative, or vice versa. An up-down-up-down approach may be visually pleasing and can stress the fluctuations. Figure 3.8 demonstrates this latter approach.

Figure 3.7 **Clustered Bar Graph**

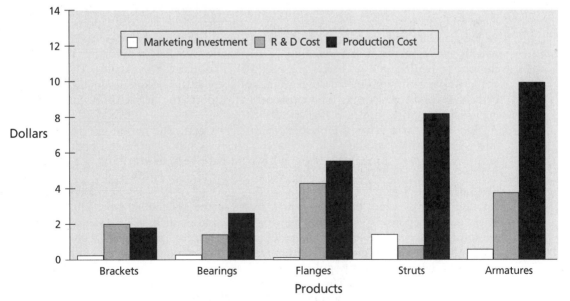

Figure 1: Retail Price Breakdown by Product

Figure 3.8 **Bilateral Bar Graph**

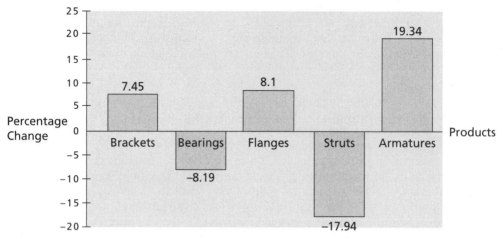

Figure 1: Percentage Change in Five Products' Co, 2000–2001

Pictographs

A pictograph is somewhat similar to a bar graph. Pictographs usually employ horizontal and vertical axes and plot data for comparison. However, instead of using bars to represent the amounts, symbols are used. For example, a picture of an oil drum might stand for 1,000 barrels of oil. Part of the symbol is used to show a fraction of the amount. Thus, in this example, half of an oil drum would represent 500 barrels of oil. Barrels stacked on top of each other show total amounts. Stacking symbols of equal size is better than increasing the size of just one item to show an increase, because most symbols represent three-dimensional things, and three-dimensional items increase in volume as they increase in height. In other words, showing a one-inch-tall oil barrel and a two-inch-tall barrel to suggest a 100 percent increase is misleading because the actual increase (in volume, and therefore perception) is 16 times that. This misuse greatly affects the lie factor. A correctly drawn pictograph is shown in Figure 3.9.

Occasionally you may see a pictograph with no y-axis. The reasons are that the unit values normally on the y-axis are inherent in the symbol, and that if high accuracy was the intent, probably a bar graph would have been used.

Geographics

Another graph that uses pictures—usually maps—is the geographic type. The value of geographic figures is to compare geographic divisions, such as states or regions, on some numeric variable. Sometimes states are enlarged or reduced and shown with other size-varied states to illustrate a quantity of something by state. For example, a geographic for population would reduce the relative size of Montana and enlarge Massachusetts. The intent is not to portray precise cartographic location or distance; that is the venue of maps, which will be discussed soon. A geographic visual is found in Figure 3.10.

| Figure 3.9 | Pictograph |

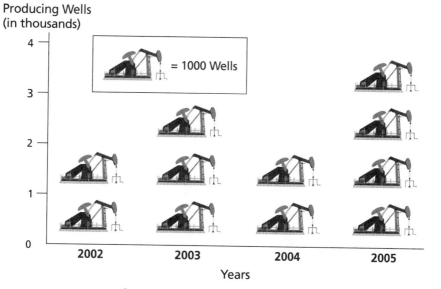

Figure 1: Producing Oil Wells by Year

| Figure 3.10 | Geographic Graph |

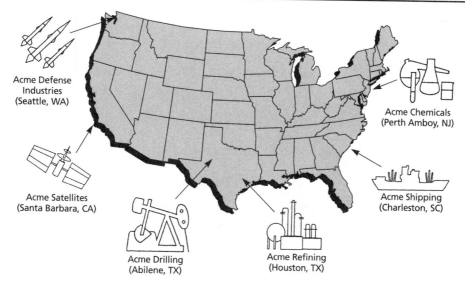

Figure 1: Primary U.S. Holdings

Pie Graphs

A popular but frequently boring and incorrectly prepared graph is the pie graph. Although commonly referred to as pie graphs or pie charts, note that they are not true graphs or charts. Pie graphs present data as slices of a whole, and the sum of the pieces totals 100 percent. According to William Cleveland,[6] author of *The Elements of Graphing Data*, these wedges are not an effective way to present percentages. His research shows that visual perceptions of pie slices are consistently inaccurate. He is also concerned about the problem of labeling narrow slices. Tufte, too, is critical of pie graphs because they do not order numbers along a visual dimension.[7]

Be cautious: Many of the computer software packages that facilitate preparation of pie graphs do not follow time-honored pie-graphing rules. These rules include:

- Always show 100 percent of something.
- Start at 12 o'clock with the largest slice and move clockwise in descending size. An exception to this rule is to place an Additional or Miscellaneous slice, no matter what its size, as the last slice.
- Use a protractor to draw each slice if you are hand-drawing the pie; each 3.6 degrees represents 1 percent.
- Consider using colors or patterns to visually differentiate the slices. Be careful, however, not to clutter the graph.
- Try to limit the number of slices to six. If you have only two or three slices, question whether you need the graph at all.
- Use the lightest color for the largest slice and move to progressively darker, smaller slices. Other alternatives are to move from darkest to lightest, or to alternate between light and dark to allow each slice to stand out. See which approach works best.

Try to use a software package that conforms to the rules above, but also be aware of its capabilities. For example, some packages allow you to "explode" a slice from the rest of the pie for emphasis.

Figure 3.11 shows six pie graph treatments of the same data. The author must decide which of the first four pies best supports the oral or written message: Does identification of the slices by product, percent, price, or a combination make the most sense? Notice the uneven exploding of the slices in Treatment D, which starts to misrepresent the data. Going to a 3-D exploded pie, as in Treatment E, introduces some of Tufte's lie factor because the amount of thickness given to the slices is not equal. Treatment F, which exaggerates the 3-D effect, amplifies the lie factor.

3-D Graphs

For variety and visual excitement, 3-D graphs are popular. On the other hand, 3-D representations can be misleading and are often difficult to draw. Software can facilitate 3-D graphs, such as the 3-D pie graph shown in Figure 3.12.

High–Low–Close Graphs

Especially valuable for financial graphs is the high–low–close graph, like the *Wall Street Journal* uses. Rather than show a single dot for a dollar amount, the high–low–close graph shows the dots (the high and the low) that indicate a range

Figure 3.11 | Pie Graphs

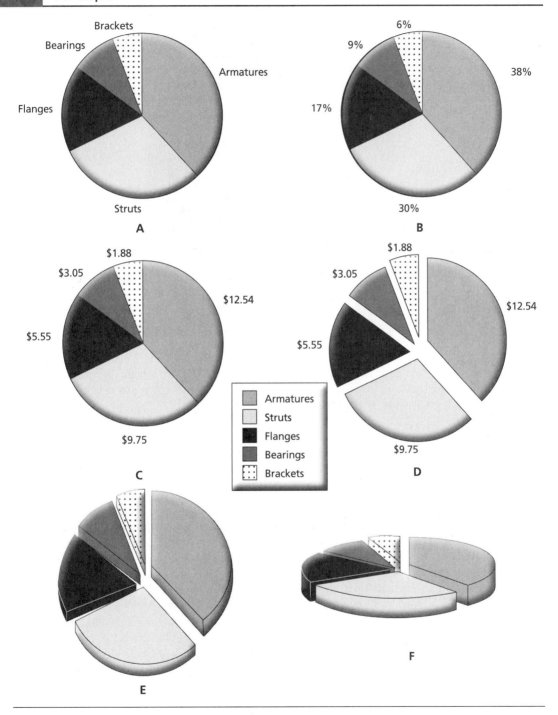

Figure 3.12 | **3-D Graph**

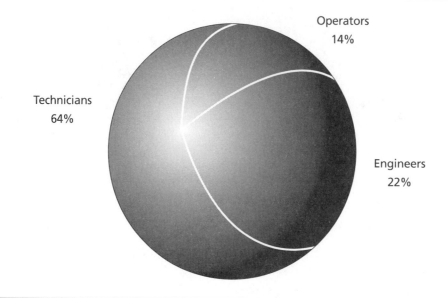

Operators
14%

Technicians
64%

Engineers
22%

and are connected with a line. The close may appear as a point on the line between the high and the low. Or, the top of the line is the high, the bottom is the low, and a cross line or dot is the close.

Gantt Graphs

The Gantt graph is used for event or production planning and process scheduling, such as for coordinating ordering, delivery, prefabrication, final fabrication, packaging, and shipping of a product. Bars on the graph show initiation and completion dates. Many software packages ease the tedious or repetitious burden of preparing Gantt graphs, and their first cousins, PERT graphs. A Gantt graph is shown in Figure 3.13. Another form of scheduling graph is found in Figure 3.21, yet to be discussed.

Scatter Graphs

A scatter graph presents dots on a two-dimensional matrix and is most often used with statistical data to show correlations. Lines may be drawn through clusters of dots to show trends or make forecasts.

Charts, Drawings, and Diagrams

Charts, drawings, and diagrams, as opposed to graphs, usually represent less-precise data, relationships, and flows of activities.

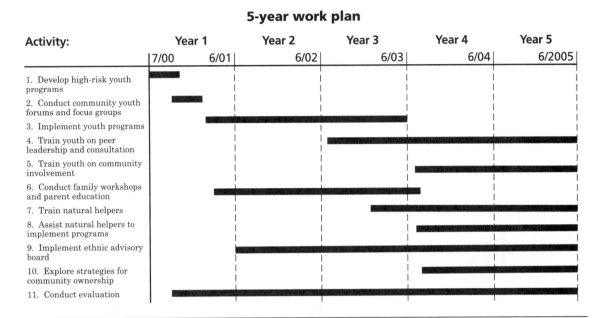

5-year work plan

Activity:	Year 1	Year 2	Year 3	Year 4	Year 5
	7/00	6/01	6/02	6/03	6/04	6/2005

1. Develop high-risk youth programs
2. Conduct community youth forums and focus groups
3. Implement youth programs
4. Train youth on peer leadership and consultation
5. Train youth on community involvement
6. Conduct family workshops and parent education
7. Train natural helpers
8. Assist natural helpers to implement programs
9. Implement ethnic advisory board
10. Explore strategies for community ownership
11. Conduct evaluation

Source: Used with permission of Union of Pan Asian Communities.

Charts

Charts often depict relationships, such as those in an organization. Within organization charts, solid lines usually connect line personnel and dotted lines link staff personnel. Organization charts show the channels that formal communication should follow. An organization chart appears in Figure 3.14.

Bubble charts present data, people, or departments inside circles (or bubbles) and then connect them with various thicknesses of lines to illustrate interrelationships. The size of the circles illustrates the amount of data or department size (see Figure 3.15).

Drawings

Drawings are beneficial for accurate representation of images that do not lend themselves to verbal descriptions, such as blueprints and technical drawings. These drawings often use standardized techniques and symbols to facilitate understanding.

Diagrams

Diagrams are often drawings, but diagrams usually show a flow between items, such as communication between people or the electrical current in a wiring scheme. The parts of a diagram relate to some actual object, such as the depiction of a laser printer toner cartridge that looks like the true component. Diagrams

Figure 3.14	Organization Chart

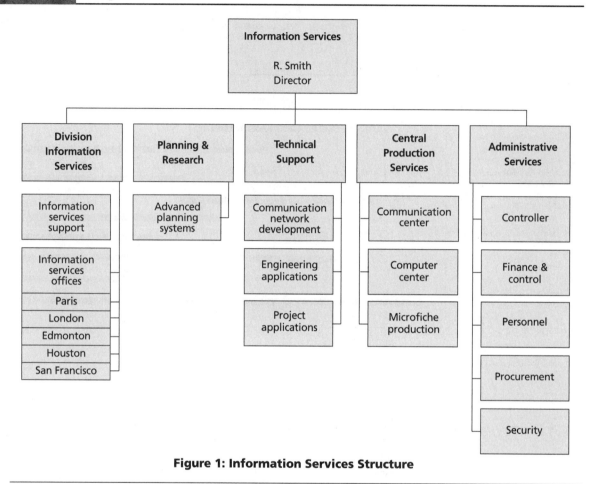

Figure 1: Information Services Structure

Source: Reproduced with permission from Computer Support Corporation.

showing steps in information processing by computer hardware and software are flowcharts. Figure 3.16 shows a diagram.

A **Venn diagram** uses overlapping circles to characterize mutuality and exclusivity. Venn diagrams can quickly illustrate what would often take many words to describe. See Figure 3.17 for a Venn diagram.

Maps

Maps are used when geographical precision is important, as opposed to a geographic graph, which might show a map but have the purpose of showing characteristics by section, such as product penetration by state. Identifying exactly where oil leases are on a piece of property may well call for a map (as well as a legal description of the location). See the map in Figure 3.18.

Figure 3.15   **Bubble Chart**

Figure 1: Relative Size of Departments

Figure 3.16   **Diagram**

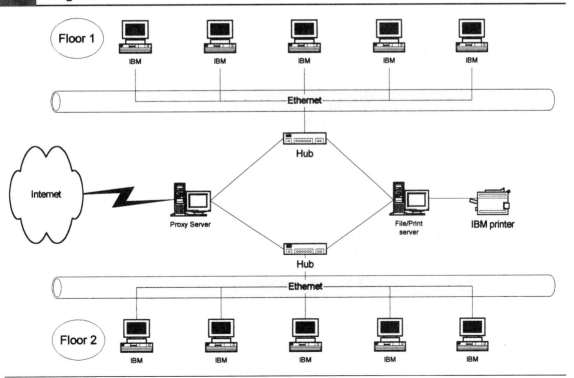

| Figure 3.17 | Model of Working Well |

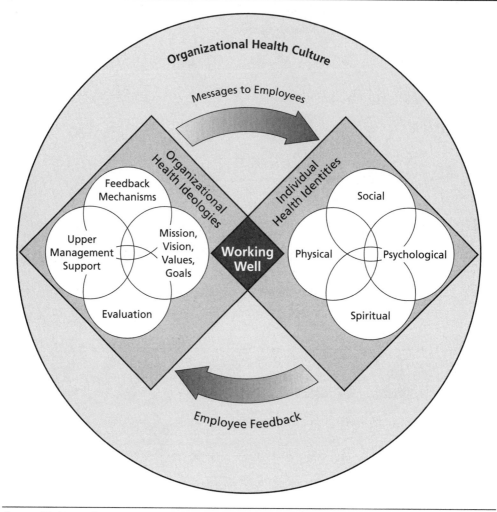

Source: "Working Well: Communicating Social Health," Angele M. Farrell.

Photographs

Most illustrations represent something; photographs often come the closest to representing what they stand for. Few people have the ability to describe a particularly beautiful sunset accurately; a photograph of the sunset can capture much of the emotion elicited by the original occasion. Photographs, then, not only effectively document a visual moment better than words but also improve on other visual means. They can, of course, be accurately duplicated as prints, prepared for print media, or scanned into a computer. A photograph that underscores these thoughts is found in Figure 3.19.

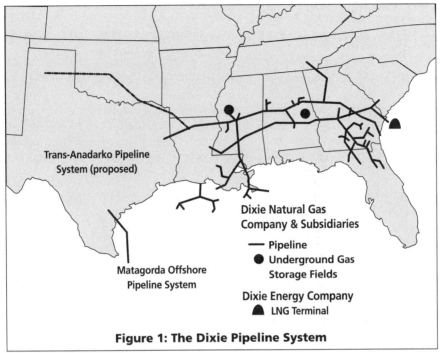

Figure 1: The Dixie Pipeline System

Source: Reproduced with permission from Computer Support Corporation.

Source: © PhotoLink/Getty Images.

Text

Because reports *are* text, the text is not considered visual support. That is not to say that reports and other forms of delivering hard-copy text do not benefit from effective formatting and appropriately bulleted or enumerated items. Such documents often are distributed prior to an oral presentation on the topic.

In support of previously prepared written documents or as stand-alone oral presentations, many visuals transmit only words. Quotes, outlines, and key thoughts are examples of text visuals that support oral presentations. Text visuals can show the direction of a presentation, give guideposts along the way, and pull together final conclusions. Text visuals can work in unison with the spoken word for emphasis or can stand alone. They are often used in 35-mm slides, overhead projector presentations, and computer slide shows. Figure 3.20 is an example of a text visual.

Some guidelines for the preparation of text include:

- Use a mixture of capital and lowercase letters to enhance readability.
- Select a simple, readable typeface if possible. Serif typefaces are easier to read than sans serif faces. (Serifs are the little lines on the ends of letters.)
- Select bullets or symbols to make items in a list show up and to clarify relative importance among items.
- Use color, boldface, or large type to differentiate among levels or to make important items stand out.

Figure 3.20   **Text Visual**

Steps in developing text slides

1. Select a background image
2. Select colors for text, back-, and foreground
3. Type in text
4. Pick a "build" effect
5. Add flourishes as appropriate

- Keep the lettering style for titles, legends, tables, and other illustrations consistent.
- Use no more than three type sizes in a single visual. More than three becomes too complicated.

In summary, you can choose from many types of visual support, but you need to know the rules for preparation and design. Learn which support is best for certain types of data; see Table 3.3 for a comparison of the support types by strengths and weaknesses. You also need some common sense. It is easy to allow visual support to become complicated, particularly when you are working with involved data. Figure 3.21 illustrates a complex graph that shows the timed steps of building an ocean-going vessel.

When to Use Visual Support

As we mentioned before, visual support can improve most written and spoken interpersonal communications. Because visual support has the ability to enhance involvement, understanding, and retention, it is used in written business reports, procedures, statements, proposals, feasibility studies, memos, and letters. Oral communications, such as individual and group presentations, speeches, seminars, training sessions, and briefings also are enriched with visual support.

When should support be used within the oral or written message? As it is needed. Visual support is support, not just entertainment. There are precise moments that call for visual support, at which point you would naturally use some visual. However, because visuals do have some value in garnering attention and in breaking up long blocks of text or extended periods of less-interesting information, you may be able to position them at a place or time when you need to rouse your audience.

As you decide whether to use visual support with your written or spoken communication, ask yourself these three questions:

1. Does the support increase efficiency?
2. Does the support increase effectiveness?
3. Does the support increase impact?

Efficiency reduces reading or listening time; effectiveness enhances understanding; and impact emphasizes the impression.[8] Your visual support should increase at least one of these qualities. If not, don't use it.

Within business reports, illustrations follow their discussion in the text. If an illustration is small—one-half page or less—it may be placed on the same page as text, with the text above or below. A larger illustration requires its own page. A separate page illustration should be placed on the first page following its mention in the text. The text will run on from its mention of the figure to the bottom of the page. The next page will be the illustration, and the page after that picks up the text. If the illustration requires a horizontal display, place it landscape (sideways) in the report so it is read from the outside edge rather than across the binding. Illustrations also can be placed in appendices at the end of a report. Rules for the preparation of illustrations described in this section apply.

Table 3.3	Visual Support Classification System	

Visual	Strengths	Weaknesses
Table	Shows precise numerical data	Tedious to prepare; slow to show relationships
Graph		
Line	Best for showing trends	Too many lines can be confusing; about 4 lines maximum
Bar	Best for comparisons; can be horizontal, vertical, segmented, clustered, or bilateral	Often incorrectly drawn; about 12 bars maximum
Pictograph	Visually interesting	Can be less immediately obvious than a bar graph; must stack numerous symbols rather than enlarge a single symbol
Geographic	Compares geographic divisions	Not drawn to scale
Pie	Popular; shows comparison of parts that total 100 percent	Wedges can be difficult to compare; too many wedges can be confusing
3-D	Visually exciting	Can be misleading
High–Low–Close	Best for financial data, such as stock prices	Complicated to prepare
Gantt	Excellent for scheduling events	Can be quite large and may need frequent updates
Scatter	Useful for statistical data and comparisons	Tedious; may require special software
Chart	Good for showing relationships; a bubble chart shows relative size or importance	Many items may require a large chart; a bubble chart is quite time consuming to prepare
Drawing	Beneficial for showing accurate representations of images, perhaps with standardized techniques	May require special knowledge or skills to prepare
Diagram	Best for illustrating flows; a Venn diagram efficiently shows overlaps of parts	May not accurately reflect relative importance of parts
Map	Shows geographic data	Relevant data can change over time
Photograph	Excellent for portraying pictures	Requires photographic ability or equipment
Text	Focuses attention on key words or phrases	Requires careful planning
Videotape	Shows motion; captures events, displays color	Requires special equipment to create and exhibit; carries high expectations by audience

Figure 3.21 A Complex Graph

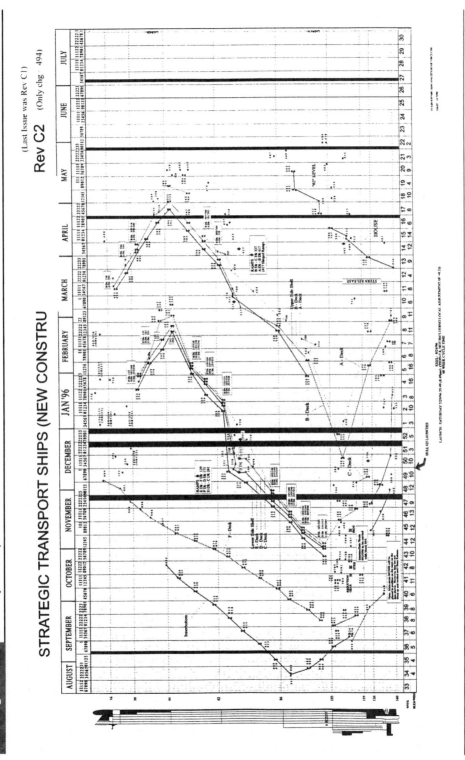

STRATEGIC TRANSPORT SHIPS (NEW CONSTRU

Rev C2

(Last Issue was Rev C1)

(Only chg 494)

Source: Reprinted courtesy of National Steel and Shipbuilding Company.

In oral presentations, visuals supplement or complement spoken words. They generally are shown concurrent with verbal descriptions when they are used to explain or illustrate. Visuals may precede oral comment for striking effect or attention value. They may follow a description to emphasize a point or summarize.

Critical skills for effective communication, then, include knowing both the value of visual support and the formal and informal rules for when to use that support. You also need to know the media available to you and how to prepare the support.

Media Selection, Preparation, and Usage

Many media are available for transmitting visual images. Paper handouts, blackboards and electronic blackboards, flip charts, overhead transparencies, and slides are the most frequently used visual media. Other popular media include computers and videotape.

Paper

By paper, we mean visuals that are prepared for delivery on paper, which probably will be prepared with a computer or typeset for inclusion in reports or used as handouts. Written words often carry a connotation of more formality than spoken words; this feeling of formality is even stronger with typeset words than computer-printed text, though the difference in perception between the two is narrowing. Therefore, if a sense of formality is desired, consider text visuals. Further, printed visuals usually carry the assumption that the audience may keep the paper for documentation or later review. The audience, of course, has the visual in its original form, not one subject to redrawing or interpretation.

One drawback to handing out visual aids prior to a presentation is that you lose control of when and how the audience receives your message. The audience is likely to page forward to sections later in your presentation and may even raise questions about that information before you are ready to discuss it.

Preparation
While the cost of black ink on white paper is relatively low, adding color to a visual increases the cost. However, the cost of high-quality color printers and copiers is falling rapidly.

Usage
If you use visual support in reports or handouts, number your illustrations. Give them titles that accurately describe the data and their relationships. Visual support should stand alone and require little explanation; the support should be carefully integrated into the presentation. Keep illustrations neat and attractive, but not at the cost of misrepresenting information. Proofread for accuracy. Aim for consistency across illustrations.

Blackboards

Blackboards, now available in many forms, have several strengths: They are flexible, usually placed to be viewed by the entire audience, and can be changed easily. Colors add clarity and are especially easy to use with white boards.

Preparation

Boards require little preparation beyond erasing them before use and perhaps putting complicated images or long passages on the board before a meeting. Make sure there are erasers and plenty of chalk or fresh markers.

Usage

Boards are usually used to put information in front of an audience as it is generated by a speaker or from a discussion. In the haste of writing on the board and with an audience watching, many people write poorly. Take the time to write legibly. Avoid standing in front of what you are writing and what you have written. Erase unimportant messages. If what is being developed on the board requires dissemination, ask someone to take notes and duplicate them later.

Audio teleconferencing with an optimum eight to ten participants at each location has recently emerged as a mode of communication superior to a telephone conference call. Among the apparatus that enhance audio teleconferencing are a microphone that picks up only one voice at a time and the teleconferencing blackboard. Typically, two remote locations are connected by telephone lines, and each may have the teleconferencing blackboard and a television monitor. What is written on either board appears on both monitors simultaneously. Thus, as one group develops a forecasting model on the board, the second group can see it and modify it.

Yet another form of the blackboard is the electronic blackboard. This board is usually a white board that requires markers. Information that appears on the board can, at the touch of a button, be sent to a built-in photocopier. On some models, the screen rotates so that the message then appears on the back of it, and a clean screen appears to the audience. Again, the touch of a button returns the first side to the front.

Flip Charts

Flip charts are not charts but, rather, large paper tablets. Speakers can mark on the sheets with colored markers and can remove sheets or flip to the next sheet with ease. Flip-chart tablets are usually supported on easels and can be moved easily. Expense is minimal, and no special skills are needed. Flip charts can help deal with unanticipated needs, such as recording an audience-developed list. Most uses of flip charts fall into one of two categories: as a visual aid for presenters, or as a way of displaying group thinking for problem-solvers or project planners.[9]

The impact of flip-chart visuals often suffers, however, from illegible writing, too many abbreviations, sloppiness, or audience frustration with someone slow at writing or drawing. Because most tablets are about three feet by two feet, viewers must be relatively close. You can't erase images; mistakes must be redrawn, crossed out, or ignored. See Figure 3.22 for a typical flip-chart image.

Preparation

Speakers can overcome some of the disadvantages of flip charts if they can plan what images will be needed and can draw or print them beforehand. The corners of pages can be coded or stick-on flags can be used so the speaker can quickly flip to the correct sheet. Most audiences do not look unfavorably on this planning step. If there is reason for extemporaneous drawing or writing during a presentation,

| Figure 3.22 | **Flip Chart** |

Source: © Ghislain & Marie David de Lossy/Getty Images.

consider lightly penciling the words or images beforehand on the sheet and then darkening the words during the presentation. Most viewers will not see the pencil marks.

When you prepare text or images in advance of a presentation, consider leaving blank sheets after each prepared sheet. The blank sheets allow you to flip a prepared sheet out of sight, thus redirecting attention back to you. The blank sheet also allows you space to write about your topic during the talk, if the occasion arises, without having to jump to the end of your prepared sheets. For especially dark or bright images, the blank sheet avoids bleed-through, where the image on the next sheet can be seen.

If you prepare your charts beforehand, consider using color. Red catches attention for key words, for example. One source suggests a maximum of three colors per sheet.[10]

Obtain a rather professional impression by making a black-and-white transparency of an image you would like on a flip chart, such as a city skyline or the face of the president. Then project the image on the tablet sheet and trace the image with a marker. Another professional touch is to use a computer to print large titles on adhesive labels.

For presentations that will be repeated and that rely on flip charts, consider investing in equipment that creates professional flip-chart pages. This equipment can produce enlarged photocopies, laser output, drawings, and text with color images on easel-pad-size paper for about $2 a page.

Until you have substantial experience with flip charts—and perhaps even then—practice giving your oral presentation while using the flip chart to coordinate the delivery of text and visual effectively.

Usage

Avoid standing in front of your flip chart, even as you write on it. A pointer can give you distance if necessary. Have a supply of markers available in case colors are unexpectedly needed or a marker runs out of ink. Consider having an audience member do the writing for you, which will free you to lead a discussion. Have plenty of paper available and do not put too much information on a single sheet. Sometimes when sheets are completed, they are posted about the room for reviewing. Companies such as 3M make a flip-chart pad that is similar to stick-on flags: The individual sheets can be stuck on walls without tape or thumbtacks.

Overhead Transparencies

As the size of an audience grows, so does the need for a larger image. One popular and inexpensive medium is the overhead projector. The projector transmits images from a low-cost transparency to a projection screen. Users find the machine quiet, movable, and efficient for large audiences. Most organizations have access to overhead projectors.

Preparation

For a high-quality black-and-white overhead transparency, start with a black original image on white paper and, from that, make the transparency by one of several methods. In one method, the image is photocopied; then, the transparency film is placed over the photocopy and the pair are run through a transparency-making machine. Many machines use infrared technology. Alternatively, the original can be placed on certain photocopiers and transparency film loaded instead of paper. Then the original is transferred directly to the film. Yet another method is to print a computer-prepared visual on a printer loaded with transparency film. This last alternative usually produces the sharpest image of the three techniques.

Computer software packages designed to facilitate presentations ease the burden and much of the expense of preparing overhead transparencies. These packages can automatically put the same border or background color on each visual, sequentially number them, size them appropriately, and allow for easy rearrangement or updating of the visuals. They can incorporate text, symbols, and graphics.

Several options for transparency film exist, including black or color images on clear film and black images on colored film. You can make transparencies of typed or drawn material in minutes with a photocopier, or you can use clear film on which you can write with special pens. If you must prepare or alter a transparency while it is being projected, use the special pens designed for this purpose. These inexpensive pens are available in both erasable, water-based ink and in permanent ink, both in a variety of colors. Color transparencies from color pictures are available, but they usually suffer in comparison to the originals. Computer programs can create color images and use color printers to print directly onto transparencies.

Key your colors in a series of transparencies to your main topics. Perhaps you will use blue for major topics and green for subthoughts. In this way your audience has a better feel for where you are in the presentation. Used effectively, color can accelerate learning, improve comprehension, and reduce errors. It can attract attention, create moods, and add vitality. You may wish to select colors based on their association in Western culture.

White	for **clarity, purity**
Red	for **stop, hot**, or **danger**
Yellow	for **caution, happiness**
Green	for **growth, money**
Dark blue or purple	for **royalty**

Be inclusive with your color associations; your colors may have different meanings with other cultures represented in your audience.
Some uses of color are to

- Emphasize words or lines
- Distinguish among parts of an illustration
- Show before-and-after changes[11]

To avoid mismatched foreground colors and background colors, apply the information in Table 3.4. Transparencies carrying text often have too much text. Use the 7-by-7 rule for text transparencies: Limit the number of words per line to seven and the number of lines per page to seven. Another guideline regarding the size of transparency images is to step away from the screen about eight times the distance from the projector to the screen to see if you can read the text. If you cannot, your image size should be increased.

For text transparencies, aim for consistency. For example, your template for a series of transparencies might include main titles in 36-point Helvetica type in all capitals; subpoints could be 24-point Times Roman in capital and lowercase letters, appearing after bullets.

Table 3.4 **Guides for Color Selection**

Background Color	Lettering Color (most readable to least readable)
Light	Black, blue, violet, red, green, orange, yellow
Dark	White, yellow, orange, green, red, blue, violet

Source: Minnesota Western Visual Support Systems, 1991, p. 202.

Consider adding overlays to your transparencies. In this case, the transparency is encased in a frame, and the overlays are then attached to the frame; they are then folded over the main transparency as needed. You may have three or four overlays on one transparency. Overlays may add bars to a bar graph, lines to a line graph, or images to a map. What is added by the overlay can be in color by using transparent colored film. As we will see in the section on computerized slides to follow, this process can be much more professionally delivered with a computer if the equipment is available.

Usage

Most users of overhead projectors quickly master the idiosyncrasies of the machine: move the transparency up to raise the image on the screen, but move it to the left to move the image to the right and vice versa. Most machines have an on–off or off–low illumination–high illumination switch and a knob for focusing the image. As the importance of the presentation increases, so does the need to have a spare bulb or an additional projector; some machines have a spare bulb in an alternate socket inside them.

Learn the correct use of the projector. Follow these guidelines:

- Place the transparency on the projector and then turn on the projector.
- Turn off the projector after the transparency has made its point or move to the next transparency.
- Try to switch from one transparency to the next quickly, because the projector is projecting light. If, however, you need to make comments before the next transparency, turn off the projector, remove the transparency, place the next one, comment, and then turn on the machine.
- Consider using relevant clip art to spice up your transparencies. Possibilities include a corporate logotype, cartoon characters, or drawings of computers or people. The art should be related to the topic.
- Avoid or minimize looking at the projector glass or projection screen. Know the content of the transparency and be able to discuss it without relying on it too much. Keep to a minimum the time you spend reading what your audience can read for themselves.
- Consider pointing to items in a list or locations in a table or figure as you discuss them. Consider using a pen or pencil on the transparency surface as a pointer or using a pointer at the projection screen if you deem that sort of focus is needed.
- Consider using cardboard frames for your transparencies. Tape the frame on top of the transparency—that keeps the transparency as close as possible to the glass. Write notes to yourself on the frames—they cannot be seen by the audience. The order of presentation can be written on the frames too.
- Use a sheet of paper to keep the transparency from being projected and then remove the sheet a bit at a time to disclose your points, such as items in a list. If you place the paper between the glass and the transparency, you will be able to read the portion of the transparency yet to be uncovered.

- If you are right-handed, try to have the projector to your right as you face your audience so that you minimize blocking views when you write on or point to transparencies. This technique also improves your eye contact with the audience.

35-mm Slides

Another popular way to support oral presentations is with 35-mm slides. Slides convey a variety of information, including texts, graphs, and pictures. The slide can be the focal point of the presentation or can support a topic. A drawback to using slides is the requirement that the room be darker than for most other presentations.

One value of a slide presentation that may escape some presenters is its professional image. A study by the 3M Company and the University of Minnesota found that using 35-mm slides for graphics caused viewers to perceive the presentation as more professional.[12] Because of its potential for improving your image, careful planning should go into a slide presentation.

Preparation

Text messages on slides follow the same guidelines as those for textual overhead transparencies, including the 7-by-7 rule.

As you prepare your slides, make a few black slides. These can be used in lieu of shutting off the projector during the presentation and are especially valuable when you are using multiple projectors simultaneously and wish to black out one projector.

Consider preparing the 35-mm-size images with a computer-presentations software package (as will be discussed soon). Then either mail or electronically transmit the file to an imaging firm that can create your 35-mm slides for you.

In planning your presentation, consider the possibility of outlining your talk for the audience with key words. First, prepare a slide (or slides) with the outline of your talk. Show only major topics. Perhaps you will have seven main topics, ranging from an introduction through conclusions. In addition to the master slide of your outline, make eight more copies. Pick a background color, such as blue, and a foreground color, such as orange. For the first slide, color all words orange. For the next, color the first heading (Introduction) orange and the rest red. Continue through the rest of the slides, moving down the outline. Conclude with another copy of the entire outline in orange on blue as a summary. In presenting your talk, first show your (orange) outline. Then, when you begin the Introduction, show the slide with that heading highlighted in orange. Continue to show your audience where you are as you progress through your talk. In between these slides, insert additional slides as required. The result: a highly structured, clear presentation that will be remembered.

Because even single-projector presentations can become complicated, you may find valuable a storyboarding technique that shows the coordination of slides and voice. If you are using two or more projectors and add music, the storyboard becomes a necessity in planning and a benefit in delivery. Figure 3.23 is a storyboard for a single projector presentation, and Figure 3.24 shows a storyboard for a more complicated presentation.

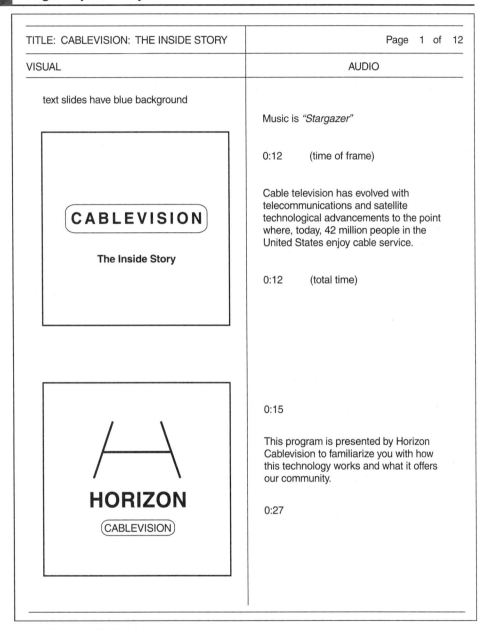

TITLE: CABLEVISION: THE INSIDE STORY	Page 1 of 12
VISUAL	AUDIO

text slides have blue background

CABLEVISION

The Inside Story

Music is *"Stargazer"*

0:12   (time of frame)

Cable television has evolved with telecommunications and satellite technological advancements to the point where, today, 42 million people in the United States enjoy cable service.

0:12   (total time)

HORIZON
CABLEVISION

0:15

This program is presented by Horizon Cablevision to familiarize you with how this technology works and what it offers our community.

0:27

Source: Courtesy of Mark Baird.

In planning your slide presentation, keep in mind that your audience grasps the point of a slide quickly. Change your slides often. A two-projector, five-minute presentation might easily consume 100 or more slides.

Figure 3.24 | **Double Projector Storyboard**

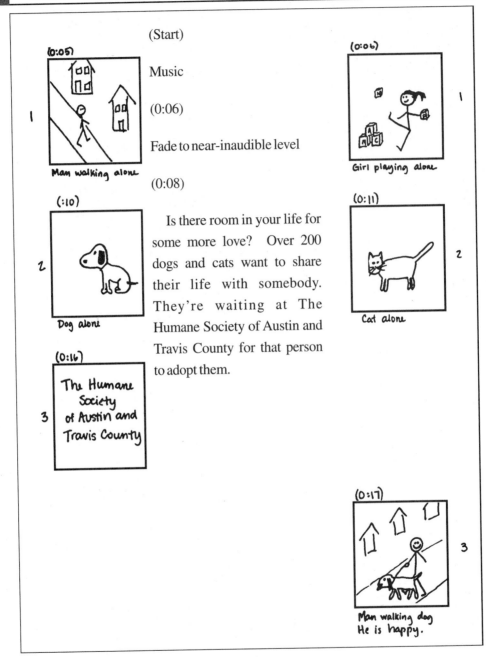

(Start)

Music

(0:06)

Fade to near-inaudible level

(0:08)

Is there room in your life for some more love? Over 200 dogs and cats want to share their life with somebody. They're waiting at The Humane Society of Austin and Travis County for that person to adopt them.

(0:05) Man walking alone

(0:06) Girl playing alone

(:10) Dog alone

(0:11) Cat alone

(0:16) The Humane Society of Austin and Travis County

(0:17) Man walking dog He is happy.

Source: Courtesy of Laura Nichols.

Usage

Learn the operation of the projector well before your presentation: Know how to focus, how to advance and reverse slides, and how to replace a bulb. Also pay attention to how the slides enter the projector. Many presentations have fallen victim to slides entered backwards or upside down. Look into increasingly sophisticated presentations as your needs grow, such as multiple projectors, fading in and out, and coordination with music or narration on several screens.

Computerized Visuals

Computers have emerged as a quick, easy, and inexpensive way to develop messages for other media, such as overhead transparencies. They have also become a medium unto themselves. In retail stores, training situations, displays, shopping-mall kiosks, classrooms, and laboratories, computers present a programmed series of "slides" on computer screens. Such slide shows can be especially beneficial in business presentations. Readily available presentation software, a portable computer, and a computer-image projection system now combine to form a portable unit capable of flashy, professional messages.

A computerized presentation in which the presenter prepares a series of slides, adds photos, graphs, audio and/or video clips, arrows, or clip art, incorporates fancy transitions from slide to slide, and adds movement by building a list item-by-item is so common that it is expected from many businesspeople and classroom instructors. Software packages such as PowerPoint facilitate development of professional, colorful, and stimulating presentations. Further discussion of these presentations appears in Chapter 11. To be consistent with the discussions of other forms of visual support preparation and usage already delivered, we do highlight some suggestions here.

Preparation

Most computer slide presentations require developing a series of slides and then ordering and timing the slides. Individual slides may include text, graphs, still pictures, clip art, sound, video, or any combination. To develop text slides, follow these steps:

1. Select a background image and slide layout (template).
2. Select colors for text, foreground, and background.
3. Type in the text in outline form.
4. Pick a "build" effect for emerging items in a list.
5. Add flourishes, such as clip art or graphs, as appropriate.
6. Choose a transition to the next slide.

Clip art picture or symbol libraries, which may be part of a presentation software package or a stand-alone package, supply popular or difficult-to-draw pictures, old photos, cartoons, or audio or video clips. A user can search the library for a desired picture, select the picture, enlarge or reduce it, and add shading or patterns if desired. Libraries can be specialized, such as for computers or new technology (see Figure 3.25). Of course, huge amounts of supporting images, sounds, and motion can be found on the World Wide Web. As long as it is not gimmicky, the addition

Figure 3.25 **Clip Art**

of a well-known voice saying something relevant or of a striking photo can add a professional feel.

When deciding which addition to use, ensure that it relates to your topic, matches the mood, and is compatible with other art and slides in your presentation.

Other hints for preparing computerized slide presentations include

- Consider having a blank slide in a single color with no images as your first slide.

- Start with a title slide.
- Consider a text slide with the outline of your presentation.
- Think about the inclusion of a concept slide.[13]
- Use graphs to help in visualizing tabular data.
- Select charts, diagrams, or photos for variety.
- Consider an occasional one-, two-, or three-word text slide for impact.
- Avoid too many text slides with lists.
- Each slide should have one—and only one—dominant visual effect that provides a starting point for the audience's eyes.
- Use color creatively.
- Avoid pictorial clichés and avoid animation overload.
- Add a conclusions slide that pulls together the main topic of the presentation.
- Seek a feeling of consistency for the entire presentation.
- End with a blank slide like your first one, or one that says "Thank you" or "Questions?"[14]

Usage

Computerized slide shows can demand attention, manage the information flow, and create a professional tone. However, they can also be boring, disorganized, or plagued by technical problems. Here are some usage suggestions:

- Keep the attention upon yourself and let the presentation support what you have to say; don't be left out of your own presentation.
- Be unobtrusive in your computer interaction during the presentation.
- Consider putting the presentation in automatic mode in which each slide (and even each item in a list) is assigned a specific and predetermined amount of exposure time.
- Don't leave simple, one-, two-, or three-word impact slides on the screen too long.
- Avoid reading what appears on the screen to the audience; paraphrase the thought.
- Consider using a remote control to forward (and perhaps reverse) the slides.
- Use the "rehearsal" option in some software to practice and perfect your timing.
- Explore the Internet for fresh templates, drawings, or photos—often at no cost.
- Anticipate problems. Consider having a backup of your presentation already prepared as 35-mm slides or overhead transparencies. The more important the presentation, the more crucial the backup.
- Seek a balance of slide types. Avoid a presentation of text-only slides. Work in graphs, drawings, photographs, or other nontext slides if possible. Audiences tire quickly of bulleted, text-only sides even when well prepared and enlivened with animation.
- Prepare a "concept" slide, if appropriate, that captures the main points of the presentation and can show individual parts, the process, or thoughts along the way. Such a slide might be a stylized drawing, a chart, or an acronym.

Videotape

In the past 25 years, videotape usage has moved from an expensive, moderate-quality, black-and-white image to an inexpensive, high-quality, color image. Professional color cameras and studio-quality productions are still expensive, but the hand-held camera and individual videotapes have become inexpensive. Many firms, such as travel agencies, real-estate brokers, and producers of computer software distribute free videotapes of their products or services. As with other media, videotapes as part of business presentations require planning and experience.

Planning and Execution

Table 3.5 compares the seven media just discussed and lists their strengths and weaknesses.

The visual and verbal portions of a presentation should support each other as part of one package.

1. Define your topic. As discussed in the chapters on making presentations and delivering case analyses, you must first determine what topic you will be addressing.
2. Determine audience characteristics. Find out about your audience (characteristics, attitudes, and so on), and what they expect from your presentation. How are they likely to respond?
3. Set learning objectives or goals. What do you want your presentation to accomplish? Awarding of a contract, development of a new product, expansion into a new market, or expanding of personnel? The information should be geared toward accomplishing observable, measurable objectives.
4. Prepare the verbal content of the presentation. Many people prefer to outline their verbal presentation first.
5. Add the visual support. Add visual support where it would enhance your verbal presentation.
6. Pretest the package. Run through your presentation to make sure it is clear and accomplishes your goals. Practicing an oral presentation with all components in place, including the visual support, prevents awkward fumbling at a meeting. Bring in peers for their reactions and modify as necessary. Check your timing. Are you within any imposed time constraints?
7. Execute your presentation. Deliver your report, presentation, or case analysis.
8. Evaluate your performance. How well did you do? What could have been improved if you had it to do over? What did you learn? Did some things work especially well?

Some Additional Hints

Here are some additional hints to help improve your visual support.

Color

Adding color to chalkboards, handouts, 35-mm slides, computerized slide shows, or overhead transparencies can grab the audience's attention and, if used correctly,

Table 3.5   **Media Selection Guide**

Medium	Audience Size	Formality	Strengths	Weaknesses	Cost
Paper	No limit	Formal	Inexpensive, flexible	Preparation required	Inexpensive
Flip charts	10–15	Informal	Inexpensive, flexible	Can be hard to read	Inexpensive
Overhead transparencies	100	Informal	Inexpensive, focuses attention	Easy to misuse; poor presentation skills	Inexpensive
Slides	Several hundred	Formal	Strong impact	Dark room required; preparation required	Moderately expensive
Blackboards	15–25	Informal	Inexpensive, flexible	Color seldom used effectively	Inexpensive
Computers	3–5 at a time (without projection capability)	Informal	Current, flexible, easy to use	Expensive; can appear childish	Expensive for hardware; software inexpensive
	100 (with projection) multi-media capable	Either	Focuses attention, flexible	Takes time and expertise	Projection system can be expensive
Videotape	15–25 with single monitor	Varies with topic	Shows motion, can be quite professional	Limited audience size; no interaction	Can be expensive

increase comprehension and understanding. However, colors can also detract from the message and even confuse or offend the viewer. In addition to the earlier comments about color, keep these hints in mind:

- Match the color to the presentation and to the audience. Members of the board of directors expect different colors than would be appropriate at a Cub Scout meeting or a garage-sale announcement.
- Arrange heavier colors, such as blues and greens, at the bottom of illustrations, if possible, and move upward to lighter colors.
- Use colors in moderation. Limit the total number of colors to six.
- Select bright colors for special effects.
- Pick contrasting colors to set ideas apart.
- Choose shades of the same color to group items.
- Be aware of cultural differences in meanings of color.

Simplicity

Whether you prepare a graphical design, a text chart, or an entire presentation, keep it simple. Too many colors, too much clutter, excessive words, too many bars or pie slices, or too many numbers overwhelm the viewer. In a study by the University of Minnesota on graphics, researchers learned that the simple presentation works best.[15] As computers increasingly are used to design illustrations, it becomes easy to add textures, patterns, and colors to graph bars and slices—but be wary. Tufte calls the overabundance of visual distinguishers "chartjunk."[16] Most of the figures in this chapter represent simple presentations.

Repress the desire to fill an illustration with too much information. Use graphs to show trends and rely on tables when specificity is needed. As the data become more complicated, consider a series of graphs to depict the information.

Professionalism

The quality of the visual images supporting your oral presentations will enhance or detract from your professional image. Therefore, in addition to presenting data accurately, make sure it looks good. When the message is an important one and the visuals are not satisfactory, call in experts. Be aware, however, that many artists, designers, and media technologists are not familiar with the principle of visual integrity; you must make sure that the final image is appropriate and not just professional looking.

In oral presentations, it is important to keep your talk moving; all too often, the visuals become the centerpiece instead of support. If a lot of time must be spent discussing a single illustration, it probably should have been distributed prior to the talk.

Visuals are no place for misspellings, too much jargon, too many acronyms, or heavy reliance on passive voice. Further, ensure both word and nonword elements do not embarrass, belittle, or ridicule any member of the audience.

The Environment

Before making your presentation, become familiar with the environment. You should learn about the equipment and the availability of backup bulbs, chalk, computers, and projectors. Know the location of electrical outlets, light switches, microphone outlets, and controls for lowering and raising screens and adjusting amplifier volumes. You need to plan ahead if extension cords or three-prong adapters are needed. You may also need to arrive early to arrange chairs, erase blackboards, distribute handouts, or set up screens or flip charts.

You may also wish to know the location of the controls for dimming lights or adjusting air-conditioning. Dimmed lights can focus attention on the screen even if darkness is not required. You may also need to know how to adjust window blinds to darken a room. An overheated meeting room distracts your audience; consider lowering the room's temperature just before the meeting begins. Conversely, a noisy ventilation system also can detract from your presentation. In that situation, cool the room first and then shut off the system for your talk.

Business Graphics Checklist

Sometimes the best way to ensure that you are abiding by the many rules for the preparation of business graphics is to follow a checklist. One such checklist, prepared by the Information Center Institute, appears in Figure 3.26.

The Information Center Institute Checklist for justifying business graphics

Computer graphics cover a lot of ground—business, engineering, manufacturing, medicine, and the arts. And the software applications to accomplish the various tasks in these fields are burgeoning at an ever-increasing rate.

The question now no longer seems to be will computer graphics help the business organization, but how much will they help and how will we measure it? In other words, how can we justify the increased use of computer graphic systems? What questions should be asked in order to start the justification process for the use of these systems? The following checklist is designed as a way to begin thinking about this process. A careful definition and understanding of needs will go a long way toward providing the information needed for justifying these graphics systems.

After determining user attitudes, especially those of management, the types of graphics needed for your situation, and the measurable and nonmeasurable costs and benefits, you will be much better prepared for the process of justifying the purchases of new graphics systems or the improvement of existing ones, and better equipped to decide on the kinds of hardware and software systems that you will need.

Note: For analysis, the estimates of the costs as well as the benefits should be divided into two categories: one-time and recurring.

No.	Item	Yes	No	N/A	Comments
	Management Attitudes				
1.	Is management interested in graphic rather than tabular presentations for decision-making tasks?				
2.	Is management comfortable with graphic presentations for spotting trends and making forecasts?				
3.	Is management satisfied with the quality, scale, and accuracy of graphs produced in the past?				
4.	Will management place a value on the availability of better graphics?				
	Use of Graphics Systems				
5.	Are business graphics desired primarily for: a. presentation of information for discussion and decision? b. summary and display of large quantities of information?				
6.	Are graphics applications already used for: a. observing statistical relationships and variable interactions? b. display of engineering results and designs?				
7.	Is there interest in image generation for: a. visualization of planned objects? b. illustration of presentation slides? c. eye-catching figures to include in presentations?				
8.	Have cost comparisons been made for: a. microcomputer-generated graphics? b. mainframe-generated graphics? c. graphics produced by specialized hardware? d. hand-generated graphics for comparison?				

Figure 3.26   **Checklist for Justifying Business Graphics (Concluded)**

No.	Item	Yes	No	N/A	Comments
	Uses of Graphics Systems cont'd.				
9.	Have costs been analyzed for downloading prepared files to minicomputers or microcomputers for graphic production?				
10.	Will the graphics costs be absorbed by information services or charged back to the users?				
11.	Have cost calculations for any software included the cost of needed modifications and extensions? Is the price of the graphics package competitive with similar packages when modifications and extensions are considered?				
12.	Are the total costs, including extra features, modifications, and maintenance, likely to remain within the budget limitations for the next three years?				
13.	Will overall costs be lowered by: a. reducing graphics production expenses? b. reducing graphics maintenance expenses? c. reducing manual effort and clerical expenses? d. reducing communications expenses?				
14.	Will controlling production costs reduce operational expenses?				
15.	Will there be faster turnaround for clients at same or reduced costs?				
16.	Will certain costs be avoided by: a. making personnel available for other work? b. employing fewer people for graphics production?				
17.	Can profit increases be estimated for: a. providing graphics for management? b. providing graphics for customers/clients? c. providing faster reaction and turnaround times? d. Improving the use of resources?				
	Intangible Benefits				
18.	Is there value in reducing errors that result in the manual production of graphics?				
19.	Is there value in having more checks and controls on designs and displays?				
20.	Are there operational cost advantages in the sharing of graphical information between files?				
21.	Are there operational cost advantages in improved planning and scheduling through the use of graphics?				
22.	Can a value be estimated for the reduction of problems and complaints?				
23.	Is there a business advantage in the improved timeliness of graphics production?				
24.	Can financial benefits be estimated for: a. improved business analysis? b. improved business control? c. improved responsiveness to customers?				

Source: Information Center Institute, a division of Chantico Publishing Co., Inc.

Summary

In many ways, visual support can have a greater impact than the spoken or written communication it assists. However, you need to know how to correctly use visual support to make it valuable. Support should be clear, precise, and efficient and reflect integrity with what it represents. Knowledge of design considerations such as emphasis, unity, balance, scale, shade and color, and texture and pattern improves the process. You also need to know the type of visuals from which to select. Major types include tables; graphs; charts, drawings, and diagrams; maps; photos; and text. Each has rules for its preparation.

Some people overuse or misuse visual support. To test your decision on including support, ask yourself whether it is efficient and effective and creates impact. Valuable support should accomplish at least one of these three goals.

Presenters can choose from many media for oral and written delivery: paper, flip charts, overhead transparencies, slides, blackboards, computers, and videotapes. A system of planning and evaluation will assist your execution, as will review of the hints that conclude this chapter.

Discussion Questions

1. What is the 7-by-7 rule? Discuss the concept with your classmates. Does the rule make sense? How much latitude is there? Does it vary by medium? Does it apply equally to flip charts, 35-mm slides, transparencies, and electronic slides?

2. Usually it is best to arrange vertical bars that have no inherent order in some order, such as of increasing or decreasing height. If you have a series of bar graphs, all with the same items as vertical bars, would you select one order for all graphs for consistency, or would you arrange each individual graph for some logical flow? Why?

3. We define graphs as data plotted on an axis, yet Microsoft Excel calls such images "charts." Why do you think they use the alternative term? Who is correct? Does it make a difference which is correct?

4. What are the best applications of pie charts? Would the same data plotted as a bar or line graph be better?

5. Is it better for the data lines in a line graph to start against the Y-axis or moved to the right? Does your graphics software package give you a choice?

Communication in Action

1. How would you apply the principles of graphic excellence if you needed to prepare a visual support element with the following data? Prepare the element.

	Year 1	Year 2	Year 3	Year 4
Net sales ($ millions)				
Compared to previous year				
Product #1	−1.75	−3.04	4.20	6.31
Product #2	−2.00	2.12	10.11	30.71

2. Create a visual aid that effectively gets across this message: "40 percent of the state's air pollution comes from 10 percent of the cars."

3. Prepare a supporting visual that makes the following point: "Research indicates that the amount of time spent in athletic exercise extends a person's life by about the amount of time spent exercising."

4. How would you graph the following concept: perfumes can be evaluated on three axes: cost, intensity, and longevity.

@ Internet

5. Search the Web for information about the U.S. population growth for each of the past four years by gender. Locate the parallel growth patterns for your state. Then locate the parallel growth patterns for Russia. Prepare a graph that seeks to demonstrate whether the three patterns are similar or different.

6. You are working on a team project that must define the American economic situation after September 11, 2001. You have been assigned the task of locating the economic indicators that best reflect the changes. Do your search and prepare a handout that covers what you found.

7. You have decided to enliven your PowerPoint presentation by adding some sounds, pictures, and brief video clips. The presentation is complete except for the following items. Use the Internet to locate these clips:

   a. Sound of thunder.

   b. Video clip of the Challenger explosion.

   c. Sound of footsteps walking on gravel.

   d. Picture of North America from space at night showing lights of cities.

   e. Sound of President Kennedy saying, "Ask not what your country can do for you. . . ."

   f. Sound of a Harley Davidson motorcycle.

   g. A picture of the capitol building of Texas.

InfoTrac

8. You have been interested in annual reports for some time. You know that such reports are often divided into an opening, narrative section, and then a financial section. You wonder whether the use of graphs in either of these two sections is allowed to "wander" from the precise data; that is, whether the graphs are intentionally misrepresenting the data to in some way enhance the image of the organization.

   You decide to research this topic and plan to examine scholarly journal articles. Using InfoTrac, see what you can find. Be sure to include at least three or four articles written by Viviene Beattie and Mike Jones.

Notes

1. Wilcox, D. L. (1985, May). The boom in business graphics. *PC Magazine*, 282–287.
2. Tufte, E. R. (1983). *The visual display of quantitative information* (p. 51). Cheshire, CT: Graphic Press.
3. Meilach, D. Z. (1985, August 6). The do's and don'ts of presentation graphics. *PC Week*, 47–50.
4. Tufte, *The visual display of quantitative information*, pp. 57–58.
5. See, for example, the parallel interviews in *Aldus* magazine: "Saying it with images: An interview with Edward Tufte," 2(4), May–June, 1991, 27–56; and "The picturing of information: A conversation with Nigel Holmes," 2(6), September–October, 1991, 18–55. A more-lengthy delivery of Tufte's views is found in Edward R. Tufte. (1990). *Envisioning information*. Cheshire, CT: Graphic Press.
6. Stoll, M. (1986, March 25). Charts other than pie are appealing to the eye. *PC Week*, 138–139.
7. Tufte, *The visual display of quantitative information*, p. 178.
8. Lefferts, R. (1981). *Elements of graphics: How to prepare charts and graphs for effective reports* (p. 5). New York: Harper & Row.
9. Wallace, M. (2000, August 1). Flip charts: Low-tech powerhouses. Retrieved June 11, 2002, from **http://www.llrx.com/columns/guide42.htm**.
10. Low-tech training. (1995, April). *Workforce Training News*, 13–16.
11. *Minnesota Western Visual Support Systems*. (1991), 200–204.
12. Goldberg, C. J., & Kunkel, G. (1987, March 10). Charting a course through graphics software. *PC Magazine*, 113–117.
13. Endicott, J. (2002, March). Concept slides flesh out ideas in ways words can't. *Presentations*, 22–23.
14. Grauer, R. T., & Barber, M. (1999). *Exploring Microsoft PowerPoint 2000*. Upper Saddle River, NJ: Prentice-Hall.
15. Santarelli, M. B. (1986, November 11). The zen of business graphics. *Information Center*, 2(11), 42–47.
16. Tufte, *The visual display of quantitative information*, pp. 107–121.

Part Two

Written Communication: Brief Messages

CHAPTER - 4

A Strategic Process for Effective Managerial Writing

Effective writing has certain characteristics. Some of these characteristics relate to the overall writing process, such as conceptualizing, researching, drafting, and revising. Other characteristics focus specifically on formal features, such as organization, tone, and readability. In this chapter, we will examine both of these approaches to the writing process.

The Overall Writing Sequence

You may be surprised to know how many people start writing without knowing where they are heading. Perhaps the assumption is that they will figure out their direction as they wander through various thoughts. In order to achieve efficiency and clarity of writing, however, avoid this method.

Most writing goes through many steps. Usually, the more complicated, lengthy, or important the project, the more steps you include. Here are the eight steps through which most of your written communications will go. The order is typical; however, you may relocate some steps.

1. Define your problem.
2. Determine and analyze your audience.
3. Do your research.
4. Consider your layout, format, and elements.
5. Draft your project.
6. Revise, edit, and proof the written copy.
7. Produce the finished package.
8. Conduct a postwriting evaluation.

At various times in your college and business careers, you will probably place more effort or emphasis on some of these steps than on others. For example, as a first-year composition student, you may have wrestled with finding a topic and defining it. Later in college, you no doubt prepared a paper that called on you to do research. As a middle manager, you may not prepare the finished version of a report, which upper managers do, but you write the initial draft. As a top manager, you will revise and edit the work of others. Nevertheless, each of these steps plays an important part in effective business writing, and each deserves examination.

Define Your Problem

When a superior gives you a writing project, you probably know the parameters you are to cover. No doubt you have a specific goal. You may even have a formal letter of authorization. Occasionally, however, your assignment will be vague. For example, how would you react to these written directions from your boss if you were in the management consulting division of a major public accounting firm?

> Sorry not to be able to give you more lead time, but by the time you read this I'll be in Madrid working on a hot project. This trip will keep me from completing the proposal for Nelson National Bank that's due this Friday. I've been working on it alone, although Bill and Tracy supplied some data. I want you to finish it and submit it to Nelson by the deadline. This package could be quite lucrative for us now and in the long term.
>
> In the attached folder are most of the supporting materials and my text so far. My assistant, Phyllis, typed and formatted a proposal something like this once before, and you can ask her to work on this one.
>
> Wish I could be more available to help you on this. See you a week from Wednesday.

Your assignment is to prepare the proposal. To know how to accomplish that, however, you need to know topic-oriented answers to questions such as these:

- What are we proposing?
- What (and who) is Nelson National Bank?
- What level of profit do we seek now and in the future?
- What is the time period reflected by the proposal?

In determining your approach, you'll also want to know:

- How would your boss write the proposal?
- How badly does your boss want the contract?

Answers to these questions would guide you in approaching this assignment. Clearly, you would be wise to know your direction before you start writing.

Determine and Analyze Your Audience

To whom will the letter, report, or memorandum be sent? Will it be sent to a group? Will it be shared with others? What is your relationship to your audience? The answers to these and other questions may determine the response you receive to what you send.

As you identify your audience, here are some factors to consider:

- What is their position in the hierarchy and how does it relate to you? Subordinates write differently to superiors than superiors write to subordinates. Yet another approach is needed when writing to peers. Messages downward are often authoritative or motivational in tone, while those going upward may have a softer tone. When you share information with peers, you often do so (1) cautiously if you are protecting yourself or (2) quite openly if you anticipate an enthusiastic response. Also, be aware of whether the audience is inside or outside the organization. Messages going outside the organization differ from internal messages by being more formal.

- What medium is best for your audience? Skilled communicators are able to match the message to the medium from the audience's viewpoint. Some media are perceived as formal (scholarly thesis) or informal (comic book); others are quick (spontaneous meeting in the hall) or slow (printed annual report); personal (face-to-face discussion) or impersonal ("to whom it may concern" letter); friendly (Christmas party) or stern (disciplinary review). Many other characteristics apply. Should the message be written or spoken? If it is to be written, for example, would a facsimile, e-mail, memo, letter, report, or printed document be best? See if you can match each message to its medium in Table 4.1. Make the best pairing you can. The suggested correct answers are open to interpretation, of course.

- How much does the audience know about the subject? Ideally, your message will be appropriate to their level of understanding. They will not be confused when you use relevant jargon or be offended when you define unfamiliar concepts or words. You do not want to waste their time sharing information they already know.

- What is the educational level of the audience? Often writing somewhat below the education level of your readers is desirable (as we will discuss a little further on in this chapter). However, you should not write much above their level. Target your audience level—substantial damage to accurate reception of the message may occur by writing above the audience's level.

Table 4.1	Match the Message to the Medium

Message	Medium
1. Your voice mail has a message from a colleague suggesting a lunch meeting tomorrow.	a. e-mail
2. Company president delivers appreciation to an employee for 25 years of service.	b. facsimile
3. You have been told that one of your direct report subordinates is stealing company supplies.	c. collaborative writing software
4. Six company peers need to plan the organization's strategy for the next five years.	d. on a computer network
5. A supplier in another state has misplaced your order form. He needs it now and must verify your signature.	e. business letter
6. College professor invites a businessperson to speak to her class in six weeks; this is the first contact and details are included.	f. videotape
7. Four managers must co-write a report for the board of directors.	g. face-to-face
8. A student seeks feedback on her business presentation skills.	h. group function
9. You must set forth the steps involved in submitting a request for business travel.	i. telephone
	j. 1-on-1 interview
	k. policy and procedure statement

Answers: 1=a, 2=f, 3=h, 4=g, 5=b, 6=i, 7=c, 8=e, 9=i

- What is likely to be their reaction? If the content is heavy with negative information, think out the best organization for the message. Consider the indirect approach described in Chapter 6. Lay out a different plan if you anticipate acceptance of what you propose from a plan you would use if you expect resistance. Will the current economic environment affect their reaction? Are funds scarce or is the economy in decline, and might these conditions determine acceptance of your proposal?

- How will your message affect or be affected by organization politics? Are favors owed among the readership? Is there animosity among readers? Are you challenging anyone's sacred cow or pet project? Are you sure which members of the audience are nominal leaders and which are true leaders? What does the grapevine say about what you are proposing or sharing? Sometimes trying out your message on politically savvy colleagues can save embarrassment. Do not underestimate the strength of corporate power, political cliques, or old-boy networks.

- Are there major differences in demographics you should take into consideration? If there are dramatic distinctions in religion, age, upbringing, values, income, or other background characteristics that will affect interpretation or acceptance of what you transmit, consider tailoring your message to those characteristics.

- Is this cross-cultural communication in which your message will be translated into another language, or where any reader is using English as a second language? Keeping the message simple and avoiding slang, idioms, and euphemisms will help the reader.

In our example of the unanticipated assignment to write a proposal, to identify your audience you would want to know such things as:

1. What is the size of the bank in numbers of employees, customers, profit, and assets? Are these characteristics improving or declining?

2. Who are the principal players for the bank? Who has the formal and the informal power? What do you know about them in terms of age, experience, education, and so on?

3. How do the bank representatives feel about what you are proposing? Is there a need for what you are proposing? How do they perceive your competition?

4. Who authorized the report? What were the directions regarding the contract? What do they expect?

Answers to these questions will have great impact on what you say and the tone you use to say it. You may need to review the corporate organization chart, make some phone calls to colleagues or secretaries, talk with others in your department, use the company library, or consult peers in other organizations to answer some of these questions.

Do Your Research

As an advanced student, you have learned efficient and effective research techniques. Some of those techniques will benefit you in the corporate world. Well-written reports and proposals are based on data from research, not opinion alone.

If necessary, refresh your memory of such research techniques as library usage; computer, Internet, and electronic database searches; unobtrusive observation; sampling techniques; experimentation; and interviewing. Do not neglect key corporate contacts who may be experts on the subject. Pay attention to company files and records for historical perspectives, guidelines, past mistakes, and suggestions made earlier by others.

Imagine the assignment of working on a feasibility study for a new shopping mall on the outskirts of a major metropolitan area. Research results, more than intuition, will support your conclusions. Topics for research will include

- Competition
- Traffic patterns of potential customers
- Tax rates
- Potential customers
- Government influences
- Building costs
- Perception of your firm by others
- Labor force
- Financial considerations
- Anticipated profit

Think of generating information on these ten topics as doing your job. It is also important research. Inaccurate, biased, or incomplete data will contaminate the quality of your study. The two main characteristics of solid research are reliability and validity. Reliability means that others researching the same topic in the same way would draw the same conclusions. Validity means that the research measures or reports what it is supposed to measure. Thorough research should lead logically to a proposed solution to a problem. The defense of your solution lies in the depth and quality of your research, as well as skills in argumentation.

The discussion that follows guides you in how to conduct electronic research.

Electronic Research

Computers and new technology have redefined the way we do research. Much of your research can be done from a computer that is connected to the Internet, which has enabled access to an increasing amount of information. From that computer you can connect to a library's online catalog, review electronic databases, or search the World Wide Web for information on companies, products, statistics, pictures, or publications. Below is a discussion of some useful research tools.

Step 1—Using the Library's Electronic Resources

Online Catalog. The first place to start when researching a topic should be the library's online catalog. Most research can be completed using this resource alone. Typically, libraries have electronic card catalogs, which include automated systems that check availability, computerized searches of databases for author's names or key words, and regular reviews of periodicals.

Electronic Databases. Many large libraries subscribe to electronic databases that contain full journal articles along with bibliographical information and/or abstracts of articles. The fact that entire articles can be downloaded or printed from the computer decreases the amount of time spent retrieving information. Thus, to save time, many researchers will begin their search within electronic journal databases rather than look up articles via the library's catalog. These databases can be especially helpful if the library has a limited number of journal titles. There are a myriad of specialized databases, but their availability depends on the home institution's needs and resources. Here is a partial list of some of the more popular databases.

- ABI/Inform: Contains articles in business research journals and important industry trade publications. Many of the articles are full text, while lengthy summaries exist for the rest.
- EBSCOhost Academic Search Elite: Contains many full-text journal articles.

All of these databases provide keyword search utilities that can greatly speed up data gathering.

- ERIC (Educational Research Information Center): Is a federally funded database of research-oriented documents intended for the educational practitioner and researcher.
- InfoTrac: Has over 11 million articles from periodicals and journals dating back to 1980. Includes both subject and key word searches.
- LEXIS/NEXIS: Provides access to the complete text of national and international news articles, and to business, legal, and reference information.
- ProQuest Research Library: Provides access to articles across a wide range of academic disciplines. The database features the full text of articles from over 1,400 periodicals.

Step 2—Employing Internet Resources

Access to the Internet provides the researcher with invaluable research tools that can locate information on practically all topics. At one time, researchers put great effort into finding the desired information. Today, huge amounts of information can be acquired in just a few seconds. We now have to put our effort into filtering the information. The problem with Internet research is that many times the researcher must sort through extensive irrelevant information in order to extract the desired materials.[1] Moreover, the Internet is not as well organized as the library. While many Web directories attempt to catalog each Web site, a single Web directory will never completely represent the entire Web. Thus, it is important to know which Internet tools to employ when trying to locate research materials on the Net.

Library Home Page. Often the best place to start is the home institution's library Web page. Every college/university library has at least one informative Web site that often provides access to electronic journal databases as well as the school's online catalog. Most library Web sites will also include several links to Internet information resources and research tips and techniques.

Web Directories and Search Engines. It would be difficult to research and organize information on the Net without the help of some sort of Web directory or search engine. One popular place to start on the Web is Yahoo! Yahoo! is a useful search tool when looking for specific information such as company news or general reference.

Yahoo! is more of a subject-oriented search engine in that all Web matches are placed into categories. Lycos is another such Web directory.

Search engines offer highly accurate findings, since keyword searches are applied to the full text of the Web site rather than just the title and/or description of the site. To gather information on more general or arcane subjects, such as how to buy a car, the following search engines offer better results:

- AltaVista (**http://www.altavista.com**)
- Excite (**http://www.excite.com**)
- HotBot (**http://www.hotbot.com**)
- Infoseek (**http://www.infoseek.com**)
- Google (**http://www.google.com**)
- Northern Light (**http://www.northernlight.com**)

All of these search engines operate in a similar fashion, although search options and syntax differ. It is best not to rely on just one search site, since all engines extract Web information differently: A search on one site may produce results different from another.

Using all search engines in combination is probably the best research strategy. To save the researcher time and effort, a couple of search sites offer the ability to search several different search engines simultaneously. MetaCrawler (**http://www .metacrawler.com**) is the most popular meta-search engine. A simple search from MetaCrawler's interface will generate results from almost a dozen different search engines. While technically not a meta-search engine, Ask Jeeves (**http://www .ask.com**) is a convenient starting point when the researcher has no idea where to start looking for information because it offers plain-English searches. Thus, typing "where do I find a listing of jobs in Los Angeles" will yield useful results from many of the big search engines.

Search Techniques and Strategies. When using search engines to do research on the Web, practice a few effective strategies. Since Internet search engines cover literally millions of Web pages, the researcher must exert extra effort to narrow the search to relevant Web pages.

The first step of any Web-based search is the identification of appropriate keywords. If your topic is already distinctive, such as the Battle of Antietam, then typing the word *Antietam* or even *Battle of Antietam* will generate useful results from all search engines. However, many times your topic will not contain specific keywords. In this case, Web directories can be particularly useful in generating a list of related keywords. For example, if your topic is "travel trends in America," you can start with Yahoo! subject directories to take advantage of human indexing. Searching just within the travel directory will already eliminate millions of Web sites that contain the words *travel, trends,* and *America.* If the Web directory doesn't help, Ask Jeeves is also a good place to generate a list of keywords related to a certain research topic. Typing in plain-English searches such as "where can I find information on current travel trends in America" will yield helpful results while leading the researcher to more useful keywords.

The researcher can narrow down a search even further with the use of Boolean logic. Boolean logic simply allows the user to add search criteria to the array of keywords, using the operators *and, or,* or *not.* For example, to search for Web sites pertaining to "Mexican oil" you might search for:

Mexic	To allow selection of Mexico and Mexican
not New	To avoid selection of New Mexico
and (oil **or** petroleum)	To select both Mexic and oil, place the "and" between them; to allow selection of petroleum as well as oil, use the "or." Note that the parentheses are necessary to group the last **or** statement together

When using Boolean logic in your searches, syntax may differ from search engine to search engine. Every search engine will have a search help page that can be found next to the search text box. Each search engine has an increasing amount of logic tools that can help you refine your search. Use these help pages as a tool to become a skilled Internet researcher.

Still other search features that may help narrow down a query. If you want to find Web pages that contain a specific phrase, the use of quotes would limit the search to only those sites that matched the entire phrase. Thus, typing "give me liberty or give me death" as your search criteria will yield dozens of pages on Patrick Henry. As you can see, quotation marks can be useful when you need to cross-reference information such as direct quotes.

Many search engines offer the user advanced search options such as limiting the search to only specific parts of the Web document. For example, within Yahoo! it is possible to search only the Web title or the actual URL by typing in "t:" or "u:" respectively before the keyword. Sometimes you will want to search only within a specific company's Web site. In this case typing "u:cnn" followed by another optional keyword would search only within CNN's Web site. Many search engines offer these features, but be sure to check each site's help pages to determine the correct syntax (Infoseek uses "title:" and "site:" to limit the search to a document's title or URL) as well as additional search options.

Search engines are key starting points to finding items in different media such as an audio clip, an image, or a short video clip. Some engines, such as AltaVista, have a special search page exclusively for audio, image, or video files. Thus, by selecting the image type, the searcher can type a keyword or two to find a particular picture. If the item searched is well known, such as the Grand Canyon, the engine may return hundreds of images to your liking. AltaVista is a particularly good site to find clip art and miscellaneous pictures, since your search will return pages of thumbnail images rather than just text descriptions. This gives the user quicker access to thousands of useful images. Thumbnail clips are also given when searching for video files, while audio searches will return a brief but useful description. Other search engines are adding such "visual" utilities, giving the user access to even more media files.

A final strategy when searching the Web is to seek useful niche sites whose main purpose is to provide the general population with useful information. Many of these sites can be found from major Web directories such as Yahoo! For example, a site that lists company information and stock quotes can easily be found by clicking on the Stock Quotes link on Yahoo! By surfing within subject directories, you will be able to find a number of informative sites. The next section describes just a handful of very useful sites on the Web.

Useful Web Sites. In addition to search engines, there are a number of large information portals on the Web worth mentioning. Getting to know the information on the following sites may speed up the research process:

- **http://www.ipl.org**—The Internet Public Library is dedicated to organizing the information on the Web, thus making it more useful to researchers. The site helps direct the researcher to relevant online magazines and newspapers while providing several helpful research tutorials.
- **http://lcweb.loc.gov**—The Library of Congress site offers online catalogs, journal collections, and numerous research services.
- **http://www.census.gov**—The Census Bureau is an excellent reference site in terms of specific statistical and demographic information.
- **http://www.ed.gov**—The U.S. Department of Education's Web page offers useful statistics and news related to education.

When you encounter a useful site such as those above, bookmark it for future reference. It may be helpful when researching a topic later.

Newsgroups. Depending on the research topic, newsgroups can be an excellent source of information. There are thousands of newsgroups covering every topic imaginable. These newsgroups hold ongoing discussions that relate to topics ranging from the C programming language to teaching. Most of the information provided in newsgroups is unstructured and usually based on opinion. Thus, newsgroups do not make good references when writing purely academic papers. However, many times, newsgroup moderators can help steer the researcher to other useful and relevant sources. Liszt (**http://www.izwa.co.za/demo/lisztnews.html**) contains an exhaustive directory of all known newsgroups. By employing Liszt's search utility, a researcher will be able to locate several newsgroups related to a certain topic.

As you gather information it is important to retain source citations for later attribution—but especially from electronic sources. Be sure to note the URL or address and make note of the date you retrieved the information. You are likely to need this information later as a footnote or bibliographical entry if you use the original data. What style to use to attribute electronic information still is evolving and you find little agreement among the major style manuals.[2] However, most manuals require the address and date as part of the attribution.

Step 3—Using Other Electronic Sources

Many commercial products, often produced on CD-ROM, are available to enhance your research without connecting to a library database or using the Internet. Encyclopedias, such as the Encarta 2003 Encyclopedia, are rich with statistics, pictures, text, and sounds.

Consider Your Layout, Format, and Elements

Letters differ from memoranda in appearance. Procedure statements look different than justification reports do. A research paper has different elements than a case analysis. As you think out your writing project, consider which elements, such as salutations, copy distribution notes, tables of contents, abstracts, or appendices will appear in your final presentation. These considerations affect the content and organization of your message.

Layout

Layout considerations recently have become especially important with the power contained in our word-processing software. Here are some layout considerations that can affect the final appearance of your product:

- Color of ink and paper
- Size and length of finished package
- Quality of appearance, including such printing techniques as color ink jet versus black-and-white laser printer output
- Use of illustrations and graphics
- Image to project
- Established corporate guidelines
- Longevity of message
- Interaction with other messages, such as periodic reports or brochures
- Treatment of headings and subheadings
- Decision on if and where footnotes should appear

Format

Closely related to layout is format, which relates more to the consistently delivered, computer-prepared items, such as headings, bulleted points, or bibliographical citations. With the power of today's word-processing software, templates can enhance the appearance of documents and provide efficiency to the writer as well. See step 5 of the electronic writing process later in this chapter for more information.

Part of layout and format is the appropriate use of headings, bulleted lists, and numbered lists. Headings can dramatically affect a person's ability to know the location within a document, the relationship to other headings or parts of the manuscript, and to "signpost" progress. Bulleted lists should be used to deliver a group of items in no particular order, such as "Here are the main characteristics of an effective manager." Numbered lists, on the other hand, should deliver stepped or staged information that has an inherent order or sequence, such as "Here is the process to get to my cubicle in Building 83."

The logic of the order of the parts also comes into play as your determine the flow of your headings and subpoints. Use the concept of classification to determine the best order. For example, in a lengthy report that starts with an introduction and ends with conclusions and recommendations, there might be five major headings. How do you determine the order of the five headings? They may be organized by chronology, importance, size, value, or even just alphabetized. You should also put careful thought into the order of the subpoints under a heading. You should have a defense for whatever order you select, and that logic should be obvious to your reader as well. If you include language such as "When we first contacted Smith Electronics about partnering with us on this project," the concept of chronology comes through. In other cases, you may want to inject such an explanatory comment as "Here are our four options, in decreasing financial attractiveness to us."

Readers will assume you are using logic in presenting items. You help them by making the logic obvious or injecting a phrase of explanation. Further, if you can't create a logical order, at a minimum inform the reader: "In no particular order, here are our five competitors."

This concept of classification is especially useful for messages that are lengthy, complex, or important. It works equally well for written documents, such as reports and proposals, or for oral presentations, such as business meetings, sales presentations, or oral reports to the board.

Elements

Just as decisions about layout and format are part of the overall writing process, so are decisions about which elements you will include in the finished package. As the length and formality of what you are writing increase, so will the number of elements you add. While a simple letter may have few elements beyond the body, a formal report will have many elements. Here, for example, are the required and optional elements that one university lists for the MBA professional report, a project often required in lieu of a thesis. Many proposals and government reports will require even more elements.

- Bound cover with author's name and report title on spine
- Fly page, blank
- Approval sheet, with original signatures
- Dedication
- Title page
- Preface or acknowledgments
- Abstract
- Table of contents
- List of tables
- List of figures
- Body of the report, with chapters and sections
- Appendices
- Bibliography
- Vita
- Fly page, blank

While these elements surround and package the main content of the report—the body—they also influence writing decisions on such things as tone and formality. For example, adding a list of figures or a bibliography may increase the formality, while inclusion of dedication, acknowledgments, and a vita may affect the tone because of the personal nature of the content. Anticipate, then, which elements to include in your writing project.

Draft Your Project

For most people, effective writing takes more than one attempt. When the message you wish to transmit is simple, your familiarity with the situation high, the consequences unimportant, and the length short, you may be able to draft a finished letter or memorandum on the first try. However, as complexity, familiarity, consequences, and length change, you are more likely to draft and revise.

People approach drafting in different ways. For some, drafting is writing down main ideas, no matter how rough they may be, then adding lesser thoughts. Finally, these writers work on smoothness. Others place initial emphasis on careful word selection and sentence development, simply adding transitions by the completion of the finished draft. Few writers expect perfection after just one draft. There is no best approach. Stick with what works for you. Just keep in mind the main value of drafting: to start the writing process.

An initial and important decision has to do with organization of the information. Organization has various meanings. At one level, a message is organized if its main thoughts flow together well and it reaches its goal. (In Chapters 5 and 6 we will discuss this type of organization, in depth, from the viewpoint of direct and indirect message approaches. Because of this attention later, we discuss overall organization only superficially here.) Your first decision may well be whether to use

- Direct organization, when you expect little resistance from the reader; or
- Indirect organization, when the reader is not disposed to do as you suggest or does not want to read what you write.

As you select an organization or format, plan to outline your message. (Sample outlines appear in the Business Presentation chapter.) Many effective writers work from an outline of important topics because they know an outline saves time and is more likely to produce a smooth, flowing final product. As you draft an outline, try to include as many main thoughts as possible. Add lower-level ideas as they occur to you, but do not let them get in the way of your planning. As you revise and edit your outline, you can add such outlining principles as parallelism (such as starting each item with a similar part of speech) and having at least two subdivisions under each heading.

While outlining works well for many writers, it may stifle creativity or lock the writer into a set format. Some writers, therefore, benefit from looser drafting techniques aimed more at idea generation than organization. Among these techniques are listing random ideas and using free writing, brainstorming, creativity matrixes, or idea trees.

Hints for overcoming writer's block appear later in this chapter.

Revise, Edit, and Proof

Having prepared a draft, your next step is to polish it. Realize that many writers spend almost as much time editing as they apply to the drafting process. Often, allowing some time to elapse between drafting and revising permits fresh thoughts and a different perspective to emerge. This may be the stage where you send your draft to an immediate supervisor, colleagues, or a content specialist to seek suggestions. The approach to having more than one pair of eyes look at the draft is especially valued here. Check to ensure that the manuscript still solves your definition of the problem.

Check for good transitions from thought to thought. Lead thoughts, such as quantifying the points to follow (four main criteria affect the decision) facilitate numbering the points as they occur (second, next, then, or last). Help your reader by supplying phrases that connect thoughts, such as when you show addition (furthermore, additionally), contrast (but, however, nevertheless, on the other hand), concession (as you've stated, I agree, admittedly), or conclusion (in summary, to conclude). You may also assist your reader by clarifying causation (because, therefore), comparison (likewise, similarly), explanation (in other words, to state differently), or example (such as, for example).

Additionally, worthwhile revision steps include seeking out clumsy words, typos, misspellings, and overly long sentences. Many computer software packages can assist with the tedious chore of finding these elusive errors. For example, you can use software to scrutinize for spelling errors, grammar, punctuation, style problems, and readability level. The grammar, punctuation, and style checkers help you spot many of the writing and typing errors that work against clarity, coherence, tone, and other attributes of effective writing. It is also helpful to use a computerized thesaurus. While these various packages cannot guarantee perfect spelling or word usage, they can help you identify common problems. Personally proofread to catch the correctly spelled but out-of-context errors (*there* for *their*). In the absence of software, elicit the help of people whose writing ability you respect.

Next, work on the organization of sentences, paragraphs, and the message as a whole. Is there an inherent logic to the entire manuscript? Does it flow smoothly within paragraphs and from section to section?

Depending on the goal of the message and the medium selected, such as an annual report, letter to all employees, procedure statement, or sales brochure, extensive review by others may be needed. Legal experts, technical content specialists, and editorial reviewers may be part of the revision cycle, as will your immediate supervisor, who reviews the work.

Because editing and revising your own work and the work of others is so important, you may wish to examine the edited paragraphs in Figure 4.1. The shaded text is new; the strikeouts show what would be omitted. While it maintains the integrity of the original message, the revision is briefer, clearer, and more active.

Many people who edit someone else's writing prefer to do so in a pencil-and-hard-copy mode and use widely accepted notation. Figure 4.2 shows some of this notation.

Produce the Finished Package

Final production may be the word processing of your manuscript or the sending of copy to a printer for design, layout, typesetting, and printing. Now may also be the time for you to confirm final layout and element decisions you made earlier. Perhaps you will use your computer to boldface text, switch among different typefaces or sizes, switch to multiple columns, or add bullets in front of items in a list.

Even today's low-cost word processors can deliver some features of desktop publishing, and the top-end word processors and desktop publishing programs have powerful control over the appearance of printed words. In addition to needing artistic understanding of style, balance, and unity, effective design and layout require knowledge of such elements as grid layout, headings, borders, columns, typography, white space, and graphics. Most desktop publishing and design guides stress the need to keep layouts simple, clean, and attractive while you are gaining

Information Gathering

The ~~most important~~ key issues to ~~be addressed~~ address in negotiations should be ~~those sections of~~ the contract sections that surfaced most often ~~under the past contract~~ during the contract term. Typically, the negotiating teams ~~in the traditional environment~~ will ~~try to patch~~ focus on these areas ~~as a priority~~. ~~What is critical is to gain~~ Gaining feedback from ~~the~~ management, ~~and~~ especially ~~the~~ first-line supervisors, ~~as to what~~ concerning areas they wish to modify is critical. Any issues ~~that are brought forward by~~ the ~~bargaining unit~~ employees raised ~~is~~ are also key to understanding ~~what is really expected of~~ the union negotiators' role.

The ~~single~~ most powerful resource ~~you can possess~~ in any negotiation is superior information. This ~~information~~ should be ~~then~~ blended with ~~similar input from~~ the union leadership's ~~relative to their~~ desires. Through parallel, small group sessions ~~of small group sensing~~ with management and union leadership, many key issues will surface (see Appendix A). ~~Additionally, those areas that are of common importance~~ Common concerns will also ~~become obvious~~ emerge and should ~~therefore gain a high~~ command top priority ~~for resolution~~. ~~One should not rely on instincts when~~ When the long-term stakes are high, ~~for in the long run,~~ instincts are no match for accurate and accessible information.

Determining Causes and Effects

~~Once the assemblage~~ After a list of ~~contracual~~ contractual problem areas ~~has been accomplished, it now requires an analysis for the causes of the undesirable effects~~ has been compiled, analyzing why they created problems is the next task. This process will help to ~~bring out~~ emphasize the issues that are ~~key to making significant gains in~~ fundamental to productive negotiation. ~~It is advantageous to facilitate a~~ A joint review ~~of~~ by human resources and line management personnel will help to ~~clarify and delineate what~~ define the action ~~are really~~ needed ~~for problem resolution~~ to resolve problems. If ~~it is a common issue with~~ the union has similar concerns, then ~~they should also be requested to clarify~~ their ~~understanding of the causal factors~~ input is also vital.

During this ~~activity it may become apparent that~~ process some ~~of the~~ earlier issues ~~brought about by the initial feedback is less important than was expressed~~ may appear less significant. These data should be set aside in a follow-up file for last minute review ~~prior to the beginning of~~ before negotiations begin ~~for any last minute concerns~~. They may be ~~of use~~ useful later ~~during negotiations if it arises during that time frame. Again, it noteworthy to remember that historical information gained must be accessible at all times. It is at this stage where~~ Now information sharing should ~~be initiated~~ begin. By distributing the information gained in the ~~sensing~~ parallel, group sessions, ~~the beginnings of collaboration and a trusting relationship~~ mutual collaboration and trust can ~~progress~~ develop. Openness and sharing also ~~facilitates the lowering of~~ help to lower barriers to communication that will benefit both parties ~~during the negotiation process~~ in negotiations.

Figure 4.2 | **Common Correction and Proofreading Symbols**

Abv	faulty abbreviation	*DM*	dangling modifier	*jar*	avoid jargon
Awk	awkward	*frag.*	sentence fragment	*sp*	spelling error
(*cap*)	capitalize	∧	insert	*pv*	passive voice
⌒	close up	*mm*	misplaced modifier	*w*	wordy
e	delete			*wc*	word choice

experience. Novices all too often clutter their layouts with the many variables under their control and end up damaging the appearance of their documents rather than enhancing them.

Conduct a Post-writing Evaluation

Now that you have transmitted the message, how would you change it? What mistakes did you make and what did you learn that will guide you in the future? Too many of us complete a major project only to shelve it in relief. However, before separating yourself from the project completely, review it to help guide you in the future. The time to conduct your evaluation is now, while the rationale for your decisions is fresh in your mind. Ask questions such as these: What are the strengths and weaknesses of the manuscript? Are there any unusual or unique aspects of the finished product that might be used again? How did others perceive the manuscript, and what suggestions did they make?

While you may proceed through all eight steps in the writing sequence, doing so does not guarantee effective writing. Effective writing has other characteristics.

Specific Writing Features

Effective writing is achieved when it has certain features. Your writing will be effective if it is organized, has appropriate tone, and is readable.

Organization

As we briefly discussed in the section above on drafting, organization can mean direct versus indirect order. A second form of organization has to do with the flow of words within and between sentences. Of particular interest are coherence and emphatic sentences.

Coherence

Coherence grows when sender and receiver perceive the transmitted thought in the same way. Unfortunately, often what we think we are sending does not resemble the interpretation by the receiver. Standard grammar often overcomes incoherences.

Using words such as *it, that,* or *this* at the beginning of sentences frequently leads to confusion about the word's referent. For example:

The value of the stock rose nine points and made over $2,000 for us. It was great! (Revision: The stock rise was great!)

A second grammatical contributor to incoherence is misplaced modifiers, such as in this sentence:

The subordinate had a phone call talking to his boss. (Revision: While talking to his boss, the subordinate had a phone call.)

A third incoherency grows from lack of clarity between multiple subjects followed by a singular pronoun, such as:

Seldom had Kristi experienced the friendship of a co-worker like Stephanie. She was delighted. (Revision: Kristi was delighted.)

Standard grammar often overcomes problems with indefinite meaning. Here is an example of such a problem:

His mother had worked the dough into a thin pizza crust with her own hands. Have you ever seen such smooth texture?

(Clarify: Did the crust or the mother's hands have the smooth texture?)

Emphatic Sentences

Your writing style can increase the emphasis of your messages. When you seek to add emphasis to specific sentences, consider these techniques:

- Put the action at the beginning of the sentence rather than bury it. "Dierdre proposed . . ." gets things moving; " . . . as proposed by Dierdre" does not.
- Build to a crescendo. "The three regions report improvements in sales of 12, 21, and 37 percent" accomplishes this goal.
- Place emphasis on important words and create memorable statements, such as "We try harder" or "Just point and click to shop our online catalog."
- Show causation. "Because of her timely investment, she quadrupled her profit" is more emphatic than reversing the two thoughts.

A growing practice related to emphatic writing is the use of visual emphasis in business messages, such as through boldface to make key words stand out. Direct mail advertisers and others have used this technique, usually with a sales orientation. Now authors of e-mail, letters, memos, and résumés are using the technique to add other forms of emphasis. In a résumé, for example, power verbs describing abilities, such as "reorganized and improved the department" or "cited for outstanding performance," might be boldfaced.

In addition to writing coherent and emphatic sentences, you will improve your sentences and paragraphs by having effective transitions, as described earlier in the discussion of revising, editing, and proofing.

Appropriate Tone

The second major characteristic of effective writing is appropriate tone. Three main ways of affecting tone are (1) writing with the *you* attitude, (2) using positive phrasing, and (3) avoiding tactless wording. Readers are egocentric. They like to read about themselves and to see references to themselves. Conversely, readers lose interest and attention when the topic turns to others. Business writing shares with direct-mail advertising the technique of personalizing messages to audiences to obtain a desired response. When you employ words such as *you, yourself,* or the person's name, you are using the *you* attitude. On the other hand, words such as *I, me, myself, our, we, us,* or the company's name illustrate the *I* attitude.

To view how detrimental the *I*-ish orientation can be, read Figure 4.3, which delivers the body of a cold contact letter from someone seeking tax work.

Consider how easy it is to remove most *I* references and to either replace them with, or to inject, *you* references; it is surprising that more writers do not follow the *you* attitude. Effective writers learn quickly the positive response that the *you* technique elicits.

Next read Figure 4.4 to see how the body of Figure 4.3 could be improved through *you*-ish tone alone. Although other improvements can still be made, the change in focus from author to reader helps this message.

Another level of the *you* attitude is more elusive but perhaps even more important. Beyond just the inclusion or exclusion of key pronouns is the goal of applying

---

Figure 4.3   **Example of an *I*-Attitude Letter**

Dear Taxpayer:

We all are willing to pay our fair share of taxes, but we don't want to pay more than is necessary. I can help avoid taxes through my expert planning and preparation.

I have the experience, knowledge, and background to do your taxes. I also have a Ph.D. in accounting. My fees are competitive while my service is excellent.

I invite you to enjoy the personal and professional service that I'm known for. I will be sending you more information soon. Call me at 555-2121 to make an appointment with me. Do so before March 1 and receive a 10-percent discount.

Sincerely,

Figure 4.4 **Example of a _You_-Attitude Letter**

Dear Taxpayer:

You, no doubt, are willing to pay your fair share of taxes, but you don't want to pay more than is necessary. You can benefit by not paying unnecessary taxes by using my expertise in tax planning and preparation.

You will find I have the experience, knowledge, and background needed to best serve your individual needs. You'll also benefit from my Ph.D. in accounting when tricky accounting questions arise. These abilities are available to you at competitive fees that include excellent service.

Please call 555-2121 to make an appointment. You'll experience my personal and professional service that will help you avoid unnecessary taxes. And if you make an appointment by March 1, you'll receive a 10-percent discount.

Cordially,

the _you_ attitude to make the message sound as if it is written to the reader, not sent by the author. A message prepared for the reader conveys sincerity, personalization, warmth, and involvement on the part of the author. It is these and other attributes that can bring about a positive reaction.[3] Positive versus negative phrasing also affects tone. If you regularly communicate negatively phrased thoughts, you project a negative and undesirable image of yourself. Most of us prefer to associate with winners and with those who hold an optimistic outlook. While the Pollyanna principle can be overdone, you are usually better off to transmit a message that the glass is half-full, not half-empty. Politicians, of course, are well known for seeing the bright side of things. Top-level managers, too, seldom associate themselves with losing ideas, projects, products, or people unless they must do so. Such associations can taint careers. Apply this philosophy—avoid the negative, seek the positive, phrase the negative from the positive viewpoint—to your business writing.

While you may think that negative situations call for negative phrasing, just the opposite is true. Unpleasant messages are only exaggerated by negative tone. A more desirable approach is to state the bad news as positively as possible. For example, compare these two sentences:

Your bid for the project was rejected.

We selected another firm for the project.

Both transfer negative information, but the second does so in a more appealing fashion.

A third way to affect tone is through tactful wording. Tactless writing offends the reader, perhaps by stereotyping, challenging intelligence, inappropriately referring to religion or ethnic background, or using humor in poor taste. Tactful writers appreciate the delicacy of a situation and say the fitting thing.

Even though most businesspeople have learned to identify and avoid inappropriate ethnic references, many still need to have their awareness raised in regard to sexist language. For example, as the percentage of women in business and in executive positions increases, there are more women who dislike receiving letters addressed "Dear Sir" or being referred to as one of the girls. If you are using gender-specific language that is offensive to the reader, that language may work against you. The trend in U.S. business is away from sexist and other forms of discriminatory language.

Readability

A third major component in the writing process is making the writing readable. Readable writing builds on some of the concepts discussed above but adds additional dimensions: clarity, conciseness, parallel structure, and activity.

Clarity

Clear writing is coherent and avoids muddy, incorrect, overly complex phrases and jargon. Muddy phrases are those that cloud the issue or idea by using too many words or skirting the issue. Here are some examples of muddy phrases:

a number of	(use *many*)
at your earliest possible convenience	(use *soon*)
fullest possible extent	(use *fully* or *completely*)
it has come to my attention that	(omit)
it would be reasonable to assume	(use *I assume*)

Many nonstandard phrases are current in our language. Clear writing, however, shuns errors. Here are some examples of frequently used but nonstandard words and phrases. Although a dictionary may list them, they are not good usage.

irregardless	(use *regardless*)
enthused	(use *enthusiastic*)
impacted	(avoid; *impact* is a noun, not a verb)
interfaced	(avoid; *interface* is a noun, not a verb)
between (three items)	(use *between* when comparing two items)
among (two items)	(use *among* when comparing three or more items)
can't hardly	(avoid; double negative)
virtually	(means "essentially the same" and is not necessary)

Occasionally, people try to make their writing sound more impressive by adding to its complexity. Usually they fail in this attempt and detract from readability at the same time. Anyone who has taken a simple, direct sentence and looked up long, abstract substitutes knows the approach. Instead, try to use simple, familiar words. Here are a few examples:

as per this date	(use *today*)
attached hereto	(use *attached is*)
contact the undersigned	(use *write me*)
considerable magnitude	(use *large*)
inasmuch as	(use *because*)

utilize	(use *use*)
necessitates	(use *needs* or *requires*)
at the present time	(use *now*)
prioritize	(use *rank*)
it is worth remembering that	(use *remember*)

Jargon, too, can detract from readability. Within any organization there will be many buzzwords and acronyms. Sometimes using this jargon will simplify and shorten complex or lengthy terms; other times it will confuse or obscure meaning. For example, FIFO immediately means "first in, first out" to an accountant, but it may be meaningless to nonaccountants. Try to avoid jargon; if the receiver is not familiar with the jargon, it makes the reader feel like an outsider or as if he or she is being used to make the author sound intelligent. Ask yourself, "Am I using jargon that is appropriate to my audience?" If in doubt, avoid the jargon.

Conciseness

A second major determinant of readability is conciseness. Avoid wordy phrases and long, complex words; opt instead for short, familiar words. You can also improve conciseness by eliminating redundancies, such as:

the consensus of opinion	(use *the consensus* or *the opinion*)
the first and foremost	(use *the first* or *the foremost*)
over and over and over again	(use *over*)
near future	(use *future* or *soon*)
desirable benefits	(use *desirable* or *benefits*)
all in all	(omit)
in the week/month/year of	(omit)

You can also improve conciseness (and coherency) by avoiding oxymorons, combinations of two words with opposite or contradictory meanings. Here are some examples:

found missing
almost perfect
intense apathy
silent scream
old news
working vacation

Parallel Structure

Your reader or listener probably will be able to understand the point of your message when you do not employ parallelism—but when you do, your message will be more polished, readable, and professional. There are four main applications of parallelism: in lists, word pairings, series, and headings.

In lists—be they found on a transparency, computerized slide, or in a written report—items should be presented in grammatically parallel structure. Consider this brief list.

- Consider your audience
- Prepare your message
- In delivering your talk, think about nonverbal communication

The third item doesn't "match" the first two, which start with a verb. Perhaps the third item would start with "Think about. . . ."

In English, there are pairings of words that are usually delivered together, such as either/or, neither/nor, and not only/but also. When you use one part of a pairing, use the other as well. Further, place each part of the pairing at the beginning of its portion of the sentence. Here is a violation:

You are either the best employee in the department, or I am mistaken.

Here is the rewrite:

Either you are the best employee in the department, or I am mistaken.

Parallelism in a sentence that contains a series is important as well. Consider this sentence, which is not parallel:

At the grocery store I need to buy some potatoes, bread, and I'll get some milk.

To make this sentence parallel, remove the extraneous "I'll get some" so it reads:

At the grocery story I need to buy some potatoes, bread, and milk.

Here is another example:

The main duties of a supervisor are generating enthusiasm, providing guidance, and to ensure that workers come to work on time.

One rewrite among several parallel alternatives could be:

The main duties of a supervisor are generating enthusiasm, providing guidance, and ensuring that workers come to work on time.

Notice that the sentence could also be rewritten to employ infinitives: to generate, to provide, and to ensure.

Finally, use parallelism in delivering your headings and subheadings in reports and proposals. Much as with the items shown above in "Lists," use grammatically similar wording across headings and within headings.

Activity

You can make your writing more readable by using the active instead of the passive voice. The passive voice discourages the reader from becoming involved with your message. You can identify passive voice by finding a form of the verb *be* plus a past participle that often ends in *-n, -en, -t, -d,* or *-ed.* In your efforts to avoid passive voice, also try to use present tense; both aid readability. Here are some examples of passive and active voice:

Passive	*Active*
has been sent	I sent
it was discussed	we discussed
were brought by	someone brought
you were mailed a	I mailed you a
were studied by	someone studied

Sometimes passive voice is desirable, such as when you do not know who did the action (The electricity was installed in the plant about 1911), when you want to bury the identity of the doer (The funds have been misappropriated), or when the action is more important than who did it (Corporate profits were increased 72 percent).

Readability Formulas

You may find the concept of readability—and even effective writing—to be elusive. Many scholars have tried to quantify readability; the outcome has been the creation of many readability formulas. Since the 1950s, when many such formulas were created, only a half-dozen or so viable formulas remain. The survivors are similar in that most attempt to measure prose through a ratio of difficult words or syllables to total words or sentence length. Some computer word processors include a readability tool that will calculate the approximate reading level of a piece of writing.

If you wish to use a readability formula to guide your writing, you should write at a level appropriate for your audience, or lower. Most of us prefer to read easy writing if it still conveys what we need to know and does not sound like the author is writing down to us. Readability formulas deserve a word of caution: While they can effectively guide you in matching your writing to the level of your audience, they can be imprecise, or overly mechanical, and may overlook important aspects of style and content. Use them to help catch problems, but take personal responsibility for the final output.

As you approach your writing and revising, seek a balance among the three main writing process considerations just presented: organization (including ways of organizing the entire message, coherence, and writing emphatically), tone (including *I* versus *you* attitude, positive and negative phrasing, and tactful writing), and readability (including clarity, conciseness, active voice, and reading ease).

Getting Writing Started

The assumption so far has been that once you know what you need to write, you can write it. Unfortunately, some people have very real problems getting started, and others start but have difficulty finishing. Here are some suggestions for increasing your writing output.[4]

1. Schedule a regular writing time and place. Then, when in that place, you will fall into the writing mood. Some people find the habit of writing at a certain time—but not necessarily a place—is all they need to enhance the process. Little changes from your regular routine will emphasize that here and now is the time and place to write. Change to a different desk. Alter the lighting. Select different music. Focus more on the periodic aspects of writing rather than on setting aside large blocks of time. Efficient use of 30 minutes a day may generate better results than setting aside a single three-hour period during which you tire or your mind wanders.

2. Set a writing goal. Pick a realistic goal, such as writing five double-spaced pages of draft in two hours. Modify your goal if you find you easily exceed it or have trouble achieving it. Try not to fall below your goal. If you are experiencing a good session, do not stop. If you must stop, jot down the ideas still in your mind to help to pick up in the same place. Review your progress periodically. You will be surprised how productive you can be.

3. Use a buddy system. Identify good writers and involve them in your writing. Find peers in your study group or people at your level in your organization who will be willing to assist you in the writing process. Be willing to help them. As you share ideas about each other's writing, all will benefit.

4. Overcome your writing blocks. Break large writing projects into small chunks. In writing your professional report, thesis, or other major academic writing project, work on and complete one chapter at a time. Then start on another chapter. Avoid writing several chapters at once. If you have trouble getting started, consider freewheeling. This process stresses writing something, no matter what, for a period of time. Then go back and revise and expand what you have created. If this approach does not work, try talking to a tape recorder to capture your thoughts. Conversations with others may help you, too.

5. Employ time-management concepts. Spend your time writing, not getting ready to write. Some people must first clean the desk, get out a favorite eraser, sharpen all pencils, and make other preparations. Instead, use this time to get ideas on paper or diskette. Rank your writing and work on the most important project first. Lay out a list each day of what you need to accomplish and start working on the first item.

Thus far this chapter has focused on when and how to write; we now turn to computer techniques that can enhance the writing process.

Electronic Writing Processes

Writing has two components: composition and transcription. Historically, in U.S. businesses, managers composed and secretaries transcribed. Managers may have started the process with dictation and asked for a typed rough draft. The revision process may have gone through several iterations and involved the editing of others before achieving a finished product. The personal computer (PC) has changed this process in several ways. First, those doing the keyboarding save time by inserting changes into an electronic file, which avoids retyping copy that is correct. They also quickly and easily make changes in appearance, such as adjusting margins or spacing.

Second, PCs have facilitated the transcription of many messages by their authors rather than by secretaries or administrative assistants. For an author who drafts on a PC, it may also be easier to make revisions and to print the finished product than to explain the desired changes to someone else. Research suggests that more employees at increasingly higher levels of management are keyboarding their drafts themselves. They also are increasingly manipulating text and data in spreadsheets, databases, and financial and accounting packages before they start a draft. Not long ago, these duties were assigned to the people in charge of the computers.

Computers can help you identify, search, record, organize, and modify relevant text. Computers can then help you write, edit, and revise your document. They can sharpen the skills discussed so far in this chapter—but they can never replace poor writing skills.

This next section shows you how computers can help you improve your writing output. The steps apply especially to longer writing assignments, such as a thesis, grant proposal, feasibility study, or case study, but they also relate to short writing situations.

Writing Using a Computer

Your use of the electronic writing process will be dictated by the facilities, hardware, and software available. The following steps incorporate computer equipment available at most universities and at most businesses. The order of the steps is not absolute, and steps may be skipped. (Refer also to the section earlier in this chapter on using the computer and the Internet to do research.)

Step 1—Note-taking. Skeletonize your notes as you take them in the library (ideally on a laptop computer or personal digital assistant (PDA)). Use abbreviations, such as J. for *Journal.* Then, on your desktop computer, record the notes to a file. Next, use the word-processing feature called search and replace to search for each occurrence of *J.* and replace it with *Journal.* Do the same with your other abbreviations.

Step 2—Searching. Especially if you are writing a lengthy research paper or working on a long-term project at work, place your research data in a database. Put similar topics under one heading. Later, when you are writing, seek out that heading to see your sources. Careful entry of bibliographic information will almost eliminate typing a bibliography later.

A variation on using the computer to help with your research is the recent introduction of report-writing software. These packages help authors of especially complex reports, which may be periodic but whose data change, to generate reports without instructions on how to organize the report or what to include. The packages typically can search many database files, join the data into one file, and paste it in appropriate locations. Many users of these report writers note increased productivity.[5]

Step 3—Word-polishing. If your word processor doesn't have a built-in dictionary, load separate packages now. *The American Heritage Dictionary for Computers* has a "wordhunter" feature that helps you find the right word when you are stumped. What's the right side of a ship called? Type in *right, side,* and *ship* and get *starboard.* What is the name of the boat used on the canals of Venice? *Boat, canals,* and *Venice* yield *gondola.* Pronunciation question? Have the computer say the word to you.

Now also is the time to load stand-alone grammar- and style-checkers if your word processor doesn't have them. Be careful, however, of too much reliance on these checkers. Spell-checkers typically are unable to interpret context and therefore would not catch a misspelling such as "I have two left feat." Grammar-, style-, and punctuation-checkers have different capabilities; they seldom catch the same errors. You need to know the rules and then use checkers to help you uncover the problems. You, however, are the final editor.

Step 4—Outlining. Another valuable feature is an outliner, which may be a separate program or part of a word-processing package. Outliners allow you not only to outline your thoughts quickly but also to rearrange sections rapidly, change levels, and so on. Usually you can import text from other files to the outliner, and you can send the outline to other files.

Step 5—Changing defaults. Open your word-processing software. Do some setting up as you create your new file. This setup will enhance document appearance on your screen and layout later. These commands can alter the appearance on the screen and/or affect the printed output. Some word-processing software packages allow definition of a template or master page that automatically carries such information as margin widths, typeface, and size requirements for body and heading text, headers and footers, and page numbers to each page of the document. If your word processor can automatically correct typing errors, such as TWo INitial CApital letters, noncapitalized days of the week, or *don;t* for *don't* and *teh* for *the*, turn it on. Also, if available, turn on controls for widows (the first line of a paragraph that falls on the last line of a page) or orphans (the last line of a paragraph that appears at the top of a page). Decide whether your finished manuscript needs a table of contents or index, because it is best to start your writing with special instructions to prepare these elements.

For a professional look with little effort for long documents, make the right headers list the chapter number with the page number, such as *Page 4-19*, and format the left header to carry the title of the chapter, such as *Data Analysis*. Depending on the length, complexity, and formality of your document, you may also want to establish a template for your document. With a template, you can assign style treatments of titles, headings, subheadings, footnotes, and bibliographical entries in terms of centering, indentation, font family, size, and treatment (boldface, italic, and so on). Then, as you work within your document, if you need a subhead, you merely click on that style in your menu and the treatment is automatic. In addition to the time saved, you also now can automatically generate a table of contents of all levels of headings, and page numbers will show as well. Finally, you can save and name your template for future use. You might create alternative templates for reports, proposals, letters, and memos and they will always look consistent.

Step 6—Using multiscreens. If your word processor supports division of the screen into two or more parts (called windows), split your screen and place your outline in one window. Then start writing your draft in the other window. Split windows also work well for entering superscript numbers for citations with the text in one window and entering the footnote or endnote in the other window.

Consider creating a "fast draft." Research indicates that some writers are held back by watching the monitor as they draft. Turn down the brightness on your monitor so you cannot see any display, check that your fingers are on the right keys, and start typing. For some, this approach helps to get them started. Any errors can be cleaned up later.

Remember that when you draft, you do not have to start at the beginning of your manuscript. If you have outlined your report, you know where you are and where you are going. Often, starting some place other than the beginning is easier, more logical, or more desirable. Start anywhere you wish. Your computer will help you assemble the parts later and you can then add transitions.

Step 7—Searching and replacing. As you edit or revise, take advantage of the search-and-replace function of your word processor. Find a word you now realize you misspelled, such as *convence*, and replace it with *convince*. Most search-and-replace functions allow you to choose between individual decisions on each occurrence or an entire text search-and-replace.

Step 8—Linking. Data in your database can be transferred to another program—say a spreadsheet—for statistical analysis and graphical presentation. While these statistical-analysis and graphical-presentation steps should occur before you start writing, the results of the steps find their way into the manuscript initially as you draft and later as you revise. You can ask some "smart" word-processing software to realize you are updating data in a spreadsheet and to automatically bring that new data to the manuscript as you work on it over time. Some software will isolate the graphical presentation from the text portion.

Step 9—Adding attribution. Most word-processing software facilitates adding footnotes or endnotes. For example, a superscript number is inserted into the text and then the footnote or endnote is filled in for insertion at the correct location. Users can later add a new citation within the text and the other citations will renumber and reposition. Other software allows the user to switch among major citation styles, such as MLA or APA, in a single keystroke.

Step 10—Using e-mail. E-mail has moved from being a convenience for a few people to a necessity for most people. According to Hamilton, e-mail ranks with the printing press, telephone, and television in mass impact.[6] Just a decade ago hard-copy letters and memos were the primary written medium for most businesspeople. Today, receiving 25, 50, or even 100 e-mail messages a day is not uncommon. Growing out of the three-billion-plus e-mail messages a day is the ten-year prediction of 1,000 e-mail messages per person.[7]

E-mail is much quicker to deliver, cheaper to send, and more formal in perception than hard-copy messages such as letters and memos. Unfortunately, the widespread use of e-mail has allowed many to become lazy. Business letters and memos in hard copy were expected to be letter perfect; e-mail messages, however, often contain spelling and grammar errors. Even worse, we seem to be growing complacent about these errors.

For all the many benefits of using e-mail, authors still must judge when an alternative medium would be more appropriate. Where, for example, would you "draw the line" and not use e-mail exclusively in the examples below?

1. Announce that part of the parking lot will be out of use for the next three days.
2. Congratulate a subordinate for a success and share the message with the department.
3. Ask a group of subordinates, peers, and superiors to let you know their availability for a meeting next Thursday or Friday.
4. Send a message of inquiry to a company to see if they have job openings.
5. Apply for a job and include your résumé as part of the message.
6. Send a formal thank-you message to a person who had publicly bestowed an honor upon you.

E-mail messages can also overlap with ethical and legal considerations. While we may think that we discard or erase our e-mail messages, many businesspeople are learning to their dismay that presumably deleted messages can have a long life. Retrieved messages have been used to show company harassment against employees, for example. Microsoft chairman Bill Gates's e-mail containing the sentence, "Do we have a clear plan on what we want Apple to do to undermine Sun?" stands as an example of how high up in an organization a retrieved message can be found.[8]

Apply these ten steps to your writing projects and you will see, with a little experience, substantial improvements in the speed with which you write, the quality of that writing, the quantity of output, and the appearance of the finished product.

Because good etiquette in business and social settings enhances the communication exchange, and because rules for electronic etiquette are still emerging, you may wish to review the suggestions found in Table 4.2.

Table 4.2	Suggestions for Electronic Etiquette*

e-mail Avoid words all in capital letters; in e-mail it is the equivalent of shouting.

Do, though, use appropriate initial capitalization, such as proper names and start of sentences. To disregard capitals appears lazy.

Avoid writing things you may regret if seen by other than those anticipated. Most e-mail is not confidential.

Proofread your message before sending it, because few e-mail messages are printed first and then proofread, spell-checked, or grammar-checked.

Avoid sarcasm and satire: They don't translate well over e-mail.

Use urgent, priority, or receipt-requested judiciously—only when necessary.

Don't overload or intrude by "dumping" long articles or questionnaires that haven't been asked for.

If a message is unusually long, warn your reader early so he or she can decide how to handle it.

Respond quickly, but after you have had time to consider your response.

Use valuable, descriptive subject lines, because recipients may decide whether to read your message based on them.

Ensure the message is relevant to your audience. Because it is so easy to send a message to multiple receivers, people often send messages that are of no interest or value to some on the distribution list.

Be watchful of your tone. People tend to be harsher with e-mail messages than when face-to-face.

Don't write in anger. Put your response aside for a day or two and then send it if you still feel the same way.

If sending a message to a large number of people, put that list in the blind-carbon-copy (bcc) line and send the message to yourself. Then they see the message only, not the list.

Be judicious in keeping preceding message as part of new messages.

Use abbreviations such as "LOL" for "laughing out loud," or emoticons, such as 0-: or   the ubiquitous "smiley face" only with close friends or family.

Don't forward chain letters or the joke-of-the-day to a list of friends.

Keep signature lines brief; four lines is the upper limit for most people.

Be careful when you forward messages. The new recipient(s) may not know the context of the original message, you may unintentionally embarrass someone, or you may be creating an undesired paper trail.

Desktop Publishing

Desktop publishing, which uses computers to design and prepare camera-ready copy, facilitates this gathering of text and nontext (such as graphics) and then shows the page on a screen as it would appear when printed. The finished product can look quite professional and be relatively inexpensive. See Figure 4.5 for an example of how desktop publishing software can manipulate graphic images. Figure 4.6 illustrates how text can flow around a graphic image through the power of desktop publishing.

voice mail	State your name clearly at the beginning of your message. Spelling it out is valuable for anyone who speaks quickly, doesn't enunciate, or has a name spelled in an unexpected way.
	Share the main point of the message early. This gives the listener a framework upon which to "hang" your comments.
	Give your phone number(s) next, clearly and slowly. Include when you are available.
	Next, give details, if necessary, regarding the message.
	Keep your message as brief as possible.
	Be sure to give the time of day and date of your call.
	Answer your voice-mail message quickly. Some experts recommend writing down your response before returning the call to ensure you know what you want to say before you say it.
fax	Do not tie up the receiving fax machine for long periods of time.
	Do not send junk faxes (of potentially little interest) to lengthy distribution lists.
	Do not send private messages over organization fax lines.
	Call first before sending a long fax or send it after hours.
	Don't use faxes for personal notes of thanks, congratulations, or condolence.
	Unless specifically requested to do so, don't bother sending your resume by fax unless you don't want the job.
cellular phones and pagers	Unless absolutely necessary, don't use them in public places.
	Don't use phones in restaurants, theaters, concerts, or church.
speaker phone	Use only for conference calls; ask permission of the other person before turning on the speaker phone.

* For additional information about cell-phone etiquette, see **http://www.csuchico.edu/plc/e-etiquette.html**, **http://www.cellmanners.com/index2.htm**, **http://www.bizforum.org/etiquette.htm**, **http://www.10meters.com/manners_tips.html**, or "A Sharper Image: Young Workers Get Back to the Basics of Business Etiquette," *San Diego Union-Tribune*, June 17, 2002, p. E-8. See also A. Sabath, *Business Etiquette, 2d ed.* (Franklin Lakes, NJ: Career Press, 2002).

A: The original

B: Pulled horizontally

C: Pulled vertically

D: Selecting part of the original

Source: Logotype courtesy of MBA for Executives Program, San Diego State University.

To customize the shape of an existing graphic boundary:

1 *Select the graphic to display the graphic boundary.*

Graphic handle ⊢

Graphic boundary ⊢

Graphic boundary handle ⊢

Lorem ipsum dolor sit amet, consectetuer adipiscing elit, sed diam nonummy nibh euismod tincidunt ut laoreet dolore magna aliquam erat volutpat. Ut wisi enim ad minim veniam, quis nostrud exerci tation ulamcorper sus- cipit lobortis nisl ut aliquip ex ea commodo consequat. Duis autem vel eum iriure do- lor in hendrerit in vulputate velit esse moles- tie consequat, vel illum dolore eu feugiat nulla facilisis at vero eros et accumsan et iu- sto odio dign- issim qui blandit praesent lupta- tum zzril delenit augue duis dolore te feugait nulla facilisi. Lorem ipsum dolor sit amet, consectetuer adipiscing elit, sed diam nonummy nibh euismod tincidunt ut laoreet dolore magna aliquam erat volut- pat. Ut wisi enim ad minim veniam, quis nostrud exerci tation

2 *Create new graphic boundary handles as necessary by clicking boundary.*

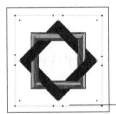

⊢ *New graphic boundary handle*

3 *Drag the handles to change the shape of the boundary. To keep PageMaker from reflowing text until you have finished reshaping a graphic, hold down the spacebar while you drag the graphic handles. The text will reflow when you release the spacebar.*

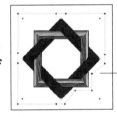

4 *Drag graphic boundary handles to outline shape of graphic.*

5 *The text flows around the customized graphic boundary.*

Lorem ipsum dolor sit amet, consectetuer adipiscing elit, sed diam nonummy nibh euismod tincidunt ut laoreet dolore ma- gna aliquam erat volutpat. Ut wisi enim ad minim veniam, quis nostrud exerci tation ullamcorper suscipit lobortis nisl ut al- iquip ex ea com- modo consequat. Duis autem vel eum iriure dolor in hendrerit in vulputate velit esse molestie consequat, vel il- lum dolore eu feugiat nulla facilisis at vero eros et ac- cumsan et iusto odio dignissim qui blandit praesent luptatum zzril de- lenit augue duis dolore te feugait nulla facilisi. Lorem ipsum dolor sit amet, consect- etuer adipiscing elit, sed diam nonummy nibh euismod tincidunt ut laoreet dolore magna aliquam erat volutpat. Ut wisi enim ad minim veniam, quis nostrud exerci tation ullam- corper suscipit lobortis nisl ut aliquip ex ea commodo

Source: © Aldus Corporation 1990. All rights reserved. Aldus® and PageMaker® is/are either [a] registered trademark[s] of Adobe Systems Incorporated in the United States and/or other countries.

Multimedia Presentations

A final computer technology that involves communication and is becoming a major application area is multimedia presentations. These computer programs can combine graphics, text, colors, animation, picture blends and dissolves, high-resolution photos, and sound to generate dazzling sales pitches and brilliant proposals. They can appear as a slide show on a computer, include video clips with motion, and incorporate interactive features for the viewer to respond to. They often use CD-ROM and stereo sound. Multimedia has uses in education, training, advertising, retail merchandising, and public access in addition to its obvious business presentation uses.

Two more important writing concepts are emerging with ever-changing technology: collaborative writing and international communication.

Collaborative Writing

For years some businesspeople have co-authored text, edited each other's writing, and worked on the same projects concurrently. As they did so, they learned that there are as many different ways of writing as there are facets to interpersonal behavior. Within a writing team there may be different approaches to writing (each person does a part versus all work together on all), hierarchical influences, ability and knowledge differences, time or job pressures, and various political effects. Sometimes the output of collaborative writing is a beautifully crafted message that is the result of team synergy, balanced abilities, a common goal, and plenty of effort. Often, however, the result pits writers against each other, takes too much effort, lacks seamless writing, and is at the level of the lowest contributor, not the group average or the highest contributor. Writing collaboratively can be challenging.

However, computers and computer networks can enhance this process. Because using computers for collaborative writing can increase quality and quantity and improve decision making, writing with others is becoming commonplace.

Collaborative writing goes well beyond trading diskettes containing text files. Today, group-oriented software tracks changes to files and records who made the changes. Queries to others can be implemented, and reactions to proposed alterations can be shared. Some software will allow any number of writers, all writing on one document at the same time if they wish, to generate a group document. They can include text and voice-based instant messaging, text chat, and threaded discussion, and can share files, pictures, and other documents.[9] Using e-mail to transmit attached documents is a common way of sharing manuscripts. Other hardware and software will permit many participants at one time, at multiple locations, at individual PCs, to brainstorm a topic, share reactions, statistically chart members' deviations from the group, and make a record of all comments.

Collaborative writing is enhanced when most of these conditions are true:

- All authors are equally competent with the hardware and software.
- Each author's contribution can be tracked.
- Each revision is shown along with the original, and the author making the change is identified.

- Authors realize that not all authors need to work on the document at once.
- Authors can add comments and questions to other authors.
- Authors work well together and are willing to give and receive constructive criticism.
- Authors meet agreed-upon deadlines.
- All authors agree upon the goal of the writing assignment from the outset.

Both academic writing experts and business practitioners see collaborative writing as a technique that will increase in value. Today's advanced business writer needs to be aware of the move toward this writing process.

International Communication

We discussed briefly in Chapter 1 that communication across cultural boundaries is becoming increasingly important. Indeed, Victor states that "the ability to compete in the world economy is arguably the single greatest challenge facing business at the end of the twentieth century."[10] Tung adds, "With the globalization of the world economy, it is imperative that managers, both present and future, be sensitive to differences in intercultural business communication."[11] To this Victor adds, "Few things, in turn, are more important in conducting business on a global scale than skill in communication."[12] Victor sees seven main variables in international communication: language, social organization, contexting, authority conception, nonverbal behavior, temporal conception, and environment and technology. Of these factors, the last is changing most quickly and making the greatest impact.[13]

Communicating internationally has always been a slow or expensive proposition. Letters were slow, long-distance phone rates were exorbitant, and time-zone differences were inconvenient. Today's technological innovations are fixing these constraints. E-mail delivers inexpensive messages quickly throughout the world.

When you employ international e-mail, be aware that people of other countries and cultures are likely to have differing views from yours on such items as formality, length, format, and tone of an e-mail message.

These e-mail messages are often limited to text, though attachments to e-mail contain color, files, or pictures. Facsimile (fax) machines, on the other hand, send and receive any black-and-white image, including drawings, handwriting, and graphics. Even the price of color fax machines is decreasing rapidly. Part of the reason for the heavy use of fax machines at the international level is that the price of a long-distance phone call, which carries the fax message, is decreasing. Such relatively new technologies as fiber optics and satellite transmissions help bring the price of a five-minute morning phone call from California to Japan to $5.40.

As U.S. businesses continue to seek out international markets, international branches, and foreign business partners, and as technology continues to make communication less expensive, quicker, and easier, one can see why international communication is such an important topic. Most business schools are readjusting their curriculum to include global trade, and international communication is a major element of that interaction.

Summary

Advanced writing calls on many skills. At the composition level, you will need awareness of the writing sequence, from defining the problem through performing a post-writing evaluation. You will also employ techniques that relate directly to writing. For example, organized writing follows some logical approach to the goal of the message, is coherent, and uses emphatic style efficiently. Another skill involves applying appropriate tone through such techniques as the *I* versus *you* attitude, positive phrasing, and tactful wording. Skill is also needed to write readable text; attention to writing with clarity, conciseness, and activity influences readability.

To make the most of your time, follow the suggestions for efficient writing, which include some time-management principles. Conducting research electronically is both time-efficient and powerful; knowledge of this skill can produce thorough research results with ease. Further, the electronic writing process can dramatically influence the quality and quantity of your output. By using shortcut techniques, selected software, and the power of the computer, you can enhance the transcription level of advanced writing.

In addition to the process of writing, the advanced business writer needs to be aware of how technology is affecting communication and business through collaborative writing and international communication, as well as the potential dangers of violating electronic etiquette.

Discussion Questions

1. What are the most commonly used electronic research tools? When you enter the same words into several search engines, do you get the same results? What is the relationship between an engine and the number of hits it generates?

2. What is the sequence of writing from beginning to end of a long, complex message? Do you start "small," such as with word choice, and move toward "large," such as overall organization, or vice versa? Does it depend on the person, the topic, or some other factor?

3. What are the different ways a computer and software can facilitate collaborative writing? Are some methods better than others?

4. How far does editing go? When is it easier to just rewrite someone else's message? At what point do her or his feelings become an issue when you are doing extensive editing?

Communication in Action

1. In society, having good manners is desirable, and violating social norms should be avoided. The same is true in business. Form a student group and assign the following items to group members. Have them conduct this mini-research assignment and then report back to the group. Discuss the results.

   a. Walk around campus or work and observe cell-phone use. Where and under what conditions are people using cell phones?

    b. Examine some of your recent e-mail messages. What violations of business etiquette do you see?

    c. Listen carefully to voice-mail messages on your phone. How well do the people follow the suggestions for phone voice-mail etiquette?

    d. Of a typical group of e-mail messages that accumulate when you have not logged on for a while, determine how many are "spam" that have little to do with you or your job. How did the senders get your address? What do the messages seek? How to resolve the danger of opening messages from unknown sources?

2. Using as many of the six electronic databases discussed on page 100 as your institution has available, search for articles by the well-known management professor Peter Drucker. How did the results compare for the various databases? What do you conclude from this?

3. Divide a writing project, such as a group report, among group members so that each person writes a section using the same word-processing program. Give each team member a hard copy of each section for editing. Unite the sections into one document. Working together on the same computer, edit and smooth out the flow so the document has consistent tone and coherency. Evaluate the document against the writing skills described in the chapter.

4. Discuss with your classmates how you would go about searching for information for the following items:

    a. A map of your state taken from space

    b. Quotes relative to the value of information by Thomas Jefferson

    c. An audio clip of Richard Nixon relative to criminal activity

    d. Information on how to put together a crisis management plan

    e. Three years of financial performance by company number 23 out of this year's Fortune 500

    f. The highest and lowest elevations for the 42nd state to join the Union

    g. The latest scholarly article on communication apprehension

    h. The ethnic breakdown of the freshman class at your university for last fall

5. Use whichever electronic or other sources you wish to track down a word that means "every fourth year." How long did it take you to find the answer? Where did you find it?

@ Internet

6. Using an Internet search engine, see what information you can find on collaborative writing software. Then, research the capabilities of the software. What are the similarities and differences of the software?

7. You are considering opening a motorcycle business in some location north of Denver, Colorado, and south of Laramie, Wyoming. Those cities have motorcycle shops that carry the same brand of motorcycle you are thinking of selling. As part of the research you are conducting that will become an element of your written business plan, determine the population size and

annual income of residents found between the two cities and in those two states.

8. Some companies develop a style manual for their employees to answer usage questions, help with frequent questions, and enhance achieving a common appearance to company documents. Search the web for such manuals. Compare them on length and topics.

InfoTrac

9. Search for scholarly journal articles for the topics *I* tone, *you* tone, *I* attitude, and *you* attitude. Compile the articles, read them, and prepare a synthesis of this literature regarding the topic.

10. Your job includes working on the corporate newsletter for employees. You have been given the assignments of preparing articles on the following topics:

    a. writing process. Using InfoTrac, find articles on this topic and see how much they agree. What are the major steps in the process?

    b. specific articles on SEC policy. What can you find?

    c. the plain-English movement. What is it, and where is it going?

11. As an employee of a global organization, you have been asked to prepare a handbook for American employees who travel to some of the international locations of the company. You plan to include a section on cultural differences and expectations for Japan, Spain, and Turkey. Use InfoTrac as your research method.

12. To add visual effect to your writing, you want some fresh suggestions and examples of it. Search for that type of emphasis along with writing emphatic sentences. What does the current literature have to say about the practice?

13. You often listen to KPBS (89.5) radio's "A Way With Words" program on Sundays. You have noticed the two hosts, who are experts on words and their usage, seem to know answers to every question readers ask them. They often discuss types of words, spellings, confusions, misuses, and origins. It occurs to you there are many ways of looking at words, but you would like some overarching resource of the study of words, such as a taxonomy. Search the InfoTrac articles to see if you can find a taxonomy of word usage.

Notes

1. Interactive media in education: An interview with Chris Dede. (2002, June). *Syllabus*, p. 13.
2. Kronholz, J. (2002, May 2). How do you cite a web page? That's a matter of debate; Arguing over a period. *Wall Street Journal*, p. A-1.
3. For a thorough review of dimensions of the *you* attitude, see Shelby, A. N., & Reinsch, N. L., Jr. (1995, October). Positive emphasis and *you*-attitude: An empirical study. *Journal of Business Communication*, *32*(4), pp. 303–328.

4. Svinicki, M. D. (1986, September). Increasing written output. *Newsletter of the Center for Teaching Effectiveness, 8*(1), p. 1.
5. DelRossi, A. (1993, September 27) SQL report writers collect information from your database and make it presentable. *Infoworld*, pp. 83–95.
6. Hamilton, J. O. (1999, October 4) Like it or not, you've got mail. *Business Week,* pp. 178–184.
7. Hamilton, Like it or not, p. 184.
8. Hamilton, Like it or not, p. 184.
9. Groove Workspace software. Retrieved May 30, 2002, from **http://www.groove.net/ products/all/workspace/comparison.html**.
10. Victor, D. A. (1992). *International business communication*. New York: Harper-Collins, p. xiii.
11. Tung, R. L. in Chaney, L. H., & Martin, J. S. (2000). *Intercultural business communication* (2nd ed.). Upper Saddle River, NJ: Prentice Hall, p. ix.
12. Victor, *International business communication*, p. xiii.
13. Victor, *International business communication*, p. 14.

CHAPTER - 5

Writing Direct Messages

Written business messages vary in directness. For instance, most congratulatory messages should be direct. In terms of directness alone, you may wish to start with your main idea (such as congratulations). In other cases, such as in most persuasive messages, you may work up to your primary thought carefully by preceding it with other information; this is an indirect organization. You should consider your message's goal and your audience, among other things, as you select between the two organizations or pick a different approach altogether.

While many messages clearly fall into either the direct or indirect categories, others do not. Examples of those messages that do not fit the direct or indirect organizations are messages that combine aspects of both, such as those that place the main point at both the opening and closing, and messages that are neither, such as those that have more than one main thought. This book uses the term *situational message* for those messages that do not overtly apply the direct or indirect approaches.

The purpose of Chapters 5, 6, and 7 is to discuss the writing of direct messages (Chapter 5), indirect messages (Chapter 6), and situational messages (Chapter 7). Of the three, Chapter 7 is probably the most important for advanced writers for three reasons: because many messages are situational; because complex audience analysis and message skills are involved; and because the higher the writer is in the organizational hierarchy, the more likely this category of message will be required. But because the logic behind preparing many situational messages grows from concepts associated with direct and indirect organizations, we will explore those approaches first. In this chapter, we will examine message formats briefly and then turn to writing direct messages.

Message Formats

Once you delete the inside addresses, attention lines, or dates, the bodies of letters, memoranda, and e-mails are organized in much the same manner. Further, as electronic message systems such as e-mail continue to pervade the business environment, content receives more emphasis than does appearance. For these reasons, this book does not differentiate between direct organization letters, direct organization memoranda, or direct organization e-mail messages. Most companies will dictate the desired format for their letters and memoranda. However, if you are in doubt about the appearance of most business correspondence, see Figure 5.2 for a letter and Figure 5.3 for a memorandum.

While the preparation of the bodies of memoranda, letters, and e-mail is similar, differences between the three do exist. Memoranda tend to get down to business more quickly than letters. Their *To, From, Subject,* and *Date* approach streamlines important information for the reader and creates a different visual impact. A Recommendation section may lead off a memorandum to quickly clarify its goal.

Another approach to writing direct memoranda is the simplified format, which delivers three main sections: *Facts, Discussion,* and *Recommendations.* As an internal, brief, and focused message for the busy executive, this order of information presents background, interprets it, and draws a logical recommendation for action. Although building to the recommendation suggests an indirect orientation, the straightforward delivery and short length, coupled with no intention to hide or manipulate the recommendation, identify this message as plainly direct. Do not confuse direct and indirect message organizations with deductive and inductive logic, which involve working from the general to specific concepts or from aiming at the general by examining the particulars, respectively. See Figure 5.1.

E-mail and memoranda tend to be rather informal, internal messages that use a format different from that of a letter; they also vary in length and distribution. While letters are usually only one page, memoranda and e-mail range in length from one or two sentences to many pages. Memoranda often are distributed to entire departments or groups, while letters typically go only to certain individuals. E-mail messages carry the additional distinction of being able to have attachments, such as electronic letters, scanned images, pictures, or audio or video clips.

One aspect of a message's format is its length. Hard-copy business letters are typically short; one page is the norm. Memoranda may be quite short—a single paragraph is acceptable—or many pages in length. E-mail messages should be brief, ideally about one screen total. However, they may be multiple screens, they may have attachments that extend the message, and as they get tossed back and forth among multiple viewers who keep prior messages, they can become quite long.

Of the three media, letters are perceived as most formal; thus, certain messages should always be delivered by letter. Before you can prepare effective written messages you must be aware of the available approaches, the reasons for their organization, and the appropriate occasion for each.

The Direct Approach

In the direct approach, the sender's primary goal agrees with the receiver's primary goal: What is foremost in the mind of the recipient is what the author most wishes to transmit. The direct approach immediately and clearly presents your main or most important thought. Additional thoughts follow by order of importance.

Substantial research exists to support the logic of the direct approach. For example, decades ago McGuire found that presenting desirable information first, followed by less desirable information, produces more change than would presenting information in the reverse order.[1] Janis and Feierbend also have found that when a message has both positive and negative content, the positive content should appear first.[2]

Figure 5.1 Simplified-Format Sample Memorandum

To: Senior Management
From: Jonah Iverson, CFO
Date: September 1, 200X
Subject: Illegal access of employees' records

Facts

On August 14, the payroll software database maintained by Ace Consultants for our employees was accessed illegally. We learned of the "hacking" of the system yesterday when Ace conducted their normal system analysis.

Discussion

The employees' records include social security records, addresses, and payroll information, such as various deductions. A review of the database shows no damage to or modification of the data, and we believe there was no malicious intent to destroy the data. Individual bank account information for employees is not part of the file. Names may have been copied, but no other data were copied.

The computers holding the database were immediately taken offline, and were thoroughly examined for corruption. New, more-extensive firewalls have been added to the security protection system.

Recommendations

A letter from me to all employees, as well as the same message on the company Intranet, will go out this afternoon. Please do what you can to minimize concern among employees and ensure them that their personal data have not been harvested, and that we have taken appropriate steps to avoid future hacking.

Some writers enjoy building up to the delivery of the most important information. However, while this indirect approach may be rewarding to the author, it is frustrating to the reader and does not evoke as beneficial a reaction as the direct approach. Three main categories of information that can be delivered with the direct organization are:

1. Positive information, which pleases the reader.
2. Neutral information, which may not elicit either a positive or negative reaction but which may have strong information value.
3. Negative information, which the reader will not want to read.

Assumptions about your audience and your tone are likely to vary with these three categories. Therefore, we shall review each category individually.

Delivering Positive Information

When you have only positive information to present, rank your information with the most positive first, followed by the next most positive, and so on. Work your way down to the least positive details.

When reading the most positive information first, the reader encounters the next thought in a more receptive mood. Assuming the second thought is the second most positive comment, these thoughts combine to place the reader in an even more favorable frame of mind for the third thought, and so on. This cumulative effect helps the reader receive the message with a better overall reaction than would be derived from an indirectly organized message.

Because substantial positive feelings can reflect well on the sender, you should make optimal use of this message category. You can achieve even more benefit by using direct statements that follow a subject/verb–first organization, selecting active voice, picking present tense, using strong verbs, organizing sentences for emphasis, and involving the reader through the use of the *you* tone. One example of such a message:

> Congratulations! Your proposal for the restructuring of the R&D team is right on target. You saw the heated personality conflicts sooner and more clearly than anyone else. We're adopting your proposal effective immediately.

The positive messages you deliver will vary greatly from extremely positive (You're hired!) to only slightly positive (Here's our regular quarterly parts order for the usual items). The more positive your information is, the more positive and strong your language should be, and vice versa.

With positive-content messages, the most difficult writing steps are (a) correctly ranking the importance of the various items from the reader's viewpoint; (b) omitting extraneous information; and (c) writing transitions from thought to thought.

Business messages that typically provide positive information include those granting requests, announcing favorable information, extending credit, showing gratitude, and accepting or sending invitations. See Figures 5.2 and 5.3 for additional examples.

Delivering Neutral Information

Neutral messages can carry information of equal or even higher importance than positive messages, but their emotional content and involvement are usually lower. Order acknowledgments, inquiries, requests for credit information, personnel evaluations, and compliance with requests can be neutral messages. The distinction between neutral and positive messages is open to interpretation: One person may see the information as positive while another perceives it as having so little positive information as to place it in the neutral camp. The perception by the receiver, not the sender, is crucial.

Use the direct approach with neutral messages. Instead of placing the most positive information at the top, however, report the most important information first. Smooth transitions from thought to thought will be necessary for coherence. Occasionally, you will need to place the less-important information earlier in the message to avoid illogical or awkward construction. For example, you may need to

Figure 5.2 **Example of an Effective Positive Information Letter**

The Computer Source
278 Electronics Avenue
La Costa CA 93008
February 12, 200X

Jorge Hernandez, President
Chips and Stuff, Inc.
1093 Upper Knob Drive
San Francisco CA 96060

Dear Mr. Hernandez:

Thank you for your recent bid to supply us with 100 GB Ultra DMA/100
hard drives; we have decided to accept it. Yours was the lowest bid we
received, and we very much want you to sign the enclosed contract
pertaining to supply of these drives.

You may be interested to know that you are being awarded this contract
not only because of your competitive pricing, but even more because of
the availability of these 100 gigabyte units. These drives are crucial to us,
and your competition would not guarantee delivery within 30 days on
orders of 1,000 units, as you do.

This new business venture should be rewarding for both of us. We look
forward to developing a close working relationship with you and to
many mutually beneficial contracts. Please sign and return the contract
by March 1.

Cordially,

Hans Sturgeon

Hans Sturgeon
President

HS/gw
Enc.: contract

---

discuss your firm's recent name change before you request an extension of credit.
Figure 5.4 illustrates an effort to organize the most important facts first while still
incorporating the needed yet unimportant facts as transitions.

You are likely to write many neutral internal messages to accompany other written information. These messages often are transmittal messages. Letters and memoranda transmit reports, illustrations, internal proposals, and other data from sender
to receiver. They briefly explain the content of and reason for transferring the data.

INTEROFFICE MEMO

To: All Employees
From: Quentin Harris, Senior Vice President
Subject: Appreciation
Date: November 23, 200X

Yesterday, Francine Smith, management consultant with Long Beach
Management Consultants, won the coveted Consultant of the Year
award from her national association. Please join us in extending our
appreciation and congratulations by signing the 2′ x 3′ congratulations
card that we will send her on Tuesday. The card is in the reception area.

Francine has spent the last 11 months, as most of you know, reviewing
our structure, financial position, and movement toward our goals. Her
recommendations have been insightful. The restructuring has improved
production and accountability, our profits are on the rise, and we're now
moving aggressively toward our corporate goals.

Sh-sh-sh-sh! Please keep this quiet. She doesn't know we are sending her
the card.

In some cases, they summarize the conclusions or recommendations of the report.
These messages usually end with an offer of availability for questions. Chapter 9 discusses transmittals. As mentioned above, e-mail messages can carry attachments, such
as reports or proposals. While it might be inappropriate to send an e-mail message
with a formal proposal attached in response to a Request for Proposal, this process
might be quite efficient and desirable for circulating the draft of the proposal internally among co-authors.

Delivering Negative Information

A decision that is often difficult is whether to use a direct or indirect organization
to carry information with negative content. Do you agree with these views?

1. "I'll bet I've received 20 job rejection letters this semester. At first I
   appreciated the gentle letdown, but now I just wish they'd tell me the
   bad news up front."

2. "Sure, I want the contract. I also know from the return address who the
   letter is from and, therefore, the general topic. So just tell me: Did I get
   the contract?"

3. "Don't try to placate me. I'm a grown person. I don't need a wishy-washy
   indirect opening. Get to the subject. That's the way I like to be handled."

Figure 5.4   **Example of a Direct Neutral Message**

Dataproducts Corporation
6200 Canoga Avenue
P.O. Box 746
Woodland Hills, California 91365-0746
(818) 887-8000   Telex 67-4734

Thank you . . .

for your recent request for information regarding products manufactured by Dataproducts Corporation. We are enclosing descriptive literature and hope it will answer any questions you may have.

Dataproducts manufactures a broad range of computer printers, printer components and supplies, and telecommunications equipment for the computer industry.

If you would like to discuss pricing and/or technical details please telephone us at (800) 555-2121, and we will connect you to the Dataproducts sales or distributor/dealer office nearest you.

We would also appreciate your completing and returning the enclosed postpaid reply card. The information you supply will be helpful to us in providing you with additional literature and service.

Sincerely,

Keith Bauserman
Vice President
North American Sales

KB:adk
Enc.

Source: Reproduced with permission from Dataproducts Corporation.

You probably can see some logic in these views. The problem for the writer is that most people do not feel these ways all the time. Many people prefer all job rejection letters, contract denials, and negative information to follow an indirect order. Your challenge, then, is to decide:

1. Does this information or occasion justify a direct approach?
2. Does this person prefer a direct approach?
3. Is this a routine message, one that is "business as usual"?

If your answer to all three questions is yes, use the direct approach. If the answer to any one of these three questions is no, pick the indirect approach. If you are unsure of the answers, you are probably safest with the indirect approach because inappropriately using the direct organization can create strong antagonism toward the author and the author's business.

Inappropriate use of the indirect organization, on the other hand, may cause the reader some frustration but is unlikely to bring about extreme negative reactions. (More discussion of the indirect approach appears in Chapter 6.)

Prepare your negative messages that follow the direct organization with these thoughts in mind:

- Place the negative information first because you assume it is the most important information to the reader. Do not try to gloss over the bad news.
- Deliver the negative information gently. The passive voice may be appropriate. Use some finesse. Be tactful. Do not dwell on the bad news.
- Give reasons that support the decision, if possible. Avoid saying that you are sorry; instead, let the rationale of the decision work for you. Give selected details but do not pass the buck or blame company policy.
- Try to include some positive information, particularly at the end.
- Sound sincere. Insincere-sounding messages, especially carrying the negative information, can be destructive.
- Work for continued goodwill.

Accomplishment of this last objective may take the form of describing what you have done to avoid similar problems in the future, offering personal attention to the customer, or providing some free service or replacement. See Figure 5.5 for an example of an effective negative message that uses direct organization.

Additional Direct Negative Message Considerations

Sometimes you will want to use the direct negative approach, such as when writing to friends who might be offended by an indirect approach. Here is an example:

You're a good friend, but I still need payment for the money I loaned you last month so you could take advantage of your company's stock investment program. Please send me the $500 right away.

You may also wish to use the direct negative approach when trying to avoid a patronizing tone, which most of us dislike. When we are clearly at fault for something, sometimes we would rather just hear the bad news instead of being toyed with. Here is an example:

The Yellow River Project report was due yesterday. We both know how important the completion of the report is to the overall strategic plan. Submit the report to me no later than 5 P.M. tomorrow.

Figure 5.5	**Negative Message Using Direct Organization**

```
From:server@net.com
Date:Tue, 08Nov 200X 011:51:06 -4000
Organization:@net.com.net
X-Mailer: BX 98.7 [cba] V-atnet.com.net 0773 (Win2000; U)
X-Accept-Language: cba.774
FROM: Samantha Chen <samchen@net.com>
TO:ExecMgmtTeam.list@net.com
SUBJECT: This weekend's Executive Management Team retreat
```

This past weekend's retreat at the Big Pines Resort was,
in my mind, a big flop. We had hoped to emerge from the
two days of meetings and discussions with a firm business
strategy for the coming year in place, a decision on
whether to move ahead on production of the X-14 or Z-19
audio chips, and a clearer understanding of the role
electronic commerce should play in our future. We did not
achieve the first two and made only slight progress on the
last goal.

In retrospect, I think there are several reasons why the
outcomes were not better. First, rather than functioning
as a committee-of-the-whole and seeking consensus on every
decision, we needed more structure. Second, inviting our
partners, while most enjoyable for us, seemed to interfere
with our getting to sessions on time and staying focused.
Finally, the afternoon of golf on Sunday afternoon cut into
our total time together, and occurred just as we were close
to accomplishing our goals.

Therefore, I'm calling a day-long work session for Saturday,
the 23rd of this month, in our executive conference room,
starting at 8 a.m. to complete our work. I've arranged for
Bill Finegar to serve as facilitator.

You know the issues, so be thinking about them. The sooner
we meet our objectives for the meeting, the sooner we can
join our partners for the balance of the weekend or get out
to the golf course.

Additional Direct Information Messages

In addition to the positive, neutral, and negative information types of messages that use the direct organization, there are two others. Routine messages and directives may carry any of the three information types, but they have some unique characteristics as well.

Routine Messages

Routine messages occur at periodic intervals, such as quarterly reports, or regularly, such as in-progress reports. See Figure 5.6 for an example of a routine form letter.
Here are two provisos exclusive to routine messages:

- First, if the routine message has negative content, it is often wise to emphasize the routine aspect of the message. For example, you might emphasize that this is your regular semiannual product order, that you plan to pay for it within 30 days after billing as usual, that you want it sent to your St. Louis plant as before, and that you appreciate the excellent service you have come to associate with the supplier. An example of routine negative information in such a message might be that your orders vary in size dramatically during the year, and this happens to be an order much smaller than the last two orders.

- Second, you might undercut your objective to inform the reader of your periodic sending of this type of message. "This invitation goes out to all persons whose names appear in the weekly listing of 'Marriage Certificates Approved' for a special 10-percent discount" misses the opportunity to focus on an event that is for the reader infrequent and individually exciting.

Routine messages may appear as form letters or may be individually prepared as the occasion requires. Form letters, of course, often are impersonal and mass produced. Nevertheless, time and cost considerations frequently dictate the form message.

The messages discussed so far—especially the similar positive, neutral, and routine messages—and goodwill messages, to be discussed in Chapter 7, have an interesting, complex relationship, as can be seen in Figure 5.7. Some of the information in a positive message (most likely the portions further down in the message) may be neutral; some early portions of a neutral message might be perceived as positive by some people. When you, as an insurance agent, send out holiday cards to your policyholders, you are sending a routine goodwill message that is also positive. When a person automatically places orders for parts with you every three months, it is a routine neutral message. Envisioning the relationship of these four message categories will help you to prepare any one of them.

| Figure 5.6 | Example of a Routine Form Message |

EMMAUS, PA 18049

Welcome!

Dear Subscriber,

Thanks for your subscription order to NEW SHELTER Magazine. Enclosed you'll find your FREE booklet which comes as part of your subscription to our magazine.

Your first issue should be arriving shortly. Once you've read through it, you'll agree that a subscription to NEW SHELTER is a great investment for any homeowner—one that's sure to pay for itself many times over in the course of a single year!

NEW SHELTER is really the complete home magazine. If it's home improvement you want, you'll find lots of help in enhancing the value . . . the beauty . . . and the overall "livability" of your home.

You really should be congratulated on the wise decision you've made! We thank you again for subscribing to our magazine, and we're confident you'll be glad you did and will want to stay with us for many years to come! Again, welcome to NEW SHELTER—it's nice to have you with us!

Sincerely,

Ed Fones

Ed Fones
Circulation Manager

P.S. For the latest from NEW SHELTER or for inquiries about your subscription, visit our web site at http://www.newshelter.mag.

EF:iss
Enc.

Source: Reproduced with permission from Rodale's *New Shelter* magazine.

Figure 5.7 **Relationship of Some Messages Using Direct Organization**

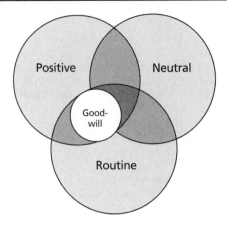

Directives

Directives are internal messages issued to employees to identify desired or undesired behavior. As a manager, you will write directives not only for the obvious reason of giving direction but also to provide a written record to which employees can be held accountable and to which they can refer over time for details. You may also use directives to establish or reinforce your authority or to build a framework of policies and procedures.

Many directives follow the direct approach. Your main purpose is to direct behavior; identify that behavior clearly and firmly at the beginning of the message. Effective directives do more than just direct; they also present the rationale behind the directive. Therefore, your second step is an explanation for the desired behavior. Support your explanation with reasons when appropriate. Your explanation and reasons are your second-most-important information.

Finally, you may wish to include a motivational thought, such as "Let's follow safety rules for our own protection and for the good of the company." Be careful, however, not to undermine your authority, lose your tone of firmness, or appear too warm or friendly. Warmth and friendliness are valuable commodities to share with employees, but not in every communiqué; omit them from your directives. You seek compliance without emotional involvement. To avoid involving your readers too much in the message or even offending them, use an impersonal tone with relatively few adjectives, adverbs, similes, metaphors, or other colorful language.[3] See Figure 5.8 for an example of an effective directive.

Another direct message type is the direct persuasive message. This message is so unique that it receives special attention in Chapters 6 and 7.

Figure 5.8	Example of an Effective Directive

```
From:server@comcom
Date:Wed, 08Dec 200X 011:41:06 -8000
Organization:@comcom.net
X-Mailer: MX 4.7 {xn} B-atcom.net 0443 (WinXP; U)
X-Accept-Language: xn
FROM: William C. Griggs <wcg@comcom>
TO:employeeslist_all@comcom

DATE: December 8, 200X.

Many employees have been bringing privately owned laptop
computers to work and have been using these computers on the
job. While employee involvement and dedication are valuable
assets, please do not demonstrate them by bringing computers
to work, effective immediately.

The presence of noncompany-owned computers has created
problems of control of confidential company data, has wasted
work time while employees demonstrated the machines to
colleagues, and has caused compatibility problems in the
production department, where the word-processing specialists
are familiar only with Microsoft Word and WordPerfect on
Windows PCs.

To involve computers more in your tasks and to assist those
of you familiar with computers, we are exploring a bulk
purchase of compatible computers for use by salaried
employees. Your suggestions regarding which equipment best
meets your needs, and assignment of these machines, if
purchased, would be appreciated.
```

Summary

In business writing, you can choose between direct and indirect approaches. Go directly to the main message (a direct organization) if your information is positive or neutral in nature. Consider a direct organization for negative information only if the information or occasion calls for it, if you think the reader prefers it, or if the message is routine.

The direct approach assumes there will be little or no resistance from the reader and that what is most positive or most important to the sender is also most positive or important to the reader. Thus, the direct approach orders thoughts from most positive to least positive (or, for the neutral message, from most important to least important). For the transmission of negative information in a direct order, be gentle in your language and use logic to your benefit. The direct organization also can be used effectively with two other types of messages: routine messages and directives. Sometimes it is advisable to indicate the routineness of the message and other times it is not. With the directive, information is firm and clear about desired behavior on the part of employees.

Because a variety of message types appear in this chapter, Table 5.1 summarizes the three major message types (positive, neutral, and negative) and shows subcategories and additional categories.

Memoranda, letters, and e-mail messages using the direct organization are relatively easy to organize and write. But despite their ease in preparation, these messages—especially the positive and neutral ones—sometimes go unwritten because they are often not a response to a request. These messages, therefore, are not missed if not received. Because of their perceived expendability, they are among the first messages neglected by the overworked writer. This neglect is unfortunate because these messages reassure, reconfirm, and give attention to existing clients, employees, and customers.

As a portion of the total writing effort, direct messages are a mainstay—one often skipped by less-concerned communicators and weaker managers. These messages can help distinguish you as a person who makes the extra effort to send such often-ignored communications as congratulations or acknowledgments. Enhance your image with these messages.

Table 5.1	**Summary of Direct Message Approaches**	
Major Message Type/Subcategory	**Goal**	**Example**
Positive	Reception of positive information by receiver	Extension of long-term financing for a major project
Letter of Recommendation	Help someone obtain a job	Recommendation of employee or friend for employment
Goodwill	Elicit positive reaction back to sender	Appreciation for continuing business
Neutral	Reception of neutral information by receiver	Acknowledgment of receipt of order
Transmittal	Transport other written media	Transmittal letter in a report
Negative	Clear, immediate delivery of negative information	Rejection of a bid
Additional Types		
Routine	Transmission of frequently recurring information	Sending clients a reminder that you need their tax information by February 1
Directives	Internal messages to direct behavior	Changing the deadline for outgoing mail

This chapter introduces aspects of another major organization: the indirect approach, which is the subject of Chapter 6. Chapter 7 goes on to examine situational writing, which brings together many of the underlying concepts supporting direct and indirect organizations.

Discussion Questions

1. Your boss has to write a letter to the Board of Directors explaining to them that the company's last investment has resulted in a $1-million loss. She is really concerned about the Board's reaction and is seeking your help in preparing the letter. What organization would you use?

2. You need to ask your supervisor for an increase in your advertising budget. You know he is a straightforward person so you don't want to be indirect in your message. On the other hand, you definitely want a positive response. How would you approach the message?

3. What types of people are more likely to prefer a direct organization message no matter what the topic?

4. Which categories of messages are always prepared in direct format, and which may be either direct or indirect? How does one decide which to use for the latter?

Communication in Action

1. Conduct a survey of business e-mail users. What percentage of their messages are formal versus informal, internal versus external, one screen in length verses longer, have attachments, and are sent to a distribution list of five or more people?

2. Find some examples of positive messages. First, evaluate them by how well the authors followed the guidelines for ordering the information. Next, how successful were the authors at avoiding extraneous information? Finally, evaluate the quality of the transitions from thought to thought.

3. Think about the body of a message, such as praising a subordinate for a job well done on a medium-size project. How would you modify the message depending on whether you used e-mail, memorandum, or letter medium?

4. What types of goodwill messages have you received, and how did you feel about those messages and the sender of them?

@ Internet

5. Select some companies and use the Internet to locate their annual reports. Read the letters of introduction. What types of organization do these letters employ? Is there a relationship between the type of organization of the letters and how well the companies performed financially?

6. The literature that formed the logic for the direct approach to message organization is about 50 years old. Use InfoTrac to locate current literature that discusses the approach. Be sure to review the following journals: *Journal of Business Communication, Journal of Business and Technical Communication,* and *Management Communication Quarterly.* Does current literature support the classic approach?

Notes

1. McGuire, W. J. (1969). The nature of attitude and attitude change. *Handbook of social psychology* (2nd ed.), *3.* Reading, MA: Addison-Wesley, p. 212; and McGuire, M. J. Order of presentation as a factor in 'conditioning' persuasiveness, in Hovland, C. I. (ed.) (1957). *The order of presentation in persuasion.* New Haven, CT: Yale University Press, pp. 98–114.
2. Janis, I. L., & Feierbend, R. L. (1957). Effects of alternate ways of ordering pro and con arguments in persuasive communications, in Hovland, C. I. (ed.) *The order of presentation in persuasion.* New Haven, CT: Yale University Press, p. 23.
3. Dulek, R. E., & Fielden, J. S. (1990). *Principles of business communication.* New York: Macmillan Publishing Co., pp. 283–284.

CHAPTER - 6

Writing Indirect Messages

In Chapter 5, we explained that when the writer expects the reader to agree with the contents of a message, it is best to present the message directly. In business, you may also select the direct approach because you think the occasion dictates it or the reader prefers it—because the information is routine or because it is easy to write (direct messages usually take relatively little planning). There is no resistance to overcome in direct messages. Resistance means that the reader may be opposed to what you are proposing (or to you or your company), may be disinterested, or may not be able to comply. You will encounter many other occasions when resistance is likely—for instance, when transmitting strong negative information or when persuading someone to act. This chapter presents writing approaches for these two message categories, both of which usually use an indirect organization. Chapter 7 discusses those messages for which there are no clear-cut formulas.

If positive messages with direct organization are among the easiest to write, then those with negative information or persuasive content are among the most difficult. The difficulty of writing a negative message stems from its bipolar objectives: (1) to transmit the bad news clearly and (2) to maintain the reader's goodwill. Picture, for example, writing a supplier to reject a bid but trying to maintain interest so that the company will continue to bid in the future. To accomplish either objective by itself is fairly easy; to accomplish both takes skill. Persuasive messages by nature are usually indirect messages because they try to overcome a reader's resistance. Using the approach that we outline below for a negative or persuasive message often makes the writer's job less burdensome.

Writing effective indirect messages entails understanding the rationale behind the indirect approach. The rationale emphasizes the steps in the formula.

Negative Messages

The formula for negative messages grows from the dual objectives of transmitting bad news and maintaining goodwill. Occasionally, maintaining goodwill is not of primary concern and is even subordinate to the message delivery. Such an occasion might be the fifth in a series of progressively more-stern letters seeking payment for goods or services. For most of us there is a point at which positive perception of us or our business is no longer a primary goal. Occasions such as these either use direct organization or are handled in a situational approach.

The pattern for transmitting negative messages has four steps: (1) a delaying opening; (2) the reasons for the upcoming bad news; (3) the bad news itself; and (4) a positive ending. These steps follow an indirect organization, which means that the primary reason for the message—the bad news—receives a location of low emphasis. Opening sentences and paragraphs carry high impact (that is why in positive messages the most positive thought is placed there), and so does the ending of a message. Using the principle of place emphasis, bad news most often appears in the middle of the message to diminish its impact.

The underlying logic supporting the indirect approach is that preparing the reader for the message can determine the reader's perception of the message. While the reader will not be happy hearing the bad news, the reader may at least understand the writer's position if the information appears in such a way that the recipient reads all the message and if the reasons are believable, realistic, and logical.

Understanding the rationale behind the order and preparation of the four steps is useful not only in preparing negative messages but also in writing more complicated messages, such as situational messages.

The Delaying Opening

The purpose of delaying the opening is to present the general topic without hinting about the upcoming negative news. Writing a delaying opening that does not sound as if it is delaying the bad news can be difficult. If you have ever read an opening that you recognized as a delaying tactic, then you have read an ineffective opening. For example, this opening is weak because it leaks the upcoming bad news: "Over the last year you've met most of the essential deadlines." Other characteristics of weak openings are those that start too far from the general subject and those that have too positive a tone.

Because many negative messages are in response to earlier messages or inquiries, the readers of those messages often eagerly anticipate the answers. This anticipation puts pressure on the delaying opening. For example, how would you react to this opening?

> Thank you for your recent letter of application for our position of management consultant. You were correct in your observation that our consulting division is one of the largest and best of the major public accounting firms. Because of this size and quality we always carefully review the education, experience, and other characteristics of job applicants.

If you are especially eager for this job, you might find the delay of the important news, whatever it may be, frustrating. On the other hand, you might find the personal references a positive way to get in the mood of the topic. At least the opening does not give away the upcoming bad news or start too far from the subject.

The astute reader may well argue that any response that does not immediately state the good news must be delaying the bad news. If all messages were prepared following either the direct or indirect organizations and were written effectively, this observation would be correct. However, there are many writers who inappropriately apply the indirect organization to positive messages and still others who use a direct organization for strong negative content. In other words, there are enough writers who are poor at organizing messages that most readers will not see through your intentions when you write an effective delaying opening.

Writing an effective delaying opening is often the most difficult of the four steps in the negative message formula. For many writers, starting with a more positive opening than is necessary is easier than the neutral-to-slightly-positive delaying opening. However, an opening that is too positive forces awkward transitions to the rapidly approaching bad news. For example, "You have consistently prepared better marketing analysis than others in your department" makes difficult the switch to negative information.

Another reason—a major one—that delaying openings are so difficult to write is that they often appear manipulative. As soon as your reader thinks he or she is being tricked or coerced or is receiving biased or one-sided information, he or she will reject your message. (Indeed, this reaction applies to indirect messages as a whole!) On the whole you are manipulating the reader as you make such decisions as word selection and order, message organization, format, and delivery timing. However, if the reader does not recognize your manipulation, you probably will achieve your goal.

The Reasons

Probably the most crucial step in the negative message formula is the second, which establishes the reasons for the upcoming bad news. The goal of the step is to seek reader acknowledgment of the reasons; acknowledgment at this point establishes a relationship with the yet-to-be-announced decision. Returning to the example of a response to a job application, does this example accomplish the step's goal?

> Because of the fine reputation of the Management Consulting Division, our well-known training program, and the firm's solid national standing, many dozens of applicants—a large percentage with MBAs—are seeking positions. Both the large number and the high quality of the applications make our job of selecting the top interviewees difficult. Our strong appreciation for experience in consulting guides us in our selections.

The example presents three reasons: the number of applications, the quality of the applications, and the focus on applicants with experience.

In preparing your reasons, empathize with your reader—the reasons should be logical to the reader and not just to you. Avoid reliance on such weak reasons as company policy. Instead, explain the reasons for the company policy. Do not pass the buck, blaming someone else for the decision. As the author of a letter being sent to someone outside the company, you represent the company; it is poor form to transfer the decision elsewhere. If possible and appropriate, each reason should build on preceding reasons.

If the reasons step appears logical, the upcoming bad news will emerge naturally. Further, this second step also should not leak bad news, even though that news is the next step.

The Bad News

Step three in the indirect organization of a bad-news message delivers the negative information. While the delaying opening and the development of the reasons may take from several sentences to a paragraph each, this third step can be quite short, sometimes taking only a part of a sentence. The bad news often follows from and can be appended to the reasons step. Avoid putting bad news in a separate paragraph. A stand-alone paragraph, such as "For the reasons stated above, we must sever our contract," is undesirable because it receives too much emphasis.

In appending the bad-news step to earlier steps of the sample message, the goal is the reader's agreement with your decision.

Applicants other than you, ones with equally solid educational background but extensive consulting background, have been selected to be interviewed.

Despite its relatively short length, this third step is still important and requires careful wording. Too blunt a negative message can destroy effectively prepared earlier steps. To maintain the goodwill of the reader, it is necessary to present the negative news as positively as possible. Sometimes you can leave the interpretation of the bad news to the reader by establishing what you are doing as opposed to not doing. For example, stating that you are awarding a bid to another firm tells the reader that he or she did not receive it.

Most often the active voice is best for business writing to add interest, clarity, and movement. In the third step of a negative message, however, the active voice may be too forceful; the passive voice may be softer. For example, the passive "Your firm's services are no longer required" is softer than the active "We no longer want to employ your firm."

The negative step can also be too personal. Seek an impersonal style by avoiding people's names and personal pronouns. Be especially cautious of first names, *I*, and *you*. Some writers, in an attempt to show personal involvement with the decision, declare their sympathy or extend an apology. Such statements weaken the strength of the earlier logic and usually add little to soften the bad news. An "I'm sorry" is likely to elicit a "me, too" or a bitter "I'll bet you are." Further, the unnecessary sympathy or apology only underscores the bad news, thus emphasizing it.

Once you deliver the negative message, leave it. Do not dwell on it. Change the subject to something more positive, such as the topic of the positive ending.

The Positive Ending

The last step seeks to change the tone from negative to positive. The reason for this step is to maintain goodwill. Positive information at the end allows the writer to end on a nice note, avoids closing on bad news, and uses the location—at the end of the message, which provides emphasis—to push a positive overall tone.

At a minimum, the ending can extend thanks for the offer, the bid, the suggestion, the application, the idea, the message, or whatever you have decided to reject. Make sure that this thanks sounds sincere; even heartfelt appreciation stated as, "Thanks again, and don't hesitate to write," will make little impact on the reader. The phrase sounds insincere and overused. The same idea, rephrased to sound sincere and individualized, might be, "Perhaps your next idea will be the award-winner, so don't hold back on sharing other suggestions with us in the future."

Look for stronger endings than just "thank you." Perhaps you can alter the declined inquiry so that you can give an affirmative answer. For example, if asked for reprints of an article, respond by saying, "If photocopies of the report rather than reprints are acceptable, we can mail them immediately." You may also be able to suggest an alternate source for something you could not provide: "We no longer manufacture the pressed glassware you seek; Art Products bought the molds; they may be able to help you. Their address is. . . ."

A third technique for stronger positive endings is suggesting that in the future you might be able to extend a *yes*. To exemplify this approach, we again turn to the response to a job application:

> As our Management Consulting Division continues to grow, we expect to have new openings. As you acquire additional accounting experience elsewhere, please keep us in mind as a possible employer.

Resist the desire to toss in a final reference to the bad news such as, "Again, know that we're as sorry about this as you are." Once you deliver the negative in the third step, do not resurrect it. End on a positive thought.

The four steps in the negative message should flow from idea to idea. Let's look again at that letter responding to a job application with its parts consolidated.

> Thank you for your recent letter of application for our position of management consultant. You were correct in your observation that our consulting division is one of the largest and best of the biggest public accounting firms. Because of this size and quality we always carefully review the education, experience, and other characteristics of job applicants.
>
> Because of the fine reputation of the Management Consulting Division, our well-known training program, and the firm's solid national standing, many dozens of applicants—a large percentage with MBAs—are seeking this position. Both the large number and the high quality of the applications make our job of selecting the top interviewees difficult. Our strong appreciation for experience in consulting guides us in our selections. Applicants other than you, ones with equally solid educational background but extensive consulting background, have been selected to be interviewed.
>
> As our Management Consulting Division continues to grow, we expect to have new openings. As you acquire additional accounting experience elsewhere, please keep us in mind as a possible employer.

Transitions are important in all writing. Negative messages are no exception. A smooth transition is especially crucial between steps one and two. Look for a phrase that links thoughts occurring at the end of step one to the first thoughts in step two. (A discussion of writing transitions appears in Chapter 4.)

Avoiding such reversal words or phrases as *on the other hand, however*, or *unfortunately* will smooth the transition from step one to step two, as well as avoid alerting the reader to the upcoming bad news.

As discussed, the transition from step two to step three is usually an easy one. Although there is a major tone change from step three to step four, the transition is not as important because the tone is now positive. The author may even wish to accentuate the change by starting step four with a reversal word or phrase, such as "In the next few months, however, . . ." This technique serves to tell the reader, "The bad news is over; now we're changing to more pleasant topics." See Figure 6.1 for an effective indirect negative message.

First National Bank
P.O. Box 987
Ft. Worth TX 78206

April 23, 200X

David Hertfelder, Executive Director
Substance Abuse Program for Children
Dallas–Ft. Worth Region
P.O. Box 2322
Ft. Worth TX 78210

Dear David:

Thank you for your letter describing the substance abuse program.
While I was aware of the existence of your program, I had not
realized the extent of your services. Your request for financial support
for your upcoming Awareness Fair honors us. As you mentioned in
your letter, we do believe in community duty and seek out those
programs that focus on children. That you know of our involvement
is reassuring to us. As part of our giving program, each January we
establish our contribution budget and then, in February, we announce
our contributions to the public. Our contributions for 200X already
have been announced and distributed.

If you decide to hold your Fair next year or wish to be considered for
a contribution to another aspect of your program, please submit a
proposal before January 1, 200X. Your proposal will receive careful
consideration.

Thank you again for thinking of us. Good luck with your program
and your Fair.

Cordially,

Traci Petalek

Traci Petalek
Director, Community Relations

Not all negative messages nor all companies follow the steps described here. A few years ago one of the largest merchandisers in the United States, in rejecting requests for credit, responded with computer-generated form letters that started

Dear Credit Applicant:

Thank you for the opportunity to consider your request for credit. We regret, however, that we cannot, at this time, accommodate your specific credit needs.

As noted below,

ACTION TAKEN

Application for credit denied.
You have the right to. . . .

Place yourself in the position of the applicant. How would you feel toward the company that sent this letter?

Persuasive Messages

The second major category of messages that relies on the indirect organization is persuasive messages. Most business writing tries to persuade others to act in a desired way. Those who are successful at altering the behavior of others make their readers want to take the proposed action. If the reader already wants to do what you propose, you should not resort to a persuasive message. Write a direct request to act. When it is necessary to change an opinion toward an action or product, however, work up to the request. You are guaranteed a rejection if you start with a request when resistance is present. Therefore, build your message following the indirect organization, which saves the request for the desired action until last. (Request messages that do not fit this concept are discussed in Chapter 7.)

Writing persuasively usually follows a series of specific steps; these steps parallel the behavior we follow each time we take an overt action. For example, analyze this vignette:

You need some parts for your old car, so you go to the dealer. The parts department is closed for another ten minutes so you decide to wait in the showroom. You immediately notice a bright red, new BMW in the middle of the room. You admire the sleek lines and take in the rugged, powerful beauty. "Now there's a car," you say to yourself.

As is usually the case, you have been near the car for only a short time when you are greeted by a salesperson: "Great little car, isn't it?" he says. "Just check this baby out!"

"You're right! It's a beauty. How much is it?" you respond.

"It's probably the best buy we have. Here, sit behind the wheel in the real leather seats. Have you ever seen a better dash? Looks like the car was made for you," he responds.

"It's comfortable, all right. I'll bet it costs a fortune. How much is it?" you query again.

For the next few minutes the salesperson continues to sidestep your inquiries about price. Instead, he maneuvers you around the car, getting you to look here, feel there. His conclusion of each exchange with a question such as, "Feels great, doesn't it?" or "How does that compare to any other car you've seen?" eludes you. Next, there's a transition in his comments. He now tries to get you to say in a different way how much you want the car. "Picture yourself pulling into the parking lot at work. Everyone's looking at you. Feels good, doesn't it?"

"Sure does," you reply. "There's no doubt I'd love to have the car. I just can't afford it."

"Hey, wait a sec'. We've just announced a new, low, 9-percent interest rate, and this car is on special this month, as well. Payments can be made over 60 months, so that they're so small you barely notice them. What? You have a car you could trade in? So much the better. Let's go back to my office and run some scenarios on my calculator."

Your head is spinning, but you know you're under no obligation yet. This is exciting.

Concurrently, the salesperson is planning his strategy; he's moving in for the kill. He punches the calculator for a while, looks at some tables, hits the calculator some more, smiles, and says, "We can put you in that new BMW today so you can drive back to work in it today for under $400 a month. Of course that includes full warranty and service for 50,000 miles, and we'll take your old car off your hands. Let's go ahead and sign the contract; what do you say?"

Whether you sign the contract now, wait weeks or even years to buy a similar car, or never buy the BMW, you still have been through a common behavior process. Something caught your attention—in this case the bright color of the car shining in the showroom's spotlights. In other cases, advertisements or jingles might be the attention-getter.

Next, and quickly, your interest was piqued. In the vignette, the salesperson spoke of general and major attributes he felt sure you would acknowledge affirmatively.

Third, the salesperson created in you a desire for the car. He listened to your needs and filled them with his product. You started to feel you needed the car. At the same time, hesitations emerged in your mind—cost, payments, trade-in, and so on. Even before these thoughts were verbalized, he struck them down with counter-arguments and opposing logic. Having convinced you not only that you needed the car, but also that you were willing to make certain trade-offs to get it, he moved to the final step: action. The concluding step reiterated some strengths, made it easy to say yes to the request, and contained the big question: Would you sign the contract?

As an advanced business communicator, your application of persuasion will have little to do with buying or selling cars. Nevertheless, as you will see, the steps are important to writing effective persuasive messages in other aspects of business. The vignette exaggerates the five steps we go through with each major action we take: attention, interest, desire, conviction, and action. Just as these are the steps we follow to action, they, too, are the steps of a persuasive message.

As we examine the writing steps in a persuasive message, be aware that there are other elements in the persuasive encounter that need consideration, such as perception of the sender, hierarchical differences, the context, nonverbal factors, degree of rapport, and others.

Attention Step

The less disposed your reader is to respond favorably to your request, the stronger and more highly defined should be the attention step. Conversely, the more likely your reader is to act as desired, the less you need an attention-getting opening.

When writing strong attention-getters, you may apply several techniques. Questions are good openers because they involve the reader. Few of us can resist answering even the silliest rhetorical question. Perhaps because of the effectiveness of the question as an attention-getter, questions are prevalent.

Attention-getting devices include making a startling statement, using mechanical or printed grabbers, focusing on a single word, giving something away, stressing low cost, describing some enticing mood or situation, or personalizing with the reader's name or address. Often, even the envelope is personalized in such a way as to encourage the recipient to read the information inside.

No rule exists about how closely related to the ultimate action the opener should be. Many magazine subscription mailings, for example, open with contests and giveaways even though these devices have no apparent connection to the action they want you to take. Compare these three openings by how they relate to the action step:

Unrelated to action. "Would you pick the $800,000 house or the year-long vacation around the world if you won this contest?" Action: subscribe to magazines.

Semirelated to action. "For only one penny you can have any 12 CDs or tapes from the hundreds listed." Action: join a CD/tape club.

Related to action. "Just as the bright, shiny penny that is glued to this letter says, 'In God We Trust,' we trust you to support our Children's Hospital." Action: financially support a children's hospital.

The goals of an attention step are (1) to get the reader's attention and (2) to develop enough attention to carry the reader into the next step. Those attention-getters that do not accomplish both objectives are in a message that will probably not result in success.

Interest Step

The interest step is one of transition; it carries the reader from the attention-getting opening to the desire step. The interest step also starts to give some direction to the message (if the opening did not do so). The step takes the undirected momentum of the attention-getter and points toward the ultimate action. The step also encourages some involvement by the reader. Interest develops through blending the strengths of the opening and the enticements of the upcoming desire step. The interest step often is relatively short.

Avoid just telling the reader to become interested; give information that creates interest. Replace "You'll be interested to know that . . ." with "Five of seven people in your job classification are desperately untrained in using a computer spreadsheet."

Desire Step

The third step develops desire in the reader for the ultimate good, service, or action. The desire grows solely from positive attributes. The goal is for the reader to feel that he or she would like the service or product. The attributes of the service or product will determine how much information to include in this step. At this step, there is no concern with the counterarguments or hesitancies against what will be proposed. These are handled in the next step.

Here is an example of a desire step that pushes the positive attributes without yet talking about their cost: "Successful businesspeople at the beginning of the twenty-first century—those making the big salaries and having job security—will have technological competence, entrepreneurial skills, and international business expertise."

Conviction Step

Before the reader has a chance to organize arguments against the upcoming action, the conviction step lays out the counterarguments. While these may sound like positive attributes, similar to those in the desire step, they actually are positive ways of looking at the action's weaknesses. For example, saying that time payments are available may disguise an unusually high price, or that the position holds great opportunities and a promising future offsets its long hours and low starting salary.

The desire and conviction steps are closely related and should flow together. Both will sound positive, but desire is inherently positive information while conviction may be seen as displacing negative information and using positive tone.

Central to all persuasion is the concept of need. A reader must feel the need to take the suggested action to satisfy some personal motivation. Without the feeling of need, the persuasion is likely to be hollow and short lived. Need is developed across several of the steps of the persuasive message but is primarily in the desire and conviction steps. The wording of the presentation of the attributes creates the feeling of need. Sometimes effective need development is as simple as employing empathy and using you words and the *you* attitude. For example, look at these statements:

Positive but impersonal and ineffective. "Underwriting this venture will be financially rewarding."

Positive, personal, and need-developing. "Enhance your image as a venture capitalist by taking advantage of this opportunity."

While the use of the you attitude is desirable in most forms of communication, including written and spoken, you will find its use especially fruitful in developing the need in the desire and conviction steps.

Action Step

Only after you are sure that the reader is convinced of the need to take the action that you plan to propose should you propose it. An action statement that occurs too early will meet defeat. Each of the first four steps sets up the next one; if any one is ineffective, the reader will not be carried to the culmination of the message. The reader may stop somewhere in the sequence or read the balance of the message but decide not to accept the proposed action.

Not only does the action step build on earlier steps, it also uses selected information from them. This last step reemphasizes the reader's benefit from taking the proposed action, makes it easy for the reader to do as suggested, and asks for the action. These three parts may be in any order within the action step.

Here is an example of an action step that incorporates the three parts:

So, start your membership in the City Club, where the Dallas business and financial world conducts the real transactions. To qualify for the special rate, just complete the brief application form and mail it in. Your membership starts once we receive your form.

The benefits are (1) to have access to critical events; (2) to pay a special rate; and (3) to begin membership soon. Ease of response is shown by the short form that is mailed back. The action request is simple: "complete the form . . . and mail it in."

Ways to Stimulate Action

Two main categories of techniques to stimulate action are (1) punishment and reward and (2) emotional and rational appeals. Both are used in business.

You can change behavior by threatening punishment: "If you don't pay the balance due by March 1, we'll contact our lawyers." Or you can change behavior by offering a reward: "If you pay your balance by March 1, your credit rating will remain unblemished." While these approaches may both be successful, the positive tone of the reward approach is preferable in business settings. Long-term business relationships especially benefit from the reward approach.

In developing persuasive messages, you may also pick from emotional and rational appeals. Emotional appeals seek a quick action based on limited thought and perhaps incomplete logic. See how this example works on our emotions:

Select us as your management consultants. We've had a long-term relationship with your firm that dates to its founding by your father, the insightful Mr. John Jones.

Rational appeals, on the other hand, seek a stronger commitment and one the reader is likely to feel comfortable with for a longer time. Rational appeals are based on logic. Here is the example above, rewritten with a rational appeal:

The proposal to serve as your management consultant satisfies the three needs you have identified: sharing of intensive experience on a temporary basis, acting as a catalyst to complete the Smith project on schedule, and providing impartial advice.

Some topics, such as children or animals, are rich with potential emotional content. Other topics, including many in business, rely more on logic. Be aware of your message's strengths and weaknesses and of your goals as you select between rational and emotional appeals. Either can be effective depending on the content. Of course, a single persuasive message can hold punishment, reward, logic, and emotion. Take care, however, not to clutter the message with divergent thoughts.

Hard Sell Versus Soft Sell

Not all persuasive messages can be characterized as the hard-sell type that push magazine or record-club subscriptions. When you describe a promising new product to a regular customer, your job is easier than if the reader is unfamiliar with you. Writing a reminder to place a periodic order would be even easier. Some persuasive messages are soft sell. In preparing soft-sell messages, you must make judgments about whether the goals of the early steps can be assumed. If, for example, you think you already have the reader's attention, you will check off this step and move on to the next one. If you have the reader's interest, you will go to the desire step. When you check off the first two steps, you start your letter with the desire step and then complete the message with the rest of the steps, in their correct order. As a manager, you are more likely to write these more subtle, softer persuasive messages.

Figure 6.2 illustrates the relationship among the five persuasive steps and hard- and soft-sell messages. The hard-sell message, such as a magazine subscription letter, will have all five steps. An extremely soft-sell letter might have only the action step: "You're invited to the office holiday party next Tuesday at 3 P.M. Hope you can be there." Other persuasive messages fall between these two extremes.

Although the illustration represents the five steps as being of equal size, that is seldom the case. The characteristics of the reader and of the proposed action will dictate the extent to which each step is developed. In one letter, there may be a brief paragraph that combines the attention and interest steps followed by well-developed desire and conviction steps. Another letter might reverse the emphasis. There is no rule regarding length of the steps.

The harder the hard-sell message, the more emphasis (and probably the more space) is needed for attention. In other words, as you move in Figure 6.2 to the left, you increase the attention step and then write the remaining steps.

Figure 6.2   **Steps in Developing Hard- and Soft-Sell Indirect Messages**

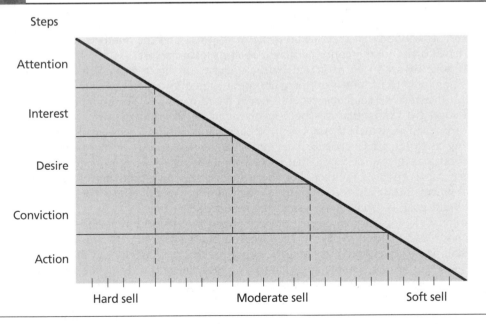

One of the major problems in writing an indirect persuasive message is deciding where on the spectrum between hard and soft sell your reader and the message fall. If in doubt, it is better to include an earlier step rather than assume that it has already been met. Further, reiteration usually does not hurt persuasion other than by lengthening the message.

Hints for Writing Persuasive Messages

Other hints may ease the task of writing persuasive messages or make the message more effective.

1. Although the steps dictate the order of information, you still need to organize your thoughts. Be careful not to let your steps overlap too much. Each step has its own goal and content. To intermix the content dilutes the impact.

2. Seek a blending from one step to the next. While each step has its own content, use transitions from step to step. Doing so will unify the entire message.

3. Consider writing your action step first. Preparing this punch line may guide the development of the earlier steps.

4. Finally, in general, try not to let your desired action leak out until the action step. In the vignette about buying a car, the salesperson avoided answering questions about cost until closing the deal. Had he told you the BMW cost $73,000 at the beginning, or even in the middle, of the conversation, he might have lost the sale. The price was so close to the desired action that the salesperson sought to hold it until the end.

When we read typical mass mailings, many of us speed through or omit passages and search at the end for what it will cost. This cost usually appears graphically with a dollar sign and some numbers. This characteristic behavior has not gone unnoticed by mass-mailing experts. They counter by hiding the dollar amount. Often you will find that they spell out the word dollar and the numbers so that we will have to endure the entire persuasive spiel to learn its cost.

Although we may be frustrated by the quantity of direct mail we receive that does not apply to us, much of it is quite sophisticated in design and employs techniques that may be adaptable to even our soft-sell messages. For example, direct-mail advertisers know that the more involvement on the reader's part, the greater the likelihood that their message will be successful. How do they involve us? By getting us to put paper coins or keys into slots, to paste music or magazine selections on a card, to pick a potential prize from a list, or to scratch off gray ink to disclose a sweepstakes number. For the manager, this may translate into seeking involvement through appreciation for a job well done, mentioning a common and important goal, or occasionally using the person's first name.

Second, these experts at persuasion recognize that the more time and effort we expend, the more likely we are to keep working our way through the message. For example, how often would we admit to ourselves that we have wasted 30 minutes placing keys, pasting stamps, or picking prizes and then not mail in the gift entry form—the form that can also be used to order a magazine subscription?

Third, these advertisers know that usually they have but one moment of your time to persuade you. If you stop to answer the phone, put the information away until later, have to search for your credit card number or checkbook, or have to look for a stamp for the envelope, you will probably not return to complete the action. Therefore, these advertisers employ techniques to encourage immediate action. For instance, they include a small pencil in the packet, supply the postage, or offer to bill later. They also know an interesting thing about human behavior: Once the return information is completed and sealed in the envelope, few people have second thoughts and decide not to mail the envelope.

In addition to Figure 6.1, which relates to negative messages, see Figure 6.3 for an example of an effective, moderate-sell, persuasive message. Figure 6.4 shows a well-written soft-sell message.

Figure 6.3   **Example of a Moderate-Sell, Persuasive Message**

YOUNG EXECUTIVE MAGAZINE

Editorial Offices:
680 Northland Blvd. / Suite 107
Cincinnati, OH 45240-3137
(513) 825-0309   Fax: (513) 825-0220
e-mail: yexec@young.com
http://www.yexec.com

Dear *Young Executive* Reader:

As a subscriber to *Young Executive* you are aware of the magazine's uniqueness. Only *YE* meets the interests and needs of America's aggressive, educated, fast-track young executives. You've seen such articles as "Investing in Condos," "Using Nonverbal Communication to Exert Your Power," and "Mexico's Best Executive Vacation Spots." You're familiar with our popular columns: CEO Gossip, Power to the Women, and Dressing the Part.

Your subscription ends in six weeks. You can continue to receive *YE* for another year with no break in your subscription, and at a $3 savings, by returning the enclosed card right away. Just check the number of years by which you wish to extend your subscription and mail the card. More great *YEs* will be on the way.

Executively,

Harrison Christopher

Harrison Christopher
Subscription Manager

Enc.

Figure 6.4 | **Example of a Soft-Sell, Persuasive Message**

Dear Customer,

Typically, our policy is to keep all boats until we have received payment for the work done on them. Since we have extended the courtesy of delivering your boat and then mailing your bill, please help us keep our costs down by mailing the payment today. Perhaps you selected Bitsy Boats to detail your boat because, as a small firm, we focus on a select clientele. As a small business, we will notice and appreciate your help.

Thank you.

Finally, personalization of form letters can enhance positive responses. As a reader, you like to see your name and comments about yourself. Computers that merge lists of names with form letters, inserting personal references from the database, make personalization easy. Letters appear individually typed with such techniques as the inclusion of phrases using the recipient's name or address. The efforts are especially likely to appear at places where the reader may lose interest: the very beginning, at the bottom of pages, and at the request for action. While the techniques may differ, knowledge of such elements of human behavior and persuasion as these can assist you in your persuasive writing.

Summary

Many messages are those that receivers do not want to see. Most negative and persuasive messages typify such messages. For the negative message, because the goals of the sender (to maintain goodwill as well as to transmit the negative news) differ from the desire of the receiver (to hear good news), use an indirect approach. For the persuasive message, when you expect to encounter resistance, use the indirect approach.

The indirect approach to a negative message has four steps: (1) an opening that delays discussion of the bad news; (2) a presentation of the reasons for the upcoming bad news; (3) the bad news; and (4) a positive ending. The first step is difficult to write because often it comes across as a delaying tactic and thus reduces its value. Instead, it should prepare the reader for a discussion of the topic and the reasons behind the decision.

Often the second step is the most important of the four. If you do not have good reasons for the bad news or if you do not present those reasons well, the reader is unlikely to accept the news or the logic of it. However, well-developed reasons will encourage acceptance of the news without hostility. Readers may not like the decision, but at least they will understand your reasoning. Further, well-planned and well-explained reasons, written with the reader's viewpoint in mind, make the delivery of the bad news much easier. After relating the bad news, change the subject to a more positive one. Do not go back to the bad news. Close on a pleasant note.

Persuasive messages follow the steps of overt behavior: attention, interest, desire, conviction, and action. Some persuasive messages are hard sell and therefore require development of each of the five steps. Soft-sell messages may assume attention and interest on the reader's part and can start with desire. Authors of persuasive messages need to calculate carefully where on the spectrum between hard and soft sell their messages fit.

Indirect message organization delays the main message component—the bad news or the request for action—because resistance is anticipated by the sender. Other message organizations that do not fit the criteria for either direct or indirect organization appear in Chapter 7.

Discussion Questions

1. Think about the spectrum of persuasive messages from soft sell to hard sell. Where on the spectrum are the most difficult-to-write messages? Which are most likely to elicit the desired response?

2. What is the intent of the delaying opening? Does it ever frustrate or anger a reader? What would it take to prepare a delaying message that would not be offensive?

3. What are the main ways of attracting a reader's attention? Which are more effective than others? Why?

4. Think about a time when you were searching for a job. How would you feel had you received a direct negative message? Why is the job-getting process so ego-involving, and why are feelings so easily hurt? Is this why almost all job rejection letters are written indirectly?

Communication in Action

1. Critique some of the hard-sell direct mail that you have received. Does each piece follow the five steps presented in the text? Do different products and services require different treatments of any steps? Where does each piece fall on the soft-to-hard-sell spectrum?

2. As an extension of Discussion Question 2 above, survey some colleagues or classmates on this thought: "How often do you prefer to receive a negative message in a direct organization?" How many said "often"? Do you believe them? How much chance is there that they think they prefer the direct organization until the message is really negative to them?

@ Internet

3. As an employee of a public relations firm, you have been given the task of preparing a fundraising appeal for money from alumni of a local university, which is a client. You have selected the concept of "the importance of one" as the thrust of your appeal. You plan to prepare a hard-copy flyer to alumni that spells out how one person has made a difference, such as one vote that took us to war, passed some major legislation, or changed history; or how one person solved a crucial puzzle or made a medical discovery. You'll list these outcomes and then persuade the reader that he or she is important, too, and should contribute to the fund. Research the "importance of one" and locate examples that you could use in the flyer. Then, write the text for the flyer.

4. As a member of the marketing department, you have been asked to locate some Web sites that excel in marketing for their companies. Locate some sites that are especially well designed for (1) ease of access to the Web site; (2) friendliness of appearance and use; (3) strong sales message; and (4) customer service.

5. You have noticed that many of your subordinates don't follow the principles of writing indirect messages, but you don't feel well-enough prepared to teach a refresher course on the topic. Also, an outside consultant may bring more authority to the situation. Use the Internet to locate some writing consultants who could help you.

6. Use the Internet to view some home pages of companies that sell either products or services. Compare the sales pitches in terms of directness versus indirectness.

InfoTrac

7. What can you find in the published literature of the last three years that connects e-mail use to the delivery of negative messages? Locate at least two full-page articles and then summarize them in an outline format. As starter topics, examine the legal and ethical issues of messages sent within Enron and Andersen Consulting in 2002.

8. Refer to Discussion Question 2 above. Use InfoTrac to see if there is literature regarding the use of the delaying (or buffer) opening. Be sure to check the business communication journals.

9. After the September 11, 2001, terrorist attacks, huge amounts of money were raised for victims and families of the event. Much of the money was sent to the Red Cross, which was then challenged over not dispersing enough money quickly enough. How might the Red Cross have written a letter to potential donors seeking contributions to the disaster fund that would have misled them? Use InfoTrac to see what articles emerged that discuss the topic.

10. Some of the classic literature from social psychology reviews types of people who are most easily persuaded, such as those with low self-esteem. Use InfoTrac to locate literature that deals with groups easily persuaded.

CHAPTER - 7

Writing Situational Messages

Many written messages can be classified as positive, neutral, negative, or persuasive and can follow the direct or indirect organizations described in Chapters 5 and 6. Others, however, cannot be classified so easily; they combine two or more of the four formulas or fall outside the formulas altogether. They are called situational messages. Although situational messages may account for only a small percentage of all messages, they deserve careful attention from the advanced business communicator because they are difficult to prepare.

Many executives forget that a well-written situational message can distinguish its author and its company from competitors. Situational messages often require deeper understanding of the business organization and of the environment than do other messages. Important concerns such as tone and audience analysis play an even more crucial role in situational messages, where achieving a goal is particularly difficult. Standard instruction in business writing usually stops with the four basic categories of messages. This chapter will help you develop a more sophisticated approach, one more suitable for advanced managerial communication.

This chapter divides the discussion of situational messages into two parts: those messages that are a combination of formulas and those that fall outside the formulas. The chapter also examines selected memoranda as unique applications of situational writing.

Situational Writing That Combines Formulas

As we discussed in Chapters 5 and 6, a direct organization is usually applied to positive and neutral messages, but either a direct or an indirect organization may be applied to negative and persuasive messages, depending on many variables. The steps in writing these messages create formulas for their construction; a formula-based situational message rearranges the steps and principles of the individual formulas in a manner appropriate for an individual, specific situation.

Because of the great similarity between the positive and neutral formulas, for instance, it is quite easy to prepare a message that contains both positive and neutral information. Indeed, the positive formula, which prioritizes information starting with most positive, would place neutral information immediately after the last bit of positive information. To show you techniques for writing effective situational messages, this chapter focuses on the more difficult-to-write combinations of direct positive and indirect negative and persuasive messages. While other combinations exist, your understanding of these combinations will prepare you for writing the others.

The four combinations that we will discuss are (1) positive/negative, (2) positive/persuasive, (3) persuasive/negative, and (4) positive/persuasive/negative. These four represent most of the situational messages you will write and capture the technique of generating a plan for how to organize these messages.

In reading this discussion, refer to the summary in Table 7.1, which presents the organization of the five main message types we have already examined. Additionally, whenever you write situational messages using a combination of formulas, keep these principles in mind:

- Identify your goals and prioritize them.
- Empathize with your reader. What reaction will be likely? As with other messages, carefully analyze your audience.

Table 7.1   **Formula Message Steps**

	Positive Message	Neutral Message	Negative Message	Negative Message	Persuasive Message
Organization	Direct	Direct	Direct	Indirect	Indirect
Principles	Positive impact is additive; most benefit occurs when starting with most-positive information	Send important information first (unless negative); seek clarity and write to avoid follow-ups	Readers prefer the direct explanation of the bad news, or occasion calls for direct organization	De-emphasize the negative by placing it in middle of message; maintain goodwill; precede negative with explanation	Persuasion to action requires movement through all steps; softer-sell messages can assume early steps; action must come last
Steps	Most-positive information	Most-important information	Negative, presented gently	Delaying opening	Attention
	Next-most-positive information	Next-most-important information	Details	Explanation	Interest
	Next-most-positive information	Next-most-important information	Positive closing	Negative message	Desire
	Next-most-positive information	Next-most-important information		Positive closing	Conviction
					Action (request, easy to do, reader benefit)

- Try to maintain the integrity of the formulas; there are reasons for the order of the steps in each formula.
- Employ effective writing rules and techniques, as with any other written message, by making it readable, using the *you* tone, and including smooth transitions.

The Positive/Negative Combination

A message containing both positive and negative information is difficult to prepare because of the opposite approaches for negative and positive messages. Poorly prepared good-news/bad-news messages receive regular attention from many comedians with their line, "I have some good news and some bad news." To be effective, this combination needs to apply principles from the respective formulas.

In deciding how to mesh the two formulas, it may be helpful to place them side by side, as in Table 7.2. Positive information appears in two places in the negative-message formula—at the beginning and at the end. They are the two most likely places to report your good news. In deciding where to place the positive information, consider the following:

- Is the information so positive that if placed first, it will make the transition to the negative information extremely awkward? If so, move the positive information to the end.
- Is the positive information only moderately positive? If so, start your message with it.
- If you do not place the positive information first, will the receiver read the message? If not, present the positive information first. (This might occur when you are responding to a direct request from the reader.)
- Is the negative information only slightly negative? If so, it is easier to start with the positive and make a smooth transition to the negative. If the negative message is very strong, then start with a delaying opening and move to the explanation and the bad news before presenting the positive information.

In Chapter 6, the discussion of the indirect organization negative formula includes two important principles: bury the negative information in the middle of the letter, and always precede the negative information with an explanation. Adhere to these rules in your positive/negative combination message.

Table 7.2	The Mixed Direct Positive/Indirect Negative Message	
Positive Message Steps	**Negative Message Steps**	**Positive/Negative Mix Formulas**
Most-positive information	Delaying opening information	Positive opening
Next-most-positive information	Explanation	Explanation
Next-most-positive information	Negative message	Negative message
Next-most-positive information	Positive closing	Positive closing

Table 7.3 highlights the four steps in a positive/negative message through an example that indicates the person may receive venture capital but not at the amount requested. The two formulas retain their identity while accomplishing their goals.

The Positive/Persuasive Combination

While the direct organization of the positive message and the indirect organization of the persuasive message conflict, the clash can be resolved by using the positive information as an attention-getting opening. Even in soft-sell persuasive messages, little harm is done by starting with positive information and then turning to interest, desire, or even conviction. Table 7.4 compares the two formulas and shows a resulting situational formula. Table 7.5 illustrates how the steps of the two formulas can be combined effectively.

The Persuasive/Negative Combination

Persuasive and negative messages share the indirect approach but follow different formulas. Table 7.6 compares the steps of these two formulas. In developing the situational message, retain the principles of both formulas: place the negative in the

Table 7.3 **A Sample Positive/Negative Message**

Positive/Negative Mix Formula	Example Thoughts from Steps
Positive opening	You are being considered for $200,000 in venture capital.
Explanation	XYZ Co. has limited assets available now; the economy is tight; others are also seeking our support.
Negative message	You are not receiving the full $250,000 you requested.
Positive closing	Entering into this venture will be to our mutual benefit; the project is promising.

Table 7.4 **The Mixed Direct Positive/Indirect Persuasive Message**

Positive Message Steps	Persuasive Message Steps	Positive/Persuasive Mix Formula
Most-positive information	Attention	Positive attention-getter
	Interest	
Next-most-positive information	Desire	Desire
Next-most-positive information	Conviction	Conviction
Next-most-positive information	Action (request, easy to do, reader benefit)	Action with emphasis on reader benefit

Table 7.5   **A Sample Positive/Persuasive Message**

Positive/Persuasive Mix Formula	Example Thoughts from Steps
Positive attention-getter with interest	Congratulations on being nominated for this year's Grant Wolford Young Manager Award.
Desire	Each year the Little Rock Jaycees select one of their members for this award; you are one of five nominees; the winner of this prestigious award receives $500.
Conviction	Each nominee must complete a seven-page questionnaire and take part in a 30-minute interview with the selection committee.
Action with emphasis on reader benefit	Complete the enclosed questionnaire and call us to schedule your interview. This is an impressive award.

Table 7.6   **The Mixed Indirect Persuasive/Indirect Negative Message**

Persuasive Message Steps	Negative Message Steps	Persuasive/Negative Mix Formula
Attention	Delaying opening	Attention/interest opening serves as delaying opening
Interest Desire	Explanation	Explanation
Conviction	Negative	Negative message
Action (request, easy to do, reader benefit)	Positive closing	Desire, conviction, and action steps, with stress on reader benefits, form positive closing

middle of the message after its explanation and end with a request for action after preparing the reader for that request.

The attention and interest steps of the hard-sell persuasive message can serve as the delaying opening of the negative message. The same is true if the persuasive message is softer in nature; still, use the desire or even conviction steps to delay the bad news. Follow with an explanation and the negative information. Once you present the negative information, leave it. Switch tone to the conviction or action step. Place special emphasis on the portion of the action step that reiterates the reader benefits. These benefits then serve as your positive closing. Table 7.7 shows one scheme for combining the steps of these two formulas.

| Table 7.7 | A Sample Persuasive/Negative Message |

Persuasive/Negative Mix Formula	Example Thoughts from Steps
Attention/interest opening serves as delaying opening	You've worked for us before and have submitted bids for contracts to us.
Explanation	Oil prices are down; prospects for prices increasing are poor for the immediate future; as oil speculators, we are being hurt by the economy, too.
Negative message	We need to pay less than usual for oil-well drilling.
Desire, conviction, and action steps, with stress on reader benefits, form positive closing	There's still money to be made in oil; it's important to keep people on the payroll, to keep the equipment active, and to maintain a cash flow.
	Please submit a bid for drilling the nine shallow wells described in the attached specifications sheet; we both can benefit from you giving a low bid.

The Positive/Persuasive/Negative Combination

When you combine three of the formulas, it becomes more difficult to incorporate individual steps and principles. Table 7.8 shows positive, persuasive, and negative formulas and illustrates one situational approach that might grow from a need to combine them.

As with earlier combinations, positive information appears in the positions of primacy or recency, negative information follows the explanation, and the required persuasive steps are woven into the message prior to the action step. Depending on the relative strengths of the positive and negative information and the degree of persuasion required, you can design various situational formulas. Table 7.9 uses the situational formula from Table 7.8 and illustrates its steps with sample phrases.

If these various formulas and mixes seem confusing, there is a general technique you may use to generate your own situational formula. This technique has four steps:

1. Is the occasion indeed one that can be answered with a basic formula, or is a situational message necessary? If a simple formula can be used, apply it. Otherwise, go to step two.

2. If a situational message is required, which of the types of formulas are present?

3. Of the various types of formulas present, which one is the primary thrust of the message?

4. Using the primary message formula as a skeleton, apply the elements of the remaining message formulas to it. These elements may be inserted between steps of the primary formula or appended to the end, depending upon the situation.

Table 7.8   **The Mixed Direct Positive/Indirect Persuasive/Indirect Negative Message**

Positive Message	Persuasive Message	Negative Message	Positive/Persuasive/Negative Mix Formula
Most-positive information	Attention	Delaying opening	Positive attention-getter with interest, delays negative message
Next-most-positive information	Interest Desire	Explanation	Desire and explanation serve as second-most-positive information
Next-most-positive information	Conviction	Negative message	Mention negative and weave in counterarguments for upcoming action
Next-most-positive information	Action (request, easy to do, reader benefit)	Positive closing	Request action with emphasis on positive aspects

Table 7.9   **A Sample Positive/Persuasive/Negative Message**

Positive/Persuasive/Negative Mix Formula	Example Thoughts from Steps
Positive attention-getter delays negative message	About a century ago, Butch Cassidy was offered amnesty; recently illegal aliens were also offered amnesty.
Desire and explanation serve as second-most-positive information	Amnesty can take on various forms; we need customers and payment for goods delivered; we dealt with you in good faith; you need our goods and a good credit rating.
Mention negative and weave in counterarguments for upcoming action	Pay us what you owe us; your credit rating is in jeopardy; we may need to contact credit services.
Request action with emphasis on positive aspects	We'll grant you amnesty on the penalty portion of your bill if you'll pay by Nov. 1; no questions will be asked, and you'll keep your credit card; mail your remittance today.

Nonformula Situational Writing

Not all situational messages are combinations of formulas—some reside outside the sphere of the formulas. As an advanced business communicator, you will need to follow formulas and write nonformula messages. Over time, your instincts will develop; you will gain experience and acquire knowledge from reading well-written nonformula situational letters written by others. Examples of nonformula situational messages are those that transmit goodwill, serve as a reference, encompass the collection-letter series, present negative-only content, serve as complaint letters and responses to complaints, deliver disciplinary reprimands, and are overt requests for action.

Goodwill Messages

Goodwill messages are a unique category of positive message. Like other positive messages, goodwill messages carry information likely to elicit positive responses from their readers; but with goodwill messages, the author makes an extra effort to garner an affirmative reaction from the reader that will benefit the author. This ulterior motive usually takes advantage of some pleasant event; letters or cards are sent to clients, customers, or employees for birthdays, promotions, reasons for congratulations, thank-you's, appreciations, anniversaries, special programs or sales, and holidays. These messages may benefit the author through increased business or strengthened loyalty. For similar reasons, it can be good business to send messages to new residents, new customers, regular customers, or prompt payers. As a manager, you are more likely to direct others to write goodwill messages than to prepare them yourself.

The goodwill message follows the same direct organization as other positive information messages by presenting the most positive information first. Figure 7.1 presents the body of a goodwill message.

A special case of the goodwill message is the extension of sympathy as a matter of course to a regular customer or employee on the occasion of a family member's illness or death. Clearly the topic is unpleasant. What sets this direct message apart is the potential for indirect reward, perhaps in the form of appreciation, on the part of the sender. As with other direct messages, start with your main thought.

The Recommendation and Reference Letters

In applying for jobs, usually you are asked to supply a list of references, as well as names of past and present supervisors or employers. If people on your list of references are contacted, assuming you sought their permission to supply their names, they most likely will deliver positive comments written in a letter of recommendation. Supervisors and employers, on the other hand, write letters of reference. Letters of reference often are unbiased and may be directed To Whom It May Concern. These two message types are often confused.

As a supervisor, you may receive requests for letters of reference after having allowed your name to be supplied by former or current employees who are applying for jobs or school. Your loyalty to former and current employees is likely to travel the grapevine; you will want to save copies of these letters. After having written a few letters of reference, you may find yourself following a certain pattern, in which case you may wish to develop a letter outline template that can be used for other employees. These outlines can be filled in with individualized information for each employee. Each letter—including those that follow your own form—should be individually typed and personalized to the applicant. See Figure 7.2 for an example of a letter of reference.

Figure 7.1 **Example of an Effective Goodwill Message**

Gardner, Givens
Certified Public Accountant
P.O. Box 1423
La Jolla CA 98192

November 23, 200X

Professor Adrian McGuffey
San Diego State University
San Diego CA 92183

Dear Professor McGuffey:

This is just a quick note to thank you for inviting Gardner, Givens into your classroom. We very much enjoyed describing our perceptions of the importance of communication to the accounting profession. The feedback received on this end from the students has been quite positive. We hope you, too, feel the time invested was worthwhile. I welcome any comments you wish to share about the speaker or presentation.

Gardner, Givens looks forward to participating in your classroom activities again. Such discussions afford us an excellent exposure to your high-caliber students.

For your leisure reading, I've enclosed our hot-off-the-press brochure describing the accounting services we provide.

Cordially,

Gerald Givens

Gerald Givens

GG: cs
Enclosure

When you write a letter of reference, you should (1) directly state the purpose of the letter; (2) explain the conditions and time frame of the acquaintanceship; (3) describe the applicant's attributes that would be of both general and specific value to the position; and (4) end with a willingness to expand on comments or answer questions.

Adams Advertising
Baton Rouge LA 52063

May 7, 200X

Scott Burkette
Accounting Supervisor
3-A Advertising
845 Lost Creek Road, Eleventh Floor
Dallas TX 75213

Dear Mr. Burkette:

Thank you for the pleasant opportunity to recommend to you Mr. Bill Andersohn for your position of Account Executive. Not only is he one of our top Assistant Account Executives, he is also an especially mature, personable, and insightful individual. It is only because our comparable positions are and will continue to be filled for some time that we are not promoting him.

Two years ago Mr. Andersohn joined us as an intern; six months later I enthusiastically recruited him to assist me with consumer research. In evaluating consumers by a variety of characteristics, he showed an understanding of advertising and marketing and exhibited particular skill in working with sales and persuasive materials. These latter skills also have served him well in his pursuit of becoming an Account Executive.

He is a self-starter and a person who predictably meets deadlines. I often notice his impressive creativity—a characteristic he has applied in the design of some brochures.

I most sincerely believe that you would benefit from the abilities Mr. Andersohn has to offer. I enthusiastically recommend him.

Sincerely,

Jackson Adams

Jackson Adams
President

You help an applicant the most by giving relevant examples of his or her skills (the third step above). Rather than say, "She's a good manager," for example, say:

She has demonstrated a superior ability to work with peers. Her colleagues cite her understanding of human nature, ability to direct subordinates, and achievement of high productivity. They say she is a team player.

Further, a comparison of the applicant to others can be beneficial. Generally, the more relevant information you write about the applicant, the more favorable the reaction. Readers know these letters take time, and they view your efforts accordingly. Conversely, a few checkmarks on a form and no responses to open-ended questions, such as "What makes you think this applicant might have a future with us?" do little to help the applicant. In some letters of reference, of course, you will find it necessary to be less than positive about the applicant. Not all the employees—current and past—under your supervision deserve glowing recommendations. You do little to enhance the image of your organization to another firm by exaggerating positive attributes of an ineffective or fired employee. Your message, therefore, is likely to carry less enthusiasm and fewer examples of positive behavior.

The question of ethical messages, in light of today's frequent unethical behavior by some in business, places renewed importance on saying what is accurate and can be defended.

Collection Letters

The collection letter is another message type that can benefit from an understanding of situational writing. As a manager, you may direct the writing of collection letters. Collection letters do not fit the recommended indirect approach to negative message writing because they usually consist of not one message but a series of messages, often moving from light in tone in the first message to stern in later messages. Many businesses prepare a series of three, four, or even five messages. Frequently the series starts as a gentle, direct message, progresses to an indirect message, and concludes with a strong direct message. The first message may take the form of a card with a thought such as, "Oops, I forgot to make my payment!" A second message may still be slightly positive and relatively direct, such as the main thought, "It's now been 45 days since your payment was due."

A third letter in a series probably stresses the positive reasons for making the payment, such as maintaining a good relationship, keeping a credit card, or avoiding complications.

In a fourth letter, the tone of the reasons may change to more negative thoughts: avoiding legal issues, returning the goods, and so on. A final letter, no matter how many letters are in the series, will be the most firm. If the company has decided to take the matter to court, this letter will present that decision. On the other hand, if the decision is to give up on the effort, perhaps because the legal case is weak or the amount small, the final letter might be a letter that says, in effect, "Return your credit card, and don't shop here anymore."

Figures 7.3 through 7.7 deliver the bodies of five messages in a collection letter series. Note the progression toward sternness. These letters are adapted from a software package that contains dozens of collection letters and facilitates the merging of mailing lists containing tagged, delinquent addresses with various categories of letters.[1] In addition to many other letters from which to choose, the software includes a spell checker, ample control of the messages, and a wide variety of applications, such as service, professional, product, or trade businesses.

Figure 7.3 **First Notice Letter in a Collection Series**

Dear   :

Everyone forgets once in a while. Or perhaps our bill is buried in a pile of paperwork. However, now that I have brought it to your attention, perhaps you could dig it out right now and take care of it. The total balance due is $ _____ .

As a reminder, our credit terms are net 30 days. Past-due balances are subject to a finance charge of 10 percent per month. I'm sure you'll want to avoid any additional finance charges and get your account back into good standing by taking care of your balance now. I know we would appreciate it, too.

Thank you for your prompt response to this payment request. If you have any questions about your account, please call.

Sincerely,

Source: Adapted from One-Write Plus 8.0 © 2002 by Peachtree Software, Inc.

Figure 7.4 **Second Notice Letter in a Collection Series**

Dear   :

In scanning our accounts, we noticed that yours is still carrying a past-due balance. We had to double-check, because that seems out of character, but there the balance was.

Right now, you owe us $ _____ , including finance charges. You probably realize that past-due balances incur finance charges at a rate of 10 percent a month if they are not paid within _____ days.

Please take just a moment right now to find your checkbook and write us a check. You would be saving additional finance charges and resuming your usual good standing.

Thanks for taking care of this right away. If you have any questions about your account, please give us a call.

Sincerely,

Source: Adapted from One-Write Plus 8.0 © 2002 by Peachtree Software, Inc.

Figure 7.5 **Third Notice Letter in a Collection Series**

Dear   :

Can you help us with something? I've been trying to collect a past-due amount on your account, and up to now I haven't had much luck. Could you look into why the payment is being held up? Our records show you owe us a total of $ _____ .

You are in business, too, so I'm sure you can understand our concern. This matter really needs clearing up and you need to get your account back in order.

We would be happy to answer any questions you have about the charges and will work with you to get your account up to date. We expect either a check or a phone call in the next few days. Thanks.

Sincerely,

Source: Adapted from One-Write Plus 8.0 © 2002 by Peachtree Software, Inc.

Figure 7.6 **Fourth Notice Letter in a Collection Series**

Dear   :

Something must be terribly wrong. Your account is delinquent and has been for several months. We really need your help to get this straightened out.

As things now stand, you owe a total of $ _____ . We have made several efforts to collect, but to date they have all been ignored.

It is very important that you forward your payment immediately, or get in touch with us to tell us when you will be able to pay us. Obviously, if you fail to do so, there are alternative ways of making our point. However, I can't believe that will be necessary.

If you value your good name, personally and professionally, you will make good on this obligation. I'll be expecting your call or your check.

Sincerely,

Source: Adapted from One-Write Plus 8.0 © 2002 by Peachtree Software, Inc.

| Figure 7.7 | **Fifth Notice Letter in a Collection Series** |

Dear   :

Your account is now seriously delinquent. You owe a total past due amount of $_____. We must receive payment in full immediately.

Your negligence in this matter is of great concern to us. You have ignored numerous requests for payment and failed to contact us to explain the circumstances that have held up your payment.

You are legally and morally obligated for this bill. Further delay may force us to take legal action to collect what is owed us. This could prove embarrassing and damage your personal and professional reputation.

Please do not let this problem come to that. Write out the check now, or pick up the phone and call. Do it today. Do it now.

Sincerely,

Source: Adapted from One-Write Plus 8.0 © 2002 by Peachtree Software, Inc.

Negative-Only Messages

Sometimes you will want to disregard the goal of maintaining goodwill evident in the indirect negative formula and assumed in the direct negative formula and focus on the bad news. We've just seen how a collection letter series typically begins positively and progresses to increasingly firm letters. By the time you have mailed three, four, or even five reminder letters, you have probably lost your patience. The payment, and not customer goodwill, is now the most important issue. A negative-only message conveys the extreme urgency and severity of the situation. A negative-only message differs from a direct negative message in its lack of concern for the feelings of the receiver. The body of such a message follows:

Over six months ago you made purchases at our store totaling $795. Because of your disregard for our requests for payment and your lack of explanation, we must turn over your account to a collection agency. While its techniques for obtaining payment often are not as understanding as ours, you have left us no other option. Further, as spelled out in the state's civil code, we have the legal right to require the return of your charge card. We are exercising that right. Return your card in the enclosed envelope by April 9. If you fail to do so the matter will be remanded to the county sheriff's office for action, as prescribed by law.

The reader of this letter will have little doubt that the company is no longer gently seeking payment. The gravity of the situation is conveyed by the negative-only message. Most businesspeople resist writing negative-only messages unless absolutely necessary.

Complaints and Responses to Complaints

Another type of nonformula situational message is the complaint message and its counterpart, the response to the complaint. While, as a businessperson, you are more likely to be writing responses to complaints or directing others to do so, both situations are common in business.

The Complaint Message

Companies today are much more open to customers' inquiries than in past decades. Nevertheless, not all complaints produce satisfactory results. The likelihood of receiving your desired response largely depends on the quality of your complaint message.

Typically you initiate your complaint with the seller of the product or provider of the service. Next you complain to the manufacturer, perhaps several times and to increasingly higher levels of management. Finally, you may seek satisfaction by going to trade associations, national headquarters, consumers' rights organizations, or even to the courts. The complaint message is an important part of this process.

Complaint messages, of course, can be from individual customers or from companies complaining about products or services supplied by other companies. While the content may vary, the principles are the same. Here are some suggestions for a complaint message written by a customer.

Begin your complaint message with details, not angry criticisms. Explain what you purchased in detail—give serial and model numbers. Tell when and where you made the purchase. Be precise. What was the location of the store, and what was the exact date? You may wish to include a salesperson's name, if available. If this message is part of a lengthy complaint process, give the history of your complaint. While you want to be complete and to give important detail, do not overburden the reader with unnecessary information.

Next, explain the problem. What went wrong? What were the conditions at the time? Were you following the manufacturer's instructions? How long after the purchase did this occur?

Third, verify your purchase with copies (not originals) of sales receipts, checks, and guarantees. Check the guarantee to see if there are specific steps or information that you have forgotten, such as handling or postage charges.

Fourth, state specifically what you want. Do you seek reimbursement or replacement? By what date do you want action? Only if you have no other recourse should you threaten legal action.

You may reorganize these steps, depending on the situation, to be even more effective. However, all four thoughts are likely to appear somewhere in your message.

In writing this message, do not be sarcastic, aggressive, or negative. Let the facts present your case. Keep a copy of the message you write as documentation of what you said, to whom, and when.

Picture the complaint message as a mix of the negative and persuasive categories. The information has a negative component, and you are seeking action from the company. The negative information is in the middle of the message, and the action request appears at the end. Beyond this similarity, however, a complaint message does not follow the two formulas. See Figure 7.8 for the U.S. Office of Consumer Affairs's sample complaint letter.

Figure 7.8 **Sample Complaint Letter**

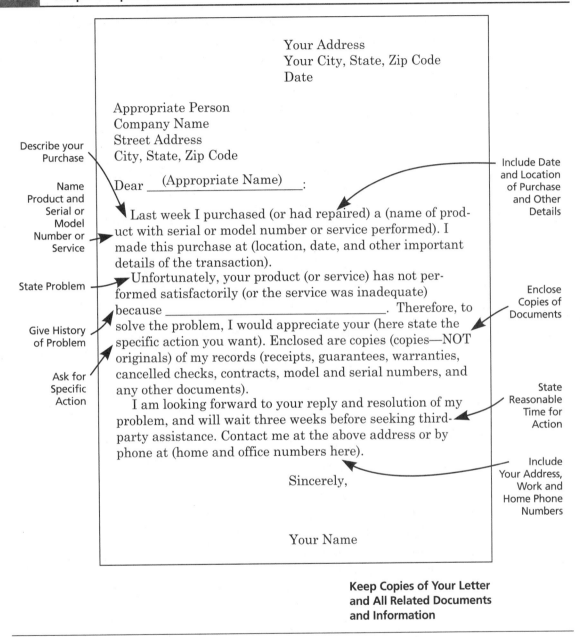

Describe your Purchase

Name Product and Serial or Model Number or Service

State Problem

Give History of Problem

Ask for Specific Action

Include Date and Location of Purchase and Other Details

Enclose Copies of Documents

State Reasonable Time for Action

Include Your Address, Work and Home Phone Numbers

Your Address
Your City, State, Zip Code
Date

Appropriate Person
Company Name
Street Address
City, State, Zip Code

Dear _____(Appropriate Name)_____:

Last week I purchased (or had repaired) a (name of product with serial or model number or service performed). I made this purchase at (location, date, and other important details of the transaction).
Unfortunately, your product (or service) has not performed satisfactorily (or the service was inadequate) because _____. Therefore, to solve the problem, I would appreciate your (here state the specific action you want). Enclosed are copies (copies—NOT originals) of my records (receipts, guarantees, warranties, cancelled checks, contracts, model and serial numbers, and any other documents).
I am looking forward to your reply and resolution of my problem, and will wait three weeks before seeking third-party assistance. Contact me at the above address or by phone at (home and office numbers here).

Sincerely,

Your Name

**Keep Copies of Your Letter
and All Related Documents
and Information**

Source: United States Office of Consumer Affairs, Washington, D.C.

The Response to the Complaint Letter

Responding to a well-written complaint letter—one that has presented evidence in a logical format—can be quite a challenge. In so doing, consider the following:

- Can you do what the writer is requesting? If so, use the positive formula and relate the good news immediately.
- Do you need more information? Use a neutral approach. Be pleasant but do not be too positive; you do not want to get the reader's hopes up and then dash them with your next letter.
- Should you turn down the request? Consider writing a standard negative formula letter.
- Do you have both positive and negative messages to relay? Apply the principles of each as discussed in formula-based situational letters.
- Is this response outside the formula-based situational letter approach? If so, why? Is a nonformula situational letter needed?
- What images are you projecting? You are the company, and the reader's image of the company may well depend on how you write this letter. Avoid hiding behind such weak phrases as company policy. Use solid reasons, such as expired warranties or lack of proof of purchase.
- Is an apology or indication of sympathy appropriate? Although your reasons should generally speak for themselves, there are times when you should express sympathy or state an apology.
- Is the message tailored for the individual, if possible? A form response can be irritating in and of itself.

You may need to respond with a *yes, but* letter that agrees with many of the author's points but disagrees with one or more other crucial points. For example, if you received a complaint letter from a firm that was rejected from the proposal process because their submission missed the deadline, you might agree with their points, stressing the importance of doing the best job possible in writing the proposal, that writing proposals takes time, and that it is a service to hire college students as couriers, even though they sometimes make deliveries at the wrong address. However, you must explain the reason for deadlines and that you always adhere to them, as stated in your Request for Proposals.

Disciplinary Reprimands

Another message type with negative content that you are likely to encounter is the disciplinary reprimand. Written reprimands usually follow spoken reprimands and may substantiate some disciplinary problem. Managers typically place copies in the offenders' personnel files. As a manager, you may find writing reprimands an unpleasant but necessary activity. Although a reprimand may appear to be a situation that calls for an indirect negative formula, reprimands usually avoid that formula and use a more direct approach. Follow these three steps.

First, begin the message with a direct statement of the action you are taking and why you are taking it. Explain what behavior prompted the reprimand, and why. Tell the reader what action can help correct the problem. Be firm.

Second, support the situation with specific facts. When and where did the offense occur? What were or might have been the consequences of this behavior?

Finally, explain the consequences if your instructions are not followed. Here is the body of a sample reprimand:

> Because of your misuse of the company computer network, your access code that gets you through the internal firewall to the Internet is being revoked. Our telecommunications department has found that you have been frequenting Internet sites that do not have anything to do with your job. Over the past four weeks you were logged into the system for over nine and one-half hours during the working day to Internet auction sites such as eBay. When you were given your access code, you signed a statement saying that the Internet would be used for business only. Last August, you were reminded of the company policy regarding Internet use when three questionable sites were accessed from your computer.
>
> The company places repeated Internet misuse in the category of disciplinary problems that can lead to termination. You are advised to reread our Internet policies. A copy is attached.

Overt Request for Action

A final type of nonformula situational message is the overt request for action. Using the persuasive formula, you first decide where on the spectrum of hard to soft sell the message should fall and then begin with the appropriate step that leads to action. In a moderate soft-sell message, for example, you might assume that you have the reader's attention and interest and, therefore, begin with the desired step.

A direct, overt request for action disregards the persuasive formula and opens with request for action. This may be appropriate when the requested action embodies the attention through conviction steps. The following opening illustrates such an occasion:

> Your address places you in the North Shore Subdivision. As a North Shore resident, you are no doubt aware that no full-service banking facility exists in the neighborhood. Until now, that is. To introduce you to North Shore Bank, we'd like you to. . . .

Other occasions for the overt action request are with directives and reprimands, as discussed above.

Two Examples of Nonformula Situational Writing

As you gain experience writing your own situational letters, you will begin to notice the effective style of others. Here are two examples.

Rise in Insurance Costs

In Figure 7.9, a letter from a boat owners association informs members of a rise in insurance costs. The letter is unusual because it presents the bad news (rise in costs) at the beginning and even in negative terms (unpleasant, and none of us like that). The second paragraph explains the true goal of the letter: not to deliver the news of a rise in costs but, rather, to promote understanding of the reasons for the rise.

The letter switches from the explanation to a more upbeat persuasive twist to help sell the insurance program and concludes on a positive note.

Figure 7.9   **Example of an Effective Situational Letter**

BOAT OWNERS ASSOCIATION of THE UNITED STATES

Washington National Headquarters
880 South Pickett Street, Alexandria Va. 22304

(703) 823-9550

Dear Member:

This year we are faced with the unpleasant fact that insurance rates are rising. None of us likes that. I, for one, have never filed an insurance claim on my home, autos, or boats, pay my premiums faithfully every year, and see my rates going up with everyone else's.

It is only natural to want to know why, and the purpose of this letter is to provide some of the answers.

The reasons are both complex and simple: Complex because they involve concepts such as increasing numbers of lawsuits and society's view of legal liability. Complex because they involve an insurance company philosophy called "cash-flow underwriting" (pursued for the past seven years) that depends on high interest rates and return on investments to cover claims and make profits. Simple because for several years now insurance companies have not been making profits.

Insurance companies won't continue business as usual when they lose money in successive years. They are going to make changes. The question is, What do they change and how? In most cases, the answer is higher rates. In a few, it is canceling or nonrenewing coverage.

Inevitably the question arises, Why not have those that filed claims pay the increase? In fact, those with claims at BOAT/U.S. do pay a heavier price as they lose their 10% "no-loss" credit for one year. Repeat claimants whose claims reflect a lack of reasonable care are refused future participation in the Group. Since we do not know which of us will suffer an accident in 200X, everyone must share to some extent in the increase. We truly regret the necessity of the increase and hope for your continued support and participation.

On the good side, 200X saw a record number of Members participating in the BOAT/U.S. Marine Insurance Group, over one billion dollars worth of boats insured, loss prevention material distributed on hurricane preparation and avoiding sinkings at the dock, and thousands of boats assisted with problems.

Your Association staff is committed to being there to assist when you need help. We wish you a safe and enjoyable year on the water.

Sincerely,

William M. Oakerson

William M. Oakerson, Director
Marine Insurance Division

Service, Savings, and Representation for the Nation's Boat Owners

Order Canceled

Figure 7.10 illustrates a beautifully written situational letter. Unknown to some people, there is a law that requires mail-order houses to either fill orders within a prescribed time period or refund money. This letter is written to a customer to conform to this law. Read the message and note the tone: concern by the company for the customer, emphasis on high-quality products, adherence to the law, and desire for additional business.

Figure 7.10   Example of an Effective Situational Letter

Dear Customer,

Thank you for your order for the Pathfinder Pants. Your request for the purchase of this item is very much appreciated and our being able to ship it to you in a timely manner is important to both of us.

L.L. Bean is very concerned with providing quality merchandise. The fabric quality on the initial shipment of these pants was not satisfactory and shipment had to be returned to our supplier. The Federal Trade Commission requires that we fill your order within 60 days. For that reason we must cancel your order for the above item. Your refund check is enclosed.

We expect our shipment of the Pathfinder Pants by late September. You are welcome to reorder by returning the enclosed order blank; please include the stock number, color, size, and method of payment. A postpaid envelope is provided for your convenience.

I apologize for this poor service. Your patronage is valued here and we look forward to providing you with fine quality merchandise and service in the future.

Sincerely yours,

Marj Porter

Marj Porter
Customer Service
Manager

MP/klr
Encls:

Source: Reproduced with permission from L.L. Bean.

The first paragraph provides background in a positive tone. Paragraph two establishes the concept of quality and mentions the law. Before the reader can complain, however, mention is made of the refund check. To maintain the order, the reader learns how to reorder and receives a prepaid envelope. The letter concludes with an unnecessary apology for the poor service, even though the service appears quite good. This self-effacing phrase emphasizes the company's concern for the customer.

The letter breaks most of the rules established for formula messages, yet successfully creates a positive perception of the company. It also serves as a reminder that breaking rules can sometimes be quite effective.

Writing Memoranda

As mentioned in an earlier chapter, there are few differences in the organization of e-mail messages, memoranda, and letters. Further, the principles of the direct, indirect, and situational organization of messages apply equally well to all three. Hard-copy media such as memoranda and letters differ somewhat in appearance. *To*: and *From*: replace a letter's inside address and signature block, for example. Further, letters usually are sent outside the organization while memoranda usually are internal messages. As internal messages, memoranda tend to be more informal and more direct than their letter counterparts.

As chapter 4 explained, the medium of e-mail can carry any form of message. Most business e-mail messages are internal, but they may also cross boundaries, such as messages from customers to companies, or from colleagues working together in two different companies. In many cases, the hard-copy memorandum has been replaced by the e-mail message that carries the same content. However, the hard-copy memorandum still is valuable for mass distribution to large groups, some of whom may not be comfortable with e-mail systems; for establishing a paper trail; and for ease in filing for future reference.

More so than with letters, memos—either hard-copy or electronic—should start with a statement of the purpose early in the message. In other words, memos are more likely either to be direct messages or to bend the formula steps of the indirect organization to become situational messages.

Memoranda also need special visual treatment. Keep paragraphs short, much like newspaper articles. Consider using bullets (asterisks, lowercase o's, or large dots) in front of items in a list. One approach to typing memoranda—enhanced by software templates—places the main text of the memo in a narrow column and then, to the left of it, adds notes summarizing the content to the right. An example appears in Figure 7.11.

Another characteristic that can set memoranda apart from letters is the inclusion of humor. Humor—or attempts at it—requires judicious use in both memos and letters. However, when the internal message is lighthearted and relatively unimportant, humor in a memo can distinguish its author as a person with personality and depth. As long as humor is on target, does not embarrass others, is not overdone, and is not too frequent, it can reflect positively on its author. A word of caution is needed, however; what is funny to you may not be funny to others. You may wish to test your message on a neutral friend. Figure 7.12 presents a lighthearted e-mail message.

Figure 7.11 **New Memorandum Format Option**

Memo

To: Regional Managers
From: Fred Gilley, Vice President, Planning
Subject: Improving Regional Meetings
Date: December 3, 200X

Managers, I have a few thoughts for you:

AMENITIES AT MEETINGS

One of the objectives of regional meetings should be to provide opportunities for attendees to meet and talk with one another. Our decentralized organization does not lend itself to intraregional communications. Therefore, we should make the most of our regional meetings by providing the following:

- a reception for everyone the night we arrive
- a luncheon for everyone on Friday
- a reception for VIPs and speakers on Friday night
- coffee midmorning Friday and Saturday
- coffee and soft drinks midafternoon Friday.

Minimal cost is involved in providing these amenities and they provide the occasions for informal visits.

JOINT MEETINGS

Last year the Southwest region and the Southeast region met in New Orleans for a joint meeting. The regions shared common discussions for the first day and then split into their respective groups for the next two days for topics relevant only to themselves.

Those in attendance agree the sessions were valuable and that it was enjoyable interacting with those from another region. Maybe other regions should consider having joint meetings.

| Figure 7.12 | Humorous Message |

X-Originating-IP: [142, 221, 198, 916]
FROM: Alex Bartholemew <abart76@fastnet.com>
TO: Brand Management Department
<dept.list.serv@fastnet.com>
SUBJECT: Season Football Tickets
DATE: May 1, 200X

For the past few years, several members of the Brand
Management Department have banded together to submit
their season football ticket applications as a group.
As a result, we have been able to secure a large block
of seats.

This procedure has the advantage of (a) securing a very
good location, and (b) allowing you to enjoy the fine
company of your colleagues, and (c) providing the
opportunity to speculate as to who Jenny Carnahan's date
will be. It has the disadvantage that arises from the
fact that Bill Maldando and I almost always show up.
Furthermore, you might be located between me and the
concession stand, a high-traffic area.

All this notwithstanding, if you are interested, just
deliver your application and your check to my mailbox
by May 13, 200X. On May 14, depending on how many
applications I receive, I will either deliver them to
the ticket office and demand with righteous fervor that
we be given preferential seating, or head for Rio.

Remember, we play A&M here next year, so this offer is
not for the squeamish.

If you have any questions about the procedure or whether
you'll ever see the money or your tickets again after
you place your check in my hands, feel free to ask.

Source: Reproduced with permission from Robert Prentice, MSIS Department, University of Texas–Austin.

Summary

Situational messages require advanced levels of planning and audience analysis because they do not clearly fit either the direct or indirect organizational approaches. Instead, they piece together the steps and principles of other messages to create a unique approach to a specific message. This chapter illustrates the combination of a variety of message types to create plans for situational messages. The main focus of this chapter, then, is illustrating the thinking that supports the planning and writing of messages that are not obviously direct or indirect.

Several types of situational messages do not follow the combination-of-formulas approach. They include goodwill messages, the collection-letter series, negative-only messages, complaints and responses to complaints, disciplinary reprimands, overt requests for action, and selected memoranda.

The experienced writer uses the principles of writing discussed in Chapters 5, 6, and 7 to prepare specialized messages to well-defined audiences. With experience, you will learn to write according to the situation and to place less emphasis on the steps of the formulas.

Discussion Questions

1. What lies behind the concept of formula writing?
2. What is the difference between formula and nonformula situational writing?
3. How much discretion do you have in following the formulas for situational writing presented in the chapter?
4. What is the 80/20 rule? Does it apply to situational messages? How?
5. As part of a company 360-degree appraisal process, you have been asked to evaluate a colleague and friend who was in the same training class as you when you both started three years ago as consumer researchers in a marketing department of a large Internet provider company. You are to write a letter to your common boss with a copy to your colleague. You need to comment on his communication skills (you think they are excellent), understanding of the job (adequate), technical understanding (could be better), and potential for improvement (excellent). How would you organize the message?
6. Your company has long had a mission statement, but few employees know of its existence or content. Because of your communication training, the company president asked you to send an e-mail message to employees explaining the existence and content of the statement, and then seeking their active support of working toward that mission. How would you organize the message?
7. Humor in the workplace, and especially when written, can be tricky. What criteria do you apply to workplace humor? What types do you like to receive? Send?

Communication in Action

1. Perhaps you have saved some of your better-written memos or letters. If not, do so. Then examine them from the viewpoint of an organization. Were some situational? What mix of formulas was used? Did they follow the principles established in this chapter?

2. Locate an example of a goodwill message and critique it. Was it successful? Why? How could it be improved?

3. Examine a block of messages, such as a group of e-mail messages after an extended absence. What percentage are of direct organization? Indirect organization? Situational messages?

@ Internet

4. Search the Internet for web sites that give guidance on the preparation of collection letters. What advice beyond this textbook did you acquire?

5. Use the Internet to learn about the legal implications of writing a letter of recommendation or of reference. What is the degree of your exposure? Is there a difference in legal exposure between the two? What recommendations would you make to authors of such letters?

6. Use the Internet for guidance on how to write a reference request letter. Find sample letters. What are the main steps in writing such a letter?

i InfoTrac

7. Research the underlying concepts that support the various message types, such as the indirect persuasive. Also, seek out information on the order of presentation of ideas and the psychology behind message organization. (The notes section in the preceding two chapters can help you get started.) How strong is the research support? From what disciplines does this support come?

8. Using InfoTrac, search for occurrences of the concept "situational messages" in the literature. How widely used does the term appear to be? Does its wide or narrow use affect its underlying philosophy?

Note

1. One-Write Plus (Version 8.0) [Computer software]. Norcross, GA: Peachtree Software. Retrieved from **http://www.peachtree.com/onewrite/**.

Part Three

Written Communication: Expanded Messages

CHAPTER - 8

The Planning and Writing
of Persuasive Proposals

No matter what profession or area of business you enter, you will probably write a proposal. Proposals make money for a company or organization by recruiting customers, winning contracts, or closing sales. Proposals are so important that you may one day receive a promotion because of your ability to write them effectively. For these reasons and many more, it is important that you understand what a proposal is and how to prepare one.

A proposal is a marketing tool that sells your ideas to others. It is a persuasive document that

- Communicates what you plan to do or offer.
- Explains how you will implement what you propose.
- Convinces the potential customer that your organization can better meet his or her needs than the competition.
- Stresses your organization's unique qualifications to do the job or provide goods or services.
- Often stands alone in selling your solution or services.[1]

This chapter is divided into four main sections: the major purposes of proposals, classification of proposals, the planning process, and the writing process. A sample proposal appears at the end of the chapter.

Two Major Purposes of Proposals

While all proposals are selling documents, what they sell varies. The purpose of a commercial proposal is to sell a specific product or solution to meet a particular need. For instance, you may write a proposal to provide 20 hours of training on how to motivate employees as your solution to a decrease in a manufacturer's production rate. Or you may propose to sell 50 computers to an engineering firm that wants to update its office automation. Perhaps you will prepare a qualification proposal, in which you seek to sell yourself or your organization as the best qualified to solve a potential client's problem or meet a need. A qualification proposal does not offer a concrete solution but, rather, attempts to demonstrate that whatever the need, you can devise and implement the steps to an effective solution. Adver-

Figure 8.1 **Types of Proposal Situations**

Proposals are written for the following activities or situations:

To pitch advertising campaigns

To bid on construction or landscaping projects

To provide temporary help services

To provide consulting services to political candidates

To conduct issue analyses for governmental entities

To provide office furnishings

To install computer equipment

To provide employee training programs

To win contracts to write companies' business plans, marketing plans, or strategic business plans

To seek approval of academic research, such as for a doctoral or master's thesis

---

tising agencies, public relations firms, and political consultants often use qualification proposals to establish agency relationships. For other types of proposal situations, refer to Figure 8.1.

Classification of Proposals

Proposals can be internal or external; they can be solicited or unsolicited; and they can take different forms.

Internal Versus External

Proposals can be aimed at audiences inside or outside your organization. Internal proposals usually are directed at a specific level of management within your organization. They can be relatively simple, such as suggestion-box ideas, or they can be time-consuming and lengthy and can have the potential to radically change the organization, such as proposals to reorganize the company or build new facilities. On the other hand, external proposals are a marketing tool aimed at current or prospective customers. One company or organization proposes to satisfy another organization's need. External proposals are more common than internal proposals and are the main subject of this chapter.

Solicited Versus Unsolicited

Proposals either identify a need and propose to meet it (unsolicited) or respond to a request (solicited). The proposal writer initiates the unsolicited proposal; it is usually the more difficult type to write because the target audience must first be convinced that a need exists and then that the response is worth the time and money required. Preparing and presenting unsolicited proposals generally requires exceptional persuasive skills.

When a company requests a proposal to supply specific goods, to solve a problem, or to exploit some situation, the proposal is solicited. There are two types of solicited proposals. Advertised proposals are requested when the desired product or service can be defined concisely and quantitatively. Potential suppliers learn of the requirements in a detailed Invitation for Bids (IFB). These proposals favor the lowest bidder. Another type of solicited proposal is the negotiated proposal, which allows the writer to specify a proposed solution to the need. The negotiated proposal originates with a Request for Proposals (RFP) from the potential customer, which explains the need and seeks responses. Negotiated proposals usually are not awarded on the basis of price, but on the quality of the solution and the ability to implement that solution.[2]

Forms of Proposals

Proposals are delivered orally, in writing, or both. Even if a simple proposal is generated by a conversation, do not neglect the important task of spelling it out in writing. A written proposal minimizes misunderstandings or disagreements about the type, quality, and cost of goods or services provided. Many proposals constitute the basis of legally binding contracts. There are four forms of proposals, which differ by the extent of work required to prepare them rather than by their content.

Letter proposals are brief proposals written for projects that are not complex or expensive enough to warrant a longer document. Use this form to present either qualification proposals or commercial proposals.

Preliminary proposals (sometimes called short proposals) find application in service areas such as public accounting, advertising, or communications or in technical areas such as research and development. They may be either qualification or commercial proposals.

Detailed proposals (sometimes called formal proposals) are the longest and most complex proposals. They are usually commercial proposals and contain precise implementation plans and cost estimates.

Oral presentations generally accompany written qualification proposals but should not take the place of them. An oral presentation is an opportunity for experts to explain their areas of knowledge and experience, to detail the services they can provide, and to give immediate feedback to questions.[3]

A fifth form of proposal, of interest to advanced business students and graduate students, is the thesis or dissertation proposal. Because this form of proposal has such a unique audience and is not a business proposal per se, it is discussed separately at the end of this chapter.

The Proposal-Planning Process

Planning is the most crucial stage in preparing a proposal and, if done properly, will greatly increase your company's chances of producing a successful proposal.

Thorough planning will make the actual writing of an effective proposal easy; view the effort as an investment in success. There are four major steps to the planning process: (1) screening; (2) creating a capture plan; (3) formulating solution and implementation strategies; and (4) budgeting and scheduling the proposal effort.

Screening: The Bid/No Bid Decision

Within the planning process, screening is perhaps the most important aspect. Omission of this task can cost your company time and money. When your company receives a Request for Proposals (RFP) or an Invitation for Bids (IFB), you must screen the document as soon as possible. Do this even if you have discussed the project with the potential client. Screening involves asking yourself whether your company should consider competing for the job. You should read the RFP or IFB thoroughly to determine if your firm qualifies. Many government RFPs contain special requirements for firms, such as having company headquarters located in specific states or having full-time engineers on staff. Read the RFP carefully, including the fine print.

You must also determine whether your company is capable of doing the work. Do you have the resources and expertise necessary to bid on the job? If not, can you obtain the resources to enable you to meet the requirements? Many companies waste time and money bidding on work of which they are not capable. Consider how taking the job will influence your staff's workload and the work being performed for your other clients. Other strategic questions that you should ask are whether taking this job will enhance your reputation and what your chances of winning are.

A final and essential step in screening is to determine the total value of the project or sale to your company. Will this opportunity reap an adequate return or profit for your company? If not, look for a higher-value project on which to bid.[4]

Creating a Capture Plan

A capture plan is an analytical planning document prepared for internal use to ensure the creation of a winning proposal. Preparation involves careful planning to review whether all variables that might affect the proposal have been considered. The capture plan entails conducting a customer analysis and a situational analysis.[5]

Conduct a Customer Analysis

The customer-analysis step, much like the audience-analysis step discussed in Chapter 4, involves researching the entity that is requesting the proposal to discover facts that will help you formulate a proposal that responds to their needs and has a high probability of being selected. The customer analysis is analogous to doing your homework and is essential preparation for the later writing of the proposal. A customer analysis is composed of four parts:

1. *Problem Identification.* Although most requests for qualification proposals outline the problem to be solved, you should not take for granted that this is the primary problem. The problem stated in the RFP may be a symptom of a greater, underlying but unstated problem. What does the customer perceive as the solution to the problem? Can this be improved on while

staying within the scope of the RFP? In the case of a commercial proposal, the type of goods the potential customer is requesting may not be adequate for the desired tasks. The best way to get clarification is to ask questions. Meet with the contracting agent in charge of receiving proposals. In addition to obtaining valuable information for identifying the problem, formulating your strategy, and writing your proposal, by having such a meeting you let the organization know of your intention to submit a proposal. Furthermore, the meeting may provide some hints of the contractor's expectations on some issues about which you cannot ask direct questions. For example, a nonverbal cue such as tone of voice may inadvertently reveal an estimate of the amount budgeted for the project.

2. *Needs Analysis.* If a formal RFP (or an IFB) is issued, be sure that you understand what the potential customer is asking for. Do not rely on previous discussions with the customer. Do not read just the Statement of Work section in the RFP or IFB. Examine the entire document, including the attachments and exhibits, which may contain important information that is not presented elsewhere. What assumptions are inherent but not stated explicitly? Are these realistic assumptions? Restate exactly what you believe the customer is requesting in the RFP or IFB and ask why.

3. *Customer's Previous Procurement Background.* Know the buying behavior of the potential customer. Conduct research to determine

   - Background about the customer found on a Web site.
   - The goods or services purchased.
   - The quality of goods or services purchased.
   - The price paid for the goods or services.
   - The customer's satisfaction with the goods or services.

   Use the results of your research when you formulate a solution to the problem. The information could spare you from proposing a brand of product or solution that is not satisfactory, a product that is priced too high, or one that is of inappropriate quality.

4. *Proposal Evaluator.* Find out who in the requesting company will evaluate the proposal. An individual or a team may serve as evaluators. Either way, a formal list of criteria is likely to be used in the evaluation. These criteria can serve as a checklist for tailoring your proposal. If the evaluator is an individual, knowledge of personal background can reveal information that might help you. For instance, if the evaluator has an accounting background, you can anticipate concern about the financial aspects and cost containment of your proposal. Knowledge of evaluation criteria for previous projects may prove useful as well. Does the company usually award contracts or jobs to the lowest bidder, or to the bidder that offers the best solution to the problem, or to the company that offers the highest-quality goods? Are bids evaluated according to a combination of factors, and if so, what are the weightings?

Conduct a Situational Analysis

As the second portion of the capture plan, the situational analysis scrutinizes the internal and external environment to make the proposal more persuasive. It supplies the groundwork for turning your proposal into a competitive marketing tool by providing information to outdo your competition, emphasize your strengths, and highlight major selling points. There are three components to the situational analysis:

1. *Competitor Analysis.* Know your competition, their strengths and weaknesses, and what they are likely to propose or offer. In most cases, you will not be able to find out which companies are submitting proposals, and you will have to assume that all firms similar to yours will submit proposals. However, you may learn who bids on similar projects by examining public records. Especially if you are trying to win a state or federal contract, previous bids are probably in the public record. As you analyze bids in these records, keep in mind that some companies bid at a loss to gain knowledge in a new area or to establish a reputation. Wasson contends that each bidder tends to follow a consistent pattern in estimating cost. Knowing your competition can influence your final product and your chances of being awarded the job.[6]

2. *Internal Analysis.* A winning proposal convinces the proposal evaluator that your company is the one to implement the solution to the problem. Conduct an internal analysis of your firm with this criterion in mind. What strengths does your company possess that should be played up in the proposal? Are there weaknesses that will hamper your ability to perform the work? How is your company uniquely suited to perform the work required for this proposal? Do you have previous experience in this specific field? In the proposal, use the strengths identified in this analysis to demonstrate that your firm has performed well in the past and can do so in the future. Build on or sell your company's reputation.

3. *Theme Development.* Themes are major selling points that run through your proposal. Develop a few major themes that communicate that your ideas are better than everyone else's. Label your themes with key words and weave these words into your title, headings, introduction, and text. Examples of themes are high quality, cost justification, efficiency, reliability of your research, major benefits of your plan, and return on investment.

In summary, a capture plan forces a proposal team or writer to analyze crucial strategic issues before writing the proposal. Perhaps the greatest benefit of a capture plan is that it helps identify the nuances of the proposal environment as well as the major themes to which one must be sensitive in order to write a winning proposal.

Formulating a Solution and Strategies

Once you have decided to submit a proposal and have evaluated the customer and the situation, the next step is to formulate a solution. The capture plan helped you understand strategic issues and identify the problem; now use these issues to devise a solution to the problem. For instance, if the problem is that a company needs some software that doesn't exist, the proposed solution might be that your staff could develop such software. With a solution prepared, you need to devise strategies for implementing it. An effective proposal contains these three kinds of strategies:

1. *Technical Strategy.* Your technical strategy explains the solution (be it a product or service) that is being proposed and how the solution will be implemented. The goal is to convince the reader that your solution best meets the customer's need. If you are preparing a qualification proposal, you will discuss your proposed research methodology or type of analysis. Readers usually evaluate this section first to ensure that a feasible solution is being proposed.

2. *Management Strategy.* The management section establishes your company's ability to carry out the solution proposed or to deliver the goods promised. Whether you are writing a commercial or a qualification proposal, you must establish your firm's ability to implement the proposed solution through expert personnel, experience, insight, facilities, internal organization, and quality control as well as a schedule or a timetable for implementation. Customers that are governmental agencies may want to review your company policies, finances, or personnel records.

3. *Cost Strategy or Cost Estimate.* Your reader needs information to assess if his or her company can afford your products or services and if your offering is reasonably or competitively priced. Many simple commercial proposals are evaluated on the basis of cost after the evaluator determines that the offering meets the company's need. The technical and cost sections of a qualification proposal carry equal weight to the proposal evaluator.

For lengthy, detailed proposals, each of the three strategies may be presented as a separate section or even as individual volumes, as in the case of large government contracts. Letter or memo proposals devote a paragraph or two to each strategy.

Budgeting and Scheduling the Proposal Effort

The final step in the planning process is budgeting and scheduling the proposal writing process. Because some proposals take months to prepare and require considerable financial investment, it is necessary to prepare a proposal cost budget and a proposal schedule. A proposal manager monitors and controls proposal costs. Calculations in employee-hours ensure that all members of the proposal team are performing their assigned tasks.

Preparation and use of a Gantt chart (see Chapter 3, Figure 3.13) aids scheduling your proposal effort. Schedule all proposal activities to meet crucial deadlines and to ensure that all aspects of preparing the proposal have been delegated to a proposal team member. Scheduling has the positive by-product of forcing you to be organized.

The Proposal-Writing Process

If you were thorough in your planning, writing the proposal should be relatively easy. In this section, we will examine three topics: the writing process, additional types of proposals, and proposal formats.

The Writing Process

The writing stage requires strict attention to detail. The written proposal must reflect all the work you have done to this point. It is a tragedy to have a brilliant solution disqualified because of dull text, poor writing skills, lack of organization, or use of an ineffective or inappropriate format. Your proposal package requires persuasion, effective writing, and appealing graphics.

Be Persuasive

Your goal in writing a proposal is to win—to be awarded the project or job. You are selling your solution and your organization. Some suggestions for being persuasive include:

- Open with a persuasive and conclusive summary. The proposal evaluator exhaustively analyzes every detail of your proposal, but the final selection decision may be made by a busy executive who can spend only a few minutes reviewing your proposal. A concise but thorough summary that is hard-hitting will appeal to his or her needs. (This opening is often called an Executive Summary.)
- Use a hook or attention-getting device to begin your proposal. Choose your words carefully; maintain a business tone. For businesses, the most effective attention-getting device is often to focus on profits. Governmental agencies show more interest in competence and reliability.
- Use the themes you formulated in the capture plan.
- Back up your statements with facts, statistics, and expert testimony to be convincing and to build credibility for your solution.[7]

Write Effectively

Your writing should be clear, concise, attractive, and free of spelling and typographical errors. Readers interpret writing ability as an indication of how well you can do the job, especially if the job involves writing.[8] In addition to following the suggestions for effective writing in Chapter 4, you should take care to organize your proposal well. Organization is especially crucial if you are not well-known by your audience; the clarity of your language and organization are the best—sometimes the only—ways your target can judge your thinking and organizing ability.

Near the beginning of your proposal place a specific statement of what you propose. Organize your writing for maximum clarity and psychological effect. Avoid the tendency to write in chronological order; starting with remote causes can be boring and appear irrelevant. Save the background details for middle paragraphs. Locate the most important unknown information at the beginning—the proposal evaluator needs the specific details of your solution as early as possible. Consider summarizing highly detailed portions in the body of the proposal and relegating the details to an appendix to avoid a dull text.

Use Graphic Appeal

Graphic appeal refers to the look of your proposal. For better or for worse, your reader gains a first impression of your work before reading a single word of it. Several graphic features determine whether the piece invites or discourages reading, places emphasis efficiently, or adds clarity. Some graphic considerations are:

- Provide adequate margins and white space on each page. If the proposal looks tight and jammed on the page, it does not draw the reader in and could even be viewed as a chore to read.

- Construct paragraphs that vary in length and are no longer than one quarter of a page. Long, heavy-looking paragraphs discourage reading. Short paragraphs invite reading and emphasize content. Keep opening and closing paragraphs pleasingly short.

- Break up the text by section, subsection, and paragraph headings; use headings as often as possible—in every paragraph if appropriate. Exhibit an array of headings in contrasting type styles. For example, use bold capitals for major headings and lightface capitals for subsections for two degrees of emphasis. Avoid the use of too many different styles of type, though, and use consistent type styles for headings of the same level.

- Use appropriate graphics to illustrate, clarify, and summarize. Place the graphics to break up larger blocks of text.

- Employ desktop publishing techniques to add additional levels of professional impact at relatively low cost.

Additional Types of Proposals

The type of proposal prepared depends on the proposal's purpose. Three of the most common types are the sales proposal, the procurement proposal, and the grant proposal. A sales proposal sells a product, service, or idea and is primarily used for business-to-business transactions. Procurement proposals are solicited by federal, state, or local government agencies seeking to obtain goods or services. They are usually longer than sales proposals and their contents are usually specifically dictated in an RFP. Nonprofit organizations write grant proposals to obtain funding from businesses, foundations, and governmental agencies. Because the latter two types of proposal are written so frequently and have unique features, we will discuss them individually.[9]

The Procurement Proposal

Solicitations for proposals issued by government entities specify a tremendous amount of detail, and thus the process of preparing the proposal requires a special degree of care in every stage. Procurement proposals usually state who qualifies to submit a proposal, what form the proposal is to take, what specific information should appear in each section of the proposal, and many more requirements. These proposals and the subsequent work usually entail substantial paperwork. For large government procurements, your proposal may encompass three or more volumes. In preparing your proposal, use graphs, charts, and time lines to simplify complexities.

A common problem in proposal writing is nonresponsiveness—being disqualified because you did not follow the RFP or IFB directions or guidelines exactly. Review your proposal carefully to ensure that you have met all requirements. One omitted detail could disqualify you. Imagine a proposal that took three months to produce being disqualified because you did not include one topic. It is helpful to prepare, in advance, a checklist of the details so that you will not overlook any.

Finally, keep in mind that you may be required to show your accounting books to federal auditors. A plethora of government regulations that you must follow await if you are awarded the contract.

The Grant Proposal

Most nonprofit organizations obtain funding by applying for grants-in-aid from foundations, governmental agencies, and businesses. Before you prepare a grant proposal, your organization must qualify by proving its nonprofit status. Next, your project must be eligible to receive the grant. Funding sources usually specify the characteristics that establish eligibility.

It is important to demonstrate your credibility in the introduction. Build credibility by explaining your history, your organizational goals, what support you have received from other sources, and your previous accomplishments.

When explaining the reason for seeking aid (the "Need" or "Problem Statement" section of the proposal), define the problem narrowly. Do not attempt to solve all the ills of society with this additional funding. Document the problem with research and statistics. Demonstrate your depth of understanding of the problem.

Propose a specific objective that is measurable and realistic. If you intend to request additional funding in the future, the funding source will want to know what you have accomplished with the resources granted in the past. They will want tangible statements, such as: "purchased three buses for the disabled and transported 25 wheelchair patients to the physical therapy facility each day" or "renovated 22 homes for occupancy by low-income families."

Your proposal should have a special section entitled "Future Funding." Funding sources will want to know how you will continue your program when their funding runs out. You should present a plan for obtaining additional funding in the future.[10]

Proposal Formats

There is little agreement about what format to give proposals or what to name the various subject headings.[11] Often, RFPs or solicitation packages suggest an outline or contain a Business Proposal Instruction section. If so, follow that format. In following a dictated organization, your persuasiveness and the quality of your solution will distinguish your proposal from the others submitted. In the absence of such guidance, you may be able to follow a standard format that your company uses. Perhaps you will be fortunate enough to be able to design your own format. Designing your own format is your opportunity to be persuasive and creative, but do not deviate too far from the traditional format. Effective proposals, at the minimum, include a summary, a statement of the problem or need, the proposed solution, how the solution will be implemented, and what it will cost to implement the solution. The following is a suggested format that will be appropriate for many proposals.

1. *Cover Materials.* Include a letter of transmittal, a title page, and a table of contents.
2. *Executive Summary.* A persuasive summary briefly states the need or problem, the solution, the implementation plan, and the costs and resources required. Use an attention-getting device to open your summary and highlight the themes or strategy you will discuss throughout the proposal.

Make the summary persuasive and concise enough for your reader to make a decision about your offer on reading your summary, without having to read the entire proposal. At the same time, draw in and make your reader want to read the rest of your proposal.

3. *Introductory Materials.* The introduction can include the background to the situation or problem that the proposal is addressing, the most immediate cause of the problem, the purpose for studying the problem or submitting the proposal, the goals of the proposal, or the benefits to be derived from adoption of the proposal.

4. *Need or Problem Statement.* State the problem concisely. Differentiate between symptoms of the problem and the root problem.

5. *Technical Solution or Methodology.* This section is the heart of your proposal. Present your solution and prove that it is not only viable but that it is the best alternative for solving the customer's problem or meeting the need. Convince the reader of the strengths of your proposed solution. Demonstrate that your solution is based on the latest research findings and the most current or most appropriate technology. It is not enough to just state your solution; you must sell your solution. Use facts, figures, and expert testimony.

This section also outlines the implementation of the technical solution. Discuss the methods. Identify major and minor tasks. Provide a time line for completion of each task. Give the specifications of materials and products used or produced.

If you are writing a qualification proposal, describe how you will accomplish the work, how you will conduct the study, what research techniques will be employed, why they are the most appropriate measures to use, and how you will analyze the data.

Finally, many customers want to know how you will evaluate yourself and track your progress to completion. If the job will be lengthy, the customer may ask you to periodically report on the progress of the project and to evaluate your company's performance.

6. *Management Profiles.* First, introduce the individual or team who will be implementing the solution. Describe qualifications and related backgrounds. Include résumés of key personnel in an appendix. Tailor the résumés for the specific proposal. Highlight your company's previous experience or specialization in the area. List work done for other clients in the area of interest and the scope or depth of the work performed.

Second, describe how you will organize the project. Delineate lines of authority and responsibility. Design the workload and structure from start-up to completion. Create an organization chart. Include all resources and facilities to be used.

Next, present the management policies and administrative methods applicable to the project. For example, describe quality control, cost accounting, payroll, timekeeping, and reporting methods.

End the Management Profile by demonstrating that your company is stable, financially viable, and reputable. Include financial statements, letters of reference from satisfied customers (in an appendix), and awards. Close by selling your company's strengths.

7. *Budget.* Provide a thorough breakdown of costs and differentiate between direct and indirect costs. List any subcontractors and give their qualifications and costs. Describe the method of payment that will be followed and clearly state any penalties prescribed for late payment.

8. *Conclusion and Recommendations.* The conclusion is your last chance to sell your solution. Make it persuasive. Summarize the problem and your solution. Bring in key themes and strategies and highlight the strengths of your solution and your company. If the proposal would benefit from a recommendation, include it.

9. *Bibliography.* If you did research and want to project a scholarly or authoritative image, include your sources. Also, of course, avoid copyright infringement and plagiarism, which taking credit for other's work without attributing the source.

10. *Appendices.* Include résumés of key personnel, letters of reference, highly specific details of implementation that you summarized in the body of the proposal, and any other relevant material.

Finishing Touches

Flashy bells and whistles will not hide a vague, thin, or off-target proposal, but some finishing touches are essential. Spend time on appropriate packaging, evaluating, and delivering of the proposal.

Packaging

Does your proposal have a professional appearance? Type should be clean and easy to read. Avoid dot matrix printers for final drafts; the clean type of a laser printer is preferable. Print your proposal on white paper that is smooth, crisp, and heavy enough not to look cheap. Ensure that the type on one page does not show through on the previous page by using 25-percent cotton content (rag) bond, in 20-pound weight. If the paper has recycled content, which some businesses and agencies require, state this in a credit line. External proposals should always be enclosed in a binder. While bindings should be attractive, avoid obvious extravagances, such as submitting your proposal in a leather binder. You do not want to give the impression that you spend resources needlessly.

Evaluating the Proposal

After you have completed writing the proposal, evaluate it in light of the RFP or IFB to ensure that it is complete. Have you correctly identified the problem? Have you offered a solution that is feasible? Were you effective in selling your solution? Have you met all the requirements? Does the text flow smoothly? Read the proposal as if you were the evaluator; is it concise and competitive? Now read it from the viewpoint of the busy decision maker; is it a persuasive document if skimmed?

Delivering the Proposal

If you are rushed to complete the proposal, you are likely to overlook crucial last-minute details. Be sure that you are submitting the correct number of copies of your proposal. Is a transmittal letter enclosed? Is the proposal addressed properly? Are all the required forms enclosed? Careless omission of any one of these details could cost you the job.[12]

Often when a customer has narrowed the choice to two or three companies, the companies are asked to present their proposal orally. Be prepared to make an oral presentation by referring to Chapter 11 on effective presentations.

Thesis Proposals

As mentioned earlier in this chapter, some graduate students write a scholarly thesis or dissertation. These lengthy, complex, and challenging projects take an extended amount of time, effort, and planning—often several semesters' worth.

To ensure that a thesis project is well planned and its content valuable, often a thesis advisor requires a thesis proposal. With a well-thought-out plan approved, the student then has a plan of action and better understands the steps necessary for completion of the project.

A thesis proposal is a combination of planning steps and rationale for the study with a proposed outline of the final paper. Different universities have their own requirements regarding the outline of the thesis, and thesis advisors and the topics themselves also influence the content—and its organization. Here are common elements likely to be required in a thesis proposal:

1. *Problem Statement.* Establish the problem that the thesis will solve or investigate. The problem statement may well lead to the hypotheses or research questions. However, the hypotheses or questions should be a partial response to the ubiquitous question, "So what?" The essence of most problem statements should be captured in one to three paragraphs.

2. *Hypotheses or Research Questions.* Hypotheses are quite specific and able to be tested; research questions are more general and may or may not be tested by statistical means. In addition to stating the hypotheses or questions, include some dialogue that leads up to them: to why they are important, to why they need examination.

3. *Literature Review.* A literature review gives the background of the problem, connects it to a theoretical basis, discusses a void (that is at least partially answered by this thesis research), and leads to methodology. To merely reiterate what is in the literature is not especially valuable; to synthesize that information adds meaning. Connect information by comparison and contrast, show trends, and spot omissions. Draw your reader to the direction in which you are headed.

4. *Methodology.* Most theses involve some primary research; if so, it would be described here. If the thesis is a case study or other form of research, change the title of this section and include the information here.

5. *Anticipated Results.* Of course you cannot yet describe what results you will get, but discuss what you think you will find and why it is important.

6. *Statistical Analysis of Data.* Describe any statistical tests you expect to use. Perhaps you can even graph what you hope you will find. Often this will be compared to known data.

7. *Expected Value or Implementation.* Expand on your answer to "So what?" How do we benefit from this research? How might the results be used? Is the use theoretical or practical? Are there new research questions that might be raised by the research? What are they?

You may wish to include a discussion of anticipated appendices that would benefit the reader. Throughout the proposal, thorough attribution of sources is essential and leads to a complete bibliography.

While the student anticipating writing a thesis may consider the proposal a bothersome and unrewarding step, just the opposite is true. Once a thesis proposal is approved, the student has a plan of action and knows what will be necessary for accomplishment of the thesis project. Further, much of what is written in a thesis proposal carries over to the actual thesis.

Summary

A proposal is a persuasive document that makes an offer to provide goods or services to a potential or existing customer. The effective proposal convinces the customer that you are the best qualified to meet the customer's needs. Commercial proposals sell a specific product or solution. Qualification proposals sell skills, experience, knowledge, and creativity as the most capable in implementing an effective solution.

Proposals may be prepared for those inside your organization (internal) or outside (external). The writer initiates an unsolicited proposal. An entity that has need for goods or services may solicit proposals when it issues an Invitation for Bids (IFB) or a Request for Proposals (RFP). IFBs usually specify the solution the solicitor wants implemented. Negotiated proposals, on the other hand, allow the proposal writer to create a unique solution to the customer's need; RFPs are often of this type. Proposals take many forms including letter proposals, preliminary proposals, detailed or formal proposals, and oral presentations.

The planning stage of the proposal-preparation process is crucial. First, screen the RFP and decide whether to submit a proposal. Second, create a capture plan that analyzes the customer and the proposal situation. The customer analysis step evaluates the need (as stated in the RFP), the problem, the customer's buying behavior, and the proposal evaluator. The situational-analysis step examines the competition, your strengths and weaknesses, and major themes. Third, create a solution to the problem that consists of technical, management, and cost strategies.

When writing the proposal, be persuasive, write effectively, and make your proposal graphically appealing. Use appropriate content and format, depending on the type of proposal you write (sales, procurement, or grant proposal). All types of proposals should include the following: cover materials, executive summary, introduction, need or problem statement, a technical solution or methodology, management profiles, budget, conclusion, and appendices (if needed). Your proposal should have a professional appearance. Finally, evaluate the finished product carefully.

For those considering writing a thesis, careful planning of how the project will be approached and why it is valuable should be written in a thesis proposal.

Discussion Questions

1. When would you write an internal versus external proposal?
2. Why is planning so important in preparing a proposal?
3. What are the differences and similarities among an audience analysis, a customer analysis, and a situational analysis?
4. In what ways does writing a proposal differ from writing letters, reports, or e-mail messages?
5. What is the role of graphic appearance in a written proposal?
6. What should the technical solution or methodology section of the proposal accomplish?

Communication in Action

1. Discuss with your classmates how graphic appeal can be added to proposals. What are the limits—both minimum and maximum—of treatments? What part does visual good taste play?
2. What document-formatting applications are available for proposal writing, especially for lengthy and formal proposals? How would you set up your software *before* you started writing your proposal? For example, how would you set up templates? What considerations would you add for preparing multiple proposals to the same or different organizations over time? What common document design might be beneficial?
3. Most large, daily newspapers have a section for Announcements, Requests for Proposals, or Bids. Find the appropriate section and scan the RFPs. Based on the discussion of proposals presented in Chapter 8, what specific classification of proposals do you see? How specific are the requirements, such as length, headings, page limits, or deadlines?

@ Internet

4. Search the Internet for current, live Requests for Proposals, Requests for Bids, and Invitations for Bids. Limit your search to for-profit organizations seeking proposals that would resolve a problem by delivering technical training. How many hits did you get? Now search for organizations prepared to deliver technical training. What is their proportion to requests for proposals or bids for such training? Why do you think this occurs?

5. As part of an organization that is responding to a request for proposals from Philip Morris Corporation, your supervisor has asked for your help in conducting the customer analysis prior to writing the proposal. In addition to such obvious data as its annual report and its Web site, what more can you find out about Philip Morris? What are the major types of sources of this data, such as news stories or sales rankings? To get you started, visit the Dow Jones, D&B Million Dollar Database, Hoover's, or other databases identified in Chapter 9.

InfoTrac

6. Use InfoTrac to search for literature on how to be persuasive in your proposal writing. You may wish to start with persuasion in general, and attitude change, and then move on to applications related to proposal-writing. Do your sources recommend a certain type of persuasion for specific situations? Consider such key words as *persuasion, business, proposals,* and *writing.*

Notes

1. Roetzheim, W. H. (1986). *Proposal writing for the data processing consultant.* Englewood Cliffs, NJ: Prentice-Hall.
2. Roetzheim, *Proposal writing,* chap. 3.
3. Bowman, J. P. & Branchaw, B. P. (1992). *How to write proposals that produce.* Phoenix, AZ: The Orynx Press, pp. 171–184.
4. Bowman & Branchaw, *How to write proposals,* p. 31.
5. Both of the above-mentioned books deal thoroughly with the planning process and strategic issues to consider when planning your proposal.
6. Wasson, C. R. (1969). *Understanding qualitative analysis.* East Norwalk, CT: Appleton-Century-Crofts.
7. Schell, J. & Stratton, J. (1984). *Writing on the job: A handbook for business and government.* New York: New American Library, p. 126.

8. Moffat, A. S. (1994). Grantsmanship: What makes proposals work? *Science, 265,* pp. 1911–1912.
9. Schell & Stratton, *Writing on the job,* chaps. 11, 12, 13.
10. Kiritz, N. J. (1987). Proposal planning and proposal writing. *Grantsmanship Center News,* Los Angeles, CA.
11. All of the above sources discuss proposal formats extensively, as well as Pfeiffer, W. S. & Keller, C. H., Jr. (2000). *Proposal writing: The art of friendly and winning persuasion.* Upper Saddle River, NJ: Prentice-Hall.
12. Roetzheim, *Proposal writing,* chap. 10.

Appendix
Sample RFPs and Proposals

This chapter concludes with an example of an unsolicited, brief, internal proposal for a new computer (Figure 8.2), and a Request for Proposals and the response to that RFP (Figures 8.3 and 8.4). You will find that the latter proposal follows most of the observations and suggestions presented earlier in this chapter. Keep in mind that there are many forms of proposals, that authors have their favorite writing styles, and that evaluators have differences in what they expect. These proposals, then, are just two of many alternatives that could have been prepared.

Figure 8.2   **Example of a Brief, Unsolicited Internal Proposal**

Small Products World
Yuma AZ 89947

INTEROFFICE MEMO

TO: Caroline de Rosa
FROM: Carmine Vasquez
SUBJECT: Proposal to purchase new computer
DATE: January 12, 200X

The purpose of the memo is to propose that we purchase a Delta 5000 computer server. The number of orders for our products has been increasing over the last four years, and the increase is dramatic for the last two quarters. This increased business has reached the point where our current computer is holding back the shipment of goods. The Delta 5000 would overcome these problems. Immediate approval of this proposal is requested.

The Current Situation

Our reputation for importing high-quality international goods and for having exceptional service and delivery systems has resulted in a positive growth pattern over the last four years. However, orders are pouring in so fast that we are unable to give customers our usual quality service or expected delivery times. Complaints are on the rise as well.

The Problem

The reason for our slow delivery times and most of the complaints lies with the overwhelmed, slow, outdated computer we use for our customer database, billing information, and shipping information. This computer has served us well, but now, because of the amount of data submitted, the ongoing process of backing up our hard disk, and new software we have installed, the computer can no longer keep up with our demands. Updating it is cost-prohibitive.

The Analysis

As you can see from the data illustrated on the next page, 2003 showed increased profit, but at a cost of dramatically increased complaints.

Figure 8.2 | **Example of a Brief, Unsolicited Internal Proposal (Concluded)**

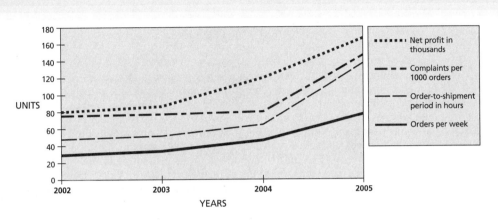

The trends of the last four years, and especially this last year, require increased computer use. Upon investigation of information in our database, I note the following inverse relationship between average order amount in dollars and number of orders per week. I believe our customers are spending less money per order because the quality of our service is slipping.

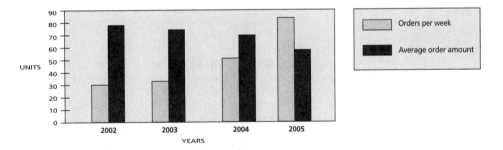

In sum, because of change in our business and because of the age of our current computer, we are offending more customers and flirting with losing some of them.

The Solution

We should purchase and install the Delta 5000 computer server (for $8,799) immediately. I forecast it will meet our needs well through this decade. I'll be pleased to meet with you if you have any questions.

Figure 8.3   **Sample Request for Proposals**

REQUEST FOR PROPOSALS

Financially well-backed private investor seeks proposals to start a rubber-stamp vending business. The purpose of the business is to solicit orders for rubber stamps and then to prepare and deliver those stamps, to retail already-prepared stamps, and to vend related materials, such as ink pads, business forms, and so on. Types of business stamps would include individually prepared Paid, Received, Filed, and Date stamps. Boutique aspects of the business would include many forms of household-use stamps, such as This belongs to Mary, A recipe from Mary, A note from Mary, animal and cartoon caricatures for children, and envelope return addresses.

Details: A storefront in Horton Plaza in downtown San Diego is under lease by the investor and is of adequate size for this business. A written business proposal should be delivered to Union-Tribune, P.O. Box 1234, no later than the 10th of next month. Proposals should address these issues: proposed vendors for prepared stamps and office materials, cost of equipment for preparation of stamps, anticipated profit margin for various products, further description of products to be offered for sale, size of workforce with salaries, and background of the person proposing to be selected as the manager of the store.

The investor has access to store fittings, such as display cases and computerized cash registers; do not discuss these needs or the monthly lease fee. The store would be open from 10 A.M. to 9 P.M. daily.

Proposals should be limited to 12 pages, single-spaced, and include a cover page as part of the 12 pages. An executive summary and table of contents are not needed. Content should reflect the degree of business opportunity available based on research or substantiated facts. A 50-percent interest in the business will be awarded to the winning proposal. The proposer may be, but is not required to be, the manager of the store.

Opportunity: For the right person, this is the opportunity to establish a financially rewarding business with no personal financial obligation and to become a store manager in a promising field.

Figure 8.4   **Sample Proposal**

PROPOSAL

A Business Opportunity:
Starting a Rubber Stamp Business

Prepared by:
Susan Jones
January 200X

Figure 8.4   Sample Proposal (Continued)

<u>**Proposal for a Rubber Stamp Business**</u>

Introduction

A financially well-backed private investor is planning to start a rubber-stamp vending business. The business would sell custom-made rubber stamps, traditional rubber stamps, and related supplies. The business would be located in Horton Plaza in downtown San Diego, in a storefront leased by the investor.

The investor has issued a Request for Proposals to provide an analysis of the business opportunity and an implementation plan.

Purpose

The purpose of the business is to sell rubber stamps and related office supplies to businesses, households, and tourists in the San Diego area. The business would actively solicit orders for custom-made rubber stamps and manufacture and deliver those stamps. The business would also sell traditional business and household stamps containing phrases such as "Paid," "Received," and "A note from Mary," as well as related supplies such as ink and ink pads.

This proposal presents a business overview, implementation strategy, and financial analysis. The implementation strategy includes the proposed rubber-stamp vendors, the cost of equipment for making rubber stamps, the anticipated profit margins by product type, the products to be offered for sale, the planned workforce, and the background of the proposed store managers.

This proposal demonstrates the viability of the rubber-stamp business and substantiates that we should be selected to initiate the business and bring it to profitability. We suggest the name "Stamp It Out" for the business.

Business Overview

Rubber stamps and associated supplies are used routinely by most businesses and many households. Businesses frequently stamp forms or checks as "Received," "Filed," "Processed," or "Paid." Households often stamp envelopes with return addresses and label personal property with name and date stamps. Rubber stamps can be customized with a company name or logo for business use or with a personal note for household use. Rubber stamps with attractive designs are often purchased as gifts.

Figure 8.4 | Sample Proposal (Continued)

San Diego's Horton Plaza is a particularly attractive location for a new rubber stamp business. San Diego is the sixth-largest city in the United States, with a population of 1.23 million as of the 2000 census (U.S. Census Bureau for 2000). According to the California State Board of Equalization (2002), there are approximately 80,000 businesses in San Diego County with a total taxable sales revenue of $36 billion per year. About half of this business occurs in the City of San Diego. Horton Plaza is located next to the historic Gaslamp Quarter in the center of downtown San Diego. Horton Plaza is a major shopping attraction in downtown San Diego and hosts 137 specialty stores (Westfield Shoppingtown Horton Plaza, 2002).

Horton Plaza is located a few blocks from the San Diego Convention Center, making it a prime attraction for convention attendees. San Diego's Convention Center was recently named one of the top three convention centers in the world by Europe's largest meetings industry trade publication (San Diego Convention Center Corporation, 2002). During fiscal year 2001, the convention center hosted 172 events, attracted 759,269 out-of-town attendees to San Diego, and contributed $544 million to the local economy. Conventions are a particularly attractive source of customers because convention organizers tend to give small gifts, coupons, and shopping recommendations to attendees as part of the conference registration process. Contracts with a few large conventions could provide significant revenue for this business.

To target convention attendees, we plan to work with the San Diego Convention Center Corporation to offer customized stamps, key chains, magnets, signs, and other personalized items to convention attendees. We also plan to target local businesses by attending trade shows and career fairs. Businesses at these events may have a particular need for rubber stamps to properly label the résumés and business cards they receive.

Implementation Strategy

This section includes the details of establishing the operation.

Proposed Vendors for Prepared Stamps and Office Materials

We propose two major vendors and other smaller niche vendors for the products.

Figure 8.4　　Sample Proposal (Continued)

Simon's Stamps

Our primary vendor for prepared stamps, ink pads, ink, and related materials will be Simon's Stamps in Amherst, MA. Simon's Stamps has been in business since 1989 and has several hundred wholesale accounts (Simon's Stamps, 2002). Simon's sells self-inking push-down stamps, traditional wood-handle rubber stamps, and three types of metal frame self-inking date stamps. Simon's provides both custom-made stamps and off-the-shelf stamps. Orders can be placed online, and net 30-day credit terms are available. Online orders are shipped within 24 hours, including orders for custom-made stamps.

Simon's Stamps is our first choice because it focuses on rapid service and provides an attractive wholesale dealer discount program. This program provides a 40-percent discount off suggested retail prices for traditional wood-handle stamps, Kwik and Trodat brand stamps, and a 25-percent discount for ink pads, ink, date stamps, numbering stamps, and heavy-duty stamps.

JLS Rubber Stamp Co.

Our second major supplier will be JLS Rubber Stamp Co., Inc. of Redding, CA. JLS has been in the rubber stamp and office supply business for 35 years (JLS Rubber Stamp, 2002). JLS manufactures and sells several types of self-inking rubber stamps, embossers and seals, engraved signs, name badges, and stencils. JLS also sells a variety of gift products such as engraved luggage tags and key chains, custom metal license plate frames, and custom name stamps. JLS specializes in serving commercial and industrial accounts.

Other Stamp Vendors

Two other stamp vendors can bring a variety of stamps to our customers. Rubber Stamps of America features over 1,000 stamps designed by graphic artists; specialties include wildlife and exotic art (Rubber Stamps of America, 2002). The Doodle Art Rubber Stamp Company provides a variety of special occasion stamps. Their Christmas stamps include pictures of trees, snowmen, Santa Claus, reindeer, and many others (Doodle Art Rubber Stamp Company, 2002).

Backup Suppliers

AllMark Identification Systems can provide rubber stamps and ink pads, and FormsPlus can supply a wide array of business forms. Both companies are located in San Diego. While they cost more than the vendors we propose, we need backup suppliers in case of emergencies.

| Figure 8.4 | **Sample Proposal (Continued)** |

Cost of Equipment for Stamp Preparation

Rubber stamps can be produced at least six different ways (Tuffley Computer Services, 2002). The most-common and least-expensive method is to use a hand-set foundry. This process involves positioning individual letters of printer's type into a holder and then creating the rubber stamp with a heated press. For this process, the necessary equipment and supplies cost about $500. Because of the smell of heated rubber associated with this process, special city permits would be required or an alternative site needed.

The newest method of producing rubber stamps uses photographic processing (Tuffley Computer Services, 2002) to make stamps from laser-printed artwork. Prices for the photo processor vary by the manufacturer, but Grantham's Polly Stamp of East Grand Forks, Minnesota, sells one for $1,095 (Home Business Line, 2002).

For this business, we recommend the photographic process because it can produce stamps from any picture or drawing, not just words and letters. This flexibility is particularly important in our proposed business because we plan to sell stamps with company logos, handwritten signatures, and personal photographs or drawings that would be difficult to produce with the foundry method. Permits would not be required.

Once the rubber portion of the stamp is completed, it must be attached to a stamp molding and handle, usually made of natural wood. A description of this process is given by rubber-stamp–making organizations (Rubber Stamp Club, 2002). Moldings and handles can be purchased cheaply in volume. Pictures of the major categories of stamps appear below.

Traditional   **Self-Inking**   **Pre-Inked**

Source: http://www.simonstamp.com/cgi-bin/webshop.pl?config=stamp

Figure 8.4	Sample Proposal (Continued)

The equipment used for making rubber stamps can also produce a variety of other custom-made gifts. We plan to make key chains, refrigerator magnets, and name plates from the same material.

To provide the best service to Stamp It Out customers, we plan to have a computer at the store displaying a variety of possible stamp designs. Our employees would then be able to work with our customers to add names, logos, or other personal items to existing designs. The customer's modified stamp would then be printed on-site and used in the photographic process. Similarly, a customer would be able to bring in an existing design, scan it into the computer, and modify it as necessary. The proposed store manager for this business offers to donate a Dell computer and a Hewlett-Packard Printer/Scanner/Copier (PSC) for this purpose. If purchased new, the Dell computer would cost approximately $1,500 and the PSC would cost $400.

Anticipated Profit Margins

Industry data for office supply firms indicates an average gross margin of 30 percent (Market Guide, 2002). We anticipate that we will obtain a similar average margin on most previously prepared stamps, ink and ink pads, note-paper, and gift items. Based on discounts provided by Simon's Stamps, we anticipate a margin of 40 percent on traditional wood-handle stamps, Kwik stamps, and Trodat stamps, and a margin of 25 percent for ink pads, ink, date stamps, numbering stamps, and heavy-duty stamps.

Custom-made stamps can be ordered from Simon's Stamps or produced directly. If ordered from Simon's, we estimate a potential profit margin of 25 to 40 percent, based on the type of stamp ordered. Much higher margins are possible for stamps that we produce ourselves. Ignoring labor costs, we estimate that the stamps can be produced for $5 to $10 and sold for $12 to $30, implying a gross margin of about 60 percent. Based on our prior experience and unobtrusive observation of similar businesses in the Los Angeles area, we estimate that about half of our business will be custom-made stamps and the other half will be previously prepared stamps and supplies.

Further Description of Products

We plan to market a variety of custom-made and off-the-shelf stamps for business and household use. The custom-made stamps will be produced in the back of our store within 20 minutes of the customer's order. The customer may provide the design for the stamp or customize one displayed on our computer screen.

Figure 8.4 **Sample Proposal (Continued)**

The computer can display thousands of images and designs for traditional business-use stamps as well as household-use stamps. The business-use designs will give the customer the opportunity to add a company name or logo to traditional stamps such as "Received" or "Paid." The household-use designs will allow the customer to add a name or slogan to stamps such as "A note from Mary" or "Property of John Smith." We can also easily create a rubber stamp of the customer's signature.

We plan to sell all six basic types of rubber stamps marketed by Simon's Stamps. The six types include both traditional stamps and self-inking stamps, as listed below:

- Trodat Self-Inking Printer. Push-down model. Efficient and convenient. Available in seven sizes. Suggested retail price: $12.50 (3/8″ × 11/32″) to $24.75 (11/2″ × 31/16″).
- Kwik Stamp Plus Self-Inking Stamp. Push-down model. Available in four sizes. Suggested retail price: $12.95 (5/8″ × 13/4″) to $19.95 (11/4″ x 3″).
- Traditional Wood-Handle Stamp. High-quality commercial-grade. Used with ink pad. Suggested retail price: $6.90 (1/2″ × 1″) to $27.00 (3″ × 5″).
- Metal Type-Band Die-Plate Dater. Changeable date stamp, custom text available. Used with ink pad. Suggested retail price: $29.75.
- Heavy Duty Self-Inking Dater. Super heavy-duty stamp. Durable, nickel-plated steel construction. Suggested retail price: $38.40 (1″ × 15/8″) to $69.95 (2″ × 23/4″).
- Metal Frame Self-Inkers. Super-heavy-duty stamp for bank tellers, tax collectors, and receiving clerks. Suggested retail price: $31.38 (1″ × 15/8″) to $56.45 (2″ × 23/4″).

These rubber stamps will include the words "Received," "Faxed," "Paid," "Billed," "Replied," and "Filed." We will also sell ink and ink pads, business forms, and notepads to go with these stamps. We will also provide customers with the opportunity to order custom-made embossers and seals from JLS Rubber Stamp Co.

For household use and for gifts, Stamp It Out will sell a variety of rubber stamps and other custom-designed products. These products are listed below:

- Custom-made name stamps, for both adults and children.
- Custom-made key chains, luggage tags, and refrigerator magnets.
- Customized license-plate holders from JLS Rubber Stamp Co.

Figure 8.4   Sample Proposal (Continued)

- Over 1,000 rubber stamps from Rubber Stamps of America (RSA), including wildlife, exotic art, and cartoons for children. We will purchase a sample of about 50 of these from RSA and provide the full catalog to customers for special orders.
- Several hundred stamp designs from Doodle Art Rubber Stamp company, including a variety of holiday and seasonal stamps. We will purchase seasonal stamps during the holiday shopping periods and provide the catalog to customers throughout the year.
- Other specialty stamps include alphabet, recipe, and hobby stamps.
- Books on stamping.
- Stamp ink (all colors, permanent and water-based).
- Embossers and desk plates.

Size of Workforce

The business will begin operations with four employees: the store manager, an assistant manager, and two sales clerks. We anticipate that the store will be open when Horton Plaza is open: 10:00 A.M. to 9:00 P.M. Monday through Friday, 10:00 A.M. to 7:00 P.M. on Saturday, and 11:00 A.M. to 6:00 P.M. on Sunday (Westfield Shoppingtown Horton Plaza, 2002). This is a total of 71 hours per week. We require that at least two employees be present in the store at any time, including the store manager or assistant manager and at least one sales clerk. We currently plan to hire two full-time (40 hours per week) cashiers but may choose to hire four half-time cashiers instead, based on labor availability. As the business grows, additional full-time or part-time sales clerks will be hired as necessary, particularly during peak hours.

The store manager will be responsible for overall store operations, including hiring of additional employees as necessary, ordering supplies, and marketing the company's products and services to convention planners. The assistant manager will be responsible for store operations when the store manager is not present and will assist in ordering supplies and training sales clerks. Sales clerks will be responsible for helping customers to find products, collecting orders and payments, and making custom stamps.

We propose an initial annual salary of $50,000 per year for the store manager and $40,000 per year for the assistant manager. Sales clerks will be paid around $7 per hour, or about $13,000 per year for full-time work. Thus, we anticipate total salary expenses of $116,000 per year. Adding an additional 20 percent of salary for benefits such as health insurance and workers' compensation insurance, we estimate initial total labor costs of $140,000 per year.

The main duties of the store manager would be inventory, bookkeeping, personnel management, and daily store operations. The assistant store manager will focus on customer service, new product selection, and marketing, and will assist with daily store operations.

| Figure 8.4 | Sample Proposal (Continued) |

Background of Store Managers

The store manager will be Susan Jones. Susan recently graduated from San Diego State University with an MBA, specializing in finance and entrepreneurship. Prior to getting her MBA, Susan worked for Staples for two years as a store manager and for Wal-Mart for three years as a department manager. During her two years at Staples, Susan initiated a marketing campaign with small businesses that increased sales by 30 percent.

The assistant store manager will be Sandra S. Davis. Sandra is currently the assistant manager of an arts supply store in Solana Beach, California, where she has been employed for the past three years. Her duties include ordering supplies, assisting customers with special orders, and training sales clerks. Sandra was previously self-employed creating arts and crafts and selling them at craft fairs. Forty percent of Sandra's craft business came from customizing existing items for individual customers by adding names or slogans. She has a bachelor's degree in business.

Financial Analysis

According to the California Board of Equalization (2002), total taxable sales of office supplies in San Diego in 2001 were approximately $1 billion for 1500 stores, or average sales of almost $666,000 per store. To confirm that this estimate applies to stores of our proposed size, we obtained annual revenue estimates for Staples and Office Depot stores and scaled these numbers downward. This calculation is shown in Table 1 and confirms that a $666,666 estimate is reasonable.

The annual revenue given in this table is taken from the firms' most recent financial statements (Staples, 2002; Office Depot, 2002). Revenue per store averages about $10 million for these large chains. To adjust the revenue to a store of our size, we computed the revenue per employee for these chains, and used this to estimate the revenue for a comparable four-person store. These values are given at the bottom of Table 1.

Table 1.
Sales for Office Supply Stores
(dollar values in thousands)

	Staples	Office Depot
Total annual revenue	$10,700,000	$10,028,200
Number of stores	1261	859
Revenue per store	$8,485	$11,674
Number of employees	21,580	45,000
Revenue per employee	$362	$259
Estimated Revenue for four-person store	$1,449	$1,038

Figure 8.4 Sample Proposal (Continued)

There is sufficient demand for rubber stamps, related office supplies, and related gift items in downtown San Diego to support these estimates. As mentioned earlier, San Diego Convention Center brings 760,000 people to San Diego every year. Based on our contacts with convention organizers, we believe we can sell a $20 rubber stamp, key chain, or other gift item to at least 5 percent of convention attendees. This alone would produce revenue of $760,000. In addition, as mentioned earlier, there are about 80,000 businesses in San Diego County. If we could generate sales of $100 per year from 5 percent of those businesses, we could produce additional revenue of $400,000. These two target markets combine to provide well over $1 million of revenue, before including sales to households for general use and for gifts. Thus, we believe that we can achieve $1 million of annual revenue within a year or two of starting this business and still have future growth prospects.

Based on an annual revenue of $1 million, the estimated profit for our proposed rubber stamp business is given in Table 2. We used a gross margin estimate of 45 percent in this analysis, assuming that half of our sales will be custom-made products at 60 percent margin and half will be off-the-shelf products averaging 30 percent margin. As shown in Table 2, we estimate a pretax profit of $310,000 per year based on this initial business size.

Table 2
Estimated Profit for Rubber Stamp Business
(dollar values in thousands)

Estimated Revenue	$1,000
Gross Margin	45%
Gross Profit	$ 450
Labor Costs	$ 140
Net Profit (before taxes)	$ 310

Conclusion and Recommendation

Horton Plaza provides an ideal location for a rubber-stamp business because it is close to downtown businesses and to San Diego's Convention Center. Estimated demand for rubber stamps and related materials in the downtown San Diego area indicates that we should be able to achieve sales of approximately $1 million per year. A small four-person store can generate pretax profits of approximately $310,000 and has the opportunity to expand into related office supplies and custom gifts. The proposed management team has significant experience and a track record of success in managing similar retail stores.

This proposal demonstrates that initiating a rubber-stamp business in downtown San Diego can be financially rewarding. We believe Stamp It Out can be operational with six week's notice. We encourage you to select us to bring this profitable venture to fruition.

Figure 8.4 | Sample Proposal (Concluded)

References

California State Board of Equalization. (2002). Taxable sales in California, second quarter, 2001. Retrieved July 12, 2002, from http://www.boe.ca.gov/news/pdf/T1_2q01.pdf.

Doodle Art Rubber Stamp Company (2002). Retrieved July 12, 2002, from http://www.doodle-art.com.

Happy Rubber Stamp Club. (2002). How to mount your rubber stamp. Retrieved July 12, 2002, from http://www.rubberstampsclub.com/tips/mountingstamps.html.

Home Business Line. (2002). Retrieved July 12, 2002, from http://www.homebusinessonline.com/downloads/R21.txt.

JLS Rubber Stamp Co., Inc. (2002). Retrieved July 12, 2002, from http://www.jlsrubberstamp.com.

Market Guide. (2002). Sales data for Staples and Office Depot. Retrieved July 12, 2002, from http://www.marketguide.com/home.asp.

Office Depot. (2002). 2001 annual report. Retrieved July 12, 2002, from http://biz.yahoo.com/e/020319/odp.html.

Rubber Stamps of America. (2002). Retrieved July 12, 2002, from http://www.stampusa.com.

San Diego Convention Center Corporation. (2002). 2002 annual report. Retrieved July 12, 2002, from http://www.sdccc.org/sdcccorp/impact/impact2.html.

Simon's Stamps. (2002). Retrieved July 12, 2002, from http://www.simonstamp.com.

Staples, Inc. (2002). 2001 annual report. Retrieved July 12, 2002, from http://ccbn8.mobular.net/ccbn/7/84/93/.

Westfield Shoppingtown Horton Plaza. (2002). Retrieved July 12, 2002, from http://www.westfield.com/us/centres/california/hortonplaza/.

US Census Bureau. (2002). Census 2000. Retrieved July 12, 2002, from http://factfinder.census.gov/servlet/QTTable?ds_name = D&geo_id = 05000US06073&qr_name = DEC_2000_SF1_U_DP1&lang = en.

CHAPTER - 9

Report Writing: From Formal Documents to Short Summaries

In the business world, report writing is a common activity. Reports may cover short meetings, analyses of customers' relationships with your company, or problems your company may be facing with manufacturing, or they may summarize the work your company accomplished under a contract won by a proposal.

At first the job of writing a report may seem overwhelming. Like other types of writing, however, it becomes easier if it is broken into small parts. This chapter introduces you to report writing and discusses several report forms, ranging from formal documents to short executive memos. After reading the sections of this chapter on the preparation and writing of reports, you will find that the job of report writing will become much easier.

Understanding the Nature of a Report

What Is a Report?

A report is the compilation of information that has been sought out, collected, sifted, organized, and written to convey a specific message. The objective is generally either to present information or to research a particular situation. Consequently, reports can be broadly categorized into information reports and research reports.

The Information Report

An information report may present a record of previous events, or it may periodically cover past and new information that will allow readers to stay current on a topic, see progress on a project, or gain insight on product development. The purpose of the information report is to convey ideas and data as clearly, concisely, correctly, and quickly as possible. Sales reports and quarterly finance reports are informative.

The Research Report

A research report is concerned with analyzing information, presenting the findings of the research, and then offering possible recommendations. Thus, two objectives of the research report are to *analyze* and make *recommendations*. In a report that analyzes data the writer looks at a problem that needs to be solved, gathers the data, analyzes the available data, arrives at a decision, and then makes recommendations. Annual reports, audit reports, and payback reports are all analytical.

The research process is much like that described in Chapter 8 on proposal writing and Chapter 15 on the case study method. Research reports may solve merchandising or production problems, offer remedies for better ways of financing an organization, or give insight into anticipated acts by competitors. The writer hopes that the reader of a research report will desire to take some action as a result of the new information gained from the report. Reports that follow the recommendation process are feasibility reports, justification reports, and problem-solving reports.

What Initial Questions Should You Ask?

Five critical things to know before you write a report are the purpose of the report, who the readers will be, what information the readers will need, what resources are available, and how you should organize your research findings. Knowing this information will help you save time and energy, and will ensure that your report accomplishes your objective. With this information in mind you will be ready to develop your topic, find and organize your resources, and then write the report.

What Is the Purpose of the Report?

Before you invest time in writing a report you need to determine the reason for writing it. Have you been assigned a topic to explore? Do you have a client you are trying to convince to use a product or service? Are you a researcher who has invented a product or process and you want others to see the benefit of your effort? Your first task is to determine why a report is needed, and the objective of that report. Understanding the purpose will help you decide how to research, organize, and write the report.

Who Will Read the Report?

After determining the purpose of the report you should then determine who will read the finished product. Knowledge about your readership will help you find the right information, develop it to meet the reader's needs, and determine the type of report format to use. In addition to your primary readers, also consider any secondary readers to whom the report may be distributed.

Upward reports carry information such as progress on production facilities or product lines, status factors, anticipated problems, requests for personnel or budgetary support, financial data, and projected business conditions. Downward reports more often take the form of policy statements, procedures of action, and decisions of which employees need to be aware.

If you find that the primary readers are on your organizational level, the report is likely to contain information to be used by others in preparing additional reports. This situation often occurs in marketing and production realms. Some reports are often intended for other companies, competitors, and the public. As you consider your readers, develop answers to the following questions:

- Are my readers likely to be receptive, indifferent, or resistant?
- If there are several readers, will their reactions differ?
- How technical can I be?

What Information Does the Reader Need?

In Chapter 4 we discussed the importance of analyzing your audiences. As you prepare for report writing the necessity of knowing your audience becomes critical. Does your reader merely want some new information? What can you share with the reader that cannot be gotten elsewhere? Does your reader need to make major decisions about a product, service, or program? What information can you provide that will serve to persuade that reader? The clearer you are about the reader's needs, the more effective you can be in doing your research and in designing your findings to meet those needs. As you think about this area answer the following questions:

- What is the reader's role?
- What does the reader know about the subject?
- How will the reader react?
- What is my reader's style? Should I adjust to it?
- How will the reader use this document?
- If the reader were to forget everything else, what one key point do I want remembered?[1]

What Research Resources Are Available?

When you know your reader's needs, you must find a way of meeting those needs. Where will you find your information? From what sources can it be collected (public, employees, customers, files, experiments, documentation)? How can the information be collected in the easiest and most cost-effective manner? Start with your mission for meeting the reader's needs, your personal curiosity, and the tools, techniques, and resources you have obtained in school and from this book. In this chapter we will give you some additional ideas for successful researching.

How Should the Information Be Organized?

After the research has been conducted the hard part of assembling it together in written form must take place. How should you organize and format the material to ensure that your reader will understand and comprehend it? A large portion of this chapter is designed to give you ideas for organizing and writing your report.

Five critical things to know before you write a report are: the purpose of the report, who the readers will be, what information the readers will need, what resources are available, and how you should organize your research findings. Knowing this information will help you save time and energy, and will ensure that your report accomplishes your objective. With this information in mind you will be ready to develop your topic, find and organize your resources, and then write the report.

A review of Chapter 4 is in order at this point. It discusses the process that advanced writers go through in defining the problem, determining the audience, matching the message to the medium, doing the research, considering the layout, drafting the message, and editing and producing the final product. Refer to Chapter 4 as you research and write your report.

Organizing Your Ideas

Develop Your Purpose

By this time you should know the purpose of the report that you will write. In your classroom assignment, it may be the major issue presented in the assigned case. At work, it may be a new product on which you are seeking to eliminate the design problems. It may be key to the question your customer has asked regarding how your product or service is not only different, but also better than what he is currently using. Regardless of the situation, it is usually easy to start from a problem-solving mode. Most problems that we encounter can be solved with a five-step process: define the key problem, describe the main dimensions of the key problem, determine the causes of the problem, describe alternative ways of dealing with the causes of the problems, and determine the best action to solve the problem.

With this five-step process in mind develop a good problem statement. "A problem statement is a specific declaration that summarizes the point of view you will express in your paper. It is the basic stand you take, the opinion you express and the point you will make about your narrowed subject. It's your controlling idea, tying together and giving direction to all other elements in your paper. Your primary purpose is to convince the reader that your thesis is a valid one."[2]

A good problem statement will be specific and restrictive, and will unify and express one major idea about the specific subject. Problem statements are not the same as topics. The problem statement will likely appear in the final report, and if so, should be placed early in the report. It will demonstrate to the reader the rationale for the report, and the value in reading it.

For example, your topic may be job-sharing. Your general purpose may be to simply inform. Developed into a problem statement it becomes: "Teach employees how to share knowledge and skills by job-sharing." Your main idea when developed might be: "Efficient job-sharing by employees saves the company time and money."

Organize Your Scope

The overall scope of your writing should match your main idea and purpose. Your scope is determined by how much information your reader will need, how much information you are able to find, and the limitations of your report (time and space). While you may start with a general idea of all that you will cover, often you will make adjustments because of the amount of research data that you can uncover, or the time limits of preparing your report.

Start by grouping your ideas around your main point. You can do this through a variety of methods. *Brainstorming* allows you to pour out as many ideas as possible without having any relative order to the flow. Your main idea may be "to propose the purchase of 20 new computers for the office." Figure 9.1 shows the result of brainstorming on a sheet of paper. This nonlinear method allows for a spontaneous way of thinking, free association of ideas, and ease in seeing relationships. This method can be as simple or as detailed as one desires to make it. Instead of the free-flow brainstorming process you might want to develop ideas on index cards, sticky notes, or a typed outline.

Categorize Your Initial Ideas

From the free-flow process of idea **generation** you need to move to idea **organization**. Grouping ideas into likeness by category is one of the easiest ways of doing

Figure 9.1	Initial Idea Brainstorming

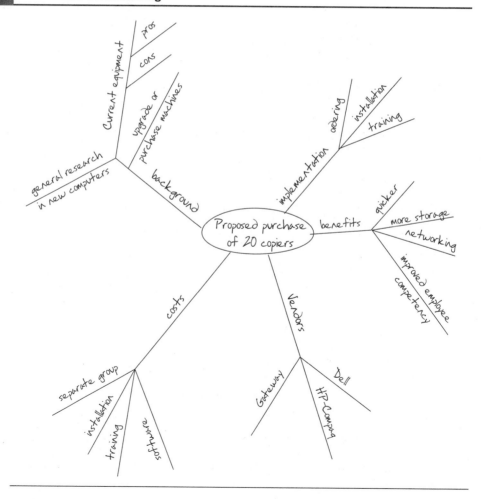

that. Following the categorization you can prioritize the numerous categories. A few of the **generic** categories are: proposal, request for action, rationale for action, process explanation, situation description, sequence of events, analysis of findings, implementation plan, and recommendations. Depending upon your general purpose, the material within each category will be different. Here are two examples of how your free-flow information could be grouped into general categories:[3]

Meeting Announcement
- Meeting time and place
- Agenda: list of topics
- Speakers and topics
- Background information

Performance Analysis
- Background
- Task analysis
- Comparison with previous process
  - Similarities
  - Differences
- Problems detected
  - Problems description
- Possible cause of problems
  - Suggested solutions
  - People
  - Costs
- Time commitment
  - Necessary change needed
  - Date for change occurrence
  - Date of next evaluation

Put Ideas in Sequential Order

From your initial categorization you should now move to make sure your ideas are in an organized sequence to properly balance both the reader's need and your desired intention. From here you will move to research and gather your information and determine whether it will actually fit your initial idea outline. At this point it is a good idea to review the concept of classification in Chapter 4. The concept will be mentioned again in Chapter 10. Several of the more popular development areas are listed below.[4] It is always a good idea to tell your audience that you are following a classification process, unless it is obvious.

Inductive order. Start with examples, facts, or reasons. Use them to lead the reader to the conclusion they imply. This format is ideal for long segments of information. It is also ideal for readers who are uninformed on a topic, or when employees are resistant to a change idea. "For example, a report written to convince management to fund an employee fitness program might begin with the advantages of a fitness program: improved job satisfaction, reduced absenteeism and turnover, improved productivity, and lower health care costs. After describing the benefits, the report writer could draw the conclusion that a company-sponsored fitness program is a wise investment. Starting with the main idea first risks the chance that readers opposed to the idea will read no further."[5]

Deductive order. You will want to make use of this direct approach to grouping information when your readers are well informed about your topic. In the deductive sequence you get right to the point. You put the main idea first and follow it with examples, reasons, and clarification. Your ease in making use of this style in the organization stage will help you when you start writing. Good report writing requires following a deductive pattern, especially in the writing of the executive summary, because it presents information in a clear and open way. In the writing stage it is also referred to as a form of journalistic writing, where the main ideas are always put up front and any material that is potentially unnecessary is placed toward the end.

Order of location. Discussing a variety of different things, all connected, are what this sequence is about. For example, a report on employee policies might discuss how new policies will be introduced at each company location, in a particular sequence.

Order of increasing difficulty. Normally a sequence of tasks will start with the easiest step and then move on to the more difficult areas. Computer instruction manuals use this format.

Sequential order. This order is used when writing a set of instructions. Since equipment must be installed in a certain order, this is the best process to follow.

Beneficial order. Examining advantages and disadvantages is a common part of the manager's job. Likewise looking at a list of possible actions and grouping them from most important to least important, or least important to most important, or best to worst, is a common process. Discussing the pros and cons of software packages or the reasoned options for a training program all fall under this organization pattern.

Chronological order. When material is introduced there is a starting and ending point. This ordering records behavior or events in the order of occurrence. Histories, sales reports, installation stages, product time lines, and progress reports all use a method of describing a series of events by using this format.

Problem-Solution order. Here the writer states the problem and then discusses the seriousness of the problem, identifying the causes. Possible solutions are identified and analyzed from an advantage/disadvantage position. Eventually one best solution is selected and recommendations made. Case studies make use of this approach, as do production reports.

Traditional order. In this sequence the writer follows a line of reasoning that has been used by the organization for some period of time. The belief is "we just do it this way," and thus all reports will have a resemblance.

Cost order. The flow of information here follows from least expensive to most expensive, or from most to least.

Create an Outline

From the categorization and sequencing of ideas the writer needs to move to creating a working outline. The outline will serve as a framework with boundaries that will help you as you conduct your research and then write your report. The outline may change as you proceed with your research. The categorization process used above makes for an easy transition into a sequenced outline. Outlines allow you to separate material into major and minor areas and then put those areas into a logical sequence. Figure 9.2 displays two approaches to outlining: alphabetic and numeric. The former is used more in general managerial business reports, while the numeric tends to be favored by technical writers. While some reports may carry the actual alphabetic and numeric postings within the finished copy, most reports will substitute headings for those designations.

Use Headings and Subheadings

The use of headings and subheadings is preferred, over alphabetic and numeric listings, because the words used will actually describe the contents of the paragraphs that follow. There are several advantages to using headings.

- They help the reader get the intended message.
- They make information easier to find, especially when skimming or browsing.
- They tend to add creativity and take the boredom out of writing.

When you use headings in your reports keep some simple rules in mind. When using second-level headings make sure you never use only one. Have at least two subdivisions (A and B). Treat headings at each level in a consistent manner: Observe capitalization, underlining, boldface, and font-change style listings.

Figure 9.2 | **Common Outline Forms**

ALPHABETIC OUTLINE	NUMERIC OUTLINE
I. First Major Point	1. First Major Point
A. First subpoint	1.1 First subpoint
B. Second subpoint	1.2 Second subpoint
1. Evidence	1.2.1 Evidence
2. Evidence	1.2.2 Evidence
a. Detail	1.2.2.1 Detail
b. Detail	1.2.2.2 Detail
3. Evidence	1.2.3 Evidence
C. Third subpoint	1.3 Third subpoint
II. Second Major Point	2. Second Major Point
A. First subpoint	2.1 First subpoint
1. Evidence	2.1.1 Evidence
2. Evidence	2.1.2 Evidence
B. Second subpoint	2.2 Second subpoint

Conduct Your Data Search

After you develop your topic and problem statement, and you have your initial outline, you should start your research. Think broadly at this point. As Wertheim suggests, "[I]t is best to *think inductively*. . . . Deductive logic involves starting with a conclusion or generalization and drawing particular implications from that generalization. Inductive reasoning follows the reverse order; it moves from the particular to the general. It leads to a conclusion rather than drawing from a conclusion."[6] Inductive research is where we start with most business problems; we analyze information and eventually reach a conclusion. That means we search for examples, facts, or reasons that will lead us to solid conclusions. With that in mind we begin our data-gathering.

Gathering the Data

Report writing often becomes time-consuming because of this particular step. Gathering sufficient data can take hours and even days. Thomas Edison once advised, "The first thing is to find out everything everybody else knows, and then begin where they left off." Your data may come from personal observations, experiments, books, questionnaires, interviews, financial records, or a variety of other sources.

The data may be primary—those generated by the researcher for the explicit purpose of the research—or secondary—any material already generated for another purpose but usable for the research. Discretionary readers are concerned about the sources that a writer uses. Primary documents can include items like surveys, questionnaires, observations, and scientific experimentations. All secondary sources—items like company records, current business survey conclusions, or census information—depend on the accuracy and validity of their sources for credibility. Always remember that the statements you make are only as strong as your source.

As you gather your data, constantly analyze and question the interpretations that you find. Question your material: Is it relevant? Is it accurate? Is it fairly representative? Is it timely? And most important: Is it necessary? Figure 9.3 presents an overview of some of the basic ways research information is collected. Before any of those methods are used most business researchers turn to electronic information sources. Again, Chapter 4 offers excellent information about electronic research. Review it for a better understanding of the following section.

Electronic Information Sources

As an advanced business student you have undoubtedly done abundant research on the Internet. There are two primary ways of conducting the research. The first is through excellent search engines such as Google or Lycos. This research can be done in your home as well as in a library. The second method is through the use of excellent electronic information databases that are primarily available in the libraries of most colleges, universities, and public libraries. Most of these resources allow for quick and extensive searches on a wide variety of topics.

Electronic resources change continually. Depending upon your institution, you may access the identical information using a Web browser, such as Internet Explorer or Netscape, or you may use an interface designed by the database producer or third-party database provider. A local or remote server may store the information.

Figure 9.3   Research Information Collection

Method	Overall Purpose	Advantages	Challenges
questionnaires, surveys, lists	• quick information gathered in non-threatening way	• complete anonymously • administer inexpensively • easy to compare/analyze • administer to many • collect lots of data	• are impersonal • can get biased responses • additional information is not obtained
interviews	• first-hand report • goes beyond survey	• can develop relationship • can be flexible • gather wider/deeper information	• time-consuming • hard to analyze • costly • interviewer bias
documentation	• review applications, finances, memos, etc.	• comprehensive data • obtains history • information exists • few biases	• can be time-consuming • info may be incomplete • need clarity in search • inflexible data retrieval • existing-data restriction
observation	• gather accurate info about actual operation	• view actions as occur • adapt to events as occur	• can be difficult to interpret behavior • complex categorization • can influence behavior • can be expensive
focus groups	• explore topic via in-depth group discussion • reactions, suggestions • used in marketing	• quick, reliable • range/depth of info in short time	• can be hard to analyze • good facilitation needed • difficult to schedule 6–8 people
case studies	• gain broad understanding	• excellent coverage of experiences • powerful learning	• time-consuming to collect, organize, describe • depth of information, not breadth

Source: Adapted from: McNamara, C. (n.d.). Brief overview of basic methods to collect information. Retrieved July 15, 2002, from **http://www.mapnp.org/library/research/overview.htm**.

Database providers and your institution's library or information center will offer training sessions, either as workshops or in conjunction with your courses, to help you get your search started. By taking the time to participate in brief workshops, you will save hours of time in the future. You can devote that time you save to analyzing your data and developing your reports, papers, and presentations.

Be sure to use the InfoTrac source provided when you purchased your textbook. This resource offers hundreds of thousands of articles on numerous topics.

It is easy to learn and use. We include at least one InfoTrac assignment with each chapter in this book.

It is also helpful to realize that electronic information resources are similar. Before you begin using a new service or searching a new database, you need to ask these questions: What is the content of the resource? Does it provide full-text information or only references to resources? Is the full text only text or are materials such as tables, graphs, and illustrations also available online? If you need retrospective information, how many years of information are available? How do you narrow or broaden a search? Does the system support Boolean operators (AND, OR, NOT) and truncation? In what order do my search results display: relevance ranked, by date, alphabetical order?

The following list augments what was described in Chapter 4 on pages 98–102. This list serves only as a starting point for your next research project.

Databases

Online services that organize material into giant collections of information are called databases. They require special protocols that are different from ordinary Web search engines. They are designed to help researchers run searches and retrieve valuable information from a large variety of sources. Sites that aggregate content allow you to search hundreds of sources at once, through a single search. They require setting up an account with a user ID or password. While your university library usually pays the access fees, you may be required to pay for any articles that you download. Depending upon the amount of research that you have to do, this charge may well be worth the time it would take you to search all the individual publication sites.[7]

- **ABI/Inform.** This database, updated monthly, indexes over 2,000 worldwide business and management periodicals. Subject areas include accounting, banking, data processing, organizational behavior, management science, marketing, advertising, sales, real estate, public administration, new product development, and telecommunications. It is backfiled from 1971. Full citations and abstracts are available for all references. Full text articles are available for approximately 500 publications.

- **Bloomberg.** This provides live, around-the-clock coverage of the national and international governments, corporations, industries, and financial markets. Bloomberg transmits 3,000 news stories daily and appears in over 160 newspapers throughout the Americas, Europe, the Middle East, and the Pacific Rim. It is designed so that researchers can instantly access all news, research, securities, pricing, and research reports directly through a single source.

- **Business Dateline.** This product is updated monthly and provides access to hard-to-find, regional business information. It covers most of the same subject areas as ABI Inform from 535 local, state, and regional business publications. These articles are the full text of the publication. Press releases from Business Wire provide a corporate perspective on events and people. Back files to 1985 are available. Updated weekly.

- **Compustat PC Plus.** This source contains 20 years of annual, 12 years of quarterly, seven years of business and geographic segment, and 240 months of stock prices and dividend data for over 10,300 U.S. and Canadian companies. It also has data for over 7,600 inactive companies no longer filing with the SEC because of merger, liquidation, or bankruptcy.

- **Dialog.** This comprehensive information resource computer-based, online system contains over 450 separate databases. The databases contain more than 120 million records and provide information ranging from a directory-type listing of companies, associations, or famous people to in-depth financial statements on a particular company. Citations, abstracts, conference papers, and complete texts of journal articles are available. Tradeline is available through Dialog.

- **Dialog Business Connection.** This service allows access to more than 11 million U.S., Canadian, and European companies. About 40 of these databases have been pulled together to form the Dialog Business Connection. Financial profiles, late-breaking news stories, investment research reports, and more are brought together in a menu system. The information in this service can be accessed by industry, product, or company. There is no subject approach. On-screen instructions or a hard copy manual, usually available at the library, guide you through this database.

- **Disclosure SEC Database.** This product consists of business and financial information extracted from 10K reports, which public companies file with the SEC. It includes all financial statements (three to seven years for comparison purposes), subsidiaries, description of the business, officers and directors, stock information, president's letter, and management discussion for over 11,000 public companies. Financial data can be converted to files that can be imported as numbers directly into spreadsheets.

- **Factiva.** This service provides business and financial data on nearly 10 million U.S. and international companies in more than 80 industries. Researchers can review financial reports on public and private companies; research corporate families and ownership structures worldwide; access SEC filings, 10Ks, and 10Qs; track the activities of the major stock exchanges; and gain insight into emerging markets information. Dow Jones provides access to more than 6,000 business, trade, and general publications, including *The Wall Street Journal.*

- **Dun's Million Dollar Database.** This database provides comprehensive business information on 1,260,000 U.S. public and private companies. Lists are limited to companies with $25 million or more in sales, or 50 or more employees, or a net worth of $500,000 or more. File records can be searched by geographical area, primary and secondary SIC codes, annual sales, and number of employees. This is a useful tool for job searching.

- **FirstSearch.** This offers access to a number of business and economic databases useful to business researchers: Articles 1st, Contents 1st, ERIC, the GPO Monthly Catalog, and WorldCat, an electronic card catalog of 24 million bibliographic records representing the holdings of 13,000 libraries worldwide.

- **InfoTrac Business ASAP.** This product contains bibliographic references to and abstracts of articles from more than 400 business, management, and trade publications, including *The Wall Street Journal, The New York Times,*

Asian Wall Street Journal, and *Financial Times of Canada*. Full-text access is provided to approximately 50 percent of the periodicals indexed. It is updated monthly.

- **LEXIS-NEXIS.** This service provides accesses to over 22,000 business, legal, news, and reference resources. Most institutional subscriptions will provide full-text access to national and international newspapers; business periodicals, including magazines, regional business journals, trade publications, and newsletters; company and financial information; statistical sources, and business directories.

- **Hoover's Inc.** Hoover's offers basic directory information, public domain materials such as 10K reports, and in-depth analysis of over 16,000 world-wide public and private companies. A unique feature is the list of competitors accompanying each profile. Hoover's Online on the Internet provides direct links to company sites and recent newspaper and magazine articles about the company.

- **Million Dollar Database Premier.** This Internet subscription site is used to search public and private companies, specific companies, or specific industries. You can search by size or new markets by using multiple selection criteria. It will list potential prospects or prospective employers in a targeted market, identify key decision-makers so you can contact them directly, and search executive biographies for hard-to-find information.

- **Moody's Company Data Direct.** This link provides immediate access to fully searchable data on more than 10,000 NYSE, AMEX, NASDAQ, and other select regional exchange companies. All financials are "as reported," providing balance sheets, income statements, expenditures, assets, liabilities, and cash-flow performance trends.

- **Moody's Investors Services.** This service provides information on national and international companies. Information available may include company histories, products, income sheets, and balance statements. The breadth of resources available at a single location is subscription based.

- **Morningstar Mutual Funds Ondisc.** This product provides such items as description and analysis, basic operating facts, and several years of statistics for total return, income, capital gains, and performance/risk factors.

- **Standard & Poor's Stock Corp.** Nine popular publications are searchable: Stock Reports, Industry Surveys, Corporation Records, Register, Stock Guide, Bond Guide, Earnings Guide, The Outlook, and Dividend Record. The breadth of resources will vary with individual institution's subscriptions.

- **The Wall Street Journal.** This is a full-text product containing every article including daily stock market reports, finance, investment, and business-oriented news. Its coverage is from 1984 and is updated monthly.

Writers who frequently produce reports should be aware of one major problem with the use of secondary material, which arises frequently, particularly in management and engineering consulting firms. The problem is called "boilerplating." Boilerplating occurs when individuals do similar work for different clients. Once a report is produced for one client it is filed, only to be reviewed later and often borrowed from so heavily that the new product does not fully communicate the message the writer wants and needs to convey.

Today, managers no longer have to save the hard copies of memos and reports and labor over them, gleaning the data they need to make reports. With computers and central integrated databases, information can be stored in single files and used in numerous ways.

Gramma describes three basic types of reports that can be generated by a computer and by the use of a database: performance analysis reports, exception reports, and special analysis reports. Periodically scheduled performance reports for marketing, finance, and manufacturing can be automatically accessed, processed, printed, or electronically distributed to readers. With graphics software, the data can even be organized to show interrelationships.

Database analysis also makes it easy to pull out exceptional information that falls outside the norm of usual business activity. Exceptionally high or low performance by individuals, lack of inventory movement, and wide fluctuation of prices are a few examples of exceptional information. Computer programs can be written to automatically generate reports when exceptional information becomes available. Likewise, managers can use databases to create special analysis reports on a wide variety of subject areas.[8]

Report Format

After you have researched your topic and have gathered your data, it is time to consider the way your finished report will look. This section covers three different formats: informal, semiformal, and formal. Two things determine formality: wants and need of your readers, and the amount of information that you must present to meet those needs.

The Informal Report

The informal report is the type most frequently used in business. This report can extend from a one-page letter or memo to several typed pages that are produced inexpensively for distribution. The topics are usually less important business issues: for example, status reports, progress reports, laboratory reports, design reports, trip evaluations, training analysis, and minor requests. The author knows the reader and does not want the many formalities of a long, formal report to get in the way of presenting information quickly. The focus of the information is usually on the text material (problem, solutions, methods, findings, conclusions, and recommendations). The writing style can be informal, contractions are appropriate, and the entire report carries a more conversational tone than either the formal or semiformal reports. Informal reports, especially in memo and e-mail formats, generally stay within the organization.

Figure 9.4 presents an example of an informal report. The staff of the Defense Nuclear Facilities Safety Board (DNFSB) prepared the report after it reviewed safety management at the Los Alamos National Laboratory. The report is written in a formal governmental tone, and yet it is informally prepared as a memo to the Technical and Deputy Technical Directors of the Los Alamos National Laboratory.

Figure 9.4   **Informal Report Example**

DEFENSE NUCLEAR FACILITIES SAFETY BOARD

Staff Issue Report

April 15, 1999

MEMORANDUM FOR: G. W. Cunningham, Technical Director
J. K. Fortenberry, Deputy Technical Director
COPIES: Board Members
FROM: D. Burnfield
SUBJECT: Review of Worker Protection Practices at Los Alamos
National Laboratory

This report documents the results of reviews of the implementation of worker protection practices at the Los Alamos National Laboratory (LANL), and highlights noteworthy practices and specific areas in which improvements may be possible, based on the staff's observations during the reviews.

These reviews examined the implementation of activity-level worker protection practices in the work planning for research and development (R&D) and facility projects for defense activities at LANL. The reviews included discussions with representatives of the Department of Energy (DOE) Los Alamos Area Office (LAAO), presentations by and discussions with responsible LANL staff, and walk-throughs of several projects in TA-55. The most recent review was conducted during April 5–8, 1999, by members of the staff of the Defense Nuclear Facilities Safety Board (Board), D. Burnfield, A. Jordan, and M. Helfrich, assisted by outside expert D. Volgenau. A previous review was led by J. Troan in August 1998.

Implementation of Safe Work Practices for R&D. LANL management is vigorously pursuing the implementation of an Integrated Safety Management System (ISMS). LANL developed Laboratory Performance Requirements (LPRs) and Laboratory Implementing Requirements (LIRs) to implement contractual requirements. These documents are supplemented by Laboratory Implementing Guidance (LIG) documents. Deviation from the LPRs and LIRs is permitted, through a formal approval process. LANL management is working to ensure that the principal investigators for R&D projects recognize their responsibility to conduct work safely. This is a strong underlying theme of the Safe Work Practices (SWP) LIRs, which are intended to implement an ISMS for R&D work.

LANL Documentation—The SWP LIRs impose significant responsibilities on the workers but do not, in our view, contain sufficient guidance to enable them to meet those responsibilities. An objective of the SWP LIRs is to ensure that principal investigators and line managers/supervisors retain responsibility for the safety of R&D work. While this objective is commendable, the requirements must be carefully and completely stated to ensure that the desired results are achieved. The LIRs require that a Hazard Control Plan (HCP) be written whenever new controls are developed, existing controls are modified, or established documentation is not adequate to communicate the hazards posed by the work. The HCP documents the hazards control system for a particular work activity. Workers are to use it directly in the field. However, the LIRs do not adequately describe the purpose and intended use of the HCP. Upon examination of a number of sample HCPs, the staff noted that this lack of specificity resulted in inconsistent HCPs that provide insufficient documentation to ensure that the activity-level safety envelope can be maintained. Additional guidance (i.e, LIGs) and improved LIRs are needed to provide the necessary flexibility and yet document the hazards analysis and implementation of controls to ensure worker safety.

The LIRs contain a matrix designed to assist in estimating risk for an activity. The matrix requires the planner to estimate risk for each combination of severity and likelihood. The estimated risks are used to establish the levels of review and line management authorization. However, in order to allow the researcher to categorize activities or hazards consistently, additional guidance may be necessary in the LIRs. Guidance and examples for selecting the frequency category for the types of research tasks normally performed would be beneficial, as would guidance for determining consequences. For example, the guidance could define the risk category for potential scenarios such as a fall from a height of 6 feet, a radiation exposure of 50 rem, or work in a glovebox containing gram level quantities of plutonium.

The LIRs could benefit from more emphasis on the effective use of integrated teams to plan work. Planning is done routinely in a serial manner. The use of environment, safety, and health (ES&H) subject matter experts (SMEs) is mentioned as a mechanism for providing assistance rather than being integral to a team approach. Also, the LIRs do not identify that an SME in an area other than ES&H might be appropriate. An interdependent team relationship for all tasks (both R&D and Facility work) not within the well-defined skill of a researcher/worker has proven successful at other sites.

Figure 9.4   **Informal Report Example (Continued)**

The LIRs could benefit from additional guidance on how to select and document the methodologies to be used for hazards analysis. If the researchers are tasked to make these decisions, they need to be provided the necessary tools. In order to assist the researchers, an annotated list of acceptable hazard analysis techniques (such as can be found in the Center for Chemical Process Safety Guidelines for Hazard Evaluation Procedures) could be developed to provide flexibility and assist the workers to choose the technique best suited for the activity. Given appropriate guidance, the researchers could develop and use their own techniques, provided they retained the documentation of the methodology. Presently, however, formal activity level hazards analyses are not routinely being conducted for R&D work activities.

The LIRs require that each organization inventory its work activities. However, the LIRs do not specify the purpose and intended use of these inventories. Review of completed work activity inventories by various groups has revealed a lack of completeness, detail, and consistency.

Performance of Hazards Analysis—TSA-11, the LANL Probabilistic Risk and Analysis Group, does qualitative as well as quantitative hazards analysis in support of DOE and LANL missions. The group has a wide range of analysis capabilities and is staffed by experienced people. However, the group participates in activity-level hazards analyses only when specifically requested. The Lab might benefit from enlarging its role and assignments. For example, this organization could serve as mentors and help develop hazards analysis tools and techniques for use by researchers on R&D projects.

Feedback and Improvement—The process for capturing lessons learned from R&D work activities is not yet mature. Although LANL personnel share information internally from such sources as periodic management walkarounds, occurrences, and new directives, there is no program for capturing the lessons learned from individual work activities.

ISMS Training—Safe Work Practices training was to be provided to personnel likely to be assigned responsibility for developing or modifying controls to mitigate R&D work hazards, as well as to line managers who might authorize work once controls are in place. More than 2000 people have been trained, yet no evaluation was performed to determine whether all appropriate personnel have been trained; and there is no plan to conduct continuing training or training for new hires. Review of the training plan indicated many strengths. A significant strong point was the use of varied analysis techniques beyond job hazards analysis to analyze workplace hazards, together with examples of their use.

Figure 9.4 | **Informal Report Example (Continued)**

Implementation of SWP by Nuclear Materials Technology (NMT). The NMT Division requested and was granted a variance from the requirements of the SWP LIRs. As justification, NMT stated that the Division's existing activity level work control processes met or exceeded the major implementing criteria of the LIRs. For the conduct of R&D work, the NMT Division uses a combination of documents mandated by recently issued internal divisional procedures. These documents, which include safe operating procedures (SOPs), experimental plans, and special work permits, provide for written work authorization and are intended for field use. They are used to identify the hazards and controls associated with potentially hazardous R&D-related activities.

The Board's staff reviewed the NMT procedures and a sample of the documents associated with work in TA-55. The following observations resulted from this review:

- NMT requires process hazards analysis for all R&D activities. Although aspects of the associated process hazards analysis did flow down to the controls section of the SOP, there was no indication that specific activity level hazards analyses were routinely conducted to ensure that proper controls were developed and implemented. In addition, the SOPs reviewed did not always have a one-to-one correlation between controls identified in the hazards identification section of the procedure and those in the body of the procedure.

- Each SOP contained a training lesson plan. However, it appeared that individuals were not trained on all the hazards identified in the hazards identification and controls implementation sections in the procedure. Nor is there currently a provision for determining whether the knowledge, skills, and abilities associated with an SOP activity have been retained when the workforce has not performed the activity for an extended period of time.

- The recently issued requirements permit review and updating of SOPs within 2 years or by the next scheduled review date, whichever occurs first. A review of three SOPs revealed that allowing these procedures to stand until the regularly scheduled update will not adequately ensure protection of the workforce. At least a cursory review of the SOPs is needed to reveal those that do not provide adequate protection.

Figure 9.4 | **Informal Report Example (Concluded)**

The Board's staff review of the implementation of safe work practices in NMT resulted in the following observations:

- TA-55 operators and principle investigators were interviewed regarding their responsibilities and knowledge of the processes. They were knowledgeable and appeared well qualified to execute their assigned responsibilities.

- In accordance with the ATLAS SOP, the operator uses data sheets containing abbreviated procedural steps to perform process operations. For each step on the data sheets a small space is provided in which the operator can make a comment or observation. The use of data sheets, without having the procedures readily available, is typical for most NMT operations. These data sheets do not stipulate the hazards or controls for the various operations. In addition, their use requires a detailed understanding of the procedure by the operator.

- Weaknesses in the manuals and codes of practice for hazard task-level screening, identification, and analysis for facility work in TA-55 were also noted during the August 1998 review. These documents could be improved in a manner similar to the LIRs and LPRs discussed above.

Conclusion. The staff considers that correction of the above will better ensure that hazards can be properly identified and analyzed, and adequate controls can be implemented. This will enable R&D and facility work to be conducted safely at the activity level with a higher degree of assurance.

Source: Burnfield, D. (n.d.). Defense nuclear facilities safety board: Staff issue report. Retrieved July 6, 2002, from http://www.deprep.org/1999/fb99126a.htm.

Copies of the memo were also sent to DNFSB members. The report highlights improvements the Board observed in its review, and practices it believed could be improved. While the concluding remarks call for improvements to be made, no timetable or deadline is made for such improvements.

The Semiformal Report

The semiformal report is longer than an informal one, yet shorter than the formal. It is typed and stapled together, although it can be informally bound. The readership for this form of report can be either small or large and is usually very targeted, as in the case of the numerous government reports completed daily. The report has a highly organized structure, is outlined, and uses major headings like those found in a formal report. However, this report carries a more informal tone and look. This report style is commonly used in daily business settings. Examples include task force reports, employee policy manuals, and regular research topics that do not include all the resource materials found in formal reports.

The Formal Report

Formal reports are usually long; they can contain all or several of the traditional elements listed in Figure 9.5. While the parts in that exhibit are listed in the customary order, few formal reports contain every part named there. Different organizations also take great liberty in rearranging report parts in different order, even deleting some parts and adding others, and in changing the names of the different parts. The report formalities and the appended parts contain material that supports the text, or body, of the report. The text portion introduces the report topic, displays the research approach, discloses the research findings, and then presents any recommendations.

Report Formalities
The various elements listed below all serve a distinct purpose for the formal report. This material introduces the reader to the report and gives an overview of what will be contained within the report content. The report formalities include: a cover page, a title page, an authorization page, the letter of transmittal, the table of contents, graphic and figures pages, and finally an executive summary. All the front-matter material found in the "formalities" section, with the exception of the cover page, should be numbered with lowercase Roman numerals.

Cover page. This lists the report title, name of the producer, and date of production. This information is usually typed to achieve a balance on the cover. The title uses a larger font than that used for the author's name and the date. Since the cover is the first thing that a reader will see, you should make it attractive. The use of color, visuals, and printing on quality card stock adds a special touch. Not every formal report will have a cover page; some start with the title page.

| Figure 9.5 | **Parts of a Traditional Formal Report** |

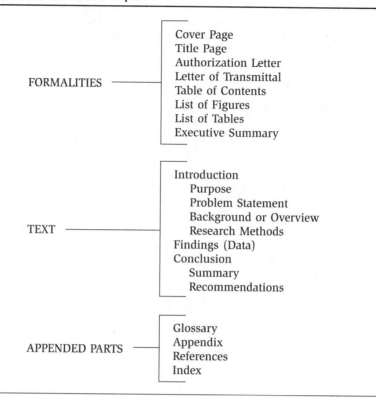

FORMALITIES
- Cover Page
- Title Page
- Authorization Letter
- Letter of Transmittal
- Table of Contents
- List of Figures
- List of Tables
- Executive Summary

TEXT
- Introduction
  - Purpose
  - Problem Statement
  - Background or Overview
  - Research Methods
- Findings (Data)
- Conclusion
  - Summary
  - Recommendations

APPENDED PARTS
- Glossary
- Appendix
- References
- Index

Title page. The title page gives the full report title, the names of the authors, the name of the company or person for whom the report was prepared, the date of transmission, and any related information. Figure 9.6 displays an example of a highly sought-after report from the Committee on Governmental Affairs concerning the behavior of the Enron Board of Directors.

Authorization letter. If included, this is a copy of the letter that shows that the report was originally requested. It serves as an authorization document to any secondary readers. Government organizations, consulting companies, and organizations that have been given grants to conduct research and then write a report will include such a letter in the final report. Figure 9.7 displays an authorization letter from the Chairman of the U.S. Defense Nuclear Facilities Safety Board (DNFSB) to the Deputy Secretary of the U.S. Department of Energy (DOE). This letter accompanies a report that the DNFSB has conducted on deficiencies in the software used at the DOE. The letter requests that the DOE conduct its own report into the software issue within 60 days.

| 107th Congress
2d Session | COMMITTEE | Report
107-70 |

THE ROLE OF
THE BOARD OF DIRECTORS IN
ENRON'S COLLAPSE

R E P O R T

PREPARED BY THE

PERMANENT SUBCOMMITTEE ON INVESTIGATIONS

OF THE

COMMITTEE ON GOVERNMENTAL AFFAIRS
UNITED STATES SENATE

JULY 8, 2002

Source: U.S. Senate Permanent Subcommittee on Investigation, Committee on Government Affairs. (2002, July 8). The role of the board of directors in Enron's collapse. Retrieved July 7, 2002, from **http://govt-aff.senate.gov/psi.htm**.

Figure 9.7 **Authorization Letter for a Formal Report**

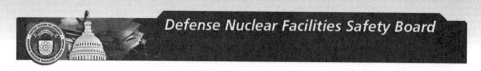

Defense Nuclear Facilities Safety Board

January 20, 2000

The Honorable T. J. Glauthier
Deputy Secretary of Energy
1000 Independence Avenue, SW
Washington, DC 20585-1000

Dear Mr. Glauthier:

Software quality assurance (SQA) is a process for the systematic development, testing, documentation, maintenance, and execution of software. The staff of the Defense Nuclear Facilities Safety Board (Board) has reviewed the status of SQA for software used to make safety-related design decisions and to control safety-related systems. The enclosed report, Quality Assurance for Safety-Related Software at Department of Energy Defense Nuclear Facilities, identifies deficiencies in SQA for both types of software. The report also describes problems with code execution resulting from a lack of guidance and training. The Board believes these problems are symptomatic of underlying deficiencies in the infrastructure supporting SQA at the Department of Energy (DOE), and they have a direct debilitating effect on safety activities in DOE.

The Board has been informed by its staff that the Quality Assurance Working Group within DOE has been aware of some of these issues since February, but that little progress has been made toward addressing these problems because no senior DOE leader has actively accepted responsibility for the function of SQA. The Board believes this to be precisely the type of important cross-cutting safety issue that could be resolved through actions by the DOE Safety Council.

Accordingly, pursuant to 42 U.S.C. § 2286b(d) the Board requests a report from DOE within 60 days of receipt of this letter that describes the actions that are needed to address the deficiencies and potential improvements identified in the enclosed report and the schedule for completing these actions.

If you have any questions on this matter, please do not hesitate to call me.

Sincerely,

John T. Conway
Chairman

c: Mr. Mark B. Whitaker, Jr.

Enclosure

Source: Letter covering Technical Report 25, Quality Assurance for Safety-Related Software at Department of Energy Defense Nuclear Facilities. (2000, January). Retrieved July 6, 2002, from **http://www.deprep.org/2000/fb00j20a.htm**.

Transmittal letter. This letter, often called a cover letter, officially sends the report to the person who requested it. If the report is mailed to the reader this letter will probably be attached to the outside of the cover page. If the report is sent internally within an organization, a memo will most likely be used instead of a letter. The letter has several purposes: to create a good initial impression of the sending organization, to briefly summarize the report and its conclusion and recommendations, to point out any interesting elements, and to describe any problems encountered. Since an individual personally writes the letter it usually carries a more informal tone.

Figure 9.8 shows a form letter used by the Farm Credit Administration (FCA) each time it issues a Report of Examination to one of its member banks. The FCA is an independent agency in the executive branch of the U.S. government. It is responsible for the regulation and examination of the banks that comprise the Farm Credit System. This generic letter, along with a report, goes to each bank that has been examined. The tone of the letter is formal. Each letter lists the component ratings that the receiving bank has been given. While a word of caution follows the ratings, placing such sensitive information bluntly in a transmittal written letter does not appear businesslike.

Contents page. The table of contents outlines, using headings and subheadings, the ordering of the parts of the report. It shows page numbers on which each part begins. This not only aids the reader in finding any desired parts, the outline serves as an analytical overview. The only items not included in the table of contents are the cover, title, and contents pages. Short reports normally list all levels of headings. Longer reports list only major headings.

Figure 9.9 presents an example of a table of contents. This was for an analysis conducted to determine the feasibility of developing and operating a technological center business incubation program in Kokomo, Indiana.

Tables, figures, illustrations, and photograph contents. Lists of this type are used in formal reports when numerous graphics are included. All nontext items within the body of the report are either tables or figures, unless they are combined and called illustrations. The format follows that of the contents page and lists the numbered items along with titles and page numbers.

The writer should refer to each table, figure, illustration, and photo in context in the report. When discussing it, first reference its name and then complete the paragraph. If space permits, insert the item; if not, start a new paragraph and then insert the item after that paragraph. A full-page item would be inserted on the page closest to its mention in the text. Insert the table or figure on the next page and continue the text on the page that follows.

When the reader must see the table or figure to understand the context, place it in the text. If not all readers need to see the items, or if they may be only a convenience to readers, place them in an appendix at the end of the report. Sometimes the appendix items will not be listed in the content page.

Tables are numbered sequentially with Arabic numbers, as are figures. Even if, say, a table appears between two figures, they would be called Table 1, Figure 1, and Figure 2. Figures and tables should be assigned a clear four- to eight-word title.

Figure 9.8 **Model Transmittal Letter for Formal Report**

Date

Mr. _____ , Chairman
Board of Directors
(Institution)
Street Address
City, State ZIP

Mr. _____ , Chief Executive Officer
(Institution)
Street Address
City, State ZIP

Dear Mr./Ms. __(Chairman's name)__ and Mr./Ms. __(CEO's name)__ :

This letter contains the Farm Credit Administration's (FCA) composite and component CAMEL ratings for the _____ Association/Bank based on the Report of Examination as of (date). These ratings are strictly for the confidential use of the board of directors and the chief executive officer. **Under no circumstances shall any person associated with the institution make public the composite or individual component ratings.**

The purpose of the FCA Rating System is to provide a uniform evaluation of the main characteristics of all Farm Credit System institutions and ensure a consistent examination and regulatory approach to institutions with similar risk. The FCA's composite rating definitions, factors considered in assigning component ratings, and other information pertaining to the FCA Rating System may be found in the FCA Examination Manual.

The _____ Association's/Bank's composite rating is "_____ ."
The individual CAMEL component ratings are:

____ Capital ____ Assets ____ Management ____ Earnings ____ Liquidity ____ Sensitivity

While these ratings provide some insight as to the overall condition of your institution, we urge the board of directors to address the conditions identified in the Report of Examination rather than focus on the ratings.

Representatives from our office will be available during the __(date)__ board meeting to discuss your institution's condition and the Report of Examination. We will discuss any questions you may have regarding the above ratings at that meeting. Should you have any questions regarding the contents of this letter or other matters pertinent to the examination prior to the scheduled meeting date, please contact me at __(phone number)__ .

Sincerely,

_____ , Director

_____ Field Office
Office of Examination

Source: Farm Credit Administration. (n.d.). FCA exam manual EM-199 Supplement 4, "Example ratings transmittal letter. Retrieved July 6, 2002, from **http://www.fca.gov/examman.nsf/d1df4b2d1f2289dc85256bea004af854/ 6fbda97edd332d54852561cd004d77bd?OpenDocument**.

Figure 9.9   **Table of Contents of Formal Report**

**The Kokomo Technology Center Business Incubation Program
Feasibility Analysis: April 2002**

Table of Contents

Source: Pittsburgh Gateways Corporation. (2002, April). Feasibility analysis report to Kokomo Technology Center, An analysis to determine the feasibility of developing and operating the Kokomo technology center business incubation program. Retrieved June 5, 2002, from **http://www.ktconline.org/**.

Executive Summary. This part of the report formalities tells the reader what the textual document is about. It is a miniature version of what the reader will read. This summary is called several things: abstract, synopsis, overview, or précis. When the word *abstract* is used, it usually indicates a technical audience. Abstracts are typically limited to a half-page. The term *executive summary* has come to be identified with managerial audiences. This summary differs from one found at the very end of a report. The executive summary is usually longer than one page but less than 10 percent of the overall report. Because this serves as an overview and not the overall report, the writer (or editor) must limit what goes in the executive summary.

There are two approaches to writing an executive summary. In the first approach, which is most widely used, the writer prepares a miniature edition of the body of the report. Concepts reviewed appear in the same order and in the same relative proportion as in the body. The second approach is interpretative. The writer might point out strengths, flaws, new information, or important implications of the report and may connect to other issues outside the report.

Figure 9.10 presents the executive summary of the U.S. Senate Subcommittee Report on the Enron Corporation Board of Directors. For a long, formal report, this summary is relatively short and encompasses only three areas: the background of the subcommittee investigation, the subcommittee's findings, and its recommendations.

An executive summary can stand alone as a short report. In fact, such a summary is the only thing some individuals in the intended audience will read. Because it presents the main points discussed in the report, it often communicates succinctly all the information a reader needs or wants. Any recommendations made in the report will be stated here. Because an executive might read only the summary and then make decisions, accuracy of information is essential. Illustrations and footnotes are generally not used. As an abstract this part of the report can serve as an enticement for what will follow.

Because of the concise way in which the executive summary presents a complete overview of the main report, it has come to serve as a stand-alone report, preferred by many executives to other types of reports. It is used between managers and subordinates, between sales personnel and customers, by consultants, and as a short report sent to the public. It can be created in memo, letter, informal, or semiformal style. There are two factors that make it an executive summary. The first is the typing of "Executive Summary" at the top of the report. The second is deductively moving the conclusions and recommendations to the front of the summary and placing a discussion of the analysis later into the report, often as appendix matter. Figure 9.11 gives an example of a stand-alone executive summary that is in outline form and takes an informal style. While at first this appears to be the minutes of a meeting, you will see the committee produced a report of its yearly work, and this was the executive summary of the report.

Long, formal reports use the inductive process that many refer to as suspense-oriented. Starting with an introduction, it weaves through a purpose statement, methodology description, data findings, conclusions, and recommendations. The real news of the report arrives for the reader in the conclusion and recommendation stages. In some reports, this may not happen until page 200 or 300. Because most managers are burdened with too much to read, they need a method of receiving information quickly. The deductive method is preferred. It starts with placing the real news first and then giving general information that is needed.

THE ROLE OF
THE BOARD OF DIRECTORS IN ENRON'S COLLAPSE

SUBCOMMITTEE INVESTIGATION

On December 2, 2001, Enron Corporation, then the seventh largest publicly traded corporation in the United States, declared bankruptcy. That bankruptcy sent shock waves throughout the country, both on Wall Street and Main Street where over half of American families now invest directly or indirectly in the stock market. Thousands of Enron employees lost not only their jobs but a significant part of their retirement savings; Enron shareholders saw the value of their investments plummet; and hundreds, if not thousands of businesses around the world, were turned into Enron creditors in bankruptcy court likely to receive only pennies on the dollars owed to them.

On January 2, 2002, Senator Carl Levin, Chairman of the Permanent Subcommittee on Investigations and Senator Susan M. Collins, the Ranking Minority Member, announced that the Subcommittee would conduct an in-depth investigation into the collapse of the Enron Corporation. The following month the Subcommittee issued over 50 subpoenas to Enron Board members, Enron officers, the Enron Corporation and the Arthur Andersen accounting firm. Over the next few months, additional subpoenas and document requests were directed to other accounting firms and financial institutions. By May 2002, the Subcommittee staff had reviewed over 350 boxes of documents, including the available meeting minutes, presentations and attachments for the full Board and its Finance and Audit Committees. The Subcommittee staff also spoke with representatives of Enron Corporation and Andersen, as well as numerous financial institutions and experts in corporate governance and accounting.

During April 2002, the Subcommittee staff interviewed thirteen past and present Enron Board members, none of whom had previously been interviewed by the U.S. Department of Justice, Federal Bureau of Investigation, or the Securities and Exchange Commission. These lengthy interviews, lasting between three and eight hours, were conducted with the following Enron Board members: Robert A. Belfer; Norman P. Blake, Jr.; Ronnie C. Chan; John H. Duncan; Dr. Wendy L. Gramm; Dr. Robert K. Jaedicke; Dr. Charles A. LeMaistre; Dr. John Mendelsohn; Paulo Ferraz Pereira; Frank Savage; Lord John Wakeham; Charls Walker; and Herbert S. Winokur, Jr.

All Board members appeared voluntarily, and all were represented by the same legal counsel.

| Figure 9.10 | **Executive Summary Sample (Continued)** |

On May 7, 2002, the Subcommittee held a hearing on the role and responsibility of the Enron Board of Directors to safeguard shareholder interests and on its role in Enron's collapse and bankruptcy. Two panels of witnesses testified under oath. The first panel consisted of five past and present Enron Board members, including the current Board Chairman and the past Chairmen of the key Board Committees. The witnesses were as follows:

Norman P. Blake, Jr. (1994–2002), Interim Chairman of the Enron Board and former member of the Enron Finance and Compensation Committees, has extensive corporate, Board and investment experience, including past service on the Board of General Electric and current service as Audit Committee Chairman of the Board of Owens Corning;

John H. Duncan (1985–2001), former Chairman of the Enron Executive Committee, has extensive corporate and Board experience, including helping to found and manage Gulf and Western Industries;

Herbert S. Winokur, Jr. (1985–2002), current Board member, former Chairman of the Finance Committee, and former member of the Powers Special Committee, holds two advanced degrees from Harvard University and has extensive corporate, Board and investment experience;

Dr. Robert K. Jaedicke (1985–2001), former Chairman of the Enron Audit and Compliance Committee, is Dean Emeritus of the Stanford Business School and a former accounting professor; and

Dr. Charles A. LeMaistre (1985–2001), former Chairman of the Enron Compensation Committee, is former President of the M.D. Anderson Cancer Center, a large, well-respected and complex medical facility in Texas.[1]

The second panel consisted of three experts in corporate governance and accounting:

Robert H. Campbell is former Chairman of the Board and Chief Executive Officer of Sunoco, Inc., and current Board member at Hershey Foods, CIGNA, and the Pew Charitable Trusts;

Charles M. Elson is Director of the Center for Corporate Governance, University of Delaware and a former member of the Board of Sunbeam Corporation; and

Michael H. Sutton is the former Chief Accountant of the Securities and Exchange Commission from 1995 to 1998.

1. Two Enron Directors, Mr. Blake and Mr. Winokur, who were members of the Board at the time of the May 7 hearing, resigned from the Enron Board on June 6, 2002.

Figure 9.10 | **Executive Summary Sample (Continued)**

SUBCOMMITTEE FINDINGS

Based upon the evidence before it, including over one million pages of subpoenaed documents, interviews of thirteen Enron Board members, and the Subcommittee hearing on May 7, 2002, the U.S. Senate Permanent Subcommittee on Investigations makes the following findings with respect to the role of the Enron Board of Directors in Enron's collapse and bankruptcy.

(1) **Fiduciary Failure.** The Enron Board of Directors failed to safeguard Enron shareholders and contributed to the collapse of the seventh largest public company in the United States, by allowing Enron to engage in high risk accounting, inappropriate conflict of interest transactions, extensive undisclosed off-the-books activities, and excessive executive compensation. The Board witnessed numerous indications of questionable practices by Enron management over several years, but chose to ignore them to the detriment of Enron shareholders, employees and business associates.

(2) **High Risk Accounting.** The Enron Board of Directors knowingly allowed Enron to engage in high risk accounting practices.

(3) **Inappropriate Conflicts of Interest.** Despite clear conflicts of interest, the Enron Board of Directors approved an unprecedented arrangement allowing Enron's Chief Financial Officer to establish and operate the LJM private equity funds which transacted business with Enron and profited at Enron's expense. The Board exercised inadequate oversight of LJM transaction and compensation controls and failed to protect Enron shareholders from unfair dealing.

(4) **Extensive Undisclosed Off-The-Books Activity.** The Enron Board of Directors knowingly allowed Enron to conduct billions of dollars in off-the-books activity to make its financial condition appear better than it was and failed to ensure adequate public disclosure of material off-the-books liabilities that contributed to Enron's collapse.

(5) **Excessive Compensation.** The Enron Board of Directors approved excessive compensation for company executives, failed to monitor the cumulative cash drain caused by Enron's 2000 annual bonus and performance unit plans, and failed to monitor or halt abuse by Board Chairman and Chief Executive Officer Kenneth Lay of a company-financed, multi-million dollar, personal credit line.

(6) **Lack of Independence.** The independence of the Enron Board of Directors was compromised by financial ties between the company and certain Board members. The Board also failed to ensure the independence of the company's auditor, allowing Andersen to provide internal audit and consulting services while serving as Enron's outside auditor.

Figure 9.10 **Executive Summary Sample (Concluded)**

SUBCOMMITTEE RECOMMENDATIONS

Based upon the evidence before it and the findings made in this report, the U.S. Senate Permanent Subcommittee on Investigations makes the following recommendations.

(1) **Strengthening Oversight.** Directors of publicly traded companies should take steps to:

(a) prohibit accounting practices and transactions that put the company at high risk of non-compliance with generally accepted accounting principles and result in misleading and inaccurate financial statements;

(b) prohibit conflict of interest arrangements that allow company transactions with a business owned or operated by senior company personnel;

(c) prohibit off-the-books activity used to make the company's financial condition appear better than it is, and require full public disclosure of all assets, liabilities and activities that materially affect the company's financial condition;

(d) prevent excessive executive compensation, including by —

(i) exercising ongoing oversight of compensation plans and payments;

(ii) barring the issuance of company-financed loans to directors and senior officers of the company; and

(iii) preventing stock-based compensation plans that encourage company personnel to use improper accounting or other measures to improperly increase the company stock price for personal gain; and

(e) prohibit the company's outside auditor from also providing internal auditing or consulting services to the company and from auditing its own work for the company.

(2) **Strengthening Independence.** The Securities and Exchange Commission and the self-regulatory organizations, including the national stock exchanges, should:

(a) strengthen requirements for Director independence at publicly traded companies, including by requiring a majority of the outside Directors to be free of material financial ties to the company other than through Director compensation;

(b) strengthen requirements for Audit Committees at publicly traded companies, including by requiring the Audit Committee Chair to possess financial management or accounting expertise, and by requiring a written Audit Committee charter that obligates the Committee to oversee the company's financial statements and accounting practices and to hire and fire the outside auditor; and

(c) strengthen requirements for auditor independence, including by prohibiting the company's outside auditor from simultaneously providing the company with internal auditing or consulting services and from auditing its own work for the company.

Source: U.S. Senate Permanent Subcommittee on Investigation, Committee on Government Affairs. (2002, May). Report on the role of the board of directors in Enron's collapse. Retrieved July 7, 2002, from **http://govt-aff.senate.gov/psi.htm**.

Figure 9.11   Example of Short, Informal Executive Summary

Providence University
Graduate Research Council
Report Presentation of the Council's Yearly Work.

May 25, 2003

EXECUTIVE SUMMARY

1. <u>2003 University Graduate Research Fund (UGRF)</u>
   a. The Research Office will notify applicants after the review of outcomes.
   b. The Research Council has decided in principle that two UGRF reviews will be held in 2004.
   c. The Research Council has decided a grant-writing seminar for potential UGRF applicants will be held before each review.
   d. The Research Council has decided that, for future reviews, supervisors must certify a student's attendance at a grant-writing seminar, the suitability of a student's attendance at a conference, and the suitability of the application's budget.

2. <u>2003 Research Infrastructure Block Grants (RIBG)</u>
   The Research Office will notify applicants of outcomes after the Review.

3. <u>Providence University External Collaborative Research Grants—2003—Round 2</u>
   a. The Research Office will notify applicants of outcomes from the review.
   b. The question of in-kind contributions by industry partners will be discussed at the next meeting.

4. <u>Dissemination of Research Council Policy</u>
   The Research Council asked that the Research Office prepare an executive summary of significant outcomes of each meeting and publish it on the Web. It is believed that Researcher's attention will be drawn to this report.

A stand-alone executive summary can take either the inductive or the deductive approach. The real purpose is to present the most information possible in an abbreviated and condensed fashion. Lengthy, detailed explanations are eliminated; only the main points are presented. When an executive report serves as a stand-alone report, and does not have a larger report that it summarizes, the material is created for a single reader. For this reason executive reports tend to grow in length unless the writer consciously strives to keep it short and concise.

Text

The formal report text is normally divided into three parts: the introduction, findings, and conclusion.

Introduction. The introduction of a report prepares the reader for the report by describing four parts of the project: purpose, problem statement, background, and research methods. The **purpose** encompasses both the thesis and the objective of the study. The **problem statement** condenses the purpose into a succinct description that gives a boundary to the scope of the research. The **background** helps orient the reader to any information needed to understand the investigation and analysis to follow. This area includes important definitions, qualifications, and assumptions. The research-methods section describes the process by which the author collected the report data and any analytical procedures that were used to show that the findings are significant. Research limitations are also important to note; they give the reader insight into how additional research might be conducted.

Findings. This is the core of the report. Within the findings section, all the report data is disclosed, discussed, and connected to the problem statement. Occasionally, statistics too detailed to be included in the body of the text are moved to charts or graphs in the appendices. To help the reader's understanding the material here is easily divided into headings and subheadings.

Conclusion. This final portion brings an end to the report by way of summary and any recommendations. A good **summary** highlights, in a logical sequence, the purpose of the study, problem statement, relevant background, research methodology, and findings. **Recommendations** direct the reader toward behavioral action. When the objective of a report is informative, recommendations are usually not given. Analytical reports, however, will present recommendations.

Appended Parts

The appended parts are often called the back matter. Four items commonly appear in the appended section: appendices, a bibliography, a glossary, and an index. The writer should continue the page numbering from the conclusion area of the report on through the appended parts.

Appendix. In an appendix an author can place a variety of supplemental material—charts, exhibits, letters, and other displays—that are too lengthy or inappropriate to include in the text. Each unique source of material should be presented as a separate appendix ordered by letter: Appendix A, Appendix B, and so on. For example, a report at a university by the Faculty Teaching Effectiveness Conference contained the following four appendices:

Appendix A: Agenda of the Conference
Appendix B: Attendance by Academic School or Department
Appendix C: List of Participant Workshops
Appendix D: List of Participant Focus Groups

References, bibliography, or works cited. Here the works consulted by the writer are listed. Because research reports draw on a number of secondary sources, a bibliographical listing can be helpful in directing readers to places where additional information can be obtained.

Glossary. Technical reports frequently present terms with which a reader might be unfamiliar. The glossary lists those terms and their definitions.

Index. A report's index serves the same purpose as that of a book. It places all report subjects in alphabetical order, and often lists page numbers.

The Final Product

Formal reports generally are bound, expensive to produce, and attractive to view. They sometimes contain illustrations or photographs. While formal reports may never be read in their entirety (because of their length and formality), the information is usually important for both present and future readers. The primary reader often learns what is contained in the formal report through an oral briefing. The public is often secondary readers of the formal report.

Other Report Formats

Design Report

Technical professionals in disciplines such as engineering and science introduce and document their work with design reports. Design reports have two audiences: other professionals who are interested in the work, and managers who are concerned with the application and effectiveness of designs. The reports' purpose is to present information about some aspect of research. In this regard they borrow from the thesis proposal process discussed in Chapter 9. "In general, a thesis involves formulating an original idea or area of inquiry that is either quantitative (e.g., typically involves either an empirically based, provable hypothesis) or is qualitative (e.g., includes explorative outcomes, along with data collection and analysis)."[9] Usually such reports contribute a new perspective or application, uncover new implications, or make fact-based predictions.

Design reports are usually semiformal or formal in nature. Their organizational layout has six parts: title page, executive summary, introduction, discussion, conclusion, and appendices. To show the intricate detail of a design, this report makes more use of tables, figures, and photographs.[10]

Title Page. This initial page carries the title of the report, authors, supporting organization, and date.

Executive Summary. The abstract or summary is written assuming that the reader has some familiarity with the topic but has not read the report. This part of the report will then provide enough background to give the reader an overview of the report.

Introduction. The design report "identifies the design problem, the objectives of the design, the assumptions for the design, the design alternatives, and the selection of the design being reported."[11]

Discussion. This part of the report contains any analysis of the design. Here the design is presented along with the theory behind it. Any problems encountered in the design creation, working process of the design, and test results are also presented. Headings and subheadings are critical in this part of the report. While other types of reports make extensive use of bullet points and white space, a design report relies heavily upon written narrative.

Conclusions. In this part of the report the reader will learn the success or failure of the design and how it can or will be changed or improved. Any recommendations will be laid out here.

Appendices. Because the design development often requires a variety of scientific experiments or empirical tests, appendices are a standard part of this report. Readers like to make use of this material to test their own hypotheses. While an appendix is the best place for material that is too detailed for the rest of the report, include only what is essential. An appendix is also the place for any references used in the work.

Figure 9.12 presents the introduction, discussion, and concluding portions of an interesting technical report, "SAFOD Pilot Hole Information: Scientific Drilling for Earthquake Research Now Underway at Parkfield." The U.S. Geological Survey prepared the report. Because this report was designed for Internet readers it omitted the executive summary and appendices. For space reasons here we have omitted the graphics from the example. An in-depth review can be made at **http://quake.wr.usgs.gov/research/parkfield/index.html**.

Progress Report

Closely related to design reports are progress reports. Often a progress report will be the next necessary step that follows the acceptance of, or interest in, a project or product design. Likewise, progress reports are a necessary follow-up to accepted proposals such as those discussed in Chapter 8. After accepting a proposal, most organizations will want periodic updates on the progress of the work.

Progress reports present information on a subject and are common in daily business life. Management and even customers want to learn the progress being made on a project. Progress reports are used following "the design, construction, or repair of something, the study or research of a problem or question, or the gathering of information on a technical subject. You write progress reports when it takes well over three or four months to complete a project."[12] Figure 9.13 displays a one-page progress report sent by a community service organization to its volunteers and supporters. This short report presents an overview of the activities performed by the organization within a six-month period.

| Figure 9.12 | Sample Design Report Content |

SAFOD Pilot Hole Information

Scientific Drilling for Earthquake Research Now Underway at Parkfield

The San Andreas Fault Observatory at Depth (SAFOD) is a comprehensive proposal to drill and instrument an inclined borehole across the San Andreas Fault Zone to a depth of 4 km. SAFOD is a component of the National Science Foundation's (NSF) EarthScope initiative, which is currently under consideration for funding by Congress. SAFOD is motivated by the need to answer fundamental questions about the physical and chemical processes controlling the initiation, propagation and arrest of earthquake ruptures within a major plate-bounding fault. To achieve this goal, SAFOD will penetrate through, or very close to, a cluster of repeating microearthquakes.

The SAFOD pilot hole is a separate, 2.2-km-deep scientific drilling experiment being carried out at the same surface location planned for SAFOD (Figure 1). This site is ~1.8 km SW of the San Andreas Fault near Parkfield, CA, on a segment of the fault that moves through a combination of aseismic creep and repeating microearthquakes. It lies just north of the rupture zone of the 1966, magnitude 6 Parkfield earthquake, the most recent in a series of events that have ruptured the fault five times since 1857. The Parkfield region is the most comprehensively instrumented section of a fault anywhere in the world, and has been the focus of intensive study for the past two decades as part of the <u>Parkfield Earthquake Experiment</u>. The pilot hole is a collaborative effort between the International Continental Drilling Program (ICDP), NSF and the U.S. Geological Survey (USGS).

There are many reasons for carrying out the pilot hole project:

- Seismic recording instrumentation deployed in the pilot hole will facilitate the determination of precise earthquake hypocenter locations that will guide subsequent SAFOD investigations in the active fault zone. These subsurface seismic receivers will also record surface seismic sources and provide depth control for several on-going and planned crustal imaging experiments, outlined below.
- Downhole measurements of physical properties, stress, fluid pressure and heat flow in the pilot hole will characterize the shallow crust adjacent to the fault zone. These measurements will be used to help calibrate physical properties inferred from surface-based geophysical surveys (e.g., seismic velocities, resistivity and density) and better constrain the thermomechanical setting of the San Andreas Fault Zone prior to SAFOD drilling.
- Long-term seismic, pore fluid pressure, strain and temperature monitoring in the pilot hole will make it possible to assess time-dependent changes in the physical properties and mechanical state of the crust adjacent to the fault zone for comparison with similar measurements to be recorded in the SAFOD hole.

| Figure 9.12 | Sample Design Report Content (Continued) |

- Approximately 60 m of granite core will be extracted from the bottom of the pilot hole. The resulting open-hole section (or core hole) will then be used for downhole measurements of permeability and pore pressure and obtaining uncontaminated pore fluid samples. Laboratory studies of these rock and fluid samples will determine the nature and extent of fluid-rock interaction along the San Andreas Fault and the sources and transport paths for fault-zone fluids.
- Real-time seismic monitoring in the pilot hole (and at the surface) during SAFOD drilling using the drill bit as a seismic source will allow high-resolution imaging of the San Andreas Fault Zone at depth.

From a strictly technological point of view, the pilot hole will provide the opportunity to obtain information about drilling conditions that will be extremely valuable in designing and drilling the main SAFOD hole.

Overview of Operations and Science Plan

Nearly the entire length of the pilot hole will be rotary drilled. An initial casing will be set at 800 m, after penetrating the sedimentary section and the uppermost granitic basement. Because of budgetary constraints, no coring or logging will be done in this interval. After cementing the 9 5/8″ casing, the hole will be rotary drilled vertically with a 8 3/4″ bit to a depth of 2.1 km (7000′). Again, because of budgetary constraints, there will be no cores taken in this section of the hole. However, rock chips (i.e., cuttings) will be continuously collected, described and logged during rotary drilling.

After drilling to 2.1 km, a fairly complete suite of geophysical logs will be run, principally by a commercial wireline logging service. These logs will be supplemented by several geophysical logs collected by the science team.

All drilling and logging information will be kept in the Drilling Information System (DIS) data base developed by ICDP and posted regularly on the SAFOD website.

After logging, the 2.1 km deep, 8 3/4″ hole will be cased with 7″ casing. After this casing has been cemented into place, we plan to collect $\sim$60 m of "HQ" core (6.4 cm diameter) at the bottom of the pilot hole. A protocol is being developed for how the core samples will be handled at the site, distributed for study and archived. We will use the DOSECC top-drive coring system successfully used in Hawaii and Long Valley.

After coring, logging of the core hole will be carried out with an ultrasonic borehole televiewer. This will make it possible to magnetically orient fractures and faults observed in the core. The core hole will also be used for fluid sampling and measurements of permeability and the least principal stress.

Upon completion of these measurements, seismic, strain and pore fluid pressure instrumentation will be deployed in the hole for continuous monitoring of seismic activity occurring within and adjacent to the San Andreas Fault Zone.

Figure 9.12 | **Sample Design Report Content (Continued)**

Geophysical Studies of the Pilot Hole Site

Over the past several years, a wide variety of geophysical investigations have been carried out at and around the SAFOD site. These studies include:

- Magneto-telluric soundings (Unsworth et al., 2000).
- Gravity and magnetic profiles (Miller et al., 2000).
- High-resolution seismic reflection and refraction profiles (Rymer et al., 1999; Hole et al., 2000).
- A number of shallow exploration techniques run at the drill site as part of the NSF-sponsored Parkfield field camp. Information about the Parkfield field camp is available at www.eos.duke.edu/Research/seismo/parkfield.htm.
- Major microearthquake experiment—the Parkfield Area Seismic Observatory (PASO)—is now underway using portable seismic instruments deployed by Univ. Wisconsin and Rensselaer Polytechnic Institute, the permanent stations of the USGS Northern California Seismic Network, and the Parkfield High Resolution Seismic Network run by U.C. Berkeley. This experiment is described on the web at http://gretchen.geo.rpi.edu/roecker/paso_home.html.
- Monitoring of the Parkfield region by the USGS and U.C. Berkeley as part of the Parkfield Earthquake Experiment continues, with networks of borehole strainmeters, global positioning system (GPS) receivers, water wells, creepmeters, magnetometers, high-gain seismometers and strong motion accelerometers. Work is presently underway to expand the continuous GPS network. Information about deformation monitoring at Parkfield is available at http://quake.usgs.gov/research/deformation/parkfield/index.html.

The next phase of the geophysical exploration of the fault zone and surrounding crust is planned for the fall of 2002, after the completion of the pilot hole:

- John Hole (Virginia Tech) has been funded by NSF to shoot a 50-km-long reflection/wide-angle refraction profile at right angles to the fault through the SAFOD site. His plan is to use conventional and turning-ray reflection methods and refraction methods to image the P-velocity structure of the fault and nearby crust. Trond Ryberg (GFZ, Germany) and Claus Prodehl (U. Karlsruhe, Germany) will expand this active source experiment to image the S-wave velocity structure.
- Peter Malin (Duke) will instrument the pilot hole with a vertical array of 3-component geophones that will be used to record both the artificial sources and nearby earthquakes.
- Cliff Thurber (Univ. Wisconsin) and Steve Roecker (Rensselaer Polytechnic Institute) will set off a series of calibration shots at the sites of their surface stations to be recorded by the seismic receivers within the pilot hole in order to test and calibrate their 3-D seismic velocity model. By traveltime reciprocity, this will create a "virtual earthquake" at the bottom of the pilot hole (Ellsworth, 1996) that will be used to refine double-difference and tomographic earthquake locations.

Figure 9.12 **Sample Design Report Content (Continued)**

This comprehensive suite of geophysical investigations in and around the pilot hole will achieve a number of critical milestones. These include determination of the absolute locations of the repeating microearthquakes we will target with the main SAFOD hole and better defining the overall structure and geophysical setting of the San Andreas Fault Zone at Parkfield.

Scientific Opportunities

The pilot hole project will present opportunities for research in three general areas:

Downhole Measurements—Due to budgetary constraints, only a modest number of downhole measurements are currently planned for the pilot hole.

A suite of open-hole geophysical logs will be conducted prior to setting the final casing string. This will include resistivity, density, porosity, dipole sonic and borehole imaging logs (both acoustic and electrical) and will provide the information needed to characterize variations in physical properties, fracture geometry and stress directions at depths of 0.8 to 2.1 km.

We welcome ideas by interested investigators for additional downhole measurements after the hole is completed and the drill rig moves off site, or to conduct detailed analyses of the geophysical logs that we already plan to collect in this hole. Other already planned downhole measurements include: 1) repeated temperature measurements (coupled with thermal conductivity measurements) for heat flow, 2) a vertical seismic profile (VSP) in the cased and cemented pilot hole to allow seismic properties measured during geophysical logging and on the core to be "scaled up" and extrapolated away from the borehole, and 3) permeability measurements and a single hydraulic fracturing stress test in the core hole.

Monitoring—The plan for completion of the pilot hole first calls for temporary installation of a 40-level 3-component array of high-frequency geophones (~ 8 Hz) that will be in place to record surface sources during the seismic surveys mentioned above. Similar arrays have been installed for use in the petroleum industry, and Peter Malin has been working closely with industrial partners to design and deploy such a system in the pilot hole.

After these surveys are completed, this seismic string will be temporarily removed and fitted with additional sensors, including:

- Pore pressure monitoring in the uncased core hole.
- Installation of strainmeters and/or tiltmeters.
- Installation of broad-band seismometers and accelerometers.

Figure 9.12   **Sample Design Report Content (Concluded)**

After reinstallation, this array will be permanently cemented in the pilot hole for long-term monitoring of nearby seismic activity and variations in fluid pressure and deformation adjacent to the San Andreas Fault Zone.

Analysis of Core, Cuttings and Fluids—Since the pilot hole will be drilled outside of the San Andreas fault zone, the opportunities for addressing many of the basic scientific questions pertaining to the mechanics of faulting and earthquake generation are relatively limited. However, we anticipate a few key areas in which important scientific progress can be made through analysis of core, cuttings, and fluids obtained from the pilot hole. These include:

- Mineralogical, geochemical and microstructural studies to determine the geometry, chemical zonation and timing of vein-filling episodes and their possible relation to the earthquake cycle.
- Geochemical and isotopic investigations of pore water and dissolved gasses—using either bulk water samples or fluid inclusions—to ascertain the origins, pathways and transport rates of fluids associated with the fault zone and the nature and extent of water-rock interactions in the country rock.
- Laboratory rock mechanics studies of the strength and transport properties of country rock, to help in the interpretation of stress-induced borehole failure and as "boundary conditions" to hydromechanical models for the San Andreas fault zone.
- Laboratory studies of P- and S-wave velocities, seismic anisotropy, mineral fabric and microcrack geometry for comparison with physical properties and stress directions inferred from downhole measurements and surface-based geophysical surveys.

Source: SAFOD pilot hole information: scientific drilling for earthquake research now underway at Parkfield San Andreas Fault observatory at depth. (n.d.). Retrieved July 8, 2002, from **http://www.icdp-online.de/html/sites/sanandreas/ objectives/pilot.html.** This report is the combined effort of the U.S. Geological Survey, the National Science Foundation, and the International Continental Drilling Program.

Figure 9.13 | **Progress Report Example**

COMMUNITY OUTREACH PARTNERSHIP

Progress Report
January 1, 2003, to June 30, 2003

The Community Outreach Partnership (COP) is made up of residential, business, health care, educational and religious groups and individuals who desire to see a revitalization of the Hazelwood and Northwood Terrace communities. This report highlights the COP efforts during the last six months.

Housing
- Community Partners established a "Housing Review" group focusing on code enforcement, absentee landlords, and fair housing issues.
- Community focus groups are being conducted to surface local needs.
- Volunteers distributed 3,000 information packets in the neighborhood providing info on tenant rights, trash, fire and safety, and other community resources.
- COP Outreach office for housing resources established in storefront next to county library.

Neighborhood Revitalization
- Tenant Council Food Pantry is moving toward self-sufficiency.
- Northwood Terrace Residents Council hired part-time business manager.
- Hazelwood Initiative hired part-time business manager.
- Catalyst for Community Builders Project launched a 10-week grassroots leadership and certificate program linked with COP and collaborations with United Way and the State Community Health organizations.
- Reform University Ministries is providing funding for summer youth programs.

Economic Development
- First neighborhood entrepreneur class completed training.
- Retired Executive Club holds weekly meetings discussing business plans.

Job Training
- New University–Community Career Development Partnership director on board.
- COP has obtained a $10,000 federal grant to develop a job training program.

Education
- The Community College "Project" Tutor Program is seeking student volunteers for outreach in Northwood Terrace and Hazelwood.
- ESL classes are taught weekly at Parkwood Presbyterian Church.

Health and Wellness
- Community Health Partnerships obtained $100,000 in welfare funding secured for community health outreach in Hazelwood and Northwood Terrace.
- Community Health officials are staging inoculation services twice monthly.

Progress reports can take the form of a letter, memo, short report, or long formal report. Information in the report will be organized into the following categories.

Project background. Because managers and funding agencies have many projects that they supervise, it is best to present a brief statement at the beginning of the report that describes the project, its objectives, and the status at the last time of reporting.

Current progress. This area brings the reader up to date on the current status of the report. This is done by showing a time line or by discussing the various parts of the project and what has been accomplished to date.

Problems experienced. Readers are interested in knowing how successful you have been and what problems you have experienced. Such disclosure might help them prevent similar problems and can even help you if they have answers for what you have encountered.

Work that remains. Detail the work that is left on the project along with speculation on when you will meet the deadlines. This step follows closely the scheduling process found in the proposal plan of Chapter 8 and often employs the use of Gantt charts discussed in Chapter 3. Figure 9.14 shows a report that is typically required by instructors regarding the progress of a term project. While this report took the form of a memo, it could have been sent in a letter or e-mailed.

The Consultant's Project Report

This style of report can take either the formal or informal format. It is presented here because many advanced business students become consultants, and because the internal design of this report differs from both the formal and informal reports.

Consultants are professional people who give expert advice. As Peter Block says in *Flawless Consulting*, they are in a position to have influence on individuals, groups, or organizations, but they have no direct power to make changes or to implement programs. The consultant's job is to identify client problems, determine reasons for the problems, decide the affect that the problems are having on the client's organization, create a vision for what the organization's future will look like without the problems, decide upon possible solutions, determine the value of the solutions, develop and refine recommendations for solving the problems, and finally, prepare and present the deliverables to the client.[13]

A consultant's deliverables consist of a final report and an executive presentation. The written report contains significant details. The presentation that accompanies it is oral, more graphical, sequenced differently from the report, and designed to stress such areas of importance as findings, recommendations, value statements, and priorities. Figure 9.15 compares the parts of the project report with those of the executive presentation.

The Consultant's Project Report Contents. The project report starts with a **cover page** like that of the formal report. An **executive summary** then gives an overview of the report along with conclusions and recommendations. Next is the list of **team members** who were responsible for researching the project. The **table of contents** lists every part of the report, along with page numbers. The **scope definition** states exactly what the client and consultant agreed upon at the start of the engagement. It identifies what is and is not included within the project boundaries.

Figure 9.14   **Example of E-Mail Progress Report**

TO: Professor Smart
FROM: Excellent Student
SUBJECT: Semester Project Progress Report #2
DATE: March 13, XXXX

Dear Professor Smart,

My Wal-Mart Corporation report and presentation are progressing
successfully. The syllabus for your course listed the following
requirements for our final project:
· A minimum of one personal interview,
· Application of at least six textbook chapters to the organization,
· Review of company Website,
· Review of company documents,
· A minimum of 20 secondary research items,
· A formal report, and
· A Power Point presentation.

In my first progress report on February 15, I indicated I had completed:
· A phone interview with Ms. June Hunt, the Wal-Mart Corporate
  College Relations Representative,
· A review of the company Website and the printing of company
  documents, and
· The acquiring of 10 quality articles on Wal-Mart's culture,
  organizational design, management training program, strategic
  planning process, and diversity effort.

As of March 13, I have completed the following:
· An additional personal interview with Mr. Petar Kljaic, a Wal-Mart
  store manager,
· Completion of all 20 secondary articles, and
· Organization of data into five major areas: corporate culture,
  organizational design, employee and customer diversity plan,
  managerial hiring and training process, and corporate strategic
  planning process.

Between now and April 15, when the third progress report is due, I
will complete the writing of the formal report. In addition I will
have a rough-draft of my Power Point presentation completed.

The project has progressed very smoothly. I appreciate the guidance
you gave me on Internet search engines. I was able to immediately find
the information that I was seeking.

The only problems I have experienced have been in the topic area of
ethics. The Wal-Mart company representatives have talked to me about
how the organization stresses ethical conduct, yet the company does
not share its corporate code of ethics. If you have any ideas on how
I might obtain a copy, please let me know.

Figure 9.15

Format Comparison Between the Consultant's Final Report and the Executive Presentation

The Final Report	The Executive Presentation
Cover page	Title slide
Executive summary	Team introduction
List of team members	Session agenda
Table of contents	Project scope definition
Project scope definition	Project objectives
Methodology	Approach or methodology
Findings	Recommendations
Recommendations	Business impact
Business impact	Implementation considerations
Implementation considerations	Next steps
Next steps	Wrap-up
Conclusions	Support documentation
Appendices	

The **objectives** state why the project was conducted. The **methodology** identifies how the project was done. The **findings** indicate what the project team identified as problems and/or opportunities for improvement. The **recommendations** indicate what needs to be done. The **business impact** describes the value to the organization if the recommendations are implemented. This usually includes benefits to be derived and costs to be implemented. The **implementation considerations** describe what the requirements or barriers to implementation are and what dependencies upon other projects may be evident. The **next steps** list things such as the recommended priorities, sequences, and funding requirements for implementation. This usually includes a proposed schedule that shows things like time frames and dependencies. The **conclusion** brings the entire report together. The **appendices** give all supporting documentation and other appropriate materials.[14]

Feasibility and Recommendation Reports

Research shows a loosely defined category of highly technical reports, referred to with a variety of names: feasibility, recommendation, evaluation, and assessment. The job of all these different types of reports is basically the same: The reports take situations, plans, or opportunities, and after a careful analysis of the data, provide guidance in the form of options and recommendations.

Feasibility Report. This report studies a situation, problem, or opportunity, and a plan for doing something about it. It then determines whether that plan is feasible, according to such factors as technical, economical, desired, or preferred. The report's conclusion provides the answer: yes, no, or maybe. In the process of reaching the decision a feasibility report rejects alternatives and shows how to implement the selection.[15]

Feasibility Report Contents. This report starts with a **title page** that gives the report title, author, and date. Next an **introduction** defines the problem, states why it is important, and describes the information that will be provided.

The **executive summary** follows. According to Hucklin and Olsen the summary does the following:

- Details the project's cost;
- Discusses any problems to be encountered;
- Details human, facility, and equipment resources;
- Shows project time schedules and deadlines;
- Discusses important recommendations for future action;
- Narrows the problem by describing what is being done and by whom;
- Suggests a feasible solution;
- Describes the specific equipment that is needed;
- Details the risks and benefits;
- Gives an estimated life of the project;
- Details all cost factors;
- Describes where the resources are located; and
- Defines any tests that need to be carried out.

Following the executive summary are the **details**. Here the facts and policies are presented, and an explanation of the preferred method is given along with criteria for judgment (effectiveness, feasibility, desirability, affordability, and preferability). As alternatives are considered, certain ones are rejected, a solution is recommended, implementation steps are explained, and the cost and time schedule is then described. The report ends with a **conclusion** and any necessary **appendices**.[16]

Figure 8.1 showed a brief proposal that makes a recommendation. Figure 9.16 presents the conclusion of a comprehensive analysis for the I-69 Evansville to Indianapolis [Indiana] transportation needs. The study examined three issues: Evansville to Indianapolis Interstate highway connection, regional accessibility, and travel efficiency and congestion. While the study shows that major problems exist in each of the issue areas, the final conclusion and recommendation could have been presented more strongly.

Recommendation Report. This approach starts with a stated need or a selection of choices and ends by making a recommendation for action. For example, you might examine different brands of automobiles comparing them by cost, quality, and features. After a careful analysis you offer a recommendation on the one that is best to buy. Basically this report answers the question, Which option should be chosen? The recommendation report provides the selection.[17]

Recommendation Report Contents. Following a **cover page** an **introduction** section is found. Here the specific audience is addressed and the specific type of report (feasibility, evaluation, or other) is indicated according to purpose. In addition, the introduction provides a substantial overview of the report's contents.

A **background** section then covers the problem, need, or opportunity that merits the report's writing. If the information here is short, it can be included in the introduction. Technical information is often needed here in preparation for the

Figure 9.16   **Example of Recommendation Report Conclusions**

The I-69 Evansville-to-Indianapolis Study
Tier 1 Environmental Impact Statement

5.0 Conclusion

The Regional Transportation Needs Analysis Summarizes the major findings of the transportation needs analysis, conducted as part of the Purpose and Need Analysis for the I-69, Evansville to Indianapolis Study. The major conclusions reached include the following:

- The connection which Evansville has to Indianapolis is the worst of any major city in Indiana. The quality of its connection, as measured by comparing a straight line connection with the actual quickest route, shows that the existing connection which Evansville has to Indianapolis is significantly worse than that enjoyed by any other major city in Indiana.
- By nearly all measures examined, the Study Area has statistically poorer accessibility than the rest of Indiana. It has poorer accessibility to population, employment, urban areas, and airports. The portions of the Study Area which are more than 50 miles from Indianapolis have poorer accessibility to Indianapolis than similarly situated areas elsewhere in the state.
- There is a demonstrable, though not overpowering, relationship throughout Indiana between accessibility and median household income. A region's accessibility, or lack thereof, partially explains the income level of its residents. The greater a region's accessibility, the greater its median household income tends to be.
- While congested conditions are not forecasted to be a major problem throughout the Study Area, some areas are forecasted to be highly congested by 2025. While congestion relief does not need to be a primary focus of this project, it would be prudent to evaluate alternative routes as to whether they would address any of these forecasted congestion problems noted above.

This analysis suggests that major issues to be addressed by the proposed project should include improving the connection of Evansville to Indianapolis, as well as improving accessibility throughout the region. Addressing congestion is a secondary issue, although it will be useful to determine whether routes would help alleviate certain localized congestion which has been forecasted. Regional safety issues, the other part of the Regional Transportation Needs Analysis, have been addressed in a separate report, *Task 3.3.4.1 Technical Report, Regional Safety Analysis*.

Regional Transportation Needs Analysis   *Page 21*
Technical Report 3.3.4   *September 26, 2001*

Source: Indiana Department of Transportation. (2001, September 26). The I-69 Evansville-to-Indianapolis study: Tier 1 environmental impact statement; Task 3.3.4: Technical report: Regional transportation needs analysis, p. 21.

comparison process that will follow in the analysis. If technical information is added, this section will lengthen substantially; therefore, avoid an analysis of the data in this section.

Next, a **requirements** section lists the standards or requirements to which you are comparing the problem. Those factors will influence the final decision, so it is necessary to state how important one requirement is compared to another. Quality definitions and descriptions are often necessary. Telling how to use secondary factors should also be considered in case no option ends up with a clear advantage.

An **options** discussion follows the requirements section because you often have to describe the process used in narrowing the number of options being considered. Options are briefly described. One of the critical parts of a feasibility or recommendation report is a discussion of the **option comparisons**. Instead of comparing option to option, use a category-by-category approach. For instance, if you were reviewing the automobile selection you would examine each brand by the specific categories of cost, quality, and features. Each category will be assigned a "best choice." A summary table, in which all key data are summarized, is an excellent way to present this report.[18]

In the feasibility or recommendation report the **conclusion** serves as a summary of the conclusions previously reached in the comparison section. For example, which automobile had the best price, the best features, or the best quality? In highly controversial cases with different comparison factors outweighing each other, secondary factors have to be considered in order to form a conclusion. For example, in the case of the automobile, cost might win out over features and quality for the college student. A final, specific conclusion must be stated here.

The final phase is the making of **recommendations**. While this may seem as obviously following a lengthy comparison process, a report often recommends several options based on different possibilities. Key factors that influenced the decision must be described.

Writing the Report

After you have analyzed and ordered your data and identified your solutions and recommendations, you are ready to write the report. Writing a report is very similar to writing a proposal (Chapter 8) and case analyses (Chapter 15). Consider the particular format you want to follow in regard to formality, and then condense your information into the necessary parts of the report.

You should produce both an initial draft and an edited version. Strive to make your writing complete, concise, and clear, using many of the tips outlined in Chapters 4 through 6.

Reports employ a variety of graphic materials, including bar graphs (segmented, group information, simple listings), line graphs, and pie charts. Graphics are used to help present information for quick comprehension and to clarify ideas that are difficult to convey with words alone. As you read in Chapter 3, with the use of computers, databases, and numerous software packages, a writer's job in seeking and presenting graphical information has been made easier.

Summary

Report writing can be frustrating and time-consuming unless it is approached in a systematic way. Reports come in several types, ranging from formal documents to short executive memos. Various exhibits were displayed to show examples of reports.

As a report writer, begin by asking these questions: What is the purpose of my report? Who will read my report? What information will my readers need? What research resources are available for me? How should I organize my information?

Several steps are involved in the organizational process of report writing. First, develop the purpose of the report. From there the scope of the writing must be clarified and the various ideas categorized. This development occurs through inductive order, deductive order, order of location, order of increasing difficulty, sequential order, beneficial order, chronological order, and problem-solving order. After the ordering is done, an outline with headings is developed.

After you organize and design your research ideas you need to gather and analyze your data. Primary research methods such as interviews, questionnaires, and examination are preferred. A variety of easy-to-use electronic sources are also available to most advanced business students.

Formatting the material occurs both during and after the data search. Reports have one of three levels of formality: the formal, semiformal, and the informal report. While there is a boilerplate format that exists, the purpose of the report and needs of the readers often dictate a change of format. A variety of different kinds of reports can be produced, such as design reports, progress reports, the consultant's progress report, and feasibility and recommendation reports.

Discussion Questions

1. The basic objective of report writing is to either present information or to present the analysis and recommendations of research. What is the difference between the two objectives? Do most reports follow one objective or the other, or both?

2. As a report writer there are things you should know before you start your research and then writing. What are the questions you should ask in the preparatory stages?

3. The best writing comes from well-organized ideas. What are the organizational steps that a wise writer takes in preparation, prior to actually researching data?

4. Ideas and information fall easily into a variety of sequential orders. Name and describe some of those orders, and the type of material in use with each.

5. For student researchers a majority of research material is obtained from the Internet. Describe the concept of electronic information sources and databases. Check the availability of such sources at your university library, and describe which sources listed in the text are available online.

6. A formal report is divided into three primary parts: formalities, text, and appended parts. While a writer is free to use or not use the various parts, knowing what each part is used for is important. Name and describe the various subparts and how they might be used or why they might not be used.

7. This chapter described a variety of different reports used in business and technical fields. Describe some of those reports, their various parts, and why each is used to present information to different readers.

Communication in Action

1. Your manager just returned from a Rotary Club luncheon where she heard a speaker claiming tremendously increased sales for firms who have outfitted their sales personnel with cellular phones. Your manager has had a company cell phone for a couple of years, and knows how convenient they are to use. She also has been convinced that sales personnel can use such a tool in numerous ways that will benefit the company.

   Your Assignment: Your manager asks you to look into how much it would cost to equip the ten salespeople in your department with cellular phones. She desires to purchase contracts with a minimum number of hours for the first year, research the effectiveness of the use, and then decide whether the contract minutes need to be increased. Your assignment is to find the top three cellular phone companies in your area and then determine cost figures for the ten salespeople. You decide to look at contracts with between 500 and 2,500 minutes per month. Compare the costs for different time limits among the three companies. Assume that most of the minutes will be used during peak times. Also calculate the cost structure for additional minutes with each company.

   After you have done your research prepare an informal report (memo or letter form) for your manager. As an addition you decide to give your boss some usage recommendations that could save the company money.

2. Your information technology instructor made comments recently in class about the increasing cases of carpal tunnel syndrome for employees who use computers multiple hours a day. He attributed the problem more to a lack of proper usage instructions than to equipment and other causes.

   You decide to research the topic for your end-of-course assignment. Collect data and prepare an informal report for your instructor. Be sure to include both primary and secondary resources for your research.

@ Internet

3. Recently you read an article in the newspaper entitled "Philip Morris Profits Take Breath Away." At first the article confused you because it talked about the company's "immense cost/benefit contribution to humanity." You thought the author was probably referring to how the organization had increased its philanthropic activities since the numerous

tobacco court cases. But as you read on you became disturbed. According to an Associated Press story the company distributed an interesting report in the Czech Republic. The report said that cigarettes are a boon to the Czech Republic economy since the early deaths of smokers help offset medical expenses. According to the report, the Czech government saved $146 million a year because of cigarette smoking. You decide to read the report for yourself. Use a search engine to search under the words *Philip Morris Czech Report*. This will lead you to a variety of analyses of the report, in addition to finding the full report itself. (If you cannot find the report go to: **http://www.infact.org/71601czh.html**; **http://www .no-smoking.org/july01/07-17-01-4.html**; or **http://tobaccofreekids .org/reports/philipmorris/**.

Your Assignment: Read the entire report. How does the report compare to the textbook description of what is contained in a formal report? What is included? What is not included? If you were required to write recommendations for this report what would you say?

After reading critiques about this report, write your own response. Be sure to discuss the ethical and social responsibility factors mentioned in Chapter 1. Put your critique in memo form and send it to your instructor.

4. Your instructor wants to expose the class to different cultures and has decided to do it through a report-writing assignment. Your task, as a small group, is to decide upon a specific country that you would like to research. You must develop a plan for marketing a specific consumer product to that country. Try to select a country that has students enrolled at your university. Through the student affairs office or international students' office, obtain names and telephone numbers of the on-campus clubs for specific countries. As a group, interview several students from the country you have selected. During the interview ask questions about their country's customs, product preferences, buying habits, prices, disposable income, competitors, and types of retail outlets.

In addition to using the information learned from the interviews, your research on the country should also inform you about the country. Look for information like: country economic profile, business customs, consumer behavior, business relationships with the United States, and export and import prospects and restrictions for that country. You should also examine customs regulations that would apply to the country. The following Web sites might be of help: **http://www.sba.gov/oit/statereports/** or **http:// www.odci.gov/cia/publications/factbook/index.html**. The latter URL is the CIA factbook site, which provides valuable information.

Your research results should be assembled into a formal report. Your instructor will specify length and other report requirements.[19]

5. To better learn how the various parts of a formal report fit together, prepare a Table of Contents using a research report outline. Go to **http://www.mintel.com/**. Mintel produces market research and analysis reports for businesses. While you have to pay for the full reports, the outlines for several of their recent research projects are available.[20] Go to the Web site, find a topic that is interesting, and do the following: First,

decide the best way to reorganize the material that you will find in the outline. Go through the process of reordering the outline. Next, put the outline into a Table of Contents format. Turn all of your work in to your instructor.

InfoTrac

6. Formal reports often contain graphical materials—especially company annual reports. For this assignment look up the following article on InfoTrac: "The Incidence and Quality of Graphics in Annual Reports: An International Comparison." Read the article and with the knowledge you gleaned, apply it to several annual reports. You can find the annual reports through a search on the Internet, or at **http://www.reportgallery .com/**.

Notes

1. Dumaine, D. (1983). *Write to the top: Writing for corporate success.* New York: Random House, p. 10.
2. *Tel 598: Research methods developing research problem statements.* (n.d.). Retrieved July 2, 2002, from **http://www.tele.sunyit.edu/Thesis-statement.html**, p. 1.
3. Dumaine, D. *Write to the top,* pp. 32–33.
4. *Some common formats for organizing technical writing.* (n.d.). Retrieved February 19, 2002, from **http://www.yorku.ca/mikes/common.htm**, p. 1.
5. *Organization is effective.* (n.d.). Retrieved March 15, 2002, from **http://www .marin.cc.ca.us/buscom/page45.html**, p. 1.
6. Wertheim, E. *Guide for written communication.* (n.d.). Retrieved March 14, 2002, from Northeastern University, College of Business Administration Web site: **http:// web.cba.neu.edu/~ewertheim/skills/writovv.htm**, p. 4.
7. Basch, R., & Bates, M. E. (2000). *Researching online for dummies* (2nd ed.). Foster City, CA: IDG Books Worldwide, pp. 15, 319–320.
8. Grammas, G. W. (1986). The management of communication flow. In J. L. Di Gaetani (Ed.), *The handbook of executive communication,* p. 63. Homewood, IL: Dow Jones-Irwin.
9. *Telecommunications thesis handbook, version 2.0.* (n.d.). Retrieved July 2, 2002, from **http://www.tele.sunyit.edu/ThesisHandbook.html**, p. 2.
10. *Design reports.* (n.d.). Retrieved July 6, 2002, from **http://filebox.vt.edu/eng/ mech/writing/workbooks/design.html**, pp. 1–2.
11. *Ibid,* p. 1.
12. *Progress reports.* (n.d.). Retrieved February 20, 2002, from **http://filebox.vt.edu/ eng/mech/writing/workbooks/prog.html**, p. 1.
13. Block, P. (1999). *Flawless consulting: A guide to getting your expertise used.* San Francisco, CA: Pfeiffer & Co.
14. Rafuse, B. S., & Loth, R. E. (1996, January). Management consulting: A skills-based workshop for success. Workshop presented to the Southern Methodist University MBA program, Dallas, TX.

15. Online technical writing: recommendation and feasibility reports. (n.d.). In *Online Technical Writing*. Retrieved July 4, 2002, from **http://www.io.com/~hcexres/ tcm1603/acchtml/feas.html**, p. 2.

16. Huckin, T., & Olsen, L. (2002). Projects in science and technology writing: feasibility reports. In *Professional communications e.textbook* (chap. 2 part B). Retrieved July 4, 2002, from **http://www.kjist.ac.kr/~slic/est/e_textbook-EST-STW-Chapter4-B .htm**, pp. 1–4.

17. *Ibid*, p. 2.

18. Online technical writing: recommendation and feasibility reports, p. 7.

19. Beisel, J. L. Forcing international communication. In *Great ideas for teaching marketing*. Retrieved March 26, 2002, from **http://www.swcollege.com/marketing/ gitm/gitm09-6.html**

20. As this book goes to press the site is being updated: **http://reports.mintel.com**. The old site can be accessed from the new one under the heading "How's it done?" Click on "Research Methods," and then click on "Report Format."

CHAPTER - 10

Writing Instructions, Documentation, Policies, and Procedures

"Pardon me, I'm new here and I'm trying to get to the mailroom and I'm lost. Which way is it?"

"Yes, you are lost. No problem. Take the elevator to the basement, G-2, go left down a long hallway until you get to a door with a funny poster on it, then take the next right, go until you hear the noise from the envelope-sorting machine, and you're there."

"Thanks, I think I can find it now."

You did find the mailroom—but only after being lost and frustrated for 25 minutes by the instructions you just received. As a new employee, how were you supposed to know that not all the elevators went to the basement? And what did she mean by a "funny" poster? There were several posters and some were humorous and others strange. And then there's the fact that you had never heard an envelope-sorting machine before. If only she had given you good instructions.

As this vignette illustrates, anyone who has been frustrated by ambiguous instructions recognizes the importance of clearly conveying them. On the job, instructions may be delivered orally from a superior on how to do a task, presented in a manual on how to use computer software, or given formally in a Policies and Procedures booklet that details operations procedures. Whether written or oral, formal or informal, good instructions have common characteristics. This chapter discusses these characteristics and then relates them to three main applications: (1) instructions, (2) documentation, and (3) policies and procedures.

Writing Instructions

Instructions are written or oral guidance that are often a one-time occurrence (such as directions to someone's office) and are likely to be given from one person to another. Documentation usually carries a degree of formality and often occurs in a form that is retrievable, such as hard copy. Often documentation is prepared by one person for many people. An example of documentation is the "wizard" help function in your word-processing utility that guides you through multiple steps, such as changing the formatting of a memorandum. Policies and Procedures are formal statements that guide employees of an organization to apply standard processes in the accomplishment of their duties.

Determining a Need for Written Instructions

Think of an organization for whom you currently work or formerly worked. Did that organization have adequate written documentation? Most do not. Use the checklist in Figure 10.1 to determine an organization's needs for written instructions.

Guidelines for Written Instructions

Good instructions are unambiguous, understandable, complete, consistent, and efficient. Each of these characteristics is a guideline.

Guideline 1: Avoid Ambiguity

The more concrete your instructions, the better. Rather than saying, "Turn at the big tree," say, "Turn left at the large oak tree between the sidewalk and the street that has a 'House for Sale' sign on it." Writing with clarity avoids words that have multiple meanings or little meaning. Precision is an important aspect of clarity.

Guideline 2: Be Understandable

Instructions should relate to the receiver. Target your audience with your message. Even though you are likely to be talking or writing to a single individual, you need to decide upon your audience's level of familiarity with the system. Jargon and acronyms may be appropriate with some audiences and inappropriate for others. Instructions can also be made more understandable with short sentences, familiar words, and good transitions.

| Figure 10.1 | Checklist: Written Instructions Needs Assessment |

Does your organization:

1. Have frequent personnel changes between jobs?
2. Have high turnover of employees?
3. Realize that people have memory limitations?
4. Have complex and often-repeated activities?
5. Tend to formalize communication by "writing things down"?
6. Have supervisors or trainers who have to repeat instructions?
7. Have employees who forget important steps in complex tasks?
8. Have employees who complain that they did not know certain steps were required as part of a procedure?

If you answered "Yes" to many of these questions, then your organization would benefit from documentation.

Guideline 3: Be Complete

Instructions can be clear and understandable but still fail because they were incomplete. Leaving out an important step in a task procedure may result in failure to complete the task. In addition to identifying all central steps or elements in your instructions, anticipate possible problems or questions that may arise.

The next time you read a newspaper or news magazine, note that most stories begin by answering these basic questions: Who? What? When? Where? How? Why? Here is an example:

> [American] Scientists announced yesterday that they have synthesized a virus from scratch for the first time, raising the possibility that terrorists could create biological killers once thought beyond their reach.[1]

The author tells us who (scientists), what (announced and synthesized), when (yesterday), where (American), and how (from scratch), and indirectly answers why (terrorist concerns). As a partial test of the completeness of your instructions, check them to see if you answered these six questions.

Guideline 4: Be Consistent

Much as parallel sentence structure improves understanding, so does consistency in giving instructions. Know the different levels of your instructions and make those levels obvious to your receiver. For example, in written instructions, treat each major step similarly, each substep in a consistent fashion, and so on. Each major step might start a new page, have the same typeface treatment and white space, and start with an overview.

When presenting lists, use bullets in front of nonsequential items, and numbers or letters in front of sequential items. Employ this concept consistently, and use parallel structure in delivering your lists.

Guideline 5: Be Efficient

Efficiency here means to achieve the other four guidelines while holding the length of the instructions to an absolute minimum. Efficiency can be difficult because clear, unambiguous, understandable, consistent instructions are likely to be lengthy. Nevertheless, seek ways to minimize your instructions. For example, rather than starting each of seven steps with the phrase, "Your next step in accomplishing your task is to . . . ," place a similar phrase at the top of the list once, end with a colon, and then list the steps in sequential order.

Efficiency can often be achieved using overviews that give the parameters of the instructions, such as, "Installing this software involves three main steps and takes about eight minutes. Before you can install the software, however, you must know your serial number and the amount of RAM available in your computer." Overviews avoid the inefficiency of getting part-way through a set of instructions only to learn you do not have the necessary equipment or information to complete the task.

Documentation

Documentation is establishing proof, information, evidence, or sequence, usually in written form. After a business trip, you will be asked to document your travel expenses, perhaps on an expense voucher, before you can be reimbursed. You may decide to protect yourself from challenges in the future by documenting in writing your request to your superior for a quieter office because your clients cannot hear you on the phone, thus reducing your effectiveness.

Another form of documentation—the form is what is of importance here—combines instructions with documentation. Instructional documentation may provide guidance on how to construct a barbeque grill, share job or specific task instructions, or give the information needed to set up a software program. The main purpose of instructional documentation is teaching a sequence of activities or serving as a reference for instructions. Software manuals, either hard-copy or built into the software, are typically divided into at least these two parts, often called "User's Manual" and "Reference Manual." This dichotomy reflects the learning process of typically examining user information only once or twice, and then longer-term, frequent use of reference information.

As you organize your documentation assignment, in addition to applying the five guidelines, also consider how the information will be used by your audience. An airplane pilot refers to a list of necessary behaviors and conditions each time before takeoff. A word-processing specialist refers to a "Help" guide to refresh the memory of a seldom-used keystroke command. A new employee follows a tutorial prepared by her predecessor to learn a complicated task. A job applicant examines a job description to evaluate interest in the position. Each of these documents has a different, focused goal based on anticipated audience use.

In preparing documentation, refer to this list of questions:

- What is the goal of the documentation?
- Am I writing to a single user or a group of users?
- Will the user refer to this documentation more than once?
- How long should this version of the documentation be used? (What is its life span?)
- Would a glossary be helpful?
- Should I pilot-test the documentation on a naive user?
- Is the writing level appropriate for the lowest-level user?
- Should I include an index?

The organization of written documentation can influence its success. For documentation that is lengthy, complex, or especially important, have a clear opening, an organized body, and a closing. Your opening may include a greeting ("Thank you for buying our product."); the purpose ("This manual will show you how to assemble your new grill."); an overview ("There are five main steps in putting together your new barbeque."); cautions, warnings, conventions, or specific language ("Whenever you see this symbol, be sure the unit is NOT plugged into an electrical outlet."); or tools or equipment needed ("You will need a Phillips screwdriver and a pair of pliers for assembly.").

For the body—especially when you have multiple steps and substeps—consider employing the concept of classification discussed in Chapter 4. Employ such comments as "You may accomplish the following four items in any order you wish," or "Follow these three steps exactly in the order presented or the product will not function."

The closing may include indication of success ("If your computer monitor shows the message, 'Do you wish to register your software now?' you have successfully installed the software.") or offer troubleshooting advice ("Check that you have adequate RAM installed by following these steps.").

The Nature of Mission Statements, Policies, and Procedures

Mission Statements

In the last decade many companies have prepared mission statements and vision statements and shared them with the public. Internal policies and procedures have been an important part of organizations for many years. However, there is little consistent use of these terms and even when the terms are used consistently, they may not be understood by all viewers.

At the highest, most general level within an organization is the mission statement, objectives, or goals: these terms are synonymous. Vision statements are sometimes part of the mission statement. They are the generalized purposes toward which the entire organization strives. Here are some examples:

- Maximizing net profits
- Keeping employees satisfied
- Keeping customers loyal
- Maximizing market share
- Being a good corporate citizen

Advantages of Mission Statements

Mission statements vary considerably in specificity across organizations and may vary from one organization to another in terms of stability, constancy, and how well-known they are. Mission statements perform five critical functions for the organization:

1. They provide orientation by depicting a desired state of affairs.
2. They set down guidelines.
3. They constitute a source of legitimacy that justifies the organization's activities and its existence.
4. They serve as standards by which success can be measured.
5. They represent a sought-after state, not one that is already available.

Figure 10.2 shows Microsoft's mission statement,[2] which includes its vision and how Microsoft seeks to deliver on its mission. For comparison, how does it stack up against Staples's brief mission statement: Great service every day in every way?[3]

Although mission statements change from time to time, they are intended to channel the efforts of all employees toward similar ends. Yet because they are so generally worded, mission statements do not provide much guidance to employees in terms of exactly how to meet them. There are many different means to one end: Policies and procedures must be written.

Microsoft's Mission

To enable people and businesses throughout the world to realize their full potential

Microsoft's Vision

Empowering people through great software – any time, any place and on any device

Delivering on Our Mission

The tenets central to accomplishing our mission include:

Great People with Great Values

Delivering on our mission requires great people who are bright, creative and energetic, and who share the following values:

- Integrity and honesty
- Passion for customers, partners, and technology
- Open and respectful with others and dedicated to making them better
- Willingness to take on big challenges and see them through
- Self critical, questioning and committed to personal excellence and self improvement
- Accountable for commitments, results, and quality to customers, shareholders, partners and employees

Excellence

In everything we do.

Trustworthy Computing

Deepening customer trust through the quality of our products and services, our responsiveness and accountability, and our predictability in everything we do.

Broad Customer Connection

Connecting with customers, understanding their needs and how they use technology, and providing value through information and support to help them realize their potential.

Innovative and Responsible Platform Leadership

Expanding platform innovation, benefits, and opportunities for customers and partners; openness in discussing our future directions; getting feedback; and working with others to ensure that their products and our platforms work well together.

Enabling People to Do New Things

Broadening choices for customers by identifying new areas of business; incubating new products; integrating new customer scenarios into existing businesses; exploring acquisitions of key talent and experience; and integrating more deeply with new and existing partners.

A Global, Inclusive Approach

Thinking and acting globally, enabling a multicultural workforce that generates innovative decision-making for a diverse universe of customers and partners, innovating to lower the costs of technology, and showing leadership in supporting the communities in which we work and live.

Source: Microsoft. (2002, July 1). Retrieved July 15, 2002, from **http://www.microsoft.com/mscorp/**. Reprinted with permission from Microsoft Corporation.

Policies

As opposed to a mission statement, a policy is a general guide to decision making and reflects the organization's attempts to achieve its goals. Policies are the framework, consistent with organizational objectives, that help managers make decisions. Yet a policy is only a guideline, as it usually gives the manager some degree of discretion in making decisions. Figure 10.3 shows some examples of policies and how they relate to mission statements.

Notice how the policy statements provide for discretion or flexibility in decision making. For example, the community-service policy does not tell the manager which or how many community organizations to join, nor does it specify how extensively the manager should be involved in any one organization.

The higher you move in a business, the more discretion you probably will have. Policy statements for top-level management are usually worded more generally than those that are used at lower levels. Figure 10.4 shows the amount of discretion given management levels in a small manufacturing plant.

Staples, an office-supply company, has a policy that it will match competitors' prices; that policy appears in Figure 10.5.

Advantages of Policies

Policies help to implement mission statements. There are other advantages, especially when they are in written form. First, policies enhance consistency in decision making. Second, conflict among employees may be prevented. Finally, policies can save time. Policies keep managers from having to make the same decision over and over.

Disadvantages of Policies

Despite the advantages of policies, they are usually not created for every decision. First, it is almost impossible to write a policy applicable to every set of circumstances. To do so would require amazing foresight and would probably result in a policy manual hundreds of pages long (which many managers would not read). Second, although policies promote consistency in decision making, at the same time they reduce the amount of flexibility decision makers have. Exceptions to nearly every policy exist, and their existence often creates frustrated reactions.

| Figure 10.3 | **Policies Related to Mission Statements** |

Mission Statement	Policy
Keeping customers loyal	If any customer is dissatisfied with a purchase, then his or her money will be refunded.
Being a good corporate citizen	Managers will use every opportunity to become involved in community services, such as the United Way, the Heart Fund, and the American Red Cross.
Keeping employees satisfied	All promotions to managerial positions will be from within the company.

Figure 10.4 **Amount of Discretion Allowed**

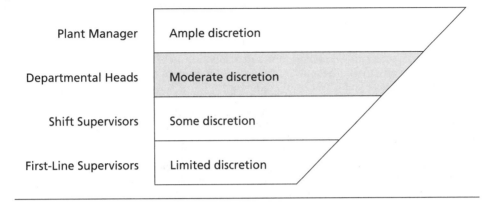

Plant Manager	Ample discretion
Departmental Heads	Moderate discretion
Shift Supervisors	Some discretion
First-Line Supervisors	Limited discretion

Policies, then, are general guides to decision making. They are created to help a business accomplish its mission. If more specific decision-making guidelines are needed, then procedures are written.

Procedures

A procedure is a specific guide to decision making, a tool for implementing a policy. While the general wording of a policy allows discretion in making decisions, procedures offer little or no discretion. When procedures give discretion, they are called guides. When procedures allow no discretion, they are called a rule. The example below shows this distinction.

Mission	*Policy*	*Procedure (guide)*	*Policy (rule)*
Keeping Customers Loyal	If any customer is dissatisfied with a purchase, then his or her money will be refunded.	Check the returned merchandise carefully to see if it has been misused.	The customer must sign the refund slip.

For just this one objective we could develop a long list of both guides and rules. However, notice first that the guide listed gives the employee discretion, whereas the rule does not. Second, notice how the chart moves from the general (the mission) to the specific (the rule). The farther we go toward the right, the more control we exert over the behavior of the employees.

You many have worked for a company that had no written policies or procedures. Many businesses do not. The larger a firm is, the more written policies and procedures (sometimes called standard operating procedures, or SOPs) the firm usually will have. If the business has unionized employees, no matter how large or small it is, most policies and procedures will be contained in what is called the labor agreement or contract.

Figure 10.5 | **Staples 110% Price-Match Guarantee**

If you find a lower price, anywhere else, on a new identical item, just show us the lower price when you buy the item at Staples or within 14 days after your Staples purchase—and we'll give you 110% of the difference.

Our 14-day price-match guarantee is good on everything from office supplies to the latest technology. The item must be in-stock and available for purchase at that price from a company located in the U.S.

- If you find a lower price in a Staples store, Staples catalog, or on our website, www.Staples.com, we will match the lower price. The additional 10% of the price difference does not apply.

- The item must be identical. For example, it must have the same U.S. manufacturer's warranty. It must also have the same model number and contain the same components. As another example, for pagers and wireless phones, the service plan, service provider, and other terms must be the same.

- Staples reserves the right to verify another company's product availability and price before issuing a price match guarantee.

- Available coupons and rebates will be deducted from the Staples price to come up with a net Staples price when calculating the price match. For example, if you buy an item from us for $100, and we offer a $20 rebate, the net price is $80. If the item is available from another company for $80 or more, there will be no price match. Another example would be if you buy an item from us for $159 and you have a $30 coupon the net price is $129. If the item is available from another company for $125, the price match will be for $4.40 (110% of the difference).

- Shipping and handling charges are included. When comparing our price to another company's delivery price, the equivalent shipping and handling charges will be included. If proof of the other company's shipping and handling charges are not supplied, then $5 will be added to the other company's price. (For example, if you buy an item from us for $100, with free delivery, and the item is available from another company for $90, with overnight shipping and handling charges of $7, then the difference is $3. You receive 110% of $3, which is $3.30.)

- If another company offers a product that comes with a free or discounted item and Staples does not carry the free or discounted item, there will be no price match. For example, if another company offers a free product with the purchase of a printer, and Staples' price for the printer is equal to the other company's price for the printer, there will be no price match if Staples does not carry the free product being offered.

- We may limit the quantity of an item that may be price-matched. For example, if the other company limits the number you may buy, we may also limit the number. In addition, Staples reserves the right to limit quantities sold to a Customer.

- We price match almost everything. We don't price match Sprint long distance service, third party providers' products and services sold through our Business Services website or through third party representatives in our stores (for example, tax preparation, payroll services and corporate logos), and items sold at local or special events (e.g., grand opening, anniversary, or liquidation sales) or on Internet auction sites. We also don't price match taxes and typographical errors.

- For more information, or a price match, see customer service, call 1-800-STAPLES or click for <u>customer service</u>.

- This policy is subject to change without notice.

Source: Staples 110% price-match guarantee. (n.d.) Retrieved October 2, 2002, from **http://www.staples.com/help/default.asp?area=protection**.

Writing Policies and Procedures Statements

As you pursue your career in business, you will most likely be involved in writing policies and procedures statements in one of three instances: (1) when a new business is formed; (2) when a new policy or procedure is needed; or (3) when old policies or procedures are being rewritten. You will probably have a chance to write policies and procedures on a variety of topics, including promotion and pay policies, actual work procedures for performing a task, and employee grievances and discipline.

Many organizations have policies and procedures for hiring new employees, ensuring employee safety, disciplining employees, hearing employee grievances, handling customers, dealing with employee absences, and evaluating employees. Although they may not be referred to as policies or procedures, companies are likely also to have government regulations imposed upon them by such organizations as the Environmental Protection Agency (EPA) or the Occupational Safety and Health Administration (OSHA), or by government standards, such as Equal Employment Opportunity Commission (EEOC) standards. In some cases, the government regulations or standards *are* the policies or procedures; in other cases, the organization writes its own policies and procedures on how to respond to the government. Yet another set of policies and procedures active in many organizations is a code of ethics. It may be called a code, but is a policy and procedure document.

You can see from this list that most policies and procedures affect the internal operation of a company. As you write your policies and procedures, apply the five guidelines presented early in this chapter in the discussion of instructions. Note how the following partial policy/procedure is concrete, understandable, complete, consistent, and efficient.

Sick leave policy. As an employee of Burns Chemical company, you are allowed time off with pay when you are unable to work because of illness. Pay for sick leave is for the sole purpose of protecting you against loss of income when you are ill.

Procedures.
1. If you are sick and unable to work, you should call your supervisor no later than one hour before your shift begins.
2. If you are unable to work for three or more days in a row, then you must bring a note from your doctor on the day you return to work. This note should be given to you supervisor.

Although this example is only part of a sick leave policy and procedure, it clearly tells the employee *who* is involved (the employee, the supervisor, and possibly a doctor). The *what* is a telephone call and bringing a physician's note. Two *whens* are in the procedure: no later than one hour before the shift begins and the day the employee returns to work. The *how* is implicit in this procedure because it links the answers to the first three questions. *Why* is answered in the policy statement: Note that the statement is consistent.

The two characteristics of a policy and procedures statement are (1) policies appear first, and (2) procedures are listed step by step. As you write policy and procedures statements, you will often find that more than one policy is covered by a given procedure. If this is the case, you will want to list all those policies first, then follow them with the procedures. The following example expands the sick leave policy we used earlier.

Sick leave policy. As an employee of Burns Chemical company, you are allowed time off with pay when you are unable to work because of illness. Pay for sick leave is for the sole purpose of protecting you against loss of income when you are ill.

1. You are allowed 8 paid sick days per calendar year.
2. If you do not need all of your sick days during a year, then you may add the days you don't use to your next year's total. A maximum of 90 paid sick leave days can be accrued.

Procedures.
1. If you are sick and unable to work, you should call your supervisor no later than one hour before your shift begins.
2. If you are unable to work for three or more days in a row, then you must bring a note from your doctor on the day you return to work. This note should be given to your supervisor.

In this example the first policy may seem to be a procedure because it appears to be a rule. However, remember that procedures are specific guides to decision making. They tell us how to take action to implement a policy. When writing procedures, you should organize them step by step. Often, following procedures results in an end product of some kind. Therefore, to be sure that the product is correct, you should organize and label the steps clearly. Here is an example:

Customer Refunds Policy. If any customer is dissatisfied with a purchase, then his or her money will be refunded.

Procedures.
1. Check the customer's sales slip. Only the store manager may authorize returns on merchandise the customer has had for more than 30 days.
2. Fill out the customer refund slip, making sure that you enter:
   - Customer's name and address
   - Date of purchase
   - Stock number and description of the merchandise
   - Sales number of salesperson who sold the merchandise
   - Your sales number
   - Reason for the return
3. Take the customer refund slip to your immediate supervisor, who will approve the refund.
4. Have the customer sign the refund slip.
5. Refund the customer's money:
   a. If the purchase was by credit card, tell the customer his or her account will be credited for the amount of purchase. Do not make cash refunds on credit card purchases.
   b. If the purchase was by cash, then refund the customer's money from your cash drawer. Place the audit copy of the credit refund slip in the drawer.
6. Take the remaining copies of the credit refund slip and returned merchandise to the customer service department.

Each step in the procedure requires a different action. Ideally, no two acts (unless they are closely connected, as in 5b) should be described in one step.

Summary

Giving good written and oral instructions in business is crucial. These instructions should achieve the guidelines of avoiding abstract language, being understandable, being complete, achieving consistency, and being efficient. Business instructions can be divided into three main categories: instructions, documentation, and policies and procedures.

Instructions are often one-on-one and may not be formalized through hard copy or other relatively permanent delivery. Documentation, on the other hand, is likely to be prepared for many users and through a medium that is likely to be available over an extended time.

An organization of more size and longevity is likely to have a mission statement, policies, and procedures. Mission statements are objectives toward which the organization moves but can never fully accomplish. Policies are general guides that help members of the organization move toward its mission statement. Procedures are specific guides for implementing policies, and they allow for some discretion (guides) or little discretion (rules).

Many of us assume we are able to give good instructions in any of their forms, but writing clear, complete, and still brief instructions is challenging, yet rewarding to the organization.

Discussion Questions

1. What is the overlap between instructions and documentation? Where does one end and the other begin?
2. What are the differences between mission statements and objectives? How firmly established are the definitions for these terms?
3. What are the two types of procedures? Who, within an organization, is likely to implement each of them? Is one likely to be more difficult to write than the other?
4. Distinguish between policies and procedures. How do they differ? At what level in a typical organization does a certain hierarchical level prepare each?
5. Compare policies and procedures issued at your organization to those of other students in the class. What similarities and differences do you note?

Communication in Action

1. Locate some software instruction manuals that are five or more years old. Compare them to some recent software that includes its documentation within the program, such as a Help file from a pull-down menu. What differences are there? Has documentation improved over time? How?
2. Analyze the Help support for some software programs that are available as part of the program. How is the documentation organized? How friendly is it? Would most users prefer documentation that is (1) delivered through a Wizard or tutorial, (2) given in an index format, (3) accessed as a formal manual in a PDF file, or (4) connected to a Web page through a link? Do you think most users prefer electronic or hard-copy support? Why?

@ Internet

3. As a staff member of a relatively young and small organization, you have been charged by your supervisor with scanning the Internet for suggestions on how to prepare effective documentation. See what you can find that pertains to length, language, and delivery media. You may wish to try using such key words as "writing and documentation," "written and

documentation," "effective documentation," or "preparing effective and documentation."

4. For the same organization as question 1 above, now assist the Human Resources department by seeking out effective examples of employee leave policies and procedures in other organizations. Include profit and nonprofit organizations, and small, medium, and large organizations. Consider using such key words as "employee and procedure and policy" in your search.

5. Use the Internet to find five substantially different organizations. Now, find their mission statements. What were their differences? Do certain types of organizations tend to adopt or write similar types of mission statements?

6. Because of the important role of e-mail in carrying messages within and between organizations, many organizations have a policy regarding how employees may and may not use e-mail. Use the Internet to locate a variety of e-mail policies. Include at least one university, one nonprofit organization, and one government organization.

InfoTrac

7. Within the management discipline, the human resources area often examines, prepares, and oversees policies and procedures related to managing employees. Use InfoTrac to identify as many human resources–oriented periodicals as you can. Prepare a list of those periodicals. Now, use the Internet to go to the Web sites of many of them. Find the mission or objective of each periodical. Attach them to the list of periodicals.

8. Use InfoTrac to locate literature that gives guidance on the preparation of mission statements. What is the current state of the literature on the topic?

9. Find an article from 1994 in *Planning Review* entitled "Rethinking Vision and Mission." Read the article. On what issues do the contributors agree and disagree? Whose opinion do you feel is most reasonable? Why?

10. User documentation for Information Systems (IS) may be directed solely to the IS group, such as how to program changes to automatically upgrade the firewall that protects the organization's server. However, the IS group often also needs to share documentation with its organization's users, who may not be savvy with the intricacies of computers and programming, such as when users are asked to upgrade their version of the company's e-mail program.

    Find an article by Kieran Mathieson entitled "Effective User Documentation: Focusing on Tasks Instead of Systems." What does she have to say about the purposes documentation serves?

11. Much of how an organization's corporate identity is formed grows from its written documents, including its mission statements. Locate Lance Leuthesser's article "Corporate Identity: The Role of Mission Statements" in *Business Horizons*, 1997. What does the article state about the role of mission statements? What does it say about their shortcomings?

Notes

1. Scientists create virus from scratch. (2002, July 12). *The San Diego Union-Tribune*, p. 1.
2. Ballmer, S. (2002, June). Microsoft's mission & values. Retrieved July 12, 2002, from **http://www.microsoft.com/mscorp/**
3. Staples (2002). Corporate information. Retrieved July 12, 2002, from **http://www.staples.com/about/policy/mission**

Part Four

Oral Communication

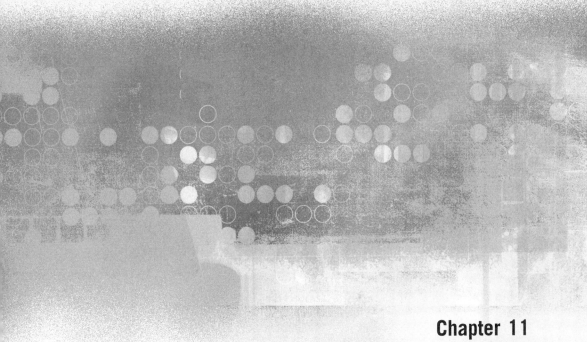

CHAPTER - 11

The Business Presentation

In this chapter, we will consider business communication situations in which you must make a presentation before an audience—usually a small group of decision makers.

Types of Presentations

While some presentations can be classified as primarily informative, most presentations are persuasive in nature. They seek agreement with a position on an issue or approval for an action proposal. Common presentations within the organization include briefings, status reports, and budget or project proposals. Outside the organization, presentations are typically occasions for selling to groups of clients or customers.

To highlight the diversity of presentations made in a typical large organization, managers attending training sessions conducted by one of the authors suggested the following as examples of presentations in their organization:

Briefing for Press on Company Plans to Handle a Crisis
Briefing for Managers on New Compensation System
    for Senior Managers
Status Report on Affirmative Action Program
Budget Proposal
Forecast Projection
Systems Demonstration for Upper Management
Briefings for Vendors
Briefings for Senior Executives on Community Issues
Orientation for New Employees
Quality Assurance Orientation
Company Position at Arbitration Hearing
Recruitment Talk at a College Career Day
Briefings for Senior Executives on Labor Relations
User Briefing on New Computer System
Talk at Company Training Seminar
Contract Award Recommendations
Briefings on Technical Subjects for Nontechnical Audience

This list reflects the range of presentations made by middle managers in most companies.

Six Propositions About Presentations

Despite the obvious differences among specific types of presentations, six propositions apply to all types.

1. Presentations are made before small audiences, which are often composed of decision makers. By decision makers, we mean people such as your boss and other senior executives who might be considering your budget proposal or status report. Or the decision makers might be your clients and customers considering your pitch on behalf of the services or products of your firm.

   Even when a presentation appears to be informative rather than persuasive (a briefing or an employee orientation talk), your audience will also be making an evaluation—an evaluation about your competence and, frankly, your future prospects with the firm.

2. Presentations are usually delivered extemporaneously. By extemporaneous, we mean that the presentation is prepared and delivered from an outline. While some executives like to deliver memorized presentations (without an outline), reading the complete text of your presentation to a small group is almost always viewed as inappropriate. The balance of this chapter presents detailed guidelines for preparing and delivering the extemporaneous presentation.

3. Presentations usually complement some type of written communication. Oral presentations rarely assume the full burden of communication on the subject. The typical oral report complements and reinforces a longer, more detailed written report. The same can be said for proposal presentations, budget presentations, project presentations, or sales presentations.

4. Presentations usually employ some type of visual aid, typically computer-generated presentation graphics (PowerPoint, for example), overhead transparencies, or slides. (See Chapter 3 for a detailed discussion of these visuals and others.)

   Although visuals serve the important purposes of highlighting main points or conclusions and clarifying statistics and financial information, they also make the presentation more interesting for the audience. Later in this chapter, we will consider some guidelines for using visuals in presentations.

5. Presentations usually have question-and-answer sessions. You rarely escape a presentation without some questions from members of the audience. This is to be expected. After all, whether you are sharing important information, seeking approval for your pet project, or selling the services of your firm, the decision makers sitting before you will probably need some clarification or elaboration of points you have made in your presentation.

6. Presentations may also involve a team of presenters. Team presentations require careful planning and coordination to ensure successful outcomes. Such presentations are increasingly common in business and industry.

Types of Delivery

As we noted in the second proposition, business presentations are nearly always delivered in an extemporaneous style. Before describing the extemporaneous style in some detail, let us consider the three other types of delivery: manuscript, memorized, and impromptu.

The Manuscript Delivery

A manuscript presentation is delivered from a full text. It is read word-for-word from a typed manuscript or from a TelePrompTer. There are occasions when a manuscript delivery is appropriate, such as when presenting testimony at a hearing, delivering a major policy statement before a large public audience, or taping a message for broadcast. Manuscript delivery offers precision and control over content.

The cost of these two benefits may be high, though. First, most managers read manuscripts poorly (without sufficient vocal expressiveness and emphasis). Second, because they are busy reading their manuscripts, they eliminate virtually all eye contact with their audiences. Third, a manuscript presentation is relatively inflexible: It is difficult to adapt to a speaking situation and depart from the prepared text. Most importantly, reading from a text is considered inappropriate for most presentations in business, especially those before small groups. Thus, the manuscript presentation is not a serious option for most presenters.

The Memorized Presentation

The memorized presentation also requires that the presenter write out the content word for word, but rather than reading it to the audience, the presenter memorizes the presentation in advance and then recites it. Naturally, some managers make brief or recurring talks that are suitable for memorization, but too many managers create unnecessary problems for themselves by memorizing long presentations.

First, as a method of delivering presentations, memorization places considerable pressure on those giving the presentation because they fear that they will forget their lines. They worry what will happen if their minds suddenly go blank, or if they lose their chain of thought. Frankly, they are in big trouble. Consider this hypothetical situation: You memorize your presentation. Midway through the presentation, you are interrupted by a question. Startled by the interruption, you momentarily forget where you are in the presentation. Unfortunately, when you resume, you skip over an important point. This creates confusion for your audience—and more questions, too.

Second, memorization of a presentation is time-consuming. Along with the time it takes to plan, compose, and practice a presentation is the time spent memorizing it. Although we recommend, below, that presenters do some memory work when preparing an extemporaneous presentation, we do not feel that the time required to memorize a full presentation is justified, especially in light of the other problems associated with this style of delivery.

Third, memorized presentations tend to *sound* memorized. There is a canned, mechanical, self-conscious quality to many memorized presentations. In fact, some speakers, eager to get through the presentation before they forget something, resemble Las Vegas slot machines, with words instead of coins spilling out of their mouths.

Fourth, the memorized presentation is as inflexible as the manuscript delivery. Speaking from a script, albeit memorized, the presenter will find it difficult to respond to the audience and the occasion.

The Impromptu Presentation

The impromptu presentation is unprepared, spontaneous, off-the-cuff. Although there will be situations in business when you will have to speak in an impromptu manner, you place your professional reputation at risk if you fail to prepare for those situations you can foresee. Unlike carefully prepared presentations, impromptu speaking tends to be relatively disorganized, imprecise, and repetitive. It is not the stuff of which successful careers are made.

Impromptu presentations, therefore, are justified only by necessity. For example, you are asked unexpectedly by your boss at a meeting to give a briefing on some problem or a status report on some project; you are asked at a presentation before some prospective clients to address an issue that you had not planned to talk about; or you are asked a rather sophisticated and unexpected open question on an employment interview—one that requires a response of several minutes.

Try to minimize these situations by anticipating them. For example, if you plan to attend a meeting, prepare for the possibility that you might be asked to speak. Then, if you are asked, what you say will be cogent. That is the stuff of which successful careers are made.

Extemporaneous Speaking

An extemporaneous presentation is carefully prepared and delivered from notes or an outline. Although the method is not without disadvantages, it is clearly superior to the manuscript, memorized, or impromptu deliveries. Once mastered, the extemporaneous method of speaking will serve you well any time you make a business presentation.

The goal of extemporaneous speaking, as a style of delivery, is to be conversational. You appear to be conversing with the audience in a natural and spontaneous manner. Although you consult your notes occasionally, you spend most of your time looking at the audience. Your voice is expressive and emphatic.

Most audience members prefer this style of communicating because you appear to be conversing with them rather than talking at them. Your image is enhanced as well. Unlike the case in a manuscript presentation, you are relatively free of written material, suggesting that you have a greater command over the content of your presentation.

Furthermore, the extemporaneous delivery provides flexibility. Given that you are speaking from an outline, it is relatively easy to adapt and modify your presentation as the occasion and audience may demand. Content may be added, deleted, expanded, or reduced without the audience becoming aware of any changes. This is much harder to do with a manuscript or memorized presentation, for reasons discussed above.

The audience-pleasing style of delivery, the flexibility it offers, and the enhanced credibility it confers on the presenter are the major advantages of the extemporaneous method of delivery. Even so, a few disadvantages do arise from the nature of the extemporaneous method, which asks you to look at your outline, construct the message in your mind, and speak to the audience.

First, there is a degree of stress associated with the process. Because you are not working from a complete text, you may worry that you will misspeak or leave something out of your presentation. These are well-founded concerns.

Second, the method sacrifices a degree of precision and conciseness compared to the manuscript presentation. Over the course of the presentation, you may make minor errors in grammar or diction, leave out an important detail, or make an error in fact. This is in the nature of the method of delivery.

Third, the extemporaneous method may be too flexible for a presentation giver. You may find it difficult to resist the opportunity to digress, to ad-lib, or to exceed the time limit assigned to the presentation. Here again, the manuscript and memorized presentations offer an advantage.

Still, the advantages of the extemporaneous method, when compared to the other three methods of delivery, outweigh its disadvantages. In the next section, as we describe the process of preparing and delivering the extemporaneous presentation, we will suggest a number of devices that will minimize those disadvantages.

The Seven-Step Process of Preparing and Delivering Extemporaneous Presentations

Step One: Plan and Organize the Presentation

You may recall from your basic undergraduate speech course that a speech consisted of three parts: an introduction, a body, and a conclusion. The introduction was said to have three primary functions: to gain the attention of the audience, to state a thesis or purpose, and to offer a preview of the main points to be covered. The body of a speech was the presentation of the main points backed by supporting material. The conclusion was said to be the obverse of the introduction: first, it reviews the main points of the speech; and then it closes with another attention-getting device. This basic plan applies to presentations in business with a few modifications.

Plan and Organize the Introduction of the Presentation

Obviously, in most cases you will plan and organize the introduction last—that is, after you have prepared the body of the presentation. Otherwise, how will you know what you are introducing? But for the purposes of this discussion, we will first consider how to plan an introduction.

As we noted above, a presenter needs to accomplish three major goals in the introduction: get the attention of the audience, state the thesis or purpose of the presentation, and preview the main points.

Attention. A number of techniques may be employed to secure the attention of an audience. Common attention-getting devices are a startling statement or statistic, an anecdote or story, a rhetorical question, a quotation, and humor. Such attention-getters must be related, of course, to the thesis or purpose of the presentation.

Be careful here: Many of these devices may be inappropriate to presentations made to decision makers. First, you usually have the attention of such an audience—your problem will be to keep it! Second, attempts at storytelling or humor may seem frivolous and a waste of time to an audience of senior executives or even to a group of important clients. Humor is highly subjective: What is funny to you may not be funny to your audience. It is a lonely feeling to be in front of an audience when your attempt at humor falls flat. A third reason to avoid an attention getter when presenting to decision makers is that the device may backfire. Suppose you pose this rhetorical question to a group of senior executives: "Why have benefits risen 20 percent this year?" You risk the following response from a crusty senior executive: "Why the hell are you asking us? You're here to answer questions, not ask them. C'mon, get to the point."

Often the best way to begin a presentation before decision makers is to skip the attention-getting device and move directly to a statement of thesis or purpose, followed by a preview of the main points of the presentation. Often the thesis will be sufficient to elicit the attention of an internal audience of decision makers: "Over this year and next, the cost of our benefit program will increase 50 percent." If that does not get their attention, check for pulses! See Figure 11.1 for a good organization for an in-house speech by a benefits manager.

Still, some presentations may benefit from a clever attention-getting device. Typically, such presentations will be before somewhat larger groups of peers and subordinates or before public audiences outside the company. See Figure 11.2 for such a use of an attention getter.

Thesis or Purpose. A presenter may or may not choose to state a thesis or main point in the introduction. If a direct plan is chosen, then the thesis will be stated in the introduction; if an indirect plan is chosen, the thesis will not be stated there. As you have read in earlier chapters, the direct plan is commonly employed when presenting information that does not evoke a strong negative response from the audience, whereas the indirect plan is used to present negative information and in cases where persuasion is necessary. The outlines in Figures 11.1 and 11.2, both of which follow the direct plan, include a clear thesis statement.

Preview. The preview prepares the listeners to consider the main points to be covered in your presentation. A preview is especially useful to an audience listening to an oral presentation, because they usually do not have a text to follow. The outline in Figure 11.2, however, shows that a preview can be omitted when the main points are easy to follow and recall.

Plan and Organize the Body of the Presentation

Conventional wisdom among speechwriters says you should plan to cover no more than three main points in an oral presentation. We agree. Most listeners find it difficult to juggle more than three main ideas in the air over the course of a presentation. If you can limit the main ideas to two, especially when speaking to non-professional audiences, consider doing so.

If the presentation is informative, the information in the body of the presentation may be organized as suggested in Chapter 2. Topical, chronological, cause-to-effect,

Introduction
Attention-getting device: None
Thesis: Over this year and next, the cost of our benefit plan will increase by 65 percent.
Preview: I'll proceed by addressing the projected cost of benefits for 2003 and then offer a projection of costs for 2004.

Body
I.   The projected cost of the benefit plan in 2003 is 25 percent over costs for 2002 because of increase in employees and premiums.
   A.   Ten-percent increase in employees
   B.   Increased premiums for medical/dental plan
II.   The projected cost for benefit plan for 2004 is likely to be an additional 30 percent over costs for 2003 because of further increases in employees and premiums.
   A.   Projected 20-percent increase in employees
   B.   Projected increase in premiums for medical/dental plan

Conclusion
Review: Actual and projected increases in both the number of employees and the medical/dental insurance premiums for 2003 and 2004 will likely increase the cost of our benefit plan by 65 percent over 2002 costs.
Attention-getting device: None

effect-to-cause, and spatial organizations are most common. (Analyze the plan of organization used in Figures 11.1 and 11.2.)

If the presentation is an oral report, you may choose to follow a specific report format, especially if the oral version is based on a written one. For example, an oral progress report may organize the body of the presentation as follows:

I. Progress to date

II. Problems encountered to date

III. Projected completion date

An oral presentation of a proposal might follow the format described in Chapter 8.

If the presentation is persuasive, the problem–solution plan works well, along with an approach similar to the one described in Chapter 6. Known as the motivated sequence (an approach introduced in 1935 by the late Alan Monroe), the presentation is organized in terms of these five steps:

1. An attention-getting step—Secure the attention of the listeners.

2. A need step—Show the audience that there is a need to be satisfied.

Figure 11.2

Outline of Presentation by President of Small Computer Firm to a Group of Industry Analysts

Introduction

Attention-getting device: You'll read tomorrow in the *Wall Street Journal* that J.D. Power & Associates has ranked our firm first in customer satisfaction among all firms in the computer industry based on their survey of mail-order customers.

Thesis: We've topped $3 billion in sales because our technology is superior, our prices are competitive, and customer service is superior.

Preview: None

Body

I.   Our technology is superior.
   A.   We install Intel microprocessors.
   B.   We have state-of-the-art assembly plants.

II.   Our prices are competitive.
   A.   We're able to bypass the high-cost dealers and deal directly with the customer through the Internet or mail.
   B.   We're able to pass on our lower costs in the form of lower prices to our customers.

III.   Our customer service is better and faster.
   A.   We customize and ship an order in five days.
   B.   We guarantee next-day, on-site service.
   C.   We provide replacement machines by overnight delivery.

Conclusion

Review: We offer competitive prices and superior service.

Attention-getting device: Let me leave with a statistic that I'm most proud of: 70 percent of our buyers are repeat customers.

3. A satisfaction step—Propose a way that the previously identified need may be satisfied; offer a plan of action.

4. A visualization step—Assist your audience to visualize the results of satisfying the need.

5. An action step—Tell your audience what action they must take to put in place the plan you have proposed.[1]

When you organize a persuasive presentation using the motivated sequence, place the attention step in the introduction; the need, satisfaction, and visualization steps in the body of the presentation; and the action step in the conclusion of the presentation. See Figure 11.3 for an outline that follows this approach. It is taken from a sales talk to prospective buyers of condominiums.

Attention-Getting Device:	What if you could sell your home in New York, buy a condo with half the proceeds, invest the balance, and soak up the sun 12 months a year while living in a secure and elegant retirement community?
Need:	While you sit on the equity of your home, your taxes keep climbing, the winters get colder, and life in the big city seems more threatening.
Satisfaction:	Buying a condo at The Vineyard, Florida's newest retirement community, will fortify your financial position, allow you to escape the harsh Northeast winters, and live the good life.
Visualization:	Just think of it: Sun warming your shoulders in January, an elegant condo in a secure community, low taxes, and your money invested and working for you.
Action:	Accept our offer to fly down as our guest and visit Florida's newest retirement community: The Vineyard.

Plan and Organize the Conclusion

Do not neglect the conclusion of your presentation. It is the last thing the audience will hear; it is the last impression you will make. Ensure that the conclusion leaves your audience with a positive impression. Use the conclusion to review and restate the main points of your presentation when presenting information. Use it to call for action when you are making a persuasive presentation. (See Figures 11.1 and 11.2.)

Finally, if appropriate and necessary, end your presentation with another attention-getter. For many presentations before decision makers, a summary or restatement may be sufficient to conclude the presentation. For other types of presentations, a concluding attention-getter will have some impact. Use any of the devices described in the discussion of introductions. (See Figure 11.2.)

Step Two: Compose the Content of Your Presentation Word for Word

Once you have decided on the essential content of your presentation, compose your oral presentation word for word as though you were preparing a manuscript speech to read.

Executives who are skillful and experienced speakers may wish to skip this step and simply prepare an outline. This may work well for some executives, but inexperienced and nervous speakers will find this extra step well worth the effort. Here is why.

When you actually make the presentation, you are likely to find that the pressure of the moment will make the process of speaking from an outline more difficult than you anticipated. As we noted before, there is likely to be a loss of precision and conciseness as you extemporize from your outline. If you have previously prepared the full text of the presentation, looking down at the outline will trigger in your mind many of the carefully chosen words and well-crafted phrases that you had composed earlier. You will sound more articulate.

As you compose the content of your presentation, because it will be an oral presentation you should bear these four suggestions in mind regarding style and organization:

1. Use relatively short sentences and avoid overly complex sentence constructions.

2. Be especially careful not to use technical expressions or acronyms unfamiliar to your audience.

3. Employ such techniques as summarization, restatement, enumeration, and transitions to help your audience follow your presentation.

4. Round off numbers and statistics, and avoid throwing too many figures at your audience. (Use handouts and other visuals to present complex quantitative data.)

In short, edit for the ear.

Finally, if you plan to speak to an international business audience composed mostly of nonnative speakers, consider these four suggestions from Patricia L. Kurtz as you word your presentation.[2]

1. Consider using more repetition (identical words) than restatement (use of synonyms) as you summarize and recapitulate main points of your presentation to avoid confusion and compensate for the relatively less-rich vocabulary of a nonnative-speaking audience.

2. Avoid English idioms and slang or explain what they mean (for example, "the 'fast-food' market—that is, food such as hamburgers cooked rapidly and uniformly . . .").

3. Avoid Anglo-Saxon phrasal verbs (a verb used with an adverb particle). This type of verb is difficult for nonnative speakers to understand because the meaning of the phrasal verb is often different from the meaning of the words considered separately (for example, *make up, bring up, stick to*, and so forth) and will change meaning depending on the context in which it is used. (Kurtz relates the anecdote of a presentation to an international audience in which the American speaker referred often to "sticking to the plan." During a break in the meeting the host, a nonnative speaker of English, arranged to have the conference table wiped clean, fearing that food or drink had made the "plan" (document) "stick" to the table).

4. Use examples and analogies that are indigenous to the audience; an analogy to baseball may be appropriate to the United States or Japan, while an analogy to soccer is more appropriate to a European audience.

Step Three: Construct Your Presentation Outline

Your outline should serve as an aid to effective delivery. Therefore, after you are satisfied with the content of the presentation in manuscript form, you should reduce the manuscript to an outline.

Outlines may be alphanumeric or decimal; outlines may be full-sentence, key-phrase, or key-word. (Figure 11.4 offers examples of the various types of outlines.) We recommend full-sentence outlines and key-phrase outlines. The key word is a bit risky because it leaves out so much information.

After you have developed your outline, you should prepare the materials in a form suitable for delivery. First, type the outline on either 8½-by-11-inch paper (20-pound) or index cards, using a large type size—for example, 18-point Times Roman. (If you plan to speak from a lectern, either the paper or the index cards will work well. If you must speak without a lectern, the index cards will be easier to handle.) Double-space between lines, allowing for 1½- to 2-inch margins at the top, bottom, left, and right of each page, and number the pages. If (when) the pages or cards fall to the floor, you will find the numbers a blessing as you hurry to reassemble the sheets in their proper sequence.

| Figure 11.4 | Types of Outlines |

FULL-SENTENCE OUTLINE (partial)

1.0 The cost of benefits has increased by 25 percent in 2003.
    1.1 The primary reason is the new employee dental plan.
    1.2 Another reason is the 5-percent increase in employees.
2.0 The cost of benefits will increase by 30 percent in 2004.
    2.1 The new employee medical plan will increase costs by about 20 percent.
    2.2 We estimate a 10-percent increase in employees.

KEY-PHRASE OUTLINE (partial)

I. Benefits increased by 25 percent in 2003.
    A. New employee dental plan
    B. 5-percent increase in employees
II. Benefits will increase by 30 percent in 2004.
    A. 20-percent increase for new medical plan
    B. 10-percent increase in employees

KEY WORD OUTLINE (partial)

I. Increased
    Dental
    Employees
II. Increase
    Medical
    Employees

Many speakers find it helpful to write reminders about effective oral delivery in the margins of the outline. Some examples are:

SLOW!
LOOK AT THE AUDIENCE!
SPEED UP!
PAUSE HERE!
RELAX!
SMILE!
WATCH POSTURE!
GESTURE!

Along with comments about delivery, important instructions for the presentation such as these should also be included:

SHOW SLIDE #1 HERE
USE TRANSPARENCY #2 HERE
START INTRODUCTIONS OF GUESTS STAGE RIGHT
ADJUST MICROPHONE

If it is important, write it on your outline.

Step Four: Memorize the Beginning and the End of the Presentation

Although we do not recommend that you memorize your entire presentation, we do recommend that you employ some memory work to enhance the effectiveness of the presentation.

We propose that you memorize the very beginning of the presentation. By doing so, you will be able to begin your presentation without looking at your notes. Instead, you will walk to the lectern, look directly at your audience, pause a moment, and begin to speak. After your opening remarks, naturally, you will glance at your outline. But the first impression you give will be one of confidence and command over the content of the presentation.

At the end of your presentation, do the same in reverse. Look up from your outline, pause, and speak directly to your audience as you conclude the presentation. Your last impression will also be one of confidence and control.

Step Five: Practice Your Presentation

You would be astonished at the number of managers who neglect this step or simply pay lip service to it. Except with a few gifted people, practice will always improve one's actual performance. You also run the risk of wasting any efforts expended on the first four steps if you do not practice your presentation.

Here are some suggestions for practicing your presentation:

- *Practice from the Beginning to the End.* Start at the very beginning of the presentation—practice even an acknowledgment or an anecdote. Continue to practice with your outline until you have worked your way through the conclusion. Do this a minimum of three times to attain command over your material and to increase your self-confidence.

- *Practice the Use of Your Visual Aids.* If you plan to use visual aids (such as PowerPoint, overhead transparencies, slides, and so on), practice using them in your presentation. Be sure to follow the advice in Step Three and indicate in your outline when to use each visual aid.

- *Time Your Presentation.* Be sure to time your presentation as you practice. Given the nature of extemporaneous speaking, you will find that the time will vary a bit from practice session to practice session. If you are an inexperienced presenter, allow your presentation to run a little longer rather than a little shorter in your practice sessions. You will find when you stand before your actual audience that your rate of speech will increase somewhat because of nervousness. Therefore, a 16-minute practice session may well be a 15- or 14-minute presentation.

- *Use Audio-Visual Feedback While Practicing.* If possible, tape your delivery during practice on a tape recorder or video camera to provide feedback. Listen to your vocal delivery; observe your body language. Use the discussion on effective delivery (Step Six) and the checklist in Figure 11.5 as a basis for self-evaluation.

- *Ask for Feedback from Colleagues and Superiors.* After a few practice sessions by yourself, ask a colleague to watch another practice session and offer some constructive criticism. This step is especially valuable if the presentation is a major one. If the presentation is to be made before your boss's superiors or some major clients, you might consider asking your immediate superior for some feedback, too. Be sure, however, to ask for specific, constructive criticism.

Step Six: Deliver Your Presentation

Your audience will both hear and see you: what they will hear is your vocal delivery, and what they will see is your body language. Let's consider both in turn and then discuss the effective use of visual aids in the delivery of a speech.

Vocal Delivery
The key factors in vocal delivery include expressiveness, emphasis, rate and volume, and articulation and pronunciation.

Vocal Expressiveness. To create the conversational style that we associate with the extemporaneous method of delivery, your voice must convey expressiveness. Simply put, vocal expressiveness is variation in the pitch, rate, and volume of your speaking voice. To sound expressive, your voice should move up and down in pitch, increase and decrease in rate of speech, and increase and lower in volume. Although you should make a conscious effort to vary these three vocal elements, an easy way to remember how to sound is to model your vocal delivery on an animated conversation. Listen to two people engaged in a lively conversation. You will hear the vocal expressiveness. That is how you should sound.

Vocal Emphasis. All words are not created equal; some are more important than others. When you write, you have a number of devices at your disposal by which you can emphasize a word or phrase—for example, underlining (italics in the printed page), bullets, indentation, and so forth. Obviously, these devices are of no help in an oral presentation. Instead, you must employ vocal emphasis.

Vocal emphasis is achieved in three ways: by the use of the pause, by variation in rate of speech, or by variation in volume. If, for example, you wish to emphasize an important phrase in a presentation, do any or all of the following:

- Pause before or after a key word.
- Slow down when you reach an important passage.
- Increase or decrease volume.

These three techniques, simple as they seem, will effectively convey to your audience the following message: This is important!

Appropriate Rate and Volume. Along with vocal expressiveness and emphasis, you must be careful to avoid two common problems among inexperienced presenters: speaking too rapidly and speaking too softly. Rapid speech is often caused by nervousness. Nervous speakers, perhaps seeking relief from the stress of delivery, seem compelled to race through their presentation, sacrificing both vocal emphasis and the comprehension of the audience. Resist the temptation. If you tend to speak too quickly, write yourself a note or two in the margins of your outline to remind yourself to slow down. A caution, however: some speakers overcompensate by speaking too slowly, a sure recipe for boring your audience. Try to speak at about 150 words per minute, slowing occasionally to emphasize a key word or phrase.

Speaking too softly is a serious problem as well. If members of your audience cannot hear you, or can hear you only part of the time, your presentation is doomed. Avoid this problem by projecting your voice with sufficient loudness so that all members of the audience are able to hear you. If volume is a problem for you, write yourself a reminder on your outline to project. You might also consider asking someone in the audience to signal to you if your volume is too low.

Articulation and Pronunciation. Pay careful attention to articulation and pronunciation as you make a presentation. By articulation, also referred to as enunciation, we mean the precision and crispness of your spoken words; by pronunciation we mean the sounds assigned to a given word. Sloppy articulation and errors in pronunciation create a poor impression. Make a conscious effort to articulate clearly, without overarticulating. When in doubt about the standard pronunciation of a word, check with a dictionary. Be especially careful about the pronunciation of names; people are not amused when they hear their names mispronounced.

Body Language

Eye contact and body movement are the two major categories of body language to consider.

Eye Contact. Eye contact—looking at members of your audience—is essential to any effective extemporaneous presentation. Here are some suggestions for effective use of eye contact:

Because presentations are usually given to small audiences, establishing eye contact from time to time with all members of the audience is expected. We recommend, however, that you linger a bit on each audience member—do not gaze rapidly around the room like a surveillance camera at a bank.

If you are speaking to a large group, it is wise to break up the audience into four sections. As you speak, shift your gaze from section to section, looking at individuals in each section. Again, linger.

Be careful with supportive and friendly audience members. Some presenters see someone in the audience smiling and nodding approval and direct the bulk of the eye contact to that person. Avoid the temptation.

Body Movement. Your body language should reflect your expressive and emphatic vocal delivery. Here are some suggestions:

- Use facial expressions to forecast and reflect the tone of your presentation.
- Gesture naturally as you speak.
- Stand with an appropriate, relaxed posture.
- Project a high energy level.
- Move with poise and confidence.
- Do not adopt a deadpan expression or a fixed smile.
- Do not employ gestures that will distract the audience.
- Avoid touching your hair, mustache, and so forth, while you speak.
- Avoid a rigid posture.
- Control such unmotivated body movement as swaying, shuffling your feet, pacing back and forth, or playing with coins or keys in your pocket.

In short, allow your body movement to convey a positive, professional image.

Visual Aids

Here are three suggestions for the effective use of visual aids during your extemporaneous presentation:

First, do not display your visual aid until you are ready to refer to it in your presentation. Otherwise, the audience will be distracted by the visual.

Second, allow your audience sufficient time to look at the visual before you remove it or replace it with another. It is most annoying for audience members to have a visual whisked away before they have fully read or understood it.

Third, do not talk to the visual aid; talk to your audience. To avoid the problem of turning your back to your audience as you point to a visual, use your inside arm.

Translation

Finally, if you find it necessary to have your presentation translated to an international audience as you speak, consider these four suggestions:[3]

1. Plan to meet with your interpreter prior to your presentation to ensure that he or she will be familiar with your phrasing, accent, pace, and idioms.
2. Review all technical terms with your interpreter prior to your presentation.
3. Insist that the interpreter translate in brief bursts and not wait until the end of a long statement, to ensure both the accuracy of translation and to sustain the interest of the audience.
4. Make a special effort to use visual aids, since the combination of both the interpreter's words and the visual message will enhance audience comprehension and accurate communication.

Step Seven: Evaluate Your Presentation

After a presentation, evaluate your performance. What did you do well? What aspects of your presentation, content, or delivery were ineffective? What feedback have you received from audience members? (Consider both positive and negative feedback.) Use the checklist in Figure 11.5 as a basis for your evaluation.

Figure 11.5　**Checklist for an Effective Extemporaneous Delivery**

KEY ELEMENTS OF DELIVERY	EVALUATION
Sufficient eye contact?	W A G E
Appropriate gestures?	W A G E
Appropriate facial expressions?	W A G E
Poised and confident?	W A G E
Vocal expressiveness?	W A G E
Vocal emphasis?	W A G E
Appropriate rate of speech?	W A G E
Sufficient volume?	W A G E
Clear articulation/correct pronunciation?	W A G E
KEY ELEMENTS OF CONTENT	EVALUATION
Appropriate introduction	W A G E
Appropriate pattern of organization/transitions	W A G E
Appropriate supporting materials	W A G E
Appropriate use of visual aids	W A G E
Appropriate use of language	W A G E
Appropriate conclusion	W A G E

W = weak　　A = adequate　　G = good　　E = excellent

Special Considerations for Team Presentations

The advice in this chapter also applies to presentations made by a team. Additional considerations for planning and delivering a team presentation include the following:

- Select a team leader for the presentation who has some aptitude for and experience with oral presentations.
- Prepare a list of team member responsibilities for preparation and delivery.
- Standardize the format for visuals by making a master slide.
- Rehearse from start to finish *as a team*.
- Prepare and practice introductions and transitions to create the impression of one seamless presentation.
- Prepare *as a team* for the handling of Q & A (anticipated questions from the audience and your answers).

After the team presentation be sure to meet and evaluate its effectiveness.[4]

Summary

Oral presentations in business and industry are common. They may be internal or external, informative (a briefing) or persuasive (a sales presentation). They may be delivered individually or as a team. The preferred style of delivery for nearly all business presentations is extemporaneous—that is, the speech is carefully prepared and delivered from an outline using a conversational tone. The effective extemporaneous presentation is characterized by such conversational qualities as vocal expressiveness and vocal emphasis, good eye contact, and appropriate body language. This chapter has outlined seven steps to follow as you prepare, deliver, and evaluate your oral presentations.

Discussion Questions

1. Many people feel more comfortable writing than making oral presentations. Discuss why they feel one way or the other. Which way do you prefer and why?
2. Why is the extemporaneous method of delivery superior to the other three methods for most business presentations?
3. What advice or cues would you include in your own presentation outline to facilitate an effective oral presentation?
4. What are the most significant differences between oral presentations and written messages? In what business situations are oral presentations more appropriate? Less appropriate? How does an oral presentation to a small group differ from an e-mail message sent to members of that same group?

Communication in Action

@ ## Internet

1. Toastmasters International says its mission is "Making Effective Communication a Worldwide Reality." Visit its Web site (**http://www.toastmasters .org**) and prepare an oral report (what else?) on how Toastmasters might help you and your fellow students to become more effective public speakers.

   Conduct a search for articles and information on "speech anxiety," "stage fright," "communication apprehension," and similar terms that refer to a "fear of public speaking." Based on your research, what are the common causes? What are some sensible ways to cope with such distressful emotions?

InfoTrac

2. Retrieve the Reinsch and Shelby article, "What communication abilities do practitioners need? Evidence from MBA students" (A20223070) and an article by Jeanne D. Maes et al., "A Managerial Perspective: Oral communication competency is most important for business students in the workplace" (A19218840). What do these articles convey about the importance of oral communication in the workplace and the importance of oral presentations in particular?

3. Retrieve James Calvert Scott's article, "Differences in American and British vocabulary: Implications of international business communication," (A68534547). As Scott notes, it is often said that "Americans and Britons are separated by a common language—English." How significant are the differences between American and British English? What are the implications for international business communication?

4. Locate N. Lamar Reinsch, Jr.'s, "Communication is fundamental to business performance." *Executive Speeches*. August 2001, v.16i1, p.20. Write an outline of the speech, identifying the attention-getting device, the main points, conclusion, and so forth.

Notes

1. Joseph A. Devito's discussion in *The communication handbook* (pp. 204–205). (1986). New York: HarperCollins.
2. Adapted from Patricia L. Kurtz's excellent primer, *The global speaker* (pp. 40–49). (1995) New York: AMACOM, American Management Association.
3. Adapted from the writing of R. E. Axtell, cited in L. H. Chaney & J. S. Martin. (1995). *Intercultural business communication* (p. 105). Englewood Cliffs, NJ: Prentice-Hall.
4. Adapted from O'Hair, D. R. Stewart, & H. Rubenstein. (2001). Appendix B: Preparing for team presentations. In *A speaker's guidebook*. New York: Bedford/St. Martin's.

CHAPTER - 12

Meeting Management

Effective meeting management is an essential business communication goal. In this chapter, we will consider the reasons for meeting, review common complaints about meetings, and offer some sensible advice for planning and leading face-to-face meetings.

Reasons for Meeting

Think of the last meeting you attended. What was the reason (assuming there was a reason) for the meeting? Was it to make a decision? Was it to solve a problem? Or was it for another reason? The 3M Meeting Management Team has identified 13 of the most common reasons for calling a meeting (see Figure 12.1); the reason for your meeting probably will be on its list.[1] We will consider each reason in turn.

To Accept Reports from Participants

Many organizations schedule meetings on a weekly or monthly basis to allow managers to report on the activities of their departments or divisions, including an account of positive or negative developments. Usually led by a senior executive, the meetings serve three vital organizational communication functions: upward communication (information is shared with superiors), downward communication (superiors provide feedback on the reports), and horizontal communication (colleagues in different departments or divisions are kept abreast of developments throughout the firm). Such meetings have a disadvantage: They run the risk that participants have little to report, especially if the meetings are weekly. This leads to trivial presentations and wasted time.

In addition to such periodic meetings, there are ad hoc meetings called to receive reports on the status of various projects within an organization. Ad hoc meetings can be as fruitful as last-minute party invitations (sometimes the most fun).

To Reach a Group Judgment or Decision

Should we discontinue a product line? Should we approve a loan to a corporate customer? Should we reorganize the human resources department? Should the firm move from a decentralized to a centralized word-processing system? Should we approve a new companywide medical benefits plan? These are some of the many issues that might be decided at a meeting of executive decision makers.

Decisions may be made in the following five ways:

1. Unanimity—All participants agree on the decision.

2. By consensus—Although some members have reservations about the decision, all participants support the decision.

3. By majority—More than 50 percent of the participants agree on the decision; it is understood, however, that the minority will support the majority's decision once it is made.

4. By a plurality—The decision supported by the largest number of participants is adopted even if the number is less than a majority.

5. By fiat—The boss makes the decision; other participants are expected to endorse it.

Figure 12.1   **The 13 Most Common Reasons for Holding a Meeting**

Reasons for Meeting

1. To Accept Reports from Participants
2. To Reach a Group Judgment or Decision
3. To Analyze or Solve a Problem
4. To Gain Acceptability for an Idea, Program, or Decision
5. To Achieve a Training Objective
6. To Reconcile Conflicting Views
7. To Communicate Essential Information to a Group
8. To Relieve Tension or Insecurity by Providing Information and Management's Viewpoint
9. To Ensure That Everyone Has the Same Understanding of Information
10. To Obtain Quick Reactions
11. To Reactivate a Stalled Project
12. To Demonstrate a Product or System
13. To Generate New Ideas or Concepts

Source: 3M Meeting Management Team, *How to Run Better Business Meetings: A Reference Guide for Managers*, McGraw-Hill, New York, 1987, pp. 8–13.

To Analyze or Solve a Problem

Why has our software lost 20 percent of its market share? Why is turnover so high at one of our subsidiaries? How can we reduce the cost of our liability insurance? How can we improve our recruitment of MBAs from the most prestigious business schools? A meeting allows the knowledge and experience of participants to be pooled and applied toward the analysis and solution of problems such as these.

Meetings called to analyze and solve a problem often adopt the following well-known approach:

1. Define the problem (as an open question).
2. Assess the significance of the problem.
3. Analyze the problem (duration, causes, effects).
4. Establish criteria for evaluating solutions.
5. Generate possible solutions.
6. Evaluate solutions (using the criteria from Step 4).
7. Select the best solution.

All seven steps are important, and they should be followed in sequence. Do not try to analyze the problem (Step 3) before you have defined the problem (Step 1).

To Gain Buy-In for an Idea, Program, or Decision

Suppose that your company has imposed a tough new security system requiring that all employees wear ID badges at all times regardless of their status or position. Anticipating resistance from many managers and other professionals in the company, you hold a series of meetings to explain, face to face, the rationale for the change in security procedures and to respond to questions and objections.

To Achieve a Training Objective

In one sense, all meetings have a training objective. Meetings offer younger executives an opportunity to observe and learn from more-experienced executives. Some meetings, however, may be called for more explicit training objectives. For example, sales meetings may be called to provide sales representatives with information and techniques required to sell new or current products, or managers may meet to review performance-evaluation procedures.

To Reconcile Conflicting Views

Staff in a department who enjoy working with background music or computer sound effects and those who prefer a more quiet working atmosphere may sharply disagree over the issue of acceptable noise levels. To ensure a sensible compromise that will allow both sides to work together peacefully, a meeting is called to air conflicting views. Such a meeting is most effective if it is chaired by an outside consultant specializing in conflict-resolution techniques.

To Communicate Essential Information to a Group

An example of such a meeting is a gathering of the officers of the trust department of a major bank to hear a briefing by a tax attorney on the implications for estate planning and management in the new federal tax bill. The presentation, supported by a variety of carefully prepared visual aids, is followed by a question-and-answer period.

To Relieve Tension or Insecurity by Providing Information and Management's Viewpoint

As an organization faces a crisis or a major change, employees hunger for authoritative information from management but often subsist on a diet of rumor and misinformation. A meeting with employees allows management to convey information personally, directly, and accurately. A meeting may also allow employees to ask questions and express their views.

To Ensure That Everyone Has the Same Understanding of Information

At times, an organization may choose to complement an important written message with face-to-face communication, especially if the message is highly controversial or complex. The major advantage of using a meeting for this purpose is the opportunity it provides for the source of the information to elicit feedback from the intended audience.

To Obtain Quick Reactions

Some managers occasionally call meetings to solicit comments about decisions or plans still being formulated. The comments may serve to alert management to possible reactions to the decision or plan, thus affecting implementation. Or input may actually be used to modify the final decision or plan.

To Reactivate a Stalled Project

When a project is stalled for lack of an administrative decision, a meeting may be called to force the decision. Such meetings can be highly political in nature.

To Demonstrate a Product or System

Meetings to demonstrate a product or service may be internal (a meeting to demonstrate the operation of the new corporate information center) or external (a meeting of automobile dealers held by the manufacturer to allow the dealers to observe and test-drive the new models). The external demonstration meeting, in particular, requires especially careful planning.

To Generate New Ideas or Concepts

Although a creative meeting called to generate new ideas or concepts is common at advertising and public relations firms, it is also employed by every type of organization from time to time. A common approach to this type of meeting, called brainstorming, is characterized by these guidelines:

1. Ideas are not evaluated positively or negatively as they are introduced; they are just recorded.
2. The emphasis is on the generation of as many ideas as possible.
3. Ideas may be combined or modified.
4. The final list of ideas is evaluated.

Brainstorming is often very productive—assuming, of course, that you have some good brains at work.

Common Complaints About Meetings

Complaints About Planning

When managers grumble about a meeting being poorly planned, the specific complaints are likely to be one or more of the following:

- An agenda was not prepared or sent out prior to the meeting; hence, the participants were unclear about the meeting's purpose.
- The wrong people were invited to attend (people who should have been there were not, while those who should not have been there were).
- The time for the meeting was inconvenient for most participants.
- The room was too small for the number of participants.
- Audiovisual equipment was not ordered.
- The meeting room was not set up correctly (wrong arrangement, too few chairs, and so forth).

Complaints About Leadership

Meetings are often criticized for poor leadership. Common complaints about ineffective leadership include the following:

- The leader did not follow the agenda; the meeting went off track.
- The leader was domineering, monopolizing meeting discussion time and attempting to impose personal views on the group.
- The leader was weak, speaking infrequently and failing to control disruptive participants.

- The leader did not facilitate communication among all the participants of the meeting.

Complaints About Participation

A third source of dissatisfaction with meetings is the performance of participants other than the leader. Some common complaints are:

- Participants were unprepared for the meeting. (They were unfamiliar with the agenda, they had not read the background materials relevant to the issues to be addressed, or they had not prepared their own presentations carefully).
- Some participants contributed too much at the meeting. (This is especially a complaint about high-status participants.)
- Some participants contributed too little to a meeting. (This is often heard about participants who felt insecure psychologically or politically.)
- Some participants were disruptive or uncooperative, either intentionally or unintentionally.

Complaints About the Meeting's Outcomes

The most common complaint about meeting outcomes is, simply put, there "ain't" any. Other complaints include these:

- Decisions are not implemented.
- Assignments agreed to by participants are not done.
- Recommendations are not passed on.
- Findings are often ignored.

Given the cost of meetings, these are serious problems. However, successful executives do not dwell on what is wrong. They do what is right. Therefore, let us consider effective techniques for planning meetings, leading and conducting meetings, and participating in meetings, as well as ensuring desired outcomes after meetings.

Planning Meetings

Effective planning always increases the probability of a successful meeting. As you plan a meeting, consider these five questions.

What Is the Objective of This Meeting?

As earlier chapters have suggested, effective business communication requires a clear understanding of one's objective or objectives. An objective is more specific than a topic (for example, "New Security Procedures at CONTECH"). An objective should describe what you expect the meeting to accomplish (for example, "CONTECH managers will be thoroughly briefed on all aspects of the new Department of Defense security requirements").

Usually, meetings have more than one objective. Beyond the first objective listed above, these two objectives also could be linked with it: "Need for changes in the existing CONTECH security system will be assessed"; and "A timetable for the implementation of mandated changes in the security system will be prepared." As you will see in our discussion of agenda items later in this chapter, the objectives may serve as items for the agenda.

Who Should Attend This Meeting?

Avoid the two most obvious problems: inviting too many people or inviting too few. Consider the objective of the meeting as you consider whom to invite. If the objective is to brief managers on a new security system, then the subset of questions would include: Who should do the briefing? Who should be briefed? Does my boss need to be there? Do other corporate superiors or additional staff need to attend? Keep the number down as much as possible, because it costs money to meet.

When and Where Will the Meeting Be Held?

Be practical. The availability of key people and corporate superiors should be determined before choosing a meeting time and date, since you will have to accommodate them. In the absence of such considerations, preferences will vary among different corporate cultures. Some people will prefer a midmorning meeting on a Tuesday, Wednesday, or Thursday, with others preferring the impact of the Monday morning meeting or the sense of closure offered by a Friday afternoon meeting.

The "where" of a meeting should be determined by two basic considerations: convenience and suitability.

First, the convenience of the location for participants should be considered, with preference accorded to senior executives. Convenience, however, also refers to how close the meeting room is to telephones if someone needs to make a call, and how accessible people are if they need to be reached by their staff or boss. Some executives deliberately select locations that are inconvenient, hoping to minimize the interruptions of telephone calls. Having the meeting offsite at a conference center or hotel is one way to achieve this.

Second, assess the suitability of the meeting room, with the size of the room as the most important factor. Is the room large enough for the number of participants selected, along with the necessary tables, chairs, and audiovisual equipment required? Other factors affecting suitability are the noise level outside the room, physical appearance, and control over temperature (heat and air conditioning).

What Materials, Equipment, Refreshments, and Room Layout Will Be Required for the Meeting?

Be prepared with whatever materials are needed, including notepads and pencils for each participant, nametags or place cards, and handouts. Have such equipment as flip charts, an overhead projector, a slide projector, a VCR, or a lectern for speakers ready if necessary. Possible refreshments include water, coffee and bagels, and soft drinks. Ensure a sufficient supply of tableware, such as cups, glasses, and napkins.

How should the room be laid out? Four popular meeting layouts are (1) the table in the center of the room with all of the participants sitting around it; (2) the U-shaped layout; (3) the classroom layout, and (4) the theater layout. See Figure 12.2 for diagrams of the four types.

To serve as a checklist for the four issues we have just addressed, you may wish to use the meeting-planning checklist from the 3M Meeting Management Team (see Figure 12.3).

| Figure 12.2 | Four Layouts for Meetings |

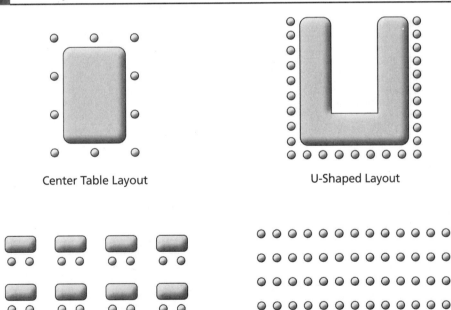

Center Table Layout

U-Shaped Layout

Classroom Layout

Theater Layout

Figure 12.3 Meeting Planning Checklist

MEETING PLANNING CHECKLIST

Meeting objective: _____

Date _____

Time _____ to _____ am/pm

Place _____

_____

Participants _____

_____

_____

_____ _____ Room reserved

_____ _____ Agenda (meeting notice)

_____ _____ Prepared

_____ _____ Sent

_____ _____ Visuals prepared

_____

_____

Meeting Materials

_____ Notepads, pencils   _____ Name/place cards   _____ Name badges

_____ Handouts _____

_____ _____

_____ _____

_____ _____

Equipment

_____ LCD panel/PC

_____ Overhead projector   _____ Spare lamp

_____ Slide projector . . . . .   _____ Spare lamp

_____ 16 mm . . . .   _____ Spare lamp

_____ Screen (Size) _____

_____ Charts   _____ Pointer

_____ Chalkboard   _____ Chalk

_____ Videotape/disc

_____ Marking pens

_____ Microphone

_____ Lectern

_____ Extension cord

_____ _____

_____ _____

Food, Beverage

_____ Coffee _____ Juice _____ Soft drinks

_____ Lunch _____

Post Meeting

_____ Action minutes

_____ Next meeting _____

Room Layout

Source: 3M Meeting Management Team, *How to Run Better Business Meetings: A Reference Guide for Managers,* McGraw-Hill, New York, 1987, p. 53. Used by permission.

What Should the Agenda Include?

An effective agenda should include the following information:

- Time of meeting
- Length of meeting
- Location of meeting
- List of participants
- Subject of meeting
- Background information
- Items to be covered
- Premeeting preparation

The sample agenda in Figure 12.4 covers all this information.

Figure 12.4   **Sample Agenda**

CONTECH SYSTEMS

AGENDA

TO: All Department Heads and Directors
FR: Dan Creange, Director of Security
RE: Meeting on New Department of Defense Security Requirements
BG: DOD has imposed a new set of security requirements for contractors engaged in classified work. We need to consider the new requirements, assess necessary changes for our present security system, and establish a timetable for implementation of the changes consistent with DOD requirements.

Time and Place
Wednesday, April 12, Room 319, 10:00 AM to 12:00 PM

Items
1. Briefing on new DOD security requirements
2. Assessment of security system changes required
3. Timetable for implementation of system changes

Meeting Prep
Attached are new security guidelines from DOD; please read. Please prepare a list of questions concerning implementation in your department.

The first five items in the list above were discussed earlier in this chapter. By background information we mean any information that will convey the reason for, or significance of, the meeting. In Figure 12.4, the background information consists of a reference to the new DOD security requirements and the need for a meeting to assess and plan modifications in CONTECH's current security system.

The items to be covered are really objectives of the meeting, and they should be specific and realistic. Some agendas specify the time that the item will be addressed or the amount of time to be devoted to each item during the meeting. These devices ensure that the group will not devote a wildly disproportionate amount of time to one item while neglecting others. Time limits should not be viewed as rigid requirements, however. Some items may require a little less time; some items may require a little more.

By including a section on premeeting preparation you inform participants about your expectations regarding their level of preparation, as well as specific responsibilities for participation at the meeting. In our example (Figure 12.4), the agenda requests that all department heads and directors read the new DOD security guidelines and that they prepare a list of questions regarding the implementation of the new security system in their departments.

Leading Meetings

The leader of a meeting has one basic goal: to accomplish the objectives of the meeting. The following guidelines will prove useful to you as you assume this role.

Starting On Time

Start the meeting on time. Nothing says more about your philosophy of meeting management than starting a meeting promptly. It happens so infrequently that starting at the time specified in the agenda will serve as an excellent attention-getting device.

Opening Remarks

Once you have the group's attention, open the meeting with an appropriate set of remarks. Offer some remarks intended to achieve the following objectives:

1. Establish the right tone—usually serious and positive.
2. Be sure to identify any participants unknown to the group.
3. Offer any background comments that might prove useful to the group— for example, why the meeting was called.

4. Review the objectives of the meeting as expressed as items on the agenda. Identify any time constraints not already expressed on the agenda—for example, when the meeting must end.

Getting to Business

After you finish your opening remarks, move to the first item on the agenda. Be careful not to let your opening remarks serve as a springboard for the group to get off track.

Participation

Facilitate balanced participation among meeting members. Some participants talk too much while others talk too little. Effective meeting leadership ensures that participation is balanced. If it is, a few members of the group will not dominate the discussion at the expense of less-assertive colleagues. Rather than muzzle the more talkative participants, issue direct, open-ended questions to the quiet ones, specifically soliciting their comments or advice.

Sometimes the group as a whole is quiet, and you may need to prime the pump. If the group appears prepared but reticent, pose open questions to them. For example, you could say, "What problems should we anticipate as we implement the new security system?" If the group's silence is related to a general level of unpreparedness, then consider rescheduling the meeting or offering sufficient information (in the form of handouts or a briefing) to improve the level of preparation.

Deal assertively but patiently with disruptive members. A storyteller, for instance, can sidetrack a meeting with an irrelevant story, especially one that walks the group down memory lane. After the first story, inquire about the relevance of any later stories to the point under discussion. Do the same for humorists and digressers. But employ some strategic leniency at times, too. An occasional story or digression may prove a harmless diversion and even provide a useful release for group tension.

Agenda

Use your agenda to keep the discussion on track. If the discussion starts to drift from the item being considered, firmly steer the group back to the item. If a meeting member resists your request to change direction, ask for justification of the relevance of the comments to the agenda item under consideration. Remind participants of time constraints: "We'd better return to Item Two. We've got only an hour left to cover four more items!"

Again, remember to exercise some strategic flexibility when appropriate. If an agenda item elicits far more productive discussion than you anticipated while planning the agenda, do not attempt to limit discussion prematurely. Otherwise, attendees may feel muzzled. If it appears that an item may require substantially more time than the agenda allows, consider holding another meeting addressed to that item.

Closing

Close the meeting at the appropriate time. Once you have covered the items on the agenda, close the meeting. Meetings sometimes continue aimlessly after the items have been covered, and it is embarrassing to have someone inquire, "Is the meeting over?"

Before you close the meeting, signal the participants by asking for any final comments or questions. Offer a summary of what has been accomplished at the meeting, and explain what will occur next. For example, let people know that minutes will be sent to all participants; another meeting will be scheduled on this subject; etc. Finally, be sure to thank the group members for their time and contributions.

Effective Meeting Outcomes

It is deeply frustrating to carefully plan and skillfully lead a meeting only to see poor results from your efforts: assignments agreed to at the meeting are not completed, decisions are not implemented, or deadlines are missed. To prevent these problems and ensure effective meeting outcomes consider the approach recommended by the 3M Meeting Network. Its approach involves two steps:

Step One: Visual Display

The first step ensures a "visual group memory." A designated recorder, using a flip chart or whiteboard, captures the important "outcomes" of the meeting. Specifically, the recorder will list these three items.

1. action items (including a description of the task, the person responsible, and the deadline);
2. decisions made by the group on either substantive (schedule press conference on most recent developments related to a company crisis) or procedural issues (day and time of next meeting)
3. open issues (issues raised but not resolved)

Step Two: Meeting Action Plan

After the meeting the recorder will copy all of the information on action items, decisions, and open issues, and send the summary to all of the participants. (See Figure 12.5).[2]

Figure 12.5 **Format for Minutes and Group Recordings**

_____ Meeting

Meeting date: _____ Recorder: _____

ACTION ITEMS

Item	Person Responsible	Deadline

Decisions

_____

_____

_____

_____

Open Issues

_____

_____

_____

_____

List of attendees attached   Time: End: _____

Start: _____

Next meeting: _____ **Length:** _____

Summary

Meetings serve a large number of important organizational purposes. They include: accepting reports; reaching a group judgment or decision; analyzing or solving a problem; gaining acceptability for an idea, program, or decision; achieving a training objective; reconciling conflicting views; communicating essential information to a group; relieving tension or insecurity by providing information and management's viewpoint; ensuring that everyone has the same understanding of information; obtaining quick reactions; reactivating a stalled project; demonstrating a product or system; generating new ideas or concepts.

Common complaints about meetings fall into four categories: complaints about meeting planning, complaints about meeting leadership, complaints about participation, and complaints about meeting outcomes. Careful planning, skillful leadership, and ensuring meeting outcomes will eliminate most of these complaints.

Discussion Questions

1. How does an agenda serve to make *both* the meeting's leader and other attendees perform more effectively?

2. Although a leader should ensure balanced participation among attendees during a meeting, what responsibilities do *attendees* have to foster balanced participation?

3. Given the widespread use of cell phones and various other wireless messaging gadgets, discuss possible standards of etiquette with respect to such technology at business meetings.

4. Sometimes meetings are highly successful. Recall such a meeting that you attended. What factors contributed to the meeting's success? Conversely, sometimes meetings are highly ineffective. Recall such a meeting that you attended. What factors contributed to the meeting's ineffectiveness?

Communication in Action

@ Internet

1. Visit **http://www.3m.com/meetingnetwork/** and discover an excellent source of information about meeting management. Be sure to find the "articles and advice" page on the site, where you will find more than 30 articles to read about meeting management.

   Write a short summary of two articles on the site and be prepared to discuss these summaries in class.

2. IDEO is a Palo Alto, California, firm that has near-mythic status in the field of product innovation and design. "Brainstorming" is one of the techniques IDEO employs to great effect. Look for some articles on IDEO and brainstorming. You might wish to start with Ed Brown's article in *Fortune*, "A Day at Innovation U.: Can You Learn Creativity?"[3]

InfoTrac

3. Search for articles on "emotional intelligence" at work, starting with Daniel Goleman's article "What Makes a Leader?" (A53221401). What are the characteristic features of emotional intelligence and how does emotional intelligence (or lack thereof) affect performance in business meetings?

Notes

1. 3M Meeting Management Team. (1987). *How to run better business meetings: A reference guide for managers* (pp. 8–12). New York: McGraw-Hill.
2. Minutes and Group Recordings. (n.d.). Retrieved October 5, 2002, from **http://www.3m.com/meetingnetwork**
3. Brown, E. (1999, April 12). A day at Innovation U.: Can you learn creativity? *Fortune, 139*(7), p. 163+.

CHAPTER - 13

Crisis Management

Employees of organizations spend large portions of their time in work-related activities that contribute to polishing the company's image. All of that work can be destroyed quickly when a crisis hits—especially a crisis of September 11, 2001, proportion. Potential crises exist in every organization. Traditional businesses prepare for the uncertainties. E-businesses have more recently learned that a few minutes of downtime can cause anger, and several hours of downtime can lose customers and cause stock to plummet. After September 11, every business understands it is susceptible in some way to disruptive crisis events. The wise organizations anticipate the potential crises and develop contingency processes that will either eliminate the threat or will create opportunities to deal with crises immediately and successfully.

This chapter examines organizational crises and methods of managing them. While we all know of large and small organizations that have been destroyed because a crisis developed, there are also many success stories of organizations that survive and do better in the future. This chapter will first examine the basic theses and stages of a crisis. Next, the crisis-management process will be explored. You will learn how organizations prepare crisis-management plans and develop communication strategies. This material will prepare you to guide your organization as it weathers the storms of crises and survives.

On the morning of September 11, 2001, the lives of all Americans changed forever. Millions of television viewers watched the World Trade Center (WTC) Towers crumble, taking thousands of office workers to their death. Over 500 businesses in the WTC were destroyed, and an additional 14,000 businesses in the lower Manhattan area were affected.[1] Every business involved in that catastrophe was suddenly thrown into an unprecedented crisis mode. One company managed the process in an almost simplistic manner.

Morgan Stanley's Plan

Morgan Stanley was the WTC's biggest tenant, with over 3,700 employees and a million square feet of space in the Towers. Following the 1993 terrorist attack on the WTC, Morgan Stanley fine-tuned its crisis plan and evacuation procedures. The company's basic principle became "you can replace the buildings but not people."[2] When the first plane hit Tower One, shortly before 9 A.M., Morgan Stanley's security and maintenance staff began moving employees out of the building. That action took place even as New York Port Authority Security used the public address system to tell occupants that the tower was fine and to stay put.[3]

In the 20 minutes between the two plane crashes, most of Morgan Stanley's employees were evacuated. President Robert Scott was giving a speech in 3 World Trade Center, and he watched the second plane hit right where his employees were located.[4] In the end, only six Morgan Stanley employees died. Ironically, one of the lost was Rick Rescorla, chief of security. In the 1993 WTC attack he was the last person out of the buildings, and on this occasion he stayed to ensure that all employees were evacuated.[5] As David Arena, managing director for Morgan Stanley Real Estate remarked, "At the end of the day, it was really about evacuation, and about people who knew where they had to be."[6]

Not only did Morgan Stanley have a low casualty rate, its crisis planning allowed operations not to be disrupted. Following the 1993 attack the company had established a backup site some 22 blocks away. By 9:20 A.M. that site was activated. Ten minutes later, at 9:30 A.M., senior management had relocated to another backup site that became the command post. With New York City phone lines dead, a credit card call center in Phoenix was converted into a toll-free emergency hotline for locating the 3,700 employees. By 11:00 A.M. that number became the first emergency number to be displayed on national television, beating even the federal government. By 1:30 P.M. over 2,500 calls had been received. By 4 P.M., Philip Purcell, the company's chairman, had posted a message concerning the attack and the company's actions on the Morgan Stanley Web site.[7]

At the command post senior managers created a usable telephone system by accessing a dedicated phone line to their London office, through which they could call their Chicago office.[8] Several emergency centers were set up to help workers. Over 300 grief counselors were hired. Twenty-four hours later, with 200 employees still unaccounted for, teams of people began calling and visiting employee homes. A process of ongoing communication then started and continued. Although located in three different New York City facilities, "[w]hen securities trading resumed on September 17, the office was fully functioning and handled the bulk of the company's trading activities that day."[9] The words of Howard Paster, CEO of Hill and Knowlton public relations firm, aptly summed up the successful results achieved by Morgan Stanley. "There are lessons here; a key one of which is that managing in a crisis requires planning, knowledge, hard work, and intangible qualities of leadership."[10]

Defining a Corporate Crisis

Crisis management, emergency preparedness, disaster response, disaster recovery, continuity planning, and risk management . . . these are all terms used in relation to business crisis. The terms have two things in common: dealing with a business interruption and protection of company assets. If a business interruption has significant impact on a company, it could mean the destruction of the organization. Such an event would be a crisis and survival would depend upon a good crisis-management strategy.[11] When a company mentions a "disaster recovery plan," it is referring to the resources, actions, tasks, and data necessary to restore operations after a disastrous business interruption. A "business continuity plan" is the process a company follows when normal operations are disrupted. Either event can be called a crisis.[12]

We define *crisis* as a significant, suddenly occurring, disruptive event that creates uncertainty and stress, and has potentially negative results. The event stimulates news media coverage. The public scrutiny may impact the organization's normal operations, and its aftermath may significantly damage an organization and its employees, products, services, financial condition, and reputation. Just as a business develops a variety of plans for marketing its sales and services, so too must it develop plans for how to survive if thrown into a crisis.

Examples of Crisis Situations

According to the Institute for Crisis Management, before the September 11 terrorist attacks the four basic causes of a business crisis were: (1) acts of God (storms, earthquakes, volcanic action, and so forth); (2) mechanical problems (ruptured pipes, metal fatigue, and so forth); (3) human errors (mistakes in making a product, and so forth); and (4) management decisions/indecisions.[13]

In the late 1990s businesses had numerous crises. Those most frequently covered by the media were white-collar crimes, labor disputes, general mismanagement, catastrophes (death, product tampering, and so forth), labor disputes, environmental disputes, defects and recalls, and class-action lawsuits. The crises that appear most frequently in news stories include sexual harassment allegations, hostile takeovers, and executive dismissals. Since September 11, crises like those above seem almost peaceful. The WTC terrorist attack struck new fear in the hearts of all Americans, including those in business. It created a feeling of impending disruption. Indeed, in the months following 9-11, the country was wracked by anthrax and bioterrorist fears; continued recession; the collapse of energy giant Enron, a Fortune top-ten company; the unraveling of the Arthur Andersen accounting firm; credibility questions with other accounting firms; and the sexual abuse revelations of the world's largest organization: the Catholic Church.

According to Ian Davies, a professor of Disaster Management at Cranfield University in England, natural hazards have cost companies in the U.S. an average of $1 billion a week since 1989.[14] Businesses often avoid the word "crisis," preferring to use words like: strike, layoff, accident, natural disaster, negative financial news, critical regulatory report, environmental problem, or legal issue.[15] Now the word *terrorism* has taken on a new meaning. "It is no longer inconceivable to imagine a scenario in which your company or facility could be confronted with a potential terrorist attack . . . , a sabotaged facility, stolen hazardous materials or trade secrets, or even the implication that one of your employees could be involved in a terrorist plot."[16]

The sample incidents listed in Figure 13.1 either resulted in significant damage or had the potential to cause significant damage to employees, consumers, the physical or financial operation of an organization, the organization's image, and even local communities or the general public. The organizational and individual victims of these unfortunate incidents ranged from large corporate companies to the federal government, from senior executives to common laborers.

Figure 13.1 Crisis Examples

ACTS OF GOD
- Oklahoma City tornado
- Florida hurricanes
- California earthquakes and forest fires

PUBLIC HEALTH AND SAFETY
- Jack in the Box hamburgers cause deaths
- Major airline crashes (Valujet, TWA, USAir, Egyptian Air)
- Mass killings of citizens and employees: McDonalds in San Diego; Luby's Cafeteria in Killeen, Texas; Columbine High School
- American Home Products: Fen-phen
- Texas A&M bonfire construction

LABOR RELATIONS
- Employee strikes at General Motors, American Airlines, and United Parcel Service

PRODUCT FAILURE
- Intel Pentium computer chip
- Dow Chemical silicone implants
- Ford Pinto gas tank placement
- Ford Explorer/Firestone tires

CORPORATE MISMANAGEMENT
- Sexual harassment (Mitsubishi, Ford, and Astra Pharmaceutical)
- Racial discrimination at Texaco and Denny's
- Bribery in the Salt Lake City 2002 Winter Olympic bids
- Cover-up of sexual misconduct in the Catholic Church
- Enron partnerships; Arthur Andersen's shredding documents

TERRORISM
- World Trade Center attacks
- Oklahoma City Federal Building bombing
- Pan American Airlines explosion
- Anthrax attacks

FINANCIAL CALAMITIES
- ADM price-fixing
- Daiwa Bank

INDIVIDUAL ACTIONS
- Falsification of individual résumés
- Office affairs
- Embezzlement by executives

CONVENTION EVENTS
- Hotel fire
- Phone system outage
- Keynote speaker collapse
- Death of attendee

Computer security expert Mark T. Edmeand has compiled some interesting statistics about companies that experience a crisis.

- Of 350 businesses affected by the 1993 World Trade Center bombing, 150 eventually went out of business.
- Of businesses that lose records in a fire, 44 percent never reopen, and the 30 percent that do reopen survive only three years after the fire.
- The equivalent of one week a year is spent by 30 percent of computer users reconstructing lost data.
- Power outages have interrupted business operations of 72 percent of U.S. companies.
- Computer hardware problems have interrupted business operations of 52 percent of U.S. companies.
- Software problems have interrupted business operations of 43 percent of U.S. companies.
- Telecommunication failure has interrupted business operations of 46 percent of U.S. companies.[17]

Every business organization should examine how many similar incidents have the potential of occurring within its boundaries and lines of operation. The organization should then create strategies for both preventing and dealing with the crises.

Basic Crisis Thesis

Steven Fink, in his book *Crisis Management*, refers to the time of crisis as "an unstable time or state of affairs in which a decisive change is impending—either one with the distinct possibility of a highly undesirable outcome or one with the distinct possibility of a highly desirable and extremely positive outcome."[18] Fink's words are important for advanced business students to remember because each crisis has the potential for either disastrous or quite positive outcomes. Consider the five crisis theses and how they apply to your organization.

A Crisis Can Be Anticipated
As part of its risk management, your organization should audit what it does and how it does it to determine every potential crisis. There are always telltale signs that, when observed, clearly can lead to crisis detection. One of the easiest times for this to occur is during the regular strategic management process in a SWOT analysis: As a company looks at its strengths, weaknesses, opportunities, and threats, potential risk areas become apparent. We discuss this process as we talk about case analysis in Chapter 15.

A Crisis Can Be Prevented
Once the potential crisis is detected your organization can take the proper measures to correct what is wrong and to ensure that a full-scale crisis does not develop.

A Crisis Can Be Controlled
Even if prevention is not possible, your organization can take steps to manage each stage of the crisis and to bring it to a complete end.

A Crisis Can Be Turned into an Advantage

While the presence of a crisis almost always means that some type of negative outcome will occur, the overall impact does not have to remain negative. Johnson & Johnson's (J&J) skillful handling of the Tylenol tampering case gives an excellent example of how the end result can be more positive than negative if your organization takes the right steps through the duration of the crisis.

James Burke, J&J's Chief Executive Officer, responded to the cyanide poisonings by referring to the company's ethical credo, and issuing a total capsule recall. J&J's market share fell from 35 percent to 18 percent. The total recall cost J&J in excess of $500 million. Yet within three years the company had recaptured the market share, had set the industry standard for tamper-resistant products, and had become the model of how to handle a corporate crisis. Remember, a crisis will run its course if it is untreated.[19]

Many of us have Intel's Pentium or Celeron chips in our computers. Yet lots of us have forgotten how close Intel came to never getting the Pentium chip to the market. The following case study concerns Intel Corporation and the crisis it encountered in the mid-1990s. Intel survived, and you will read how the survival process was managed and communicated.

Intel's Big Crisis

Intel's Hidden Crisis

Over a five-year period, starting in early 1990, Intel Corporation spent hundreds of millions of dollars on consumer advertising campaigns designed to establish its name and the first of its high-powered Pentium computer chips as household words. Between March and December of 1994, it spent $150 million on the *Intel Inside* campaign. The image-building process worked: Computer companies like IBM, Dell, Packard-Bell, and Gateway shipped millions of computers to retail outlets in anticipation of successful holiday sales. But on Thursday, November 24, 1994, Thanksgiving day, Intel's world almost fell apart.

The New York Times ran a business-section front page with the headline, "Flaw Undermines Accuracy of Pentium Chips." The *Boston Globe* business page echoed a similar warning, "Sorry, Wrong Number." This was followed with the subtitle, "Results are in: Intel computer chip sometimes makes inaccurate math." [20] While this was the general public's first inkling that a problem existed with the Pentium chip, many computer users had already heard the message. For Intel, a crisis was brewing.

Intel's Pre-Crisis

The event that triggered Intel's crisis actually occurred on June 13, 1994. A college math professor had been running billions of calculations on his Pentium computer and couldn't get the numbers to divide correctly. For four months he continued to recalculate the formula and eventually figured out the error was being produced by the computer's microprocessor. The professor contacted Pentium and learned that he was the only one of 2 million users to report the problem. Believing that he had indeed discovered a problem, and seeking to find more data, he posted a message on the CompuServe online network. The issue spread across the Internet and was discussed for weeks by a network of scientists and engineers who need precise calculations and who were wondering if their work could be impacted. So began Intel's public relations quagmire.[21]

Eventually Intel acknowledged it had discovered the bug in July 1994 but had determined there was no need for a recall. The company contacted technical and scientific users, big companies, and computer retailers. It issued press releases and held telephone conferences with Wall Street analysts. But it did not run any mass-market print or TV ads explaining the situation or publicizing the toll-free phone number that it set up for concerned Pentium users. As one analyst noted, Intel's calculations showed a casual user might encounter a problem with the chip "once every 27,000 years."[22] The message seemed to be that "for the kind of computing most of us plain folks do, a defective Pentium is good enough."[23]

Intel's Full Crisis

Intel reached a new stage in its crisis management by mid-December. Walter Mossberg, who writes a popular weekly technology column in *The Wall Street Journal*, contacted Intel about a replacement for his machine. Evidently someone unfamiliar with Mossberg's status responded grudgingly that Intel would replace computer chips for certain individuals—but before a replacement could be issued the user had to prove to the company that the work being done on the computer was "mathematically complex enough to meet Intel's self-defined rules about who needed accuracy." In addition the user had to give Intel a credit-card number and agree to a potential charge of $1,000 if the old Pentium chip was not returned within 29 days. The user also had to pay for having someone swap the chips. When word of Intel's actions reached the general public it became incensed. Mossberg found cause to describe the negative customer service he had experienced in his weekly column.[24]

On December 12, 1994, alerted to Mossberg's impending article, IBM announced that it was halting all shipments of its highest-power Intel PCs. It also stated that Intel Corporation had significantly underestimated the potential for errors to occur. This action caused Intel's stock to plummet and forced a temporary halt to trading. Andrew Grove, Intel's president and chief executive officer, shot a verbal response to IBM. "You can always contrive situations that force this error. In other words, if you know where a meteor will land, you can go there and get hit."[25] The response by Intel's president seemed to typify its handling of the crisis events. At every turn it dismissed the flaw as a small problem even when customers complained. One crisis manager commented, "Whether it happens one in 10,000 times or one in a million, the reality becomes that the customer is concerned."[26] Crisis-management expert Ian Mitroff responded, "Their [Intel's] technology may be in the Systems Age, but their management thinking is in the Stone Age." Mitroff believed the company should run high-profile ads to fully explain the issue and to commit to replace the chip for any consumer who asked. He compared the $250 million Intel had spent to build an image to how quickly its image could be tarnished for years.[27]

Intel continued to hold fast to its position until the events between December 16 and 19: A *Wall Street Journal* article described "at least 10 [law-] suits in three states" that involved securities fraud, false advertising, and a violation of state consumer protection laws. Three days later the *New York Times* article on the lawsuits quoted Florida's deputy attorney general as saying, "They've [Intel] got to stop acting like a rinky-dink two-person operation in a garage and start acting like the major corporation they are." On the same day a *PC Week* cover story urged IS managers "to protect themselves against liability claims from use of flawed chips."[28]

Intel's Post-Crisis

On December 21, 1994, Intel came to its senses. Andrew Grove reversed his stand and announced Intel would give any Pentium-based computer owner a free replacement chip—no questions asked. Figure 13.2 shows a copy of the Intel press release announcing the replacement. A full-page, letter-format advertisement appeared in most major newspapers. The letter was signed by President and Chief Executive Officer Andrew S. Grove; Executive Vice President and Chief Operating Officer Craig R. Barrett; and Chairman of the Board Gordon E. Moore.[29] The letter read:

> To owners of Pentium™ processor-based computers and the PC community:
> We at Intel wish to sincerely apologize for our handling of the recently publicized Pentium processor flaw.
> The Intel Inside® symbol means that your computer has a microprocessor second-to-none in quality and performance. Thousands of Intel employees work very hard to ensure that this is true. But no microprocessor is ever perfect.
> What Intel continues to believe is technically an extremely minor problem has taken on a life of its own. Although Intel firmly stands behind the quality of the current version of the Pentium processor, we recognize that many users have concerns.
> We want to resolve these concerns.
> Intel will exchange the current version of the Pentium processor for an updated version, in which this floating-point divide flaw is corrected, for any owner who requests it, free of charge anytime during the life of their computer. Just call 1-800-628-8686.

Intel survived its crisis. Sales of Pentium processor-based systems set new sales records over the 1994 holidays. Intel's revenue for 1994 grew by 31 percent.[30] A few months later the average user gave little thought to an Intel machine's inability to perform. From a crisis-management standpoint Intel's major mistake was in waiting so long to arrive at an appropriate response. It approached the problem from an engineering rather than a consumer perspective. In fact, as one analyst stated, "Intel's stubbornness turned what could have been a minor problem, perhaps limited to a few scientists and engineers, into a costly fiasco."[31] The entire crisis episode cost Intel $475 million and was a pretax charge to fourth-quarter 1994 earnings.

Ethically, Intel's pre-crisis decision was financially motivated. It knew that a total recall would take months and would cost millions. "Because chips take as long as 12 weeks to make . . . it would take months for Intel to start stamping out chips with revised circuitry. And because computer-systems makers also take time to cycle

Figure 13.2   **Intel Press Release**

INTEL ADOPTS UPON-REQUEST REPLACEMENT POLICY ON PENTIUM™ PROCESSORS WITH FLOATING POINT FLAW; WILL TAKE Q4 CHARGE AGAINST EARNINGS

SANTA CLARA, Calif., December 20, 1994—Intel today said it will exchange the processor for any owner of a Pentium™ processor-based system who is concerned about the subtle flaw in the floating point unit of the processor. The company has been criticized in recent weeks for replacing processors on the basis of need rather than on request. Intel will take a reserve against fourth quarter earnings to cover costs associated with the replacement program.

The flaw can produce reduced precision in floating point divide operations once every nine billion random number pairs. Intel said that while almost no one will ever encounter the flaw, the company will nevertheless replace the processor upon request with an updated version that does not have the flaw. This offer will be in effect for the lifetime of a user's PC, which means that users can conclude they do not currently want a replacement, but still have the option of replacing the chip in the future if they wish. Intel is making a rapid manufacturing transition to the updated version, and expects to be able to ship sufficient replacement parts to meet demand during the next few months.

"The past few weeks have been deeply troubling. What we view as an extremely minor technical problem has taken on a life of its own," said Dr. Andrew S. Grove, president and chief executive officer. "Our OEM customers and the retail channel have been very supportive during this difficult period, and we are very grateful," Dr. Grove said. "To support them and their customers, we are today announcing a no-questions-asked return policy on the current version of the Pentium processor.

"Our previous policy was to talk with users to determine whether their needs required replacement of the processor. To some people, this policy seemed arrogant and uncaring. We apologize. We were motivated by a belief that replacement is simply unnecessary for most people. We still feel that way, but we are changing our policy because we want there to be no doubt that we stand behind this product."

Intel will send a replacement processor to PC users who choose to do the replacement themselves, and will offer telephone technical assistance. Call 1-800-628-8686 for details. Intel also said it planned to contract with service providers to do replacements at no charge for PC owners who prefer to bring their PC's to a service location. Details will be provided in the next few weeks. Finally, Intel said it would work with its OEM customers to provide replacement for PC users who prefer to work with the manufacturer of their system.

The company said it would take an unspecified but material charge against fourth quarter earnings to cover costs associated with the replacement program announced today. Intel said it was unable to determine the amount of the reserve, but said an estimated total will be provided on or before January 17, the date of Intel's 1994 financial results announcement. Following this release is a copy of an advertisement that will appear starting on December 21 in major newspapers in North America.

Intel, the world's largest chip maker, is also a leading manufacturer of personal computer, networking and communications products.

Source: Reprinted with permission of Intel Corporation.

through their inventories, as many as 5 million flawed chips would be sold before the new ones would hit the market, analysts [had] estimated."[32]

In the end the cost was financially the same, but the company's reputation was distorted in the minds of many users. Andrew Grove was right when he said in his public letter, "technically an extremely minor problem has taken on a life of its own." Years later we recognize that Intel managed the crisis well, for few people remember or care about the event. Intel and Pentium are synonymous and positive words. Intel was fortunate. It referred to the crisis in its 1994 Annual Report as an event that brought the personal computer (PC) industry and consumers closer together. "This episode reflects a strategic turning point. Quite simply, the PC is now a standard consumer tool used by a wide range of people, from preschoolers to university researchers. Many of these PC customers have more demanding—and varied—expectations for product quality, performance, and service than computer users have in the past. In many ways, Intel facilitated this transition."[33]

Intel's Management Mindsets

Intel did not anticipate a public response to what the company considered to be a minor problem. If the company had adopted a philosophy of correcting each problem in favor of the customer, the crisis could have easily been prevented. When the company finally came to its senses, it controlled the negative spiral and quickly applied positive public relations to turn the situation to the company's advantage. It believed that it could get by without responding to the general public, issuing a recall, and answering many of the questions that had been generated.

Intel's management held the first of several mindsets: "There is only one correct approach to solving a problem." It decided to stonewall the issue, pretend that only a few Pentium users could possibly be impacted, and that all other users would eventually realize that their machines were not damaged. In doing this it fell prey to the second mindset: "Factual data is superior to subjective opinions when making a decision." While it was true that errors were generated in answers that required extremely high calculations, they failed to take the beliefs of the ordinary user into account. By using the third mindset—"*It is possible totally to separate reason and emotion*"—Intel disregarded the feelings of consumers and in essence called them "stupid" for not seeing that they would never be doing problems that could possibly generate errors. Finally, Intel believed that "Severe change is only temporary. . . . Things will return to normal if one will just wait long enough." Its problem with the waiting was that it gave those who were demanding that Intel respond more time to generate additional support, especially through the Internet. What started as a small problem became a giant one.

Four Stages of a Crisis

As the Intel case showed, four stages can be identified in every example of an organizational crisis that has run its course. If management applies itself seriously to correcting problems as they develop in Stages One and Two, a full crisis can usually be averted. However, once the crisis hits Stage Three it is too late to avoid certain consequences. It is important that the organization at that point seek to resolve the crisis as quickly as possible and minimize the costs involved.

Stage One: The Hidden Crisis

Just as when a disease invades a human body and the person is not yet aware, potential crises exist within every organization. They could be in the composition of a product, a particular response to a customer, a method of production, or any number of other items. If management is wise, and seeks to correct every problem and issue that develops, it may avoid a crisis. The organization will often not know the potential danger until the issue moves to Stage Two.

Stage Two: The Pre-Crisis

If the hidden issue is recognized but not resolved, the organization will find itself in Stage Two. Managers here often believe that a problem will solve itself over time. For Intel this stage occurred in July 1994, when one of its engineers realized that the computer chip allowed errors to occur. The fatal mistake was that management believed that no one outside the organization would ever find the problem. Consequently it chose not to act. Even when the math professor notified Intel of his findings in September the company led him to believe that he alone had made a mistake and that the chip was perfect.

Stage Three: The Crisis

Here the problems can no longer be hidden from the public. Managers operate at a high degree of stress. Entire entities within the organization are in chaos. Rapid problem-solving attempts are made, but not enough time and resources are available to quickly bring the problem to an end. Input from people within the organization is narrowed to just a few. Outside help is not trusted or sought. Panic is the norm. If the crisis goes public, the media's agenda becomes the organization's agenda. Instead of putting its attention to properly solving the problem, employees suddenly have to supply the media with information and strategy. Valuable time is wasted. Resources are improperly used.

Stage Four: The Post-Crisis

Eventually a crisis will end. It is hoped the outcome favors the organization. This stage is critical because the organization can now discover what went wrong, how it happened, and what should have been done about it in the first place. The wise organization uses this stage to re-evaluate every potential crisis and to put in motion problem-solving groups that are empowered to correct whatever problem exists before a new crisis can occur.

The Crisis-Management Process

Every organization should recognize that crisis management is a process. The time and energy spent in investigating and planning will pay off should an actual crisis develop. The preparation steps allow management to ask hypothetical questions that are not thought of or that are too emotional to ask when a crisis develops. According to a study at Oxford University, organizations that actually take the time to prepare for a crisis (recoverers) regained shareholder value within 50 days. For organizations that did not plan (nonrecoverers) recovery time was always more than a year.[34] In order to ensure a favorable result, five steps need to be taken: (1) determine the crisis potential, (2) develop appropriate crisis teams and centers, (3) write a crisis-management plan, (4) develop a communication strategy, and (5) practice and revise the plan.

Step One: Determine the Crisis Potential

Studies show few organizations critically evaluate the technical, human, natural, or contingent threats they could face.[35] Wise managers do scenario planning on how likely it is their organizations will suddenly encounter a crisis. To do this, what-if questions must be asked. Examine your organization's internal and external environments. Start with the *personnel*. For instance, what would happen if your CEO or president suddenly died? Who would take charge? What immediate actions would be necessary? What could happen to people involved in a plant accident? How would your organization handle a libel or slander suit?

The next category deals with the organization's *facilities*. Companies that manufacture, transport, and store certain chemical and hazardous products are required by federal and state regulations to have available emergency-response plans. Consequently, organizations in such industries have plans available to deal with emergencies at the incident site. Employees are usually trained as to what procedures to follow.[36]

Amazingly many companies are not prepared to deal with catastrophic events or incidents. Ask questions like: What would happen if a fire, flood, or earthquake occurred? Where would my organization meet to conduct business? If a manufacturing plant were the target, how would the organization continue to make its products? Is there a backup source that you could have continuing the production?

The Oklahoma City Chamber of Commerce experienced a disruption that impacted both facilities and personnel on April 19, 1995, when the Murrah Federal Building was bombed. The Chamber is a not-for-profit organization. It makes no product, but services dues-paying member organizations. The organization was housed in downtown Oklahoma City, a few blocks from the epicenter of the blast. At the time of the explosion, all personnel evacuated the building. Unlike Morgan Stanley on 9-11, no procedure was in place for where to go or where to meet. Because of the chaos in the downtown area, Chamber personnel went in different directions. Some volunteered to help blast victims. Some became so distraught they went home and watched the happenings on television. Because of the telephone outages, it was several days before new office space was secured and all employees were notified and reassembled for work.

Another area of concern is with *products*. What will your organization do if, like Intel, a product is shown to be faulty, causes death or injury, or needs to be recalled? What plans are in place in case a product becomes obsolete? How will your organization respond to a patent infringement?

Competition should also be considered. What will your organization do if competition suddenly undercuts your price substantially? How will it respond to a major advertising campaign? What will happen if your company suddenly becomes a takeover target? By asking many of these questions, your organization can prepare to deal with uncertain and destructive events and can develop management strategies for the inevitable.

United Parcel Service (UPS) failed to consider several of these factors when its employees, who were Teamster union members, threatened to stage a strike. According to UPS Vice-Chairman John Alden: "We didn't expect a strike. Then we thought it would last only a day or two. And we thought the vast majority of our workers would cross picket lines." UPS didn't understand its personnel were truly mad at management for holding down workers' wages while company profits and executive salaries soared. Neither did UPS understand its opponent. The union had a well-funded war chest and had prepared carefully for the battle. Finally, as we will soon see, a company should select a primary spokesperson to address the crisis. Teamster president Ron Carey consistently addressed the media, while UPS paraded as many as a dozen different human-resource executives before the press to answer questions.[37]

Figure 13.3 gives some ideas regarding the potential risk for your organization. Barton found in a ten-year study of hundreds of organizations that certain types have a much higher degree of risk for crisis events than others do. Pinkerton's Inc. determined the specific security threats that cause many of the risks. Figure 13.4 gives the 2000 list of Top Ten Business Security Threats in the United States.

Step Two: Develop Appropriate Crisis Teams and Centers

As potential crisis situations become evident an organization should develop teams that take responsibility for previewing each crisis, developing a strategy to prevent occurrence, and then managing the event should it occur. *Senior executive* teams may include two or three key executives. *Support* teams may involve several department heads, key managers, and functional specialists. *Field* response management is developed based on the nature of each organization, its facilities, and operations. The team must include multiple perspectives, such as legal, marketing, operations, communications, security, and corporate, as well as an external communications counsel.[38]

Crisis centers are places where teams can assemble and carry out their activities. Anticipatory measures like adding telephone lines to a conference room, and pre-designating computers, printers, and copy machines can help the support-response operations and will save valuable time later.

As teams develop they should be carefully trained to make decisions and empowered to be able to carry them out. If a crisis occurs and the team is unsure of what to do, the staff will sense it and the media will notice it, too. Conducting tabletop exercises or response drills exposes flaws in the support system and allows each member of the team to see how important his or her role is to the total endeavor.

Step Three: Write a Crisis-Management Plan

Crisis management implies that to some degree each crisis situation can be managed. This management process takes place before, during, and after the crisis. For instance, the following things can be managed: anticipating a crisis, developing and

Figure 13.3 Crisis Risk Categories

CRISIS RISK CATEGORIES

HIGH-RISK CATEGORY
- Manufacturing organizations, especially chemical and nuclear
- All financial institutions: banks, credit unions
- Technological firms: chip and software makers, ammunition and weapons
- Public transportation: airlines, railroads, and subways
- Lodging properties: hotels and motels
- Food producers and distributors
- Nightclubs and casinos
- Federal and state buildings and agencies
- Amusement parks
- Public personalities: politicians, entertainers
- Craft renting: helicopter, excursion planes, hot-air balloons, water rafts
- Utilities and airports
- Builders, roofers, and structural engineering companies

MEDIUM-RISK CATEGORY
- Not-for-profit agencies, churches, colleges, hospitals
- Retail concerns
- Fast-food outlets and restaurants
- Telecommunications companies
- Household products manufacturers
- Computer manufacturers/distributors
- Physicians and related medical professionals
- Mall and shopping centers
- Health clubs, preschools
- Liquor, beer, and wine stores

LOW-RISK CATEGORY
- Radio and television broadcasters
- Certified Public Accountants
- Apparel manufacturers
- Neighborhood businesses: barber shops, pet stores, video rentals, dry cleaners
- Automobile repair shops
- Law firms
- Social organizations
- Car rental companies

Source: Adapted from: Lawrence Barton, *Crisis in Organizations*, South-Western, Cincinnati, Ohio, 1993, pp. 65–66.

Figure 13.4 | Top Ten Business Security Threats in the United States

Top Business Security Threats

1. Workplace violence
2. Internet/Intranet security
3. Business interruption/disaster recovery (tie)
4. Fraud/White-collar crime
5. Employee selection/screening concerns
6. General employee theft
7. Unethical business conduct
8. Hardware/software theft
9. Drugs in the workplace
10. Sexual harassment

Source: Adapted from: Workplace violence is top security threat for Fortune 1000. (n.d.). Pinkerton.com. Retrieved April 4, 2002, from **http://www.disasteresource.com/articles/pg_110.shtml**.

training a crisis team, designing and equipping a crisis center, working through a plan for each potential crisis, developing the statements to be used in communication events, and handling media interviews. A smart organization develops all of these managerial processes into a Crisis Management Plan (CMP). Organizations put these plans into action if a crisis occurs. While the plan may not address "glass found in a company's product," it can address how the organization would respond to rumors of false media information, which executives would be responsible for talking to the media, and even things they would say.

The Crisis-Management Plan Contents

The best plan is one that is thought out and prepared thoroughly. Clarke Caywood, a crisis-management specialist at Northwestern University, assembled what he considers to be "The Ultimate Crisis Plan." Caywood contends that a wise organization writes what is essentially an autobiography. This should be ready to pull from the shelf and use when a crisis hits. Usually the plan has already been reproduced and copies sent to key members of the management team—but this document will never be leaked to the outside world. In many ways it reveals an organization in its most vulnerable form.[39]

Figure 13.5 gives an outline of a crisis-management plan. In the completed plan, each item is fully documented and all requested information is listed. While creating this document may seem overwhelming, most organizations have this information readily available—although probably dispersed throughout the organization. By dividing the creation task among a variety of managers, the overall assembling of a CMP can be done in a short time frame.

I. Mission and related items

Mission. The organization's mission statement, goals, and objectives are briefly stated.

The organization's philosophy and behavior standards are listed.

Objectives. Objectives regarding what is important for your organization are then recorded. This describes what you hope your CMP will achieve and prevent. Prioritize the items listed so that if a crisis does occur, there will be no confusion as to what to do first.

Listed with the objectives are also the things that your organization wants to protect. This section can list items like an organization's image, customer and member safety, and product quality.

Rational for the CMP. This portion states explicitly the realization that crises could occur, how they would be handled by crisis teams, and vital information about the members.

II. History of Crises and Potential Crises

History of past crises. A review and critique of previous crises that have occurred within the organization are described, along with the way the situations were handled and changes that were made.

Listing of potential crises. This area lists the potential problems that were uncovered during the crisis audit.

Survey results. Here the results of any questionnaires used during the crisis audit are discussed.

Crisis stage development. For each potential crisis that is uncovered an outline of the stages of development should be constructed along with a timetable and the personnel assigned to handle it.

III. Preparing the Crisis Center

Crisis center furnishings. Each crisis center should be furnished with the items that will aid the crisis team and help bring an end to the crisis. A variety of items like those listed below should be considered:

- Sufficient electrical outlets
- Portable computers with modems that access company files; a laser printer
- Fax machines, blast fax, and fax cover sheets
- Preprogrammed cellular telephones and standard telephones equipped with a separate line for each member of the crisis team and voice mail with call interrupt
- Telephone directories for each organizational site along with updated organizational chairs and telephone trees
- Media, governmental, business, and professional directories
- Televisions with cable to receive CNN, C-Span, and multiple networks
- Radios equipped for shortwave
- Photocopier
- VCR and audio recorder with playback and copying ability and extra tapes
- Risk area maps in hard copy and software
- Body bags in the event of crisis-related deaths
- Legal pads, pens, pencils, paper clips, and staplers

| Figure 13.5 | Crisis-Management Plan Outline (Continued) |

- Organization stationery, envelopes, rapid-delivery containers
- Clocks
- Restroom and shower facilities nearby
- Lots of refreshments
- Corporate credit cards and cash

A media room. A media briefing room should also be established and equipped with the following items:

- General press kit: list of products, background of safety record and fact sheets
- Telephones
- Podium, microphone, and portable public address system
- Chairs, tables, and desks
- Computers, modems, and printers
- Photocopiers

IV. Directories of the Organization's Stakeholders

Directories of Stakeholders. Each directory should contain addresses and telephone numbers for some of the following groups:

- Emergency response personnel
- Board of directors
- Community and civic leaders
- Media
- Customers and/or members
- Shareholders
- Clients
- Neighbors
- Financial partners
- Government agencies
- Regulatory agencies
- Vendors
- Suppliers
- Certain competitors
- Family members
- Analysts
- Legal groups
- Subsidiary heads
- Employees
- Plant managers
- Union officials
- Retirees
- Pension holders
- Sales and marketing personnel

Appropriate channels of communication for each group. Mechanisms for reaching each of the above groups must be decided along with who in the organization will be responsible for reaching each stakeholder. Any preliminary steps that can be taken to have communication items ready should be taken. Typical mechanisms include:

- Press releases
- Letters
- Personal visits

Figure 13.5   **Crisis-Management Plan Outline (Continued)**

- Telephone calls
- Employee call-in center
- Emergency toll-free hotlines
- General meetings
- Video conferences
- Media advertising
- Video news releases (VNR)
- Internal publications
- News conferences
- Interoffice memos
- Faxes preprogrammed for multiple sending ability
- Telegrams and telexes
- Electronic mail
- Overnight mail
- Accessibility of computer back-up files

Government regulatory forms. All compliance forms that would be required by government regulatory organizations should be collected.

V. Media Awareness

Organization's media policy. This section should emphasize open, honest, and proactive actions with the media during the crisis.

Organization's spokespeople. The level and type of crisis will dictate the specific spokespeople. Identifying all the potential people at this point will allow the organization to do plenty of media interview training (see Chapter 13).

Organization gatekeeper and that person's function. This person will centralize and control the flow of information to ensure that it is accurate and valid and that it reaches the right people at the right time. The person will also monitor the flow of internal and external communication to ensure that the organization speaks with "one voice." He or she should always be accessible for both good and bad news.

Media databases and media contacts. A listing of each available media representative, prioritized in favor of those that have a positive relationship with the organization, should be drafted. List also media deadlines and policies. Be sure to keep this database current.

Third-party sources. Third-party sources should be developed and then updated continually. This lists friends of the organization and experts in the organization's field. The media can call these individuals for background information during a crisis. Make sure these contacts are credible, reliable, trusted sources who are often quoted in the media.

A process for handling media inquiries. This section should provide answers to questions like, "How will the calls be recorded?' "Who will the calls be forwarded to?" "How will they be prioritized when answered?" "How will they be answered (i.e., fax or phone)?"

Designate also who will check the validity and accuracy of the stories being printed and broadcast. This person should have access to the scene of the crisis and should monitor radio, television, and wire services, along with police, hospitals, and government agencies.

Figure 13.5 **Crisis-Management Plan Outline (Concluded)**

VI. Other Action to Take

Depending upon the specific industry, each organization will need to determine when and where to take appropriate action on a variety of issues like the following:

- Have back-up office sites.
- Specify how security arrangements will be handled for facilities, possibly injured individuals, and the public.
- Cover items like what alarms will be activated, who will be responsible for first aid, and what evacuation routes to use.
- Determine how much crisis insurance to purchase. Policies normally cover types of events like securities confidence, hostile takeovers, and employment practices.
- Develop a list of professional counselors who can help "de-escalate" the crisis. Their help is often needed in the first few hours and days following an event. They can support, encourage, and listen in a caring way to traumatized employees.
- Consider establishing a reunification center, where dispersed individuals can be reunited. Make sure it can accommodate both vehicles and people. This necessity has become apparent with the major school crises.
- Create a cellular phone policy that can be put into effect for the first few hours of the situation. Often all members of a community are encouraged to avoid use to allow safety officials reliable service.

VII. Method of Evaluation

After a crisis is resolved, it is important that an organization review and analyze everything that occurred. This process should be started while the crisis is happening (the gathering of information) and completed immediately after it is resolved. Several things go into this process.

Interviews with both external and internal publics. The organization can interview, informally, people who are key to the system. They should be asked about their perception of how the company reacted and how the organization could have reacted better.

A content analysis of media clippings and tapes. Clippings collected by staff during the crisis should be analyzed for accuracy of reporting and fairness of treatment.

A cost-benefit analysis. After the crisis has ended and all data have been summarized, an organization should determine how much damage was done to the organization financially.

Modification of the crisis management plan. After all evaluations are completed, the crisis management plan should be changed to allow the organization to better manage crises of the future.

Written case study. While the information is still fresh in the minds of all involved, a case study should be developed. This can be an excellent training tool to use in preparing future personnel for new crises. This also allows the organization to be more objective in its focus.

Step Four: Develop a Communication Strategy

When a crisis hits, a company must communicate and do so quickly. History is full of organizations that did not respond and their reputation suffered. NASA took five hours before commenting on the *Challenger* spacecraft explosion. Exxon took several days. Intel also tried to avoid telling the truth. But in stories of crisis success, like that of Johnson & Johnson during the Tylenol tragedy, appropriate communication protected the organization's image.

One crisis expert defines *crisis communication* as ". . . the process of managing the strategy, messages, timing, and distribution channels necessary to communicate effectively with the media, employees, core constituencies, clients, customers, and stakeholders. The focus of the crisis-communications function is to facilitate the rapid de-escalation of the crisis through timely and effective communications methods." [40] Because time is of the essence for managers in the midst of a crisis, a communication strategy must be easy to understand and follow.

To be able to accomplish the above requires that a strategy be developed and working at the time the crisis occurs. The crisis-management plan should designate who will take charge of the communication process. Usually the public relations department takes care of the mechanics and a designated individual is selected to be the spokesperson. A good communication strategy considers several things.

Determine the Audience That Needs Information

Figure 13.6 gives a list of potential stakeholders. Not every audience member will need to receive information in every crisis. As Whitesell states, "It is crucial to communicate only with the appropriate audiences. For instance, there is no need to alert the news media to a situation occurring internally that has no impact on the general public. A contingency plan should always be developed for secondary audiences, because crises can explode beyond their initial boundaries.[41]

A key objective of a good communication strategy is that you reach your target audience with the right message and response. Finally, "identify and prioritize target audiences and then identify channels of communication; update media lists; consider alternate communications sources: newsletters, Internet, e-mail, fax-on-demand, 1-800 lines."[42] Lukaszewski gives a protocol for prioritizing the communication:

Priority #1: Those most directly affected (victims, intended and unintended).

Priority #2: Employees (sometimes they are victims, too).

Priority #3: Those indirectly affected: neighbors, friends, families, relatives, customers, suppliers, government, regulators, and third parties.

Priority #4: The news media and other channels of external communication.[43]

Determine Who Will Be the Spokesperson for the Organization

A single spokesperson is recommended, with a backup designated. Longtime crisis expert Barry McLouglin states: "A good spokesperson is someone who is technically knowledgeable, in a position of authority, has strong professional credentials, is a quick study, has an even temper, a reasonable tone, an honest face, an ear for a good sound bite, and gets along well with reporters."[44]

Figure 13.6   **Organizational Stakeholders**

Adversarial groups	International executives
Bankers	Investors
Board members	Law enforcement
Brokers	Lawyers
Business groups	News media
Community leaders	Neighbors
Competitors	Politicians
Customers/clients	Regulators
Educators	Retirees
Emergency response personnel	Senior executives
Employees	Stockholders
Employees' families	Suppliers
Financial partners	Union officers
Franchisees	Vendors
Government agencies	

Source: Adapted from "Stakeholders in a business crisis," Institute for Crisis Management, Louisville, Kentucky, 1999, at **http://www.crisisexperts.com/stakeholders_main.htm**.

In 99 percent of the cases the chief executive officer, executive director, or highest-ranking official takes charge—but some experts believe this is unwise. Larry Smitz, president of the Institute for Crisis Management, contends: "Your spokesperson should be someone high up who has credibility, but not the top person. It's better to reserve your CEO as a safety net. That way, if someone makes a statement that needs to be corrected, the CEO can step in. Deploy your top gun first and you've got no ammunition left."[45] For minor types of information-sharing a public relations member may be used. You may want to have a member of your board, a chief scientist, or the head of your board's audit committee. The real thing you should look for is, "Who has the credibility?" Usually a public relations person will be the designated receiver of all media requests, questions, and other sources of information. It is critical that each person in the organization be informed that only the designated spokesperson will comment to any outside source. Of course cases of severe crises involving deaths or public health threats make the CEO a required spokesperson.

Such was the case of New York City Mayor Rudy Giuliani, who established a new standard for the role of crisis spokesperson as he handled the WTC aftermath. He was visible almost immediately following the attacks and spearheaded every aspect of the city response effort. He provided a wealth of factual and usable information for his constituents. He answered questions concerning their needs in areas like electric power, water supply, transportation, and where families could go for help. In the midst of chaos he presented a calm personal strength, speaking with empathy, passion, and eloquence. He gave New York City residents assurance that they could get past the crisis. He refused to take credit for any of the effort under way, but directed it to his fellow New Yorkers, and to the search-and-rescue workers. Author Malcolm Fleschner commented about Giuliani's media style: "perhaps most important for the deeply shaken city and nation was the mayor's ubiquitous TV presence, whether in front of the cameras delivering a press briefing on casualty figures, at Ground Zero overseeing rescue efforts, or comforting victims at triage centers or area hospitals. Understanding the power of symbols, and to emphasize his role as emergency response chief, Giuliani never appeared on-camera without a rescue worker jacket, FDNY hat, or some article of clothing symbolizing the heroic city employees who continued to work tirelessly off-camera to save lives."[46]

Determine the Appropriate Communication Style

Information should be communicated quickly, candidly, and in a positive way. The organization must act immediately to show that it is capable of resolving the problem and then take steps to ensure it doesn't occur again. It is critical that the organization tells the truth and never lies. This, of course, does not mean revealing confidential or competitive information. Because crisis situations are related to emotions, communication should recognize those areas and be developed and delivered with compassion. Finally, as in all written and spoken communication, the information should be clear, concise, and free of technical jargon and ambiguity.[47]

Determine the Appropriate Timing

Each communication device is impacted by timely delivery. By drawing on the crisis-management plan, some data can be accessed immediately and distributed to the necessary audiences. Policy statements must be developed. A question-and-answer sheet regarding the crisis should be prepared, especially for the media. Other written materials such as news releases, press kits, or letters must also be prepared and distributed when necessary. An organization will find that it will use various means of communicating during crisis situations: meetings, press conferences, memos, e-mail, telephone calls, Internet Web site, letters, and personal interviews. Chapter 14 describes the appropriate methods of working with the news media. Media interface is one place where a well-prepared crisis-management plan is invaluable. Your CMP should contain fact sheets, backgrounds, prior news releases, prior media statements, and a general archive of your past public statements. Often such items serve as boilerplates for your required messages.

In crisis situations the media are busy compiling the story. If you want your voice to be heard, use that opportunity to speak while the news is fresh. In a hurry, the media can sacrifice quality. Realize that when the media representatives appear, you must have an organized statement that relays pertinent information. Make sure that this statement is prepared and delivered in a clear and concise manner.

Richard Brundage, at the Center for Advance Media Studies, believes an organization should take control of a crisis situation within the first six hours—not 24 or 36 hours later. "Even if you have a press release already written for incidents like this, present it and then let them know when they will get more. Then follow through. This is how to get the media off your back without making them mad."

He describes the timing used by Waterworld USA when an accident occurred at its Concord, California, location. "It was obvious they had a well-laid-out plan well ahead of time. . . . Right from the outset, control was established. Not one media [member] was allowed inside the park . . . until all details, if not completed, were launched. The parties that needed to get in and do their work could. They had a clear-cut plan in place for an interim management team to come in and deal with the day-to-day communications with all the agencies and the media."[48]

Contrast Waterworld USA to Exxon. Exxon misjudged its opportunity in the oil spill off the Alaska coast. As the public, environmentalists, government, and the media waited for the company to respond to and manage the spill, the situation grew worse. Most executives have learned to take immediate and visible action, and so a press conference seemed required. Other CEOs caught in similar crises have even jumped on a plane to head for the disaster scene. Lawrence Rawl, Exxon's CEO at the time of the accident, did none of those things. In fact, he did not comment publicly for a week, and when he did make a statement he tended to blame others, including God.[49] It quickly became evident that neither Exxon nor the petroleum industry could find a reasonable solution. At that point, the media became their enemy. As one public relations expert put it:

> There was a window of opportunity with the news media. The reporting initially and for a period of time following the disaster was factual and pretty straight-forward even though media representatives were undoubtedly as horrified as the rest of us at the scope of the disaster. But as Exxon stumbled, fumbled, stone-walled, denied, shifted the blame, ducked responsibility, and tried to manage the messages, the news media had no choice but to turn against them as well.[50]

Figure 13.7 shows the critical impact of a CEO's failure to appear at an appropriate time. Coca-Cola experienced a relatively minor European crisis, but that grew in intensity as the company failed to manage it properly. In this instance the CEO's appearance would have showed strong organizational leadership.

American Airlines shocked many when it announced just eight days after its jet crashed into the mountains of Cali, Columbia, "that human error on the part of our people may have contributed to the accident." Most corporate lawyers fear that any concessions of that type cost the company in court. Yet American, which had not had a crash in 16 years prior to that accident, had learned much from other airlines like Pan American and U.S. Air, and also from two American Eagle affiliate accidents. Travelers will stop flying your airline if they do not trust your safety. A company is "better off admitting what they know, what went wrong and whether it was their fault."[51]

Determine How to Use the Internet

In past crises, managers were primarily concerned with communicating to stake-holders primarily through other media. The Internet has changed all that. Companies today must take both a defensive and offensive posture with the Internet. As we saw in the Intel case an angry customer can send a message that is instantly received by millions of interested stakeholders. Those with complaints can go to

Figure 13.7   **Coca-Cola's Poor Crisis Response**

The year 1999 was a bad one for Coca-Cola, the world's leading brand. In an average week, 70 million French and Belgian consumers drink 120 million servings of the beverage. Yet seven days is all it took "for the 113-year-old Atlanta-based [company] . . . to go from a much admired and trusted market leader in Europe, to a company scrambling to give away product in order to pick up the shreds of consumer confidence."[1]

In mid-May people in Belgium, many of them children, became sick after drinking Coke. Over 100 people were hospitalized with symptoms of headaches, nausea, and vomiting. Two days later the company withdrew 2.5 million bottles of Coca-Cola, Coca-Cola Light, Fanta, and Sprite. But then things took a strange turn. Coke was so sure of its product's innocence that it misread the consumers' level of concern and focused on denying that its product caused the illnesses. For seven days Coke failed to give an explanation or to even discuss the matter. Governments throughout Northern Europe banned and recalled Coke soft drinks, and in some countries, all Coke products (Nestea, Minute Maid, Aquarium, and bon Aqua).[2] A Belgian health minister described the scene: "People were angry and disturbed because there was a lack of communication. They did not say whether they knew what the problem was and if they did know they were keeping it to themselves. Coca-Cola has been seriously damaged in Belgium."[3]

That action got Coke's attention and it quickly responded. In Belgium, a "created in-house" newspaper ad offered an apology. Coke's CEO, M. Douglas Ivester, known for an extremely hands-on management style, finally got on a plane to Brussels to take charge. His first words were: "My apologies to the consumers of Belgium. I should have spoken to you earlier." Soon similar ads appeared in France and Poland with Ivester saying, "I want to reassure our consumers, customers and governments in Europe that the Coca-Cola company is taking all necessary steps."[4]

What caused the problem? Coke placed the blame on a batch of defective carbon dioxide in its Antwerp plant, as well as on a fungicide in Dunkirk, France, that may have rubbed off wooden pallets onto the soda cans. Others suspect that maybe errors were committed in the selection of plants or the dosage of extracts in the Coke concentrate. But months later the blame still is unsure . . . there is no evidence linking the illness to the product.[5]

What is sure is that Coca-Cola bungled its crisis management. It was slow to address the issue, insisting that no real problems existed. An apology was belated. Coke also failed to read the social fears. Belgium had just come off a devastating dioxin-contaminated food scare with pig farmers.

| Figure 13.7 | Coca-Cola's Poor Crisis Response (Concluded) |

European government agencies were cautiously trying to protect their reputations as watchdogs. Many fear Coke got caught in the middle. But one analyst also placed the blame on Ivester. "CEOs are still regarded as the ultimate face, voice and guardian of the enterprise. No other substitute can stand for the 'real thing'—the CEO."[6] Ball agrees with this: "The golden rules of crisis management are to get the message across that you are acting, to do it swiftly and to be seen to be transparent. Coca-Cola seems to have failed on almost all these points."[7] Perhaps the stock market and Coke's board of directors agreed. M. Douglas Ivester stunned employees and investors in early December 1999 by resigning.

1. Schmidt, K. V. (1999, September 27). Coke's crisis. *Marketing News*, p. 1.
2. Ibid, p. 2.
3. Ball, S. (1999, June 24). Coke pays the price of a mis-handled crisis. *Marketing*, p. 15.
4. Ibid.
5. Michener, B., & McKay, B. (1999, August 17). EU criticizes Coke's explanation of contaminated-drinks scare. *Dow Jones Business News*.
6. Deogun, N. (1999, June 18). Coke's public-relations fiasco in Europe tests CEO. *The Wall Street Journal Europe*, p. 5.
7. Gaines-Ross, L. (1999, June 28). CEO driving lessons. *Advertising Age*, p. 34.

Web sites such as **complaints.com**, **fightback.com**, or **thesqueakywheel.com**. Wise companies monitor the Net for brand protection.[52]

In times of crisis the Internet works at warp speed. In fact, the Internet was primarily designed as a communications network that could remain operational in disaster-recovery situations—like nuclear war. Natural disasters and terrorist attacks have displayed the enormous contribution that it has made. During the Northridge, California, earthquake it was used for emergency communication. In the Kobe, Japan, earthquake the Net linked survivors to the outside world and helped rescue teams locate them. During the Oklahoma City bombing the official Internet-response site received over 27,000 hits in the first 48 hours.[53]

Brian L. Mackay, a business-continuity consultant, describes the importance of the Internet in crisis management. "The possibilities for utilization of this tool range from simple e-mail capabilities to full-blown dedicated crisis-management Web pages with press releases, pictures, situation reports, weather maps, and real-time video/audio conferencing that are 'turned on' when there is an active event. The possibilities are almost unlimited."[54] One example of a company making use of the Internet during a 1996 crisis is the California-based Odwalla Juice Company. When its natural apple juice was found to contain E. coli bacteria a nationwide recall was issued. Internet newsgroups quickly circulated news of the outbreak and recall. Consumer users wanted more information. Investment newsgroups discussed the falling price of the company's stock. Odwalla wanted to respond but had no Web site. Within a week Odwalla's public relations firm created a site and the company put up messages that expressed "ongoing concern for all those impacted." The site was simple but featured "a brief message by the company's chairman and links to the company's new releases regarding the recall, a fact sheet, a question-and-answer section, and additional relevant health resources on the Web."[55]

Following the World Trade Center attacks the Internet allowed opened communication channels so organizations could coordinate response efforts, communicate to employees, and disseminate information to the public. At the beginning of this chapter we read how Morgan Stanley successfully utilized the Web to keep its operations active. A more tragic story took place at Cantor Fitzgerald. Out of 1,000 employees in the WTC, Cantor lost 658 people. As they suddenly realized the enormity of the loss, the first priority became family communication. Cantor marketing vendors quickly volunteered their help. "Within 24 hours, digital media developer Thinkware built a crisis site [**Cantor.com**] containing news updates and contact information for friends, families, and colleagues. Rapp Collins built a database of missing and found employees as well as a memorial Web site. Edelman Public Relations Worldwide . . . donated the time of 100 employees who took calls at the financial service firm's grief center."[56]

Cantor Fitzgerald found what many organizations have found in time of organizational crisis: the Internet is the best link between the company, families, friends, customers, and the general public. Mackay encourages companies that he works with to designate either a separate Web site or a portion of the company site to crisis management. By password the site can be activated when needed. The information made available there "can range from simple call trees and announcements to detailed plans, pictures of facilities and structures, and detailed instructions for event management. A Disaster Press Kit can be made available that includes statements from management, status reports, press conference schedules, digital photos of the event, company histories, and product information sheets." In addition, companies can use multimedia packages and video and audio conference through the Net.[57]

Determine Whether to Use the Proactive or Reactive Media Approach

An organization must decide whether it wants to take a proactive or reactive approach to the media. The proactive is by far the most successful, yet often the most threatening. With this approach a company is ready to start its crisis machinery whenever an unwanted situation occurs. In fact, proactive companies often contact the media before the media have a chance to call them.

Shell Oil found that the proactive style paid off in a disaster. A blowout in the Gulf of Mexico killed four people and threatened the safety of water, beaches, and wildlife. Shell chose not to stonewall the incident. They issued 150 press releases and arranged 50 interviews and 6 press conferences. They even took reporters to the site for personal inspection. This communication technique brought the media to Shell's side as they fought the fire and finally put it out.[58]

In using the proactive approach, it is important to make a clear distinction between what you know for certain, what you assume to be true, and what you really do not know at all. Help all members of the organization involved in the crisis know the kinds of information that falls into each category. As you acquire facts try to move all information into the "known" category. Some of the members will be working with the press, some with the public, and others with the regulatory agencies that have a legitimate right to information.

The communication manager should try to determine how the media would cover the story. Because the organization's goal is to de-escalate the story, management must work hard to determine what actions will accomplish that end.[59] In relation to the media, the designated company spokesperson should tell the press only as much as the firm wants them to know, without being evasive or untruthful. How to fill white space or dead air is the media's problem, not the spokesperson's. Too many representatives keep talking well beyond the point at which they should quit, simply because they think it is their obligation to fill the airtime.

Opposite of the proactive approach is the reactive approach. Here, as Intel and Exxon did, the company takes a wait-and-see stance before making a statement. This often backfires because the lack of communication excites an already news-hungry media. The media are going to work twice as hard to cover an emergency or crisis. They will have added manpower, extra time and space allotted for coverage, and will be seeking out unknown information. Often their files and databases have facts you and your company do not have.[60]

In this age of media activism, a reactive approach combined with a defensive communication posture is seen as an indication of guilt. The proactive approach is more likely to be perceived as a sign of honesty. In addition, when an organization uses a proactive approach the media are more apt to assist in issuing warnings, informing and reassuring the public, stopping rumors, and soliciting volunteer help and public empathy.[61]

While American companies have been drilled with the necessity of creating and practicing a good crisis-management process, many foreign companies have a more difficult time developing this process. Figure 13.8 addresses the difficulty faced by Japanese organizations.

Step Five: Practice and Revise the Crisis Management Plan

Practice the Plan

Writing the CMP is not an easy task. Consequently, an organization that has a plan in place may be tempted to rest, wait, and hope the crisis never hits. But unless the plan is practiced it is like having a football team that has never practiced. At the beginning of this chapter we described how Morgan Stanley's plan for a potential crisis allowed them to evacuate all but six of its 3,700 employees, and to experience uninterrupted operations. This was possible because of the company's vigorously

Figure 13.8 | **Japanese vs. American Crisis Management**

While this chapter has concentrated on American organizational crises, it is also important to consider how international organizations relate to crisis situations. One example comes from Japan and from U.S. crisis experts who are familiar with that culture.

Previous natural disasters, such as earthquakes, and bioterrorism attacks have displayed how the Japanese excellently plan and execute crisis responses. However, they have more difficulty in responding to other types of organizational security threats. This is especially true for Japanese companies working outside their homeland. Here are several of the reasons.

- Japanese company structures tend to be centralized, with limited supply chains (two or three suppliers, compared to 15 or 20 within American firms). This creates resource and political risks.

- Japanese corporate cultures do not encourage an openness that often allows "whistle-blowers" to warn others of organizational problems or misdeeds.

- Japanese companies rotate foreign-based employees quickly through many jobs and cultures. While this gives employees exposure, it also takes those most qualified to manage a crisis out of the situation at critical times.

- Japanese organizations tend to be more stoic and less empathetic than American firms. Following the 9-11 attacks, many American firms allowed employees to take time off or to alter work schedules. At the same time many Japanese employees in the United States were expected to be at work the day after the attack.

- Japanese companies tend to use consensus building in decision making. Yet decisions about crises and media requirements are often delayed until needed.

In this chapter we learned that a wise organization has a CMP and a crisis communication strategy in place as part of good crisis preparation. Japanese employees often find that when a crisis does occur, they have not thought through sample press releases or designation of a company spokesperson. As Chapter 14 will show, when a crisis hits and the press is knocking on your door, there is little time for seeking a consensus.

Source: Adapted from: "Japanese face special challenges when preparing for a crisis," and "Crisis management for Japanese companies in America." (n.d.). Danziger.com. Retrieved April 17, 2002, from **http://www.danziger.com/crisis_management.htm**.

proactive stance on crisis prevention. Following its first exposure with disaster in 1993, the company CMP was constantly updated and employees had regular evacuation practice sessions.[62]

On July 21, 1998, the town of Dearborn, Michigan, found out how important it is to practice for a disaster. In 1980 a severe storm left the town devastated for almost 15 days. But in the mid-1990s Dearborn city officials and private industry designed a disaster-recovery process. After 18 months of preparation they conducted one of the largest mock disaster efforts ever held in the United States. More than 25,000 people participated in the two-day event. Providentially the timing was perfect: When the 1998 storm hit, it killed three people and did more than $20 million in property damage. Afterward community officials were quick to note that the training helped emergency personnel and public and private security respond in a coordinated and effective manner that minimized confusion and brought the crisis to a speedy end.[63]

Revise the Plan

The useful life of a crisis plan is three or four years. Restructuring, new personnel, and new goals require its updating. Every three years the plan should be given a major revision. Yearly, human resources and operations departments should review it. Spokespeople and organizational leaders also change. That is why annual updates are recommended.

James E. Lukaszewski, past chairman of the Public Relations Society of America, lists five of the most important crisis communication plan updating procedures. While all are useful and encourage a contingent-thinking mentality, the first and last items should be ongoing:

- Ongoing preparation with annual simulations. An untested plan is an unworkable plan.
- Sharing critical crisis communication experience case studies.
- Useful right way/wrong way video-based, situation-specific refresher programs.
- Interpreting and packaging as case studies other organizations' crises in terms of how your organization might respond if faced with a similar difficulty.
- Crisis-prevention/exposure management processes as an ongoing threat-reduction activity.[64]

Ethical lapses by organizations sometimes lead to crises. At other times a totally ethical organization involved in a crisis may use unethical behavior in an attempt to end the crisis. Called, "a fascinating case study" by Walter Kiechel, editorial director for Harvard Business School Publishing, Figure 13.9 describes an episode on crisis management and perceived ethical breaches that was lived out by the *Harvard Business Review* (HBR). At the end of that case, management had the opportunity and obligation to rebuild the reputation of an established organization that failed to stop a crisis situation at its inception.

Founded in 1922, the *Harvard Business Review* (HBR) refers to itself on its Web page as having "a proud tradition of being the world's preeminent business magazine." Although that fact is disputed by many in the academic and practical management field, the publication is the flagship of the Harvard Business School Publishing Corporation (HBSP), an organization that sells books, newsletters, business case studies, and conferences, and is a primary promoter of the Harvard Business School and its faculty.[1]

In fall 2001, HBR editor Suzy Wetlaufer conducted a series of interviews with then-recently retired General Electric (GE) Chairman Jack Welch. For years Welch had the reputation of being the greatest CEO ever. Indeed, during his tenure at GE the stock performance was unparalleled. The product of Wetlaufer's interviews was to be an article titled "Jack on Jack," scheduled for the HBR, February 2002, issue. In late December 2001, with the article in its final editing stages, Ms. Wetlaufer called Walter Kiechel, Editorial Director for Harvard Business School Publishing, and recommended the article be scrapped. Her reason? She had become too close to Welch during the interviews and writing, and that fact could give the appearance that the article was not objective.[2] As editorial director and manager of a large staff, Kiechel should have perceived the ethical and potential crisis issues. Yet he knew he could not kill the article because HBR had been promoting it. In early January 2002, he e-mailed the HBR staff explaining his scrapping of the original article and assigning it to two other HBR staffers. They reinterviewed Welch and rewrote the article that was published by the deadline.

Almost immediately after Kiechel's action, six top HBR editors wrote letters to him demanding Wetlaufer's resignation. At that point the HBR crisis had moved from its hidden stage to the pre-crisis mode. Kiechel needed to "act quickly and decisively to contain an emerging crisis . . . [and] to listen to concerns of the staff members closest to the situation."[3] As he listened Kiechel heard his staff describe how Wetlaufer "mixed her professional and personal life." Her colleagues believed she was "no longer able to lead the *Review*." Kiechel knew, "They're raising these concerns as a principled action, out of principled and courageous concern for the reputation of the *Review*." Colleagues believed Wetlaufer's actions were responsible, yet taken too late. They believed her real motivation was a phone call from Welch's wife after she had opened an e-mail between her husband and Wetlaufer, and the fear the entire episode could become public.[4] Still, Kiechel took no action against Wetlaufer. Instead he formed a task force to review policies governing ethics at HBR, and to consider changes in the ethics and conflict-of-interest policies. "The new policy will elucidate what kinds of relationships between interviewers and interviewees are appropriate and what kinds are not. We should make more explicit our policies on things like conflicts. One of my regrets is that I didn't get ahead of it."[5]

Soon, news of the HBR quandary spread to other news organizations. The *Wall Street Journal* broke the story in a March 4 article, "Harvard Editor Faces Revolt Over Welch Story."[6] HBR was in the midst of a full crisis. Kiechel still had time to get ahead of the full storm, but instead his actions focused on quashing the leaks rather than stopping the crisis. At that point in a crisis there are many events and rumors fly. This became true at HBR.

- "Four days after the [*Wall Street*] *Journal* story appeared, Wetlaufer sent an e-mail to her staff announcing she was stepping down as editor. But, she said, she would remain at the magazine as a full-time editor-at-large."[7]
- That same day two senior editors resigned because Wetlaufer was not leaving. They said she would occupy the same office and write the same stories. According to one editor, Harris Collingwood, such compromises with reality are typical of HBSP's senior leadership." Alden Hayashi, the other editor, stated, "I didn't resign because of Suzy and Jack; I resigned because I lost faith in HBR's ability to do the right thing."[8]
- *The New York Times* blasted HBR for "writing an ethics code" in the middle of a scandal. "The biggest mistake people make . . . is trying to rewrite policies to solve last month's problem."[9] In the article resigned Senior Editor Harris Collingwood agreed. "I found the decision to write a code of ethics laughable because of the wide gap between the ethics the organization professes and the ethics it practices."[10]
- The credibility of HBR as an academic journal was questioned. Mark Pastin, in the *Wall Street Journal*, stated it was ironic that the crisis HBR started with was a "conflict of interest," when the magazine had long been "a house organ of the Harvard Business School offering itself as plain truth . . . [but] displaying a bias for HBS faculty."[11] The *Boston Globe* raised questions concerning the review's "editorial policy that allows subjects of the regularly featured HBR interview to review and modify their comments."[12] The *Globe* also raised other conflict-of-interest possibilities. Wetlaufer was a former Bain & Company consultant. In May 2001, HBR ran a self-congratulatory Bain-authored piece . . . [as] the lead article the same month Bain cosponsored the review's annual management conference on Cape Cod."[13]
- It was disclosed that Welch had played a major behind-the-scenes role in Wetlaufer's negotiated reassignment. He had recommended a GE lawyer and had phoned advice to Wetlaufer's legal team.[14]
- *Vanity Fair* and *New York* magazines ran exposés on Wetlaufer, allegedly linking her to other well-known CEOs. It also revealed that her behavior with Welch was part of a larger pattern of reckless behavior on her part. One issue, which HBR management had known but never addressed, was Wetlaufer's romantic relationship with a 22-year-old editorial assistant at the *Review*.[15]

On April 24, Wetlaufer resigned. While she might have survived any of the single controversies, it was the accumulation of events that took its toll. While her behavior as a journalist writing a news story was "conflict of interest," the story is really one of HBR management failing in its responsibility to its employees. Alden Hayashi, one of the resigned editors, credited Wetlaufer's work. "Suzy was on a journey to improve the magazine, but . . . she showed signs of being in trouble and she needed guidance from her bosses."[16] Harris Collingwood echoed the concern: "This whole drama could have been avoided if . . . senior management had done its job in the first place."[17]

The *Harvard Business Review* arrived at the post-crisis stage. The crisis issue died away and management started picking up the pieces, putting the organization back together, and repairing a damaged brand. Perhaps business school students of crisis management will one day study in the classroom a Harvard Business School case written about this. As Editorial Director Walter Kiechel described it, "It is a fascinating case study, but it will take a little while to detail the lessons."[18]

1. Bandler, J. (2002, March 4). Harvard editor faces revolt over Welch story. *The Wall Street Journal*, p. B1.
2. *Ibid.*
3. Hymowitz, C. (2002, May 14). An HBR case study: How magazine failed to respond to a crisis, *The Wall Street Journal*, p. B1.
4. Bandler, p. B1.
5. Hymowitz, p. B1.
6. Bandler, p. B1.
7. Wenner, K. S. (2002, April 1). Too close to the source. *American Journalism Review*, p. 9.
8. Hymowitz, p. B1.
9. Seglin, J. L. (2002, April 21). An ethics code can't replace a backbone. *The New York Times*, p. 4.
10. *Ibid.*
11. Pastin, M. (2002, March 15). Taste: Scandalous reading—What exactly is the *Harvard Business Review*, anyway? *The Wall Street Journal*, p. W15.
12. Denison, D. C. (2002, April 25). *Harvard Business Review* editor quits. *Boston Globe*, p. D1.
13. Denison, D. C. (2002, March 19). Untarnished reputation despite staff tumult, *Harvard Business Review* retains lock on elite niche. *Boston Globe*, p. D1.
14. Hymowitz, p. B1.
15. Fee, G., & Raposa, L. (2002, April 25). Inside track: Mag tallies ex-biz review hottie's exclusives. *Boston Herald*, p. 8; Denison, *Harvard Business Review* editor quits, p. D1.
16. Hymowitz, p. B1.
17. Gatlin, G. (2002, April 25). Editor leaving *Harvard Review*. *Boston Herald*, p. 43.
18. Bandler, p. B-1.

Summary

This chapter has examined a need that every organization has: managing a crisis and crisis communication. A crisis is any event or activity that can bring harm and danger to the organization and its people. Communication needs are at the heart of all organizational crises. This chapter started with the case of Morgan Stanley and the World Trade Center attack. Because of a well-designed Crisis Management Plan and a well-thought-out communication strategy, only six MS employees lost their lives in the WTC tragedy. In addition MS's operations were uncompromised.

As an advanced business communication student, you will likely be involved in an organizational crisis some day. Other cases like those of Intel and Odwalla also showed that by knowing what to expect and do, you can help your organization survive the crisis and maintain its image and strength. We have learned from companies that have survived crises that management mind-sets constantly must be challenged. The lessons learned are these: There is more than one correct approach to solving a problem; subjective opinions do matter; emotional reactions to events must be assessed; and waiting is a decision that may have negative consequences.

Crises can be anticipated, prevented, controlled, and turned to an advantage. There are four stages that each crisis goes through: the hidden crisis, the pre-crisis, the actual crisis, and the post-crisis. There are specific actions that an organization must attend to in each stage. All of these actions are tied into a crisis-management process. This process has four steps: determining the crisis potential, developing appropriate crisis teams and centers, writing a crisis-management plan, and developing a communication strategy. While each is important, developing the crisis-management plan and a communication strategy are critical.

After having walked through the crisis-management plan and communication strategy, in Chapter 14 you will be introduced to a proactive process you can follow in developing a working relationship with the media.

Discussion Questions

1. In your general observation of the September 11, 2001, attack on the World Trade Center and Pentagon, what is your impression of the way that leaders of various organizations managed the crisis event? What stood out as some of the most effective acts, and what were some of the most ineffective? Who were the true crisis managers?

2. Early in this chapter the four basic crisis theses were described. How do you interpret the use of each thesis as the leaders of our nation prepare for possible future terrorist attacks? How about local leaders in your community and organizations?

3. Media reports regarding organizations that are involved in crises seem to always be in the news. Using recent reports from your local media describe a local organization, and determine in which of the four stages of a crisis the organization finds itself.

4. Pick a familiar local campus or business organization. Assume that organization has never considered the crisis-management process. Using the

four steps of crisis management, what are some things that organization should immediately consider?

5. Refer to the different case examples in this chapter. In relation to their crisis-communication strategy, which emerge as the most effective actions and the most ineffective actions? What specific changes would you have made if you had been in control of the communication process?

6. Considering the crises reported in this chapter, and those you remember from recent media reports, what are the ethical issues? How do the ethical issues relate to crisis management? Do ethical lapses cause most crises? Do crises naturally bring ethical quandaries? Explain.

Communication in Action

1. This chapter identified reasons management should respond quickly and correctly to crisis events. The case in Figure 13.9 revealed how the manager of one organization failed the "quickness" and "correctness" tests in a case that identified how ethical issues were at the heart of the crisis. If you have difficulty in identifying the issues, check out the following Web sites and determine what the journalism ethics code and principles would say about conflict of interest and mixing one's personal and professional lives. The Society of Professional Journalists' "Code of Ethics" is found at **http://www.spj.org/ethics.asp**. Look especially at the areas of "Act Independently" and "Be Accountable." The second site is from the American Society of Newspaper Editors, **http://www.asne.org/index.cfm?ID =886**. Under "Statement of Principles" examine Articles III and V. Finally, go to the Society of American Business Editors and Writers' site: **http://www.sabew.org/**. From its homepage click on "About SABEW," "SABEW Info," and then "Codes of Ethics." Listed under "Dow Jones," paragraphs 7 and 8 deal specifically with managers' leadership responsibility to follow and to impart to employees appropriate ethical conduct.

   Your Assignment: Write a short analysis of the case as it relates to the chapter. Describe the correct procedures that you would have followed had you been the manager of the *Harvard Business Review*. Be prepared to discuss the case and your analysis in the classroom.

2. Videotape an investigative story from a news program like *20/20, 60 Minutes, Dateline, or Frontline* that covers a recent crisis in an organization. With some of your classmates, analyze the program and discuss how successful or unsuccessful the organization was in managing its crisis. Make note of the reporter's behavior and write down some questions or concerns you have about media interviews that you would like to see answered as your read and discuss Chapter 14, "Media Management."

@ Internet

3. You have a job in your campus library working for the director. Recently your director went to a library conference and attended a session on disaster

plans for libraries. While there she realized the current library disaster plan does not have a recovery format section for photographs. She is suddenly troubled because the library was recently given a very large and valuable collection of photographs from a landmark department store. Your director gives you a Web site, **http://palimpsest.stanford.edu/bytopic/disasters/ plans/**, and asks you to review the "photograph" section of the campus library disaster plans.

Your Assignment: Review a few of the libraries' photograph disaster-recovery plans posted on the Web site. Develop an outline of the critical areas that you believe your director should consider. Send your outline to the director with a memo as the cover page. In your memo also include a few names of data-recovery companies that you found and reviewed while surveying the different sites. Be ready to discuss your findings in the classroom.

4. While reading this crisis-management chapter and searching the Internet for research materials, you found that several fast-food restaurants have experienced crises. Consequently you have a growing concern for a family member who owns a small chain of hamburger restaurants in a large metroplex community. You have shared your concern with your instructor who gave you a Web site to review: **http://www.e911.com/monos/ A001.html**. At the site you found a wonderful case summary of a crisis at the fictional BurgerMax chain. You have told your family member about your findings. He is extremely interested, but doesn't have time to read a long case analysis. He asks you to prepare a short review of the case with questions he should consider as he applies your review to his chain. Prepare your two- or three-page review, with questions.

InfoTrac

5. Much of our learning about crisis management occurs as we observe the way that organizations actually manage real crises. Listed below are the cases of several actual organizational crises. The cases are listed by general areas of crisis emphasis.

Your Assignment: Select one of the cases listed below. As you read the case create answers to the following questions:

1. What took place in the various stages of the organization's crisis?
2. How did the organization manage the crisis?
3. What communication strategy did the organization use? Was it effective?
4. What did the managers of the organization learn about crisis management as a result of the incident?

After you have read the case and have answered the questions, write a short case analysis. Take it to class and be prepared to share in a general discussion about cases of organizational crises.

Crisis Management:

"Developing the Three Levels of Learning in Crisis Management: A Case Study of the Hagersville Tire Fire," by Laurent Simon and Thierry C. Pauchant, in *Review of Business*, Fall 2000, Article No. A73183461.

Communication Strategy:

"Exploring the Boundaries of Crisis Communication: The Case of the 1997 Red River Valley Flood," by Donald A. Fishman, *Communication Studies*, Summer 2001, Article No. A80163313.

"Firestone's Failed Recalls, 1978 and 2000: A Public Relations Explanation," by Dirk C. Gibson, in *Public Relations Quarterly*, Winter 2000, Article No. A71565409.

"Integrating Public Relations and Legal Responses During a Crisis: The Case of Odwalla, Inc." by Kathleen A. Martinelli and William Briggs, in *Public Relations Review*, Winter 1998, Article No. A54116097.

"ValuJet Flight 592: Crisis Communication Theory Blended and Extended," by Donald A. Fishman, *Communication Quarterly*, Fall 1999, Article No. A67151733. Note that this case uses Fink's framework that was referenced earlier in the chapter. The author directly links ethics and crises by suggesting that a crisis situation always threatens important values.

Organizational Image:

"A Critical Analysis of US Air's Image Repair Discourse," by William L. Benoit and Anne Czerwinski, in *Business Communication Quarterly*, Fall 1997, Article No. A20041315.

Notes

1. McCarthy, M., & Backover, A. (2001, September 28). N.Y. firms strive to get back to work. *USA Today*, p. 1B.
2. Crisis planning for high-traffic buildings: A lesson from September 11. (2002, March 11). *PR Newswire* in Dow Jones Interactive. Retrieved May 3, 2002, from **http://ptg.djnr.com/ccroot/asp/publib/st. . .AAAMjAwMjAzMTIxNTE4MjcAAAAM&referrer=true**
3. Cox, B. (2001, September 29). Detailed disaster plans saved New York firms' workers and operations. *Fort Worth Star-Telegram*, Item 2W63655084125. Retrieved on October 15, 2002, from newspaper source.
4. Walsh, C. (2001, December 17). Leadership on 9/11: Morgan Stanley's challenge. *Harvard Business School: Working Knowledge*, p.1. Retrieved April 17, 2002, from **http://workingknowledge.hbs. . .m.jhtml?id=2690&pid=0&t=leadership**
5. Cox, B. Detailed disaster plans saved New York firms' workers and operations. *Fort Worth Star-Telegram*, Item 2W63655084125. Retrieved on October 15, 2002, from newspaper source.
6. Crisis planning for high-traffic buildings: A lesson from September 11.
7. Pfeiffer, S. & Denison, D. C. (2001, September 12). Businesses try to track employees. *The Boston Globe*, 3rd edition, p. A9.
8. Walsh, C. (2001, December 17). Leadership on 9/11: Morgan Stanley's challenge, 1–2.
9. Cox, Trade center recovery success stories, p. 2.
10. Paster, H. (2001, September 25). Well-prepared managers thrive in attack aftermath. *The Wall Street Journal Career Journal*. Retrieved October 31, 2001, from **http://www.careerjournal.com/myc/management/20010925-paster.html**

11. Defining crisis management (p. 2). (1996, January 19). Panact: Panaction Response International Guidelines. Retrieved October 5, 2002, from **http://www.panact.com/crisis.html**

12. Edmead, M. T. (n.d.). What can we learn from the September 11th attacks? *The Internet Security Conference Newsletter, 3*(19). Retrieved April 17, 2002, from **http:// www.tisc2001.com/newsletters/319.html**

13. Crisis definitions. (1999, December 11). Institute for Crisis Management. Retrieved October 5, 2002, from **http://www.crisisexperts.com/crisisdef_main.htm**

14. Sohlman, E. (1999, September 27). Natural catastrophes spawn surge in disaster studies. Reuters News Bureau. Retrieved October 5, 2002, from **http://dailynews.yahoo.com/h/nm/19990927/sc/environment_disaster_1.html**

15. Martin, R. (1996, February 5). Small business: Communications plan calms a crisis. *Detroit News,* p. 1.

16. O'Brien, T. (2001, December 1). Develop a contingency plan for your workplace. *Chemical Engineering,* p. 83.

17. Edmead, What can we learn from the September 11th attacks?

18. Fink, S. (1986). *Crisis Management.* New York: Amacom–American Management Association.

19. Paster, Well-prepared managers thrive in attack aftermath.

20. Markoff, J. (1994, November 24). Flaw undermines accuracy of Pentium chip. *The New York Times,* p. D5; Zitner, A. (1994, November 24). Sorry, wrong number. *Boston Globe,* p. 78.

21. Takahashi, D. (1994, December 13). Intel's chip-on-shoulder stance draws flames on Internet. *Dallas Morning News,* p. 4D.

22. Zitner, Sorry, wrong number, p. 78.

23. Mossberg, W. S. (1994, December 15). Intel isn't serving millions who bought its Pentium campaign, *The Wall Street Journal,* p. B1.

24. *Ibid.*

25. Ziegler, B., & Clark, D. (1994, December 13) Computer giants' war over flaw in Pentium jolts the PC industry. *The Wall Street Journal,* p. A8.

26. *Ibid.*

27. Horovitz, B. (1994, December 13). Intel needs damage control. *USA Today,* p. 3B.

28. Schmitt, R. B. (1994, December 16). Flurry of lawsuits filed against Intel over Pentium flaw. *The Wall Street Journal,* p. B8; Flynn, L. (1994, December 19). A New York banker sees Pentium problems. *The New York Times,* pp. D1–2.

29. Intel apology letter. (1994, December 21). *USA Today,* p. 9A.

30. Pentium's 1994 Annual Report to Stockholders (p. 1). (1994). Retrieved October 5, 2002, from **http://www.intel.com/intel/finance/annual/letter/index.html**

31. Kim, J. (1994, December 21). Intel puts chips on the table. *USA Today,* p. B1.

32. Takahashi, p. 4D.

33. Intel's 1994 Annual Report to Stockholders, p. 1.

34. Business continuity and crisis management: It's time to set the course. (2001, November 13). Barney & Barney.com. Retrieved April 19, 2002, from **http://www.barneyandbarney.com/News/Set_the_Course.htm**

35. *Ibid.*

36. Defining Crisis Management. Panact, p. 2.

37. Grant, L. (1997, September 29). How UPS blew it. *Fortune,* p. 29.

38. Mann, P. (1999, August 23). Prepare for crisis before crisis. *Plastic News,* p. 10.

39. Caywood, C. L., & Stocker, K. P. (1993). The ultimate crisis plan. *Crisis Response* (pp. 413–427). Detroit, MI: Visible Ink Press.

40. Crisis Communication Series, Part 3: Crisis. (n.d.). Barry McLoughlin Associates. Retrieved October 31, 2001, from **http://www.mclomedia.com/cc3.htm**

41. Whitesell, P. (1996). Crisis communications guidelines (p. 5-1). Charlotte, NC: Barron & Whitesell, Public Relations/Marketing. Retrieved October 5, 2002, from **http://web.sunbelt.net/pr/profile.htm**

42. Crisis Communication Series, Part 5: Development of a crisis communication plan. (n.d.). Barry McLoughlin Associates. Retrieved October 31, 2001, from **http://www.mclomedia.com/cc5.htm**

43. Lukaszewski, J. E. (1997). Establishing individual and corporate crisis communication standards: The principles and protocols. *Public Relations Quarterly, 42*(3), p. 14.

44. Crisis Communication Series, Part 4: Key goals and principles. (n.d.). Barry McLoughlin Associates. Retrieved May 7, 2002, from **http://www.mclomedia.com/cc4.htm**

45. Placing the proper figure behind the podium in times of crisis. (1999, August 30). *PR News,* p. 1.

46. Panko, R. (2001, November 14). September 11 provides lessons in crisis management. *Best's Insurance News,* p. 1; Fleschner, M. (2002, January/February). Rudy. *Selling Power,* p. 58.

47. Whitesell, p. 5-1.

48. Sherborne, P. (1999, October 4). Communication critical in crisis. *Amusement Business,* p. 30.

49. Welles, C. (1990, April 2). Exxon's future: What has Larry Rawl wrought? *Business Week,* p. 76.

50. Lukaszewski, J. E. (1990, July 1). Managing bad news in America. *Vital Speeches of the Day,* pp. 568–573.

51. Maxon, T. (1996, January 14). Weighing the financial fallout of speaking out. *Dallas Morning News,* p. 1H.

52. Helperin, J. (2001, July). Uh-oh: Crisis management is tough: Now imagine it in Internet time. *Business 2.0, 6*(14), p. 32.

53. Mackay, B. L. (n.d.). A new player in crisis management: The Internet. Retrieved March 15, 2002, from **http://www.disasteresource.com/articles/new_player_mackay.shtml**

54. *Ibid.*

55. Odwalla web site helps handle e. coli crisis. (n.d.). Retrieved February 26, 2002, from **http://www.holtz.com/tc/odwalla.htm**; E. coli poisoning leads to Odwalla juice recall. (n.d.). CNN.com. Retrieved May 9, 2002, from **http://www.cnn.com/HEALTH/9611/01/e.coli.poisoning/**

56. Hodges, J. (2001, October 1). Ads disappear but customer communication lives on: How public relations teams are dealing with the unimaginable. *Business 2.0,* Retrieved June 10, 2002, from **http://www.business2.com/articles/web/0,1653,17422,FF.html**

57. Mackay, A new player in crisis management.

58. Petzinger, T., Jr. (1979, August 23). When disaster comes, public relations men won't be far behind. *The Wall Street Journal,* p. 1.

59. "Crisis Communication Series, Part 7: Executing a crisis communications plan. (n.d.). Barry McLoughlin Associates. Retrieved October 31, 2001, from **http://www.mclomedia.com/cc7.htm**

60. *Ibid.*

61. *Ibid.*

62. Walsh, Leadership on 9/11.

63. Locke, P. M. (1999, October 1). Staying calm before the storm. *Security Management,* p. 59.

64. Lukaszewski, J. E. (1994, April-June). Keeping your crisis communication management plans current. Retrieved October 5, 2002, from **http://www.e911.com/exacts/EA014.html**

CHAPTER - 14

Media Management

While most of the communication skills of business executives are used within the business community, social issues and crises often require executives to communicate with the public through the media. Learning to work quickly and efficiently with the news media—when the situation is positive or negative—is the mark of an effective organization's communication-management program. Both the print and broadcast media have considerable power. However, a 1997 poll by The Center for Media and Public Affairs revealed that 86 percent of all Americans receive most of their information from local television news shows, while 80 percent use national shows and 77 percent use newspapers.[1]

Businesses have traditionally mistrusted the various media; however, the dramatic increase in business reporting by the media and a continuing effort by business to initiate reports during the past two decades have forced many companies to improve their ability to use the media to their advantage. The relatively recent phenomenon of the major crisis, such as product-tampering, has also emphasized the importance of a business/media relationship. Yet surprisingly, many upper-level executives still find themselves ill-prepared to meet with and talk to the press under any condition.

We want you to feel comfortable with media representatives and to be ready when your call from a reporter arrives. This chapter is designed to get you ready by examining how organizations communicate with media personnel. The chapter is divided into five parts: First we will describe how companies use press releases to gain attention for their personnel, products, and business. Part Two describes how to apply the organization's communication strategy in times of crisis. Parts Three through Five discuss media interviews and good performance techniques to use.

Inviting Media Response: The Press Release

One of the best ways to attract the media is to understand the types of material that editors use in noncrisis times. Companies always want to obtain media coverage that promotes their personnel, products, policies, and programs. But the media seek only current and genuine *news* about executive changes, emergencies, litigation, and key issues. Editors are especially desirous of covering unfavorable issues or subjects embarrassing to a company. With these two apparently different objectives, how does your company get its good news to the media and minimize the damage that bad news may represent? The answer is: the press release.

While the press release is a standard public relations tool, it is effective only when prepared, delivered, and used properly. There are five basic types of press releases: business features, consumer service features, financial features, product features, and pictorial features. Journalists can obtain news from around the world in an instant thanks to the Internet. This means that all large multinational companies need to have a global communications awareness.[2]

While most press releases are handled by a company's public relations office, you as a manager should be familiar with the format and character of releases. In a large company you may be required to supply copy for such a release. In a small company you may prepare your own release or respond to the media follow-up. Writing a good press release is the first step toward making your organization proactive in its media approach.

Rules to Follow in Preparing Press Releases

The ten rules that follow will give you an overview of how to prepare a press release.

Know the Media Outlets and Their Audience

Andrea Brooks, real-estate columnist for *The New York Times*, gives the following insider's view of press releases: While she tries to read every release that she receives, the reading is often only a scan. "I know within 30 seconds if it's worth reading in depth."[3] Scott Wenger, business editor of the *New York Daily News*, gives releases much less time. He receives over 500 faxes, letters, e-mails, and phone calls a day. If he allowed a 30-second read it would take four hours of his workday. He gives each review four seconds max. His number-one rule is: "Know the publication and its readers; then cut to the chase in no more than two pages—preferably one."[4]

To do this requires you to stay current on publications and reporters who do report on your type of business or service, and to know the types of articles and stories they want and need. According to Wenger only five percent of the releases he receives are really usable.

Present News That Is Real News

Reporters are interested in news, not in reading an advertisement for your business or products. What makes for real news? Generally news is something that is different or unusual—something that people do not already know. It solves problems or fulfills needs. This is one reason why bad news always finds an open ear with the media. Commercial airplanes fly thousands of trips a day. That is not news. When an airline crashes that is truly news. According to Beard and Dalton, a manager has to work hard to find real news in ordinary information.

> [You] have to search hard for a fresh angle that will give your story the proper appeal or "spin." This can be done by focusing on things like market share data, price comparisons, an outstanding statistic, or other numbers that play up the uniqueness, size, or quality of your company or product(s). . . . Any of these types of things may be considered newsworthy, although it all really boils down to the timing and perceived value of such pronouncements.[5]

Figure 14.1 displays a press release from US Airways announcing the creation of an online mileage-purchase program. For those who fly US Air, and for merchants

Figure 14.1 Press Release by US Airways

U·S AIRWAYS

Home | Contact Us | Search & Index

usairways.com -> about us airways -> press releases

About US Airways

usairways.com
- Reservations
- Timetables
- Dividend Miles
- Promotions

About US
- Corporate Information
- Press Releases
- Employment
- Investor Relations
- Aircraft

US AIRWAYS LAUNCHES ONLINE MILEAGE PURCHASE PROGRAM WHERE CUSTOMERS CAN BUY MILES THROUGH USAIRWAYS.COM

ARLINGTON, Va., May 17, 2002 -- US Airways and Points.com are making it easier for Dividend Miles members to purchase miles through a new online Mileage Purchase Program on **usairways.com**.

Dividend Miles members can take advantage of the online Mileage Purchase Program to buy miles for personal use or as a gift for others. A member can purchase up to 15,000 miles per Dividend Miles account per year. Access to this service is available through **usairways.com** or via a direct link to **buydividendmiles.points.com**.

This new online feature complements the current Mileage Purchase Program where members can purchase miles toward award travel or gifts by calling US Airways.

With the online service, members can purchase Dividend Miles at 3 cents per mile, which includes the 7.5 percent federal excise tax (Canadian members pay additional sales tax). Miles are available in increments of 1,000 miles with a minimum 2,000-mile purchase requirement. Now through June 15, 2002, US Airways will waive the $25 processing fee. These miles will be credited to the member's Dividend Miles account within 72 hours of making the purchase.

"Dividend Miles continue to make great gifts, and this program will help make it easier for members to offer a gift of travel for family and friends, or even themselves," said Stephen M. Usery, US Airways vice president of marketing and revenue management. "We even will send a personalized e-mail message to the recipient notifying them of the gift."

With Dividend Miles, a standard Coach Class award ticket requires only 20,000 miles for travel in the U.S. and Canada during the off-peak period between Sept. 15, and the last day of February. Peak period travel requires 25,000 miles in the U.S. and Canada.

The number of miles needed for European off-peak award travel is 40,000, with 50,000 miles needed for standard European peak Economy Class travel between May 1 and Sept. 30.

US Airways, the US Airways Express carriers and US Airways Shuttle provide service to 203 destinations worldwide, including 38 states in the U.S., Antigua, Aruba, Barbados, Bermuda, Cancun, Cozumel, Freeport, Grand Cayman, Montego Bay, Nassau, San Juan, Santo Domingo, St. Lucia, St. Thomas, St. Maarten, and St. Croix. US Airways Express also serves North Eleuthera, Governors Harbour, Marsh Harbour and Treasure Cay from Florida. In Canada, US Airways serves Toronto, Montreal, and Ottawa. US Airways' European destinations are Amsterdam, Frankfurt, London, Madrid, Manchester, Munich, Paris and Rome.

Points.com's proprietary technology platform offers a portfolio of innovative solutions for the loyalty program industry. Points.com solutions forges mutually rewarding partnerships with the world's leading loyalty players to deliver unique and compelling value propositions. Based in Toronto, Points.com is the wholly owned operating subsidiary of Exclamation International Incorporated. Exclamation shares trade on the TSX Venture Exchange under the stock symbol XI. More information is available at www.exclamation.com and www.points.com.

For additional information on US Airways' Mileage Purchase Program, contact the Dividend Miles Service Center at 1-336-661-8390, or visit US Airways online at **usairways.com**.

Reporters needing additional information should contact US Airways Corporate Communications at (703) 872-5100.

Source: Reprinted by permission of US Airways.

who have businesses in the US Airways market, this is valuable information. The release is upbeat and explains the entire program. Because this and figures that follow in this chapter were designed for company Web sites, some of the information in the press release guide, Figure 14.6 on page 372, does not appear.

The News Must Have a Local Interest

If there is no hometown angle or local discussion of a headquarters, plant, dealership, or other interest, the release will not be used. The media's need for local information is critical because international, national, and regional coverage is usually obtained by wire and syndicated services.[6] Of course, some of your company's news may impact the financial market both locally and internationally. Figure 14.2 is an example of a press release aimed at a narrow audience. Local media presented this information to the citizens of San Diego.

Use the Direct Message Approach

As your high school English teacher told you, a good news article discusses the who, what, why, when, where, and how. A good press release answers those same questions as briefly as possible in the first two paragraphs. Apply the same direct message approach that was discussed in Chapter 5. That approach called for leading with the most positive information, and then following with the next-most-positive information, and the next-most-positive, and so on, until the message is complete. This usually means following the journalistic or inverted-pyramid style discussed in Chapter 9 on report writing. As Christopher Brooks, news editor at the *Journal of Commerce* in Newark, New Jersey, states, "Don't bury the lead down at the bottom . . . because I won't get that far if I don't see a point."[7] The release in Figure 14.3 violates this rule. While the heading describes the information that should be contained in the release, that news is buried in the fourth paragraph. As you read this release, what other violations do you notice?

Figure 14.4 uses the direct approach, and also applies other general rules for press releases. Use active, energetic verbs while avoiding adjectives. Never use words not used in everyday conversation. Avoid long, drawn-out sentence structure. Sentences should be short, definite, and have no more than one thought contained in each. The same rules also apply to paragraphs. They should be no longer than two or three sentences and, similar to the sentence, should carry the same idea or thought process. The point is to make it as easy as possible for the reader to understand and comprehend.

Avoid Buzzwords, Acronyms, and Jargon

Avoiding company or industry jargon and technical talk will help readers understand your news quickly. For example, doctors when addressing both patients and the media automatically use medical terms that are common to their trade, yet uncommon to a layperson. Putting those terms into plain language helps in communicating the real content. Examples are: Angina: chest pain or pressure; Glottis: opening between the vocal cords; Hidrosis: sweating; Migrainous cranial neuralgia: a cluster headache or a variation of migraine headache; Otitis: ear infection; and Septicemia: blood poisoning.[8]

Figure 14.2   **Example of a Press Release Aimed at a Narrow Audience**

San Diego
Blood Bank
A Regional Blood Center

December 18, 1998

FOR IMMEDIATE RELEASE

News Release

CONTACT: Lynn Stedd, 296-6393, x237
or Faith Saculles, 296-6393, x283

SAN DIEGO BLOOD BANK "UNWRAPS" A GIFT TO THE COMMUNITY — A NEW NBC 7/39 BLOODMOBILE DESIGN IN TIME FOR CHRISTMAS

At 1 pm on Wednesday, December 23, the San Diego Blood Bank at 440 Upas Street, will "unwrap" a gift to the community: a colorful, bigger-than-life design on the NBC 7/39 Bloodmobile.

The bold new "buswrap" features the smiling faces of a dozen San Diego Blood Bank donors. Among them: Commander Bill Flores of the San Diego Sheriff's Department, who donated bone marrow to a patient in need in 1995 and has since been instrumental in recruiting hundreds of Latinos to the National Marrow Donor Program registry; and "Super Donors" Greg Mullendore of Mira Mesa, a CHP officer who has made 244 donations of blood components, and Luther Babers III of North Bay Terraces, who has made 60 donations of blood components. Photos of Frank Basset of Carmel Mountain Ranch, Sarah Hedrick of University City, Angela Murphy of Oak Park, Angie Ortanez of Scripps Ranch, David Park of Poway, Rebecca Parks of Rancho Penasquitos , Diane Roberson of Lemon Grove, Eva Rodriguez of La Mesa, and Christine Stepanian of Rancho Bernardo also grace the "wrap."

"Every inch of the bloodmobile is wrapped in this wonderful design to show San Diegans that donors come in all "types" -- all shapes, sizes, colors, and ages and from all heritages," says Lynn Stedd, community relations director of the San Diego Blood Bank. "We hope the new wrap will grab people's attention and remind them to share their health and give the gift of life."

Lar Kress, of Lar Kress Advertising and Design, and Robert Bruni of Ambience Photography, donated their time to create the bloodmobile wrap; 3M contributed more than $3,000 in materials; San Diego Transit contributed space for the wrap to be completed. Michele Prado, Supergraphics, and Elaine Dill also shared their expertise. For more information, please call 619-296-6393.

###

San Diego Blood Bank • 440 Upas St • San Diego • 92103 • 296-6393 • **No. County Donor Center** • 1340 W. Valley Pkwy • Escondido • 92029 • 489-0621
No. Coastal Donor Center • 161 Thunder Dr • Vista • 92083 • 945-1906 • **East County Donor Center** • 680 Fletcher Pkwy • El Cajon • 92020 • 441-1804
South Bay Donor Center • 1717 Sweetwater Rd • National City • 91950 • 336-4090

Source: Reprinted by permission of San Diego Blood Bank.

Figure 14.3   Example of a Press Release That Buries the Lead

the
White House
President George W. Bush

For Immediate Release
Office of the Press Secretary
May 10, 2002

National Defense Transportation Day and National Transportation Week, 2002
By the President of the United States of America
A Proclamation

The importance of America's transportation system became evident to all Americans on September 11, 2001. Airliners were diverted, airports closed, and travelers were stranded for days as transportation systems across the country were disrupted. In the aftermath of September 11, the men and women in the transportation industry have helped restore function and trust to a system that was traumatized. Today, Americans and America's goods and services are being more safely moved to their destinations, as our communities continue the process of important restructuring.

We have helped secure our transportation system with the passage of the Aviation and Transportation Security Act, which greatly enhanced the protections for America's passengers and goods. And we are determined to ensure that Americans have the transportation system and mobility that is necessary for a vibrant economy and meaningful quality of life.

We live in a time of unprecedented travel, when goods and services, regardless of origin, can be available in a short amount of time. Thanks to imagination, innovation, and investment in transportation, we can safely commute to work, receive overnight mail, buy fresh fruit and vegetables, and travel with relative ease to destinations around the world. We also continue to make progress in developing a transportation system that offers choices and protects the environment through cleaner, more fuel-efficient vehicles and new, environmentally sound infrastructure.

To recognize Americans who work in transportation and who contribute to our Nation's prosperity, defense, and progress, the United States Congress, by joint resolution approved May 16, 1957, as amended, (36 U.S.C. 120), has designated the third Friday in May of each year as "National Defense Transportation Day," and, by joint resolution approved May 14, 1962, as amended, (36 U.S.C. 133), declared that the week during which that Friday falls be designated as "National Transportation Week."

NOW, THEREFORE, I, GEORGE W. BUSH, President of the United States of America, do hereby proclaim Friday, May 17, 2002, as National Defense Transportation Day and May 12 through May 18, 2002, as National Transportation Week. I encourage all Americans to recognize how our modern transportation system has enhanced our economy and contributed to our freedom.

IN WITNESS WHEREOF, I have hereunto set my hand this tenth day of May, in the year of our Lord two thousand two, and of the Independence of the United States of America the two hundred and twenty-sixth.

GEORGE W. BUSH

#

Return to this article at:
http://www.whitehouse.gov/news/releases/2002/05/20020510-6.html

Source: Retrieved from http://www.whitehouse.gov/news/releases/2002/05/20020510-6.html.

Carrying it a step further, avoid using buzzwords. BuzzWhack.com's definition of a buzzword is: "A usually important sounding word or phrase used primarily to impress laypersons." Clichés abound in the business world. Words like *breakthrough, cutting edge, state of the art,* or *enterprise-wide* are common business lingo, but they drive journalists nuts. As John Walston of Buzzwhack.com states, "'Solutions' is a buzzword, but mainly because it is overused and abused. Is your company a solutions provider? Of course they are. Otherwise no one would buy from you. So there's little to gain by claiming to be one."[9]

Figure 14.4 Example of a Press Release Using the Direct Message Approach

Activism | Victim Services | Education

FOR IMMEDIATE RELEASE: MARCH 21, 2002

Contact: Misty Moyse, 214-744-6233
Tresa Hardt, 214-744-6233

MADD SAYS NBC PULLING LIQUOR ADS IS BAND-AID APPROACH, STRICTER STANDARDS NEEDED FOR ALL ALCOHOL ADVERTISING

Organization Calls for Congressional Hearings, Releases New Policy
Recommendations and Survey Showing Public Support

Washington, D.C. – Mothers Against Drunk Driving (MADD) says the NBC Television Network's reversal of its decision to air liquor ads misses the big picture and the need for stricter responsibility standards for *all* alcohol advertising, including ads for beer, wine, liquor, and malt-based beverages. Today, at a Washington, D.C., news conference, MADD and U.S. Congresswoman Lucille Roybal-Allard, D-CA, called for immediate congressional hearings to examine this issue and alcohol advertising's effect on youth and underage drinking. MADD also released its new policies on alcohol advertising and urged NBC and other television networks to adopt these guidelines.

Among the top priorities of the new policies announced by MADD:
- Restrictions on all television alcoholic beverage advertising – including ads for beer, wine, liquor, and malt-based beverages – so as to limit the exposure to underage viewers.
- Requirements for a matching amount and comparable placement of air time/ad space for alcohol-related public health and alcohol-related safety messages for young people and adults. A government agency or an independent agency or public health experts not affiliated with the alcohol industry must produce these counter-ads.

Americans back MADD's stance according to a public opinion poll where a majority (60.1 percent) of respondents said they would support stricter policies or responsibility standards for all alcohol advertising on television, including ads for liquor, beer, and wine. An overwhelming 93.5 percent of respondents said they would support television advertising to promote health and safety messages related to underage drinking and drunk driving. The public opinion survey released by MADD was conducted by RoperASW.

"MADD is not against alcohol advertising; we simply want standards in place that will protect our children from constant exposure and messages that directly appeal to them," said Wendy Hamilton, MADD national president elect. "NBC and the other television networks are giving the beer and wine industry a free pass when it comes to advertising. All should be held to the same standards, as alcohol is alcohol — a 12 ounce can of regular beer, 5 ounces of wine, a 12 ounce wine cooler, or 1½ ounces of 80-proof distilled spirits all contain the same amount of absolute alcohol."

U.S. Congresswoman Lucille Roybal-Allard, D-CA, backed MADD's positions and also called for Congress to hold hearings on this important issue. "Young people are already bombarded with messages promoting alcohol consumption. With this constant daily exposure to alcohol marketing, it's no wonder that over 10 million kids under the age of 21 consume alcohol, and that the average age at which children start to drink is now just 13 years old," said Roybal-Allard. "MADD's tough new standards for alcohol advertising would go a long way towards countering the considerable influence alcohol advertising has on our nation's youth."

Mothers Against Drunk Driving is a grassroots organization with approximately 600 chapters nationwide. MADD's mission is to stop drunk driving, support the victims of this violent crime, and prevent underage drinking. For more information about MADD or its alcohol advertising policies, visit www.madd.org or call 1-800-GET-MADD.

###

Source: Reprinted by permission of Mothers Against Drunk Driving.

Figure 14.5 is difficult to read and understand because it violates many of the suggestions made in this point. Use your current understanding of press releases, and the knowledge you have gathered about editing, and rewrite the following release to flow more smoothly and to present a clearer description.

Include All Required Mechanical Elements

Reporters look for several specific mechanical elements in a press release. To better ensure that your release will be used, include all these elements. You can use Figure 14.6, "Press Release Guide," to prepare your future releases.

Most large organizations put their releases on company letterhead to present all the vital company information and to add credibility. In the upper-left corner put the date of release and any restrictions on when the notice can be made public. If, for example, you are announcing a new product, but do not want that information to be made public until April 10, include the restriction, "For release after April 10." This type of restriction is called an *embargo*. If there are no date restrictions, mark the release "For immediate release." Occasionally a publication will break an embargo. In that instance other publications may do the same. If your material is time-sensitive, hold the release until the day that you want it released, and then fax it. Add "Pictures available" if you have them.

Figure 14.5   **Example of a Press Release That Needs Editing**

Page 1 of 2

PRESS RELEASE

For immediate release

July 1, 1998

Contact Gary Hodge, Vice President
+1 713 784 1880;
hodge@posc.org

MEMBERS ENTHUSIASTIC ABOUT POSC EVOLUTION

Houston, TX -- The Board of Directors of the Petrotechnical Open Software Corporation (POSC) reaffirmed the POSC goal of an integrated, seamless technical software environment, based on open specifications spanning the life cycle of E&P oil and gas fields. The Board also approved an evolutionary change in POSC's governance and operations to ensure ultimate achievement of the vision. The drivers of the change are two-fold:

- to evolve POSC to the original vision of a sustainable membership organization and
- to create a funding model based on value received.

The governance transition will occur over the next three years, with the composition of the Board changing to reflect the composition of the membership. The funding changes are to be achieved by broadening the range of uniquely funded activities to include not only the traditional development and maintenance of technical specifications but also the provision of professional services to support widespread commercial deployment of products, services, and data based on the specifications.

Board Chairman Bob Pindell summarized the actions as "POSC making fundamental changes that are in line with the original charter to become a self-sustaining membership organization, independent of sponsorship."

Members Express Their Support

In response to these changes, representatives of the former sponsor companies of POSC issued the following statement: "We wish to affirm our continued support for the vision of E&P technical software built on open specifications and to encourage others in the industry to do the same. Products and services that use open standards are generally preferable to those based on proprietary specifications. We will continue to encourage industry participants to build and use open specifications in their software applications. Additionally POSC, its staff, and member community represent an open mechanism for companies to work together to solve business problems. We support initiatives that leverage the work of the POSC community and that bring the industry closer to realization of the vision. We support membership and participation in POSC and E&P standards organizations because adopting open standards benefits the entire industry."

When the changes were discussed by the membership at large, David Zeh, CEO of Zeh Graphic Systems, expressed his enthusiasm: "My company joined as the very first POSC member because I believed, and still believe, in the POSC concepts and the need for industry standards. These changes reflect a move in the right direction with the governance of POSC becoming more equitably distributed to all members – oil companies and service companies alike."

The sentiment of many members was captured by Larry Bellomy of Mobil when he explained his company's views on POSC, "Mobil believes in the POSC effort to bring open specifications to E&P

Figure 14.5 **Example of a Press Release That Needs Editing (Concluded)**

computing and will continue to be a member of POSC. We will also continue to support selected POSC programs that support Mobil's technology direction and provide value-added benefits. We are not abandoning the effort, but believe it is time for POSC to stand on its own as a member-driven organization as was originally intended. We look forward to, and fully support, the continued transition of POSC as outlined in the business plan developed by the POSC staff."

Bob Pindell added the Texaco perspective: "Texaco has successfully deployed the POSC specifications in certain of our operations. As such, we fully support this evolutionary step to a sustainable, member-driven organization, and look forward to the continued deployment of POSC specifications in our industry. The use of open specifications can be a tremendous aid in effectively managing E&P assets by assuring access to the best technologies."

POSC CEO David Archer noted: "We are encouraged by the industry's movement toward widespread usage of the POSC specifications and services and by positive reactions to the current changes. Strong support will allow us to establish an identity as a trusted source for skills relating to information modeling, information sharing and integration, and as THE place to go for collaborative work relating to information sharing in E&P. When people want to work together in an open environment to solve a common E&P business problem, we want them to instinctively think of POSC. Our approach leverages risk, capital and people to arrive at quality collaborative solutions."

POSC is an international, not-for-profit, membership organization that was founded in 1990 to develop data and technical computing specifications for the E&P segment of the oil industry. POSC specifications are designed to enable the oil industry to deal with problems of integrating and sharing data over the life cycle of E&P assets. With a worldwide membership of more than 100 organizations, POSC has headquarters in Houston and an office in London. The membership includes oil and gas companies, oilfield service companies, software and hardware companies, government agencies, and educational institutions.

For more information about POSC, please visit our website at http://www.posc.org

- -

If you have questions about this announcement, please contact:

POSC
Gary Hodge, Vice President and CFO
Tel: (713) 784-1880
Fax: (713) 784-9219
hodge@posc.org

Updated: July 1, 1998. Send questions and comments to webmaster@posc.org

Source: Reprinted by permission of Petrotechnical Open Software Corporation.

Figure 14.6 **Press Release Guide**

Company letterhead with logo

FOR IMMEDIATE RELEASE   CONTACT: Name(s)
                                         Address
                                         Telephone number
                                         Fax number
                                         E-mail address
                                         Web site address

HEADLINE GOES HERE IN ALL UPPERCASE LETTERS

(leave an inch of space)

City, State, Date—use a "most important news first" approach. The first paragraph should always give the who, what, where, when, why, and how.

Second and following paragraphs should contain relevant information on people, products, or services. Include advantages, benefits, and uniqueness. Important quotes from management, customers, experts, or others with credibility should be added.

Overall, content should be short, one page preferred with a maximum of two pages. Ideally this means around 300 words.

-more-
or
continued on page 2 (if you have two or more pages)

Abbreviated Headline (page 2) at the top of each additional page.

Remainder of text

Company Summary (one brief but compact paragraph with information about

company history, products, sevices, location, and other relevant information.

If you would like more information about this topic call (person) at (number) or email (person) at (e-mail address).

###

(at the end of the review)

In the upper-right corner place the name of the contact person along with title, name of company (if not in the letterhead), address, both telephone and fax numbers, e-mail address, and Web site URL. Some managers place a nighttime cell phone number for emergency calls, because journalists work unusual hours. Some organizations place the contact information at the bottom of the release, especially if there are several contact individuals.

Headlines and subheads are technically optional. Editors prefer headlines—at the top of the page so they can tell at a glance what the story is about. The headline must contain the essence of the report. Use the subhead to further build and advance the title words. Avoid promotional and sales words, because reporters are not interested in helping you sell products. They want to convey useful information to their audiences. The heading should be in all capital letters. Because editors often want to rewrite or edit your heading, it is best to leave a good inch of space between the contact information and the heading.

The content of your release backs up and adds more information to the heading. The first paragraph is the most critical. Using the journalistic approach, apply the who, what, where, when, why, and how statements. The remainder of the text supports the heading and adds more useful information. Put all of your information in priority order, most important first. Editors love "quotable quotes" or comments that stand out in originality or strength. Try to use these in your writing.

Strive to limit the release to one page. If your release is more than one page in length, add the word *-more-* or *-continued-* at the bottom of the page. At the top of the next page place a *slug line*: a one-or-two word title that summarizes the subject. Example: New Store Opens! Always complete the paragraph on one page and never carry it over to the next page. At the end of the press release, let the editor know you're finished by centering and typing "# # #, –30-," or "ends," which signifies "the end." Below that symbol give the name and telephone number of the person to contact if more information is desired.

Most editors like to see a press release typed and double-spaced on standard, single-sided, letter-sized paper. Leave 1- to 1½-inch margins on the sides for the editor to use in placing notes or in editing. Use bold headings to draw attention.

The Appearance Must Be Flawless

The appearance of the press release is critical. Editors and other readers rely on their first impressions. If the appearance is not exactly as the editor prescribes, the article will not have the first line read. Just like a résumé, if there is one spelling error, grammatical error, or untidy appearance, the chances of being successful are almost zero. The document must be flawless.

Determine Whether to Send the Release Yourself or Through a Service

If your target market is small, you can probably afford to send out your own releases, but you should have knowledge of media representatives who cover companies within your industry. You should also have a list of local media contacts that was completed in the assembling of the Crisis Management Plan. One way to collect media names is to make a list of writers' names and contact information that you find as you read trade magazines and observe local and surrounding media reports. From a local perspective list all television, radio, and newspapers. Include the weekly, monthly, and even throwaway-type papers available in every community.

One of the biggest advantages of preparing your own media list is the ability to narrowly tailor that list. Another advantage is the cost savings. Yet, it is often difficult to carve out the time to collect the proper names, and to constantly keep your data list current. Journalists seem to be more receptive to releases that come from a source that they recognize, such as a public relations firm. Press-release services also stay up to date on the particular likes and dislikes of individual journalists. If you do decide to purchase a media list from many of the list companies that have them available, check them out with the following questions.

- What contact information is included (things like address, e-mail, fax, or preferences)?
- How often are the names updated? When was the last update?
- How specific is the list?
- How was the list compiled?
- How many times can you use the list?
- How much time will you have to devote to cleaning and updating the list?[10]

For a sample of some of the online press release services check out the following Web sites: **http://www.press-release-writing.com/**; **http://www.ereleases.com/**; **http://www.mediazapper.com**; **http://www.onlinepressrelease.com/**; and **http://www.expresspress.com**.

Make Your Press Releases Web-Friendly

As you prepare your press releases, keep in mind that the power of your releases can go beyond the general media outlets. By optimizing your releases for search engines you can get added benefit for the present and into the future. Keep key words and key phrases in mind. Use the words several times within the content of your release. After your release has been created, learn the proper way to submit it to search engines for indexing. This is especially true for search engines like Google and Yahoo that have designated areas for press releases. The benefit of using search engines is: "Your news will be available to journalists and consumers long after the initial release. However, before sending the release to both the media and Web search engines, make sure you have posted it to your own Web site."[11]

Customize Your Release to Different Media

Instead of sending a standard release to each media representative, consider customizing it to meet each representative's specific needs and format. A news magazine looks for an entirely different story than does *The Wall Street Journal* or a trade publication. Normally the major changes will occur in a rewriting of the first paragraph. Wayne Green—founder and publisher of some 27 magazines, including *Byte* and *CD Review*—indicates that he would have encouraged his employees to make three versions of the press release critiques in Figure 14.7: one each for the retail, music, and publishing industries.[12]

A Critique of a Press Release

The example in Figure 14.7 comes from a story in *Inc* magazine. The release was issued by an employee of Green's company, an $8-million magazine and music distributorship in Hancock, New Hampshire. The critique is Green's view of the release.[13]

| Figure 14.7 | **Critique of a Press Release** |

WGE PUBLISHING

Forest Road   Hancock, NH 03449-0278   603-525-4201   FAX: 603-525-4423

Contact Grace Cohen at:
1-800-722-7785

For Immediate Release:

Publisher Introduces Custom Music Magazine Rack For Retailers

CD REVIEW Magazine is introducing their new "Eight Pocket Rack Program" at SCES. The attractive, custom-designed spinner is a new way for the retailers to sell music and entertainment magazines. The rack creates maximum impact while using a minimal, $1\frac{1}{2}$ square feet of floor space, and is free to retailers participating in the program. Retail outlets will be able to choose from a wide variety of magazines, customizing the mix of their particular demographics. Some of the titles available include *CD REVIEW*, *Details, Option, Musician, Electronic Musician, Ear, Country Music, Spin*, and *Jazziz*.

Additional benefits, other than customizing product mix, include one-step billing and an affidavit program to simplify credits. Billing for all eight publications will be handled with a single statement by *CD REVIEW's* parent company, WGE Publishing. Instead of returning unsold issues for credit, retailers will attest to the number of remaining copies by affidavit. Title allotment will be monitored to maintain highest possible sales for the retail outlet. This procedure will cut the time stores usually spend processing returns to almost nothing. Retailers will make a full 40% on each magazine sold, with an absolute minimum effort.

For additional information, please contact Retail Circulation Manager Phil Martus at 1-800-722-7785.

Source: Reprinted with permission, *Inc.* magazine, August, 1991. Copyright © (1991) by Goldhirsh Group, Inc., 38 Commercial Wharf, Boston, MA 02110.

Figure 14.7   **Critique of a Press Release (Concluded)**

USE YOUR OWN LETTERHEAD

"If you use a public relations agency, supply it with your company's letterhead. If editors have to call an agency first, they might not bother calling at all."

FORMAT NOTES

"There's no date here. A press release should always be dated. You want to give editors a sense of timeliness and urgency and also let them know when to call to do a follow-up."

MAKE SURE YOUR CONTACT PEOPLE ARE INFORMED AND HELPFUL

"The name at the top of the release should be the person you want contacted. This should be someone who is fully informed about every aspect of your product or service and who will drop everything to get the editors what they need for their story angle. Names mentioned within the body of the copy, like Phil Martus's at the bottom, are those people you hope will be quoted or mentioned if your story gets into print—they are not intended to be primary contacts. However, editors may decide to dial them directly, so make sure whoever is named in the release has a file of information at his or her fingertips and is authorized to answer questions."

MAKE SURE IT'S NEWS

"Mistake! This headline simply trumpets the company's achievement. It should read like a news item and give the editor a story hook. I would rewrite the headline this way: New Concept in Magazine and Music Distribution Introduced. It never hurts to use the word *new*. This way the editor has to read on to find out about 'the concept'."

EMPHASIZE BENEFITS

"Don't tell me about the features of a product or service, tell me about the benefits. This is the most common mistake in public relations. You want the copy to get right into how easy the new product is to use or what problem it solves for the magazine's or newspaper's audience. That is what's newsworthy. It is also more difficult to write than simply listing a product's features."

KEEP TO THE POINT

"Don't try to cover the world in a press release. It's a coup for WGE that these magazines have signed on, but it's not critical to the story. I'd just say, 'eight other magazines.' If editors want to know which magazines, they can call. As a rule, try to keep product and company names to a minimum. Don't worry, if an article gets written, your company will get mentioned by virtue of the fact that it's the source of the news."

MAKE SURE IT'S ACCURATE

"This isn't even true. We aren't using affidavits, and WGE isn't doing the billing. We changed our strategy, but in the rush the writer wasn't informed. It sounds obvious, but never let a press release go out unless you're sure the facts are straight."

DON'T BURY THE LEAD

"These points are big news, but they're in the last few sentences. That's known in journalism as 'burying the lead.' This gets right to how easy the product is to use and how profitable it is. That's the kind of important, useful information you should deliver up front."

Use the Internet to Your Advantage

As we saw in Chapter 13, businesses should post their press releases on the Internet as soon as they are written. Having that source as a place where reporters, stockholders, and the general public can learn about you is tremendously cost-effective. Figures 14.8 and 14.9 are two examples of a business, Hewlett-Packard (HP), presenting exciting news to the public and the media. The election of Carly Fiorina as HP's new CEO in 1999 demonstrated that the so-called glass ceiling for women was being shattered in a previously male-dominated industry. Figure 14.8 was short and to the point. Issued at the time Fiorina accepted the post—July 19, 1999—it presented the most critical news. The announcement was of interest around the globe. The release quickly stated the essentials. Notice, too, that links to other information were available. Fiorina has been an instrumental figure in the success of HP in the last few years. She and the board of Hewlett-Packard waged a difficult fight in the merger of HP with Compaq Computer. Figure 14.9 shows the press release announcing the NYSE trading-symbol change for the two companies. Another interesting press release on May 7, 2002, "The New HP Is Ready," can be found at **http://www.hp.com/hpinfo/newsroom/press/07may02a.htm**.

Video Press Releases

In the last few years the press release has taken on a new look. Today many corporations use videos to replace the paper releases that they once sent. Perhaps you and your organization will want to consider the possibility of using video. In the past, videos were used largely to provide information to employees about their company. Today they are also used for community relations, investor relations, crisis communication, environmental public relations, and other proactive types of communications.[14]

Corporations are increasing their use of video news releases (VNRs) because they realize that many people who can then view their message would never read it in a newspaper or magazine. There is also an advantage for the television stations: VNRs provide stations with video material that is produced like a news story and can be aired as part of a local newscast. On slow news days, a VNR is often used to fill the news gap. To accomplish this, however, it must be of the highest quality.

Companies that distribute VNRs regularly have learned that they must invest heavily in the process. A quality video must be produced, and it must be camouflaged to look like a television news feature. Its purpose is the same as that of all public relations and marketing communications: It must deliver a controlled client message to a targeted audience. To view a sample VNR go to **http://www.jsptv.com/login.asp** or **http://www.cmntv.com/cmn_video_library.asp**.

A question of ethics arises because many VNRs that are furnished to stations have more relevant information and are more professionally produced than any material that the station can produce locally. Consumer activist Ralph Nader decries the VNR: "It generates deception. . . . It generates homogeneity. It generates centralized manipulation. It pollutes the diversity and independent production of news." For this reason he and others demand that TV stations identify VNRs by superimposing a title saying "sponsored source."[15]

Figure 14.8 Hewlett-Packard Press Release Announcing New CEO

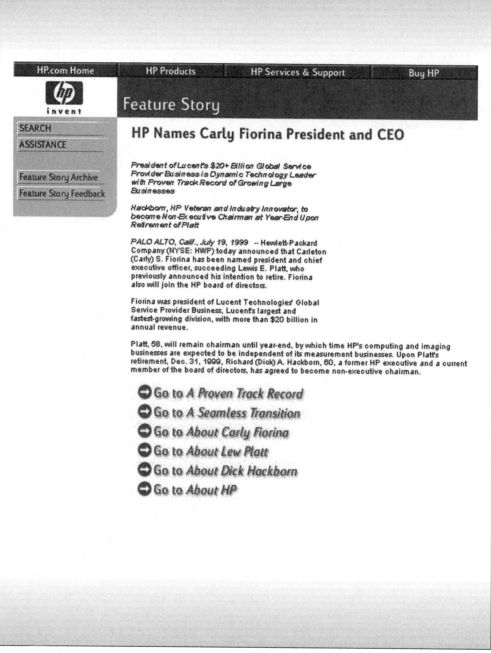

| HP.com Home | HP Products | HP Services & Support | Buy HP |

Feature Story

SEARCH
ASSISTANCE

Feature Story Archive
Feature Story Feedback

HP Names Carly Fiorina President and CEO

President of Lucent's $20+ Billion Global Service Provider Business is Dynamic Technology Leader with Proven Track Record of Growing Large Businesses

Hackborn, HP Veteran and Industry Innovator, to become Non-Executive Chairman at Year-End Upon Retirement of Platt

PALO ALTO, Calif., July 19, 1999 -- Hewlett-Packard Company (NYSE: HWP) today announced that Carleton (Carly) S. Fiorina has been named president and chief executive officer, succeeding Lewis E. Platt, who previously announced his intention to retire. Fiorina also will join the HP board of directors.

Fiorina was president of Lucent Technologies' Global Service Provider Business, Lucent's largest and fastest-growing division, with more than $20 billion in annual revenue.

Platt, 58, will remain chairman until year-end, by which time HP's computing and imaging businesses are expected to be independent of its measurement businesses. Upon Platt's retirement, Dec. 31, 1999, Richard (Dick) A. Hackborn, 60, a former HP executive and a current member of the board of directors, has agreed to become non-executive chairman.

➡ Go to *A Proven Track Record*

➡ Go to *A Seamless Transition*

➡ Go to *About Carly Fiorina*

➡ Go to *About Lew Platt*

➡ Go to *About Dick Hackborn*

➡ Go to *About HP*

Source: Reprinted by permission of Hewlett-Packard Company.

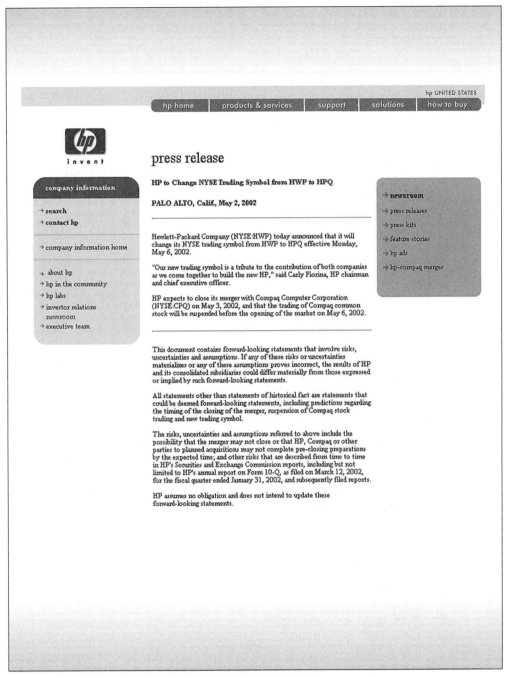

Source: Reprinted by permission of Hewlett-Packard Company.

Your company might consider producing a VNR to announce a new product that is unlike any other on the market, to illuminate an issue or fact that is making news, or to counter negative publicity. The VNR can be prerecorded or it can be a press conference or teleconference that is carried live and sent by satellite to a television station.

Applying Your Organization's Communication Strategy When a Crisis Hits

Your Relationship with the Media

In Chapter 13 we discussed the concept of crisis communication. We now turn our attention to how your organization should communicate with the media.

What the Media Will Do

If and when a crisis occurs it is time to activate your organization's communication strategy. The first thing to realize is that the media have now "put you into play." As Barry McLoughlin describes, there are seven things you can expect the media to do:

1. They will find out about the crisis quickly—often before you discover it.
2. They will monitor each other in hopes of getting more information and gaining an edge.
3. They will try to turn a local event into a national event.
4. They will go where they want, unless you establish clear boundaries.
5. They will report what they know and learn quickly, constantly, and endlessly.
6. They will try to place blame, perpetuate myths, and report rumors.
7. They will establish a process of putting the story's agenda into speculation, next steps, implications, and issues.[16]

While the media will quickly report on the crisis issue, much of their effort will help your organization. As McLoughlin reports, "They can promote pre-crisis education, disseminate warning messages, keep citizens updated with new information, and produce help requests for funds, food, supplies, and volunteers."[17] Be sure to supply media representatives with the kinds of information they request—but double-check all information before releasing it.

At the same time you are supplying information to the media you need to be monitoring the media's activity. Make a list of each media outlet and each journalist. Monitor their stories. Record each briefing, conference, and interview.[18] Recognize your vulnerable areas and work with your communication team to strengthen the weak areas.

Your Organization's Initial Communication. As you activate your communication strategy, there are several tasks you must accomplish. Within the first 60 minutes of the crisis your initial statement must be distributed. Within the first three hours the crisis-management team should be assembled. By the end of the first day your short-term operations and communication process must be up and running. From that point until the end of the crisis, regular press releases and possible press conferences will become the norm.

Your Initial Statement. This statement is critical and will determine the state of your organization's image and credibility. "The statement will serve as official notification of the accident/incident and should meet federal, state, local, and/or regulatory agency requirements for emergency announcements." In this statement you will include:

- Description of the crisis situation;
- Assessment of public and environmental danger;
- When local authorities were notified; what products, processes, or materials were involved;
- The response that has been taken;
- Additional steps to contain or remedy the emergency;
- Heroic actions of employees or emergency personnel;
- The extent of injuries or death; and
- People to contact for further information.[19]

Be careful to not make speculations in the statement, especially about the cause of the crisis. You should also not include information about damage costs, insurance coverage, possible negligence, and who will be held responsible. It is important that the media and public understand from your statement that your organization is prepared and in control of the crisis process, will keep the media and public informed of changes, is working with any regulatory authorities, and that the organization is concerned and cares about the damage and harm that has occurred. If you need to make an apology, make it, and make it clear, expressive, and ungrudgingly. The apology should be made in the initial statement and should be made to the public. This initial statement will usually be your first press release, although it is often delivered at your first press conference.

Make Full Use of Your Company's Web Site

One of the first places journalists will turn when a crisis hits is to your company's Web site. They will look for the name of the PR contact and whether a press kit is available. While there they will quickly check basic facts about your company: location, products, names of executives and board members, financial information, and a description of the crisis events. They will try to learn the "spin" you are placing on the issue. They will also survey past press releases.[20] Remember, your site is on 24/7, it's globally accessible, and it needs to be constantly updated during a crisis event.

During the 9-11 WTC attack some organizations used their Web sites well, others not very well at all. With the fear of mass Anthrax mailings, attention turned to Bayer A.G., the company that makes Cipro, one of the drug remedies for the chemical. After the first Anthrax-laced letters were found, a rumor emerged that Bayer A.G. had a limited supply of Cipro on hand and they were unable to produce enough of the drug to meet demand. On October 19, 2001, Bayer representatives told *The New York Times* that "Bayer is prepared to meet demand and is *shocked* at talk of governments allowing Bayer's patent to be mimicked by other drug makers." During that same time Bayer never discussed the active crisis on its Web site. It chose instead to defend itself in private statements to selected media outlets in the United States.[21]

One proactive Web site user in the midst of tragedy was Cantor Fitzgerald. As described in Chapter 13, it lost over 600 employees in the WTC attack. Within a matter of hours it had posted its first Web message. During the remainder of the week additional messages were used to list victims, survivors, and a variety of useful information. Because of the company's quick response and Howard Lutnick's caring and empathetic manner, Cantor Fitzgerald's actions were praised. You can review Cantor's Web sites at: **http://www.cantor.com/cantor** and **http://www.cantorrelief.org**.[22]

Make the Best Use of the Press Conference

While it is apparent that press releases are a critical tool to use in an organization's relationship with the media, press conferences are also important. In Chapter 13 the crisis management plan described the attention that should go into equipping a room where a press conference will be held. The following ideas should be considered in making sure that the conference takes place at the right time and in the right way. Later in this chapter we will go into depth on the proper communication method that you should consider using if you are the designated spokesperson for the conference.

Determine Whether a Press Conference Is Necessary

News conferences are required when a disaster or crisis has occurred. This is the time your organization will make a statement and the media will ask questions and seek answers that they can use in getting stories to their audiences. If you are tempted to call a conference merely to make an announcement that can go into a press release, don't call the conference. If the media receive little worthwhile news they will likely hold a negative impression of your organization and could possibly look for a "deeper" news story.

Pick the Right Location

Ideally your organization will have the space for a conference room and it will be equipped with many of the items described in the crisis-management plan. On the other hand, the crisis may dictate that a conference be held in a local motel meeting room or other off-site location. Avoid sites close to the disaster because scenes of the events can add negative impact to your positive words.

Choose the Right Time

As we have seen in previous examples, it is important that an organization communicate immediately when a crisis occurs. Often a conference must be called just a short time after the event happens. While the sooner the better is the norm, make sure that you have ample time to get all the necessary information and also time to prepare for the conference questions.

Proper timing also refers to the time of day. Realize that each medium has story deadlines. One expert says that the 10 A.M. conference is such a popular time that often not all conferences can be covered. He suggests 1 P.M. "It leaves plenty of time for the morning paper reporters, and you make evening drive (4 to 6 P.M.) on the radio."[23]

Be Prepared

Being interviewed by the media can be very intimidating, much more so than merely giving a speech. There is a great amount of preparation that must go into the typical press conference interview. Take the time to prepare. It will be to your advantage.

Some Final Thoughts

The following list offers some additional items that need to be considered. Attention to these can help make your conference a success.

- Provide a conducive atmosphere for the media. Consider having chairs, tables, pads, pencils, electrical outlets, telephone lines, typewriters, and microphones available.
- Prepare statements and handouts in advance—consider press releases, fact sheets, photos, typical questions and answers, biographies, product samples, and a glossary of technical terms.
- Pay attention to who is invited. Typically all media should be notified.
- Arrange for supporting people, such as experts, to be available.
- Prepare supporting visual aids. Have backup equipment and supplies, such as bulbs, available.
- Keep the conference concise and short. Don't hold the press longer than necessary.
- Follow up by telephone with those media not in attendance. Get answers to those present who asked questions requiring research.

Media Interviews

You may feel nervous and uncomfortable in delivering a planned business presentation, having a reporter arrive during an unexpected company emergency and, while holding a microphone in front of your face, saying, "What does your company plan to do about this?" In many ways, today's manager has to expect the unexpected. While most recent graduates will not be expected to respond to interviews early in their careers, most will eventually participate in both print and broadcast interviews.

This second section of the chapter will explain how you should *preview the circumstances* of the interview before it begins. You will then lead through the steps of *preparing* for the interview. Next, you will see the reasons to *orally practice* for your interview. Five *performance techniques to use* in the interview will then be given. Finally, we will present 15 items that should be asked and answered as *post-interview evaluation questions*.

Preview the Circumstances

Before you ever agree to a media interview, assure yourself that you really want to be interviewed and that you will carry a positive mental attitude into the interview. This section prescribes five things that you should investigate prior to preparing for your interview.

Determine the Reason for the Interview

Before you meet with the reporter, check out the reason for the meeting and decide whether you are the right person for the interview. Ego sometimes takes over when some executives receive a call from the press. While many would willingly dismiss the opportunity to give a speech, these same individuals often imagine themselves a star with their pictures on television or the front page of the paper. Be sure that the interview will be in your company's and your best interest. Do not let your ego damage your corporate career.

If you receive an unexpected call, make a quick excuse and do some checking before you respond. First, learn as much as you can about the reporter. What types of stories does he or she cover? What is the typical interviewing style? What are the potential reasons for the call? What are the expectations of the medium? It may not be possible to get answers to all these questions, given the usual short time frame, but try.

If the reason for the call is included in the invitation, then ask some additional questions. Is a response from you and your company necessary or appropriate? Are you the correct person to be involved? Do any company policies impinge on what you can say? An executive producer for CBS News said,

> If you cannot speak to the subject with interest and conviction, you ought not to. . . . Choose someone else in your organization who is articulate and knowledgeable.[24]

Anticipate Media Appearances

If a crisis such as those discussed in Chapter 13 has occurred, or if your company has a statement to make to the public, such as those in Figures 14.8 and 14.9, you may be the spokesperson selected. If you have anticipated a possible media appearance, you can respond quickly.[25]

Avoid a Negative Mind-Set

Some managers seek any excuse to avoid talking to reporters. They are on the other extreme from the ego star; you should avoid this position, too. Your experience is indeed likely to be negative if you hold mental impressions such as, "I've made it up the management ladder this far without going before a TV camera, so why should I risk my neck now?" or "I've never met a reporter who didn't try to crucify me with biased questions." Once you are "burned" by the media, the quick urge to respond disappears.

Jim Lehrer, host of the Public Broadcasting System's popular *NewsHour with Jim Lehrer,* cautions against taking the negative approach. He has said,

> the most serious thing that can hurt an interview is for the person who is being interviewed to think that, because a reporter asks a certain question, the reporter necessarily supports that position.[26]

While negative stories sometimes run and inaccuracies do occur, most are the result either of a reporter's ignorance about the subject matter or time pressure in doing the interview and assembling the story. Build a positive mind-set that regards the reporter as a person who has a job to do with a deadline to meet and who wants to get all the facts. This gives you a wonderful opportunity to do your homework and supply the reporter with information that is clearly organized and presented in a polished and professional way.

Recognize Your Rights

By recognizing your rights in relation to the media, you can avoid the negative mind-set and develop a positive media initiative. Gordon Andrew, a New York public relations consultant, lists several rights that a manager should remember.[27]

You have a right to check a reporter's credentials, to know the reasons for a requested interview, and to be told the nature of the questions you will be asked. You are not required to answer questions on the spot regardless of a tight time-frame the reporter may have. In fact, delaying an answer until you can call back later often gives you the time needed to assemble your thoughts.

You have a right not to discuss certain information that might be sensitive to you or your company's interests. If the reporter asks a hypothetical question, you are not required to answer it. You also have the right "to reject a reporter's facts, figures, and terminology." All of this must be done, however, calmly and with self-control.

You have a right to have your viewpoint fairly represented in an interview. This does not mean free advertising for you or your company. It merely means that you are protected from a reporter's verbal abuse.

You have a right to establish attribution rules with a reporter before the interview. Such an agreement needs to be made in advance because if you tell a reporter your comments are off the record *after* you have made them, he or she is not obligated to ignore them. Four standard agreements are normally used:

> *On the record* means that everything said may be used. *Not for attribution* means [your] statements will be attributed to a general source, such as "a company spokesperson." *Background* means that information will be used but not attributed. *Off the record* means that nothing said may be published; the interview is a means of briefing a reporter on a topic or situation.[28]

According to the public relations firm Barron & Whitesell, an organization's crisis-management plan should contain a media policy that spells out precisely the areas of a company that must be protected. Some companies by their very nature must protect proprietary information. Others need to restrict media access to certain parts of a plant or building because of dangerous working conditions or security requirements. Make sure that you and your employees understand company policy before critical events occur.

Develop a Media Initiative

First, consult with the corporate communications or public relations department of your firm. Since these groups carefully develop media policies and strategies, they may give you some words of advice, help you prepare, and especially, help you parallel your statements with those of other company employees.

Second, develop a proactive mind-set and prepare yourself to meet with the media. Familiarize yourself with the media facilities before you ever get in front of the camera: Take guided tours of the press room or studio and join in live audience situations to get a feel for the way interviewers work in media situations.

Third, remember that you need not become buddies with the interviewers, but you should become more media conscious. Develop contacts with editors and reporters. Your public relations office can supply the names of contacts. In addition, you can develop your own list by telephoning or writing media offices. Building good relations with these individuals can help you for many years. Editorial directors will generally welcome your ideas for possible stories, and while they may not agree with your position, they will certainly benefit from your input. By having a media network in place, you can respond to both the positive and negative interviews. One reporter describes what occurs when the media initiative is missing.

> We find that most people who have something positive to say don't approach us at that point, but wait until something negative develops. Then when we reach them, they're in a position of defending themselves.[29]

With media contacts in place, you will find yourself less defensive and more eager to be interviewed.

Jim Lehrer comments on how a positive media relationship helped Goodyear bridge the gap between itself and the media when a potential health hazard in the manufacturing of a vinyl chloride monomer was detected in the company's Niagara Falls, New York, plant. "I think Goodyear set a tremendous precedent in its handling of this situation. Goodyear's public relations people were on the phone saying, 'This is what happened. . . .' And every time we called Goodyear, they told us the good and the bad. . . . They answered every question we had. It was the first experience like that we've had in a long time."[30]

If you have gone from asking questions about the interviewer to developing a media initiative, you are now ready to enter the preparation phase.

Prepare for the Interview

Being anxious about an interview is normal, but there are positive ways to minimize the nervousness. Make a decision at the outset to be honest and to speak from your heart. Some interviewees ask a variety of questions about the reporter, develop their positive mind-set, and then go immediately into the interview performance. The majority of those interviews are disastrous. Instead, the wise interviewee will spend considerable time preparing for the interview. Good preparation always reaps good results.

There are five steps to good preparation: analyzing your audience, organizing your thoughts, anticipating topics and questions, developing your responses, and being aware of additional concerns. The five steps are, in essence, the same as those used for good preparation of both written materials and oral presentations, which were described in earlier chapters.

Analyze Your Dual Audience

One of the first steps in preparing for a speech or business presentation is to analyze your audience. The same holds true for a media interview, but here you have a dual audience: the reporter and the public. Learn as much as you can about the person who will interview you. If you learn your reporter is not very pleasant, develop a positive mind-set of how excited you are about the news you have to convey and how excited the reporter will be after you convey the information. Mary Munter, a communications professor at the Amos Tuck School at Dartmouth College, shares some sound words of advice for this preparation stage:

> Consider, first, reporters in general. Most of them are serious, hardworking professionals, just like you. Their job is to find newsworthy stories that will interest their audience. They are under time pressure to meet deadlines, commercial pressures to increase advertising revenues, and competitive pressures to scoop their rivals. They must compress what you say to fit space or airtime. They want to come up with something arousing and engaging.

> Consider also the individual reporters. What do they know about you? What do you represent to them? How do they perceive your expertise? What do you know about their age, their training, and background? What are their opinions and interests? What are they likely to agree with? What are they likely to disagree with? Are they expert business reporters or general reporters for whom you may have to simplify and define terms?

> Next, consider your readers or listeners. Who are they? Middle America watching a general talk show or specialists reading a technical journal? What do they know about you, your topic, and your relationship to your topic? Once you have established their level of expertise, be sure to talk in terms they will understand.[31]

Realize that an important difference exists in print and broadcast media. Newspaper and magazine reporters work on specific story lines and seek creditable sources for factual information. While they may have short-term deadlines (that evening for the next morning's newspaper edition), they often work on major stories for several days. In the latter situation, you often have more flexibility to get additional information to a reporter following the interview.

Broadcast media is a more immediate communication through which the public will first see and hear management talking about an event. Reporters who cover fast-breaking stories sometimes talk to whomever they can obtain for an interview. In emergency situations they arrive fast, cover as much territory as they can, and leave quickly to have their material on the next major newscast. While they may return for more material, you probably do not have much flexibility in establishing interviews at later times. If you, as an interviewee, are traveling to a radio or television station for an interview, you will probably find the personnel a little easier to work with, time frames more flexible, and the pressures not as great.

Organize Your Thoughts

Lewis Young, former editor-in-chief of *Business Week*, believes that effective media responses are not the result of a well-spoken person, but of much preparation.

> Before the annual meeting, the CEO will spend days rehearsing, answering hypothetical questions that his key staffpeople put to him. On the day of the meeting he appears knowledgeable, in control, deft, and impressive. I am amazed at how many CEOs just show up for an important media interview, even though the interviewer is far more skilled at asking questions than anybody who will be at the annual meeting.[32]

Once you have organized your words, consider the style that you will employ in delivering them. Some critics believe that style is more important than substance because television is primarily a visual medium. Jack Hilton, in his book *On Television*, contends that executives should remember four things before going on-camera:

(1) very few viewers will remember their names; (2) virtually all will remember their affiliation; (3) few will remember a single point they make; (4) all viewers will decide promptly whether they like them or not.[33]

The person who is prepared and in control, not the one who tries to wing it, will leave the most positive impression.

Anticipate the Topics and Questions

How do you prepare for an interview? After you have analyzed your audience, begin thinking of the possible topics of discussion and questions you might be asked. You can request a list of questions in advance from the reporter; however, you probably will not receive them. Many reporters work on such a tight time schedule that they prepare the questions while driving to your interview. Most reporters will tell you the general topics only, fearing that further disclosure might produce a dull, canned interview. You should be able to anticipate key questions, especially if the discussion is about an emergency situation. Brainstorm with your staff or colleagues. Let them play devil's advocate and help you decide on the most likely questions and the best responses. Keep in mind that any questions you are dreading will surely be asked. *Be prepared for the most difficult question and any others you can anticipate.*

As you prepare to develop your thoughts into responses consider how you can get your most positive message across. The Canadian Psychological Association makes five recommendations to its members in preparation for media interviews:

Make the Story New. Your comments should add something new to the listener's knowledge base. Whether it is a new perspective on a familiar topic, or the results of a new study, your audience will be more interested if the material is new or stated in a new way.

Make the Information Interesting. Word your ideas in ways that will make your audience want to hear more. Deliver your words with excitement.

Make the Story Relevant. Word your material so that the listeners can relate to it. Develop it to fit their lives.

Make the Story Understandable. Avoid jargon. Word your material so that an eight-year-old could comprehend the facts. Remember, the person on the street or at home watching the news is not your peer. The media love sound bites and good quotes. To help the potential listener to get clarity of your message, list your points before your speak. "I would like to make three points before I take your questions." State the number as each point is spoken. Numbering the points also makes it hard for a reporter to interject other questions until you are finished. Editors also have a harder time cutting out important material.

Make the Story Memorable. Frame your ideas with a metaphor or story. Stick to one or two key points for ease of memory.[34]

Develop Your Responses

Starting with the toughest questions you can imagine, write down simple one-, two-, or three-point responses. Later, in private or with the aid of your colleagues, practice these responses orally.[35] For now, make sure the responses fit into a 30-second time frame. For the press or television this will consist of about 75 words. Radio newscasters love one-sentence statements. Television deals essentially in headline news. A business story that rates a column in a major newspaper may command only a single sentence on a national television network evening news program.

Brundage points out the danger of top management talking too long for a broadcast. "Top management is standing there talking and talking about the incident, and the reporter is standing there with the mike thinking about having to go back and stand in line at the editing booth to edit the interview. . . . That is where there is a possibility to be taken out of context. Top management should be taught ahead to time to talk in 10- or 15-second sound bites for radio and television."[36]

There are six important things to remember in developing the response you anticipate using.

Lead with the Most Important News. Businesspeople typically present ideas by leading up to the news. But the media require a different approach. Both the press and broadcast media reorganize what you say in order to meet their needs. You can help the reporter by stating your most important piece of news first. People will remember it better if you lead with the news and then support your statement. If editors need to cut words because of time or space restrictions, your main ideas that would have come at the end of your statement will not be on the cutting-room floor. Chester Burger, a media expert, believes that most businesspeople have an inability to get across what they want to say to the media:

> They fail to make the points they wanted to make, and then they blame the reporter. Usually, it is their own fault. They have been playing what is called the "ping-pong game." The reporter asks a question; they answer it. He [or she] asks another; they answer it. Back and forth the ball bounces but the executive does not know how to squeeze in what he regards as his [or her] important points.[37]

Follow the most important news with strong and substantial facts. Cite specific times and dates. Learn names and their correct pronunciation. The use of statistics can be effective, but they should be simple, easy to understand, and of interest to the listener. Remember, the message prepared for the eye of the reader will strike the ear of the listener in an entirely different way. To say, "70 percent of the public approve of our policy and 15 percent don't care" is much better than to say, "70 percent like the policy, and this consists of 80 percent metroplex dwellers and 20 percent rural residents. The 80 percent metroplex supporters are made up of 60 percent women and 40 percent men, with 30 percent being children." While the latter may be true, few readers or listeners will take the time to figure it out. You will also sound dull and disorganized.

Use the Public Position. When developing answers, build in responses to the public's needs, desires, and wants. Tell them how they will benefit from a plan. Tell them also that they are free from danger. If plenty of time is available, you may even want to supply film footage of some specific examples.

Word Your Message with Care. Aim your message at about a tenth-grade level for understandability. Avoid technical jargon and organizational acronyms and buzzwords.

Use Positive Words. During interviews, especially those involving an emergency or disaster, examine each word for its truth and for its implied meaning. Every company and industry has a list of positive and negative words. With your colleagues, decide which ones you should use and which you should avoid. For example:

Positive Words	Negative Words
Safety	Negligence
Care	Death
Concern	Accidents
Employment opportunities	Discrimination
Long record of service	Fired
Excellent relations	Catastrophe
Equal opportunities	Layoffs
Satisfactory	Probably could happen . . .

The point is not to pick euphemisms, or words that substitute an inoffensive term for one considered offensively explicit, but to reword your thoughts by focusing first on the positive.

The usage becomes clearer when put into sentence form. Instead of saying, "The company does not consider this problem to be its fault. We have had four years without a serious accident," say:

Our safety record is excellent. We constantly monitor the process and this has resulted in four years of accident-free work. Because we are concerned for safety, we were immediately on top of the situation when it occurred.

Build Strong Transitions and Bridges. You can help media editors by flagging your most important points. This can be done with phrases like, "The main thing I would like the public to remember is. . . ."

Bridging is also a way to move a reporter off a controversial question by reiterating key messages. Bridging is done when you briefly answer a question and then form a bridge to an idea you wish to make:

Yes, I can see where that could be a possible way of chemical exposure. However, in the 15 years that our company has produced this and other dangerous, but necessary, chemicals, I am happy to say that the EPA has praised our handling procedures.

Another example of bridging is:

As your paper reported two weeks ago, in our Dallas facility 96 percent of our employees rated our safety procedures as either *excellent* or *superior*. In fact, we have received the national chemical makers award for "Safety First" every year during the last five years.

Other bridge statements include: "Let's consider the larger issue here . . ."; "Before I get to that, let me fill you in on . . ."; and even, "I don't know about that, but I do know. . . ." Remember, states Karen Berg of CommCore Communication Strategies, "once you cross the bridge, blow it up. You don't go back over it or you will pay a toll."[38]

Develop a Plan for Handling the Tough and Tricky Questions. Building a healthy respect for the media takes place as you recognize the power of influence. While you should avoid developing an adversarial impression of journalists, recognize that their questions can sometimes be tough or tricky. This is all the more reason for you to practice with someone who asks you possible questions.

As you practice with your colleagues, have them throw you very difficult questions. There are seven types of tough and tricky questions. Learn how to respond in a cool and professional manner, but not defensively. Responding to these questions is not easy, yet you can master the process with practice.

1. *False questions* are sometimes asked. Correct the false statement before you respond with an answer. Try to paraphrase the question a second time during the answer.

   Reporter: The XYZ Company has a track record for manufacturing faulty products. Does the recall of your product surprise you?

   Interviewee: XYZ Company's manufacturing record is the most solid in the industry. None of our products are faulty. We issued this recall to correct a potential problem that had been discovered and to assure our customers that they will continue to receive quality products.

2. *The loaded preface* is another problem encountered in questioning. If you miss the reporter's opening, you may find that in the final media presentation, you appear to agree with something you are completely against.

   Reporter: Mr. Jones, your company is under investigation for cost overruns and bribery in regard to one of your government contracts. Can you tell us, Mr. Jones, how are minority workers treated in your organization?

   The respondent in this example should fear that the reporter is really trying to do a story on cost overruns and bribery. The respondent should either dissect the question and handle both parts, or deny the loaded preface and then construct a bridge to the answer he or she wants to give.

3. *The what-if question* asks about something that has not happened yet. For example, "I know it hasn't been announced officially yet, but what will you do if you are asked to serve as the next executive VP?" Unless you want this information public, refuse to answer the question, make the irrelevance clear, and bridge to your ideas.

4. *The irrelevant question* asks you about material totally unrelated to the subject of the interview. For example, you are being interviewed on several legal matters pertaining to your business, and you are asked about your views on legalizing marijuana. Again, refuse to answer the question, make the irrelevance clear, and bridge to your ideas.

5. *False relationship* is another unfair question that assumes that because an event precedes an outcome, it necessarily caused it. For example, "Metro's stock went down $3.65 as soon as you were appointed to the board.

Would you care to comment on this?" Beware of the false causal relationship and do not let it go unchallenged.

6. *Popular prejudice* is shown when the reporter appeals to the popular idea rather than to the specific situation. For example, "Don't you think it's un-American for Congress to agree to support corporate stock options?" Interviewees should try to define or challenge words like *un-American* before moving on to their own points about the subject:

Interviewee: I challenge what you consider to be un-American in this bill, when it allows companies to find and hire the best managers for the jobs, and to provide dividends to millions of American stockholders. But the real point I want to make is. . . .

Turn a Negative Question into a Positive Answer. If an interviewer makes a statement or phrases a question in the negative, never answer it or repeat it. Many people have done so, only to watch themselves say the negative question on camera after it has been edited. Instead, rephrase the question into a positive statement and then add your answer.

Years ago, Carl A. Gerstacker, then-chairman of Dow Chemical Company, went on the *Today* show to discuss an explosive, six-letter word: napalm. Gerstacker, using a carefully designed game plan, told anchor Hugh Downs that yes, his company produced napalm for its country during a time of war but that it was now out of the napalm business. Gerstacker then artfully began to answer the questions by talking about the *lifesaving* products his company manufactured, including a measles vaccine. Michael Klepper, whose firm trains executives for encounters with the media, and who provided the game plan for Gerstacker, recalls: "He was able to turn the napalm issue around by concentrating on his company's lifesaving products, which he presented in a very favorable light. Downs finally told him: 'Gee, I didn't know chemical companies were also pharmaceutical companies.'"[39]

Techniques for turning negative questions into positive answers are displayed in the following examples.

Question: Isn't it true that your driver, Joe Ferguson, who was involved in this fatal collision, was cited for driving while intoxicated in 1979, and at that time was in a very serious accident?

Answer: Joe Ferguson came to work for us on February 15, 1982. He, like all our other drivers, was carefully checked and passed the Truckers' Safety Standards Test, administered by the County Vehicle Department, with a score of 89 out of 100. Since that date, he has worked steadily and up to today has had an accident-free record with our firm. Among our 65 steady drivers, he has been among the 90 percent with no reportable accident of record since June 1, 1983.

Question: Although your bank has some 35 vice-presidents, how do you explain the fact that only five are women?

Answer: All appointments to vice-president are made on the basis of Board selection and an examination. Every opening is posted and any employee of the appropriate grade is eligible to apply. In the past three years, we have had nine openings for vice president. Ten women took the examination and two were appointed. In the same period 30 men took the examination and seven were appointed. Thus 20 percent of the women taking the exam were appointed and 23 percent of the men. I would say that we had a similar level of treatment and equality in both cases, wouldn't you?[40]

Be Aware of Additional Concerns

The final step in good interview preparation is to refresh your mind with some additional concerns.

Do Not Respond to Unchecked Statistics. If an interviewer throws statistics at you with which you are unfamiliar or have not checked out, do not answer the question. Answer instead, "I'm sorry, but I do not have those figures; they are presently being calculated. I will, however, obtain them and follow up with you this afternoon," or "I have not seen the figures."

Do Not Use a "No Comment" Comment. At one time "no comment" meant simply that there was no news to share. Today when a company spokesperson uses the words it implies that there is something to hide. If you cannot answer, say why you can't answer. Saying "no comment" makes you sound evasive and secretive and it creates suspicion.[41] Say instead, "I am sorry, but we cannot make additional comments on the event until next of kin have been notified."

As the Intel case in Chapter 13 displayed, a crisis situation requires interaction with the media. You cannot hide behind a "no comment" statement and expect the media to go away. They will report the story with or without your help. If you have facts that they need, share them quickly and help resolve the issue quickly.[42]

Do Not Answer with a Simple "Yes" or "No." After uttering easy yes or no answers, you may be surprised to find them cut and pasted onto another question by an unscrupulous newsperson. Phrase your response in a yes-or-no context but expand it to at least a full sentence. For example, a reporter asks, "Will the merger be completed before the first of the month?" The answer may be yes, but you are better off saying, "Both sides are working hard to complete the merger by the month's end. I believe it will be accomplished by the first of next month."

Be Careful About Stating Your Personal Opinions. In most instances, you are representing the company. Do not cross the line and state your position as the company's position unless you clearly know your positions are the same and you have been authorized to make that position public.

Tell Them If You Do Not Know the Answer. If you are asked a question for which you have absolutely no answer, tell them, "I do not know the answer to that question at this time. I will, however, find the answer." If you know where the answer can be found, direct them to it.

Never Stonewall a Position. Since the Watergate era of the 1970s, both the news industry and the public have become very suspicious of stonewalling tactics. Issues that are unequivocally denied, or statements such as "I will be exonerated," seem to be offered by individuals who have not thought of good answers. The statements are often mere smoke screens.

Avoid Talking Off the Record. In many cases, statements made off the record have a way of appearing in the middle of news stories. A good dictum is to say nothing that you do not wish to see in print, and follow this advice:

> The press will assume you are on the record; that is, that they have the right to quote and report what was said and done to attribute statements to you. A rule that some spokespersons learn the hard way is that you are not off the record just by saying so. If reporters agree to an off-the-record comment, they are saying they will not report it. If you go off the record in a press conference, all reporters must agree, not just the one asking questions.[43]

Record Your Own Interview. You may want to take your own small tape recorder to your interview. Taping the session will not only be good for use in future practice sessions, but also to check a reporter's quotes against actual statements that you made. Be open with the reporter about wanting to make the recording. Most reporters will not care. If one does object, you should not only ask why but reconsider whether you want to go ahead with the interview.

Always Tell the Truth. The press and public accept that you may not tell the whole truth for many reasons, including competition. But if you resort to lying—even once—the press, the public, and your colleagues will never again trust your credibility.[44] The good news about bad news is that you can get it out of the way and prevent a continuing story. More often than not, lies lead to continuing probes and additional stories. A vice president of Hygrade Food Products, a meat processor that had to handle rumors that razor blades were in the company's hot dogs, makes this statement about lying, "One thing the experience taught me is that total candor can convert a reporter from a hard-nosed muckraker into a sympathetic company supporter. . . . Not only does honesty pay, it beats having to remember what you told the media yesterday."[45]

As we have seen in this section on preparation, wise interviewees spend a considerable amount of time preparing for the interview. They follow the steps of analyzing all audiences, organizing their thoughts, anticipating possible topics and questions, developing their responses, and being aware of various additional concerns.

Practice

There is a big difference between knowing the material and being able to talk about it. After you go through the preparation stages thoroughly, you may feel rather smug about the answers you have devised. Beware: Crafty reporters have reduced many overconfident executives to bumbling, incoherent, embarrassed interviewees. Just watch *60 Minutes* or *20/20* to get the picture.

To protect yourself from disgrace and to turn in a magnificent performance requires practicing your material. Spend considerable time reading out loud the responses to all your anticipated questions. After you remember the material fairly well, turn your office into a mock studio and practice with your staff and colleagues. Have them ask you the questions in the style of a reporter, including their fast pace, vocal inflections, and nonverbal gestures. If you give the wrong answer, have them repeat the question. You should practice until you feel confident of your ability to meet and answer any question a reporter might ask, no matter how tough the question or abusive the reporter's style.

The practice process used for interview questions and statements is almost identical to that described in Chapter 11 on the business presentation.

Performance Techniques to Use

On the day of your interview the focus is on you—your statements, the issues you represent, and the image you create. You hope your preparation and practice time will pay off. If a print reporter interviews you, refer to the section on preparation earlier in this chapter. The following five ideas are primarily for television interviews.

Dress for the Occasion

Pick comfortable clothing that reflects your profession. If you are warm-blooded, choose cooler fabrics. Avoid dark colors: black and navy blue look black on television and they lose detail. Try grays, a lighter navy, and beiges. Avoid tweeds, large stripes, and bold patterns. Solid pastel colors are best for dresses. Whites can cause glare and make your face look dark. The best-color shirts are off-white or light blue. Muted colors in ties are better than those with bright, large designs. According to Arnold Zenker, a media expert, "Your taste in clothing is your own business. But out-of-date, ill-fitting clothing creates an image that is out-of-date and unimpressive for an executive. Contemporary, professional clothing is a must for any television appearance."[46]

If you wear makeup, be sure it has a powder base rather than oil, so your face will not be shiny. Keep jewelry to a minimum—wedding rings and watches are acceptable. Avoid any objects, such as rhinestones, that can reflect studio lights. Glasses can be another problem. Many people who wear them do not want their pictures taken with them on and will probably not want their television image to be one wearing glasses. However, because the objects are so natural to the wearer, to be without them seems awkward, especially if the person cannot see properly. Glass lenses, on the other hand, can cause a reflection. If you appear regularly before the media, you may want to invest in a technique used by Preston Smith, a former governor of Texas. Smith felt uncomfortable without his glasses, but he grew tired of the glare they caused. He purchased a set of frames that matched his glasses and wore the frames, minus the lenses, during his interviews.

Keep Your Cool

As difficult as it may seem, you must maintain a totally calm appearance. Do a deep-breathing exercise before meeting the reporter, or before the camera is turned on. This exercise requires that you exhale all the air out of your lungs and that you very slowly inhale through your nose. Doing this a couple of times helps to lower the anxiety and give you a greater sense of well-being. If you are being interviewed during a live event, deep breathe again when there is a break for commercials. Look and act relaxed. Regardless of the turmoil in your stomach, never let the interviewer and audience suspect that you are not in control. Knowing your material and having practiced your comments are the first step in making this a reality. Second, work on maintaining the positive image of a professional executive that you have viewed so many times on television. If a reporter tries to provoke you or get you off balance, do not take it personally. Maintain your calm and unemotional manner. As Jim Lehrer says, "An executive who cannot hold his [or her] cool and who takes everything personally is a setup in an interview. I mean, you're going to get to him [or her]."[47]

A classic example is when Microsoft's Bill Gates, in 1994, got mad and walked out of a network-televised interview with newscaster Connie Chung. For watchers, that established a negative image of Mr. Gates as a rich and arrogant person. The image, in fact, was hard to overcome as Gates testified in the 1998–99 Microsoft antitrust case. Years later, it was evident as Gates was interviewed by anchorwoman Barbara Walters that he had undergone extensive media training.[48]

Jack Hilton offers this tip for those who easily perspire. "Ideally, you should discipline yourself not to perspire. Practically, if you need to wipe your brow, do it with a forefinger, and discreetly wipe your forefinger with your handkerchief. The finger will make you look thoughtful."[49]

Be Ready for the Spontaneous Questions

If you have done your preparation, you will be ready to answer all the questions a reporter might have. But here is a trick to use when a spontaneous question is asked that you were not expecting: Quickly bridge the question to a previous question or answer, or to a response that you wanted to make but were not given the opportunity. With your thought in mind, develop two or three quick statements that support or clarify your thought. Now state your ideas in a quick 30-second or one-minute response.

Let Your Body Talk

A large percentage of our information about the world comes from nonverbal cues. In interviews, the nonverbal image is extremely important. Avoid defensive-looking body language. This can take the form of clenched fists, tightened facial expressions, crossed arms, or poor eye contact. Learn to relax your body, sit in a comfortable and professional manner, and wear a warm facial expression. Here are some nonverbal expressions that are important to remember:

- Use natural hand gestures to highlight your points;
- Maintain good eye contact with the interviewer;
- Stay alert physically, even when you are not talking;
- Lean forward slightly in your chair. Do not swivel about; and
- Rest your hands naturally in your lap.[50]

Try to Ignore the Cameras

The technicians and director will take the shots they want, and you should keep your attention focused on the interviewer. The exception to this guideline is when you want to directly address the television audience. At that point, look and talk directly into the camera lens that has the red light. Even when the light is off continue to stay alert because another camera may be on you. Don't try to see yourself on the monitor. Often there is a time delay between the picture and your voice. This asynchrony can be very distracting and can cause you to lose your train of thought.[51] Have someone videotape your performance for your later viewing.

If you are delivering a prepared statement to the press, avoid reading your material. You can look at your notes from time to time, but leave the impression that you know precisely what you want to say. Likewise, if you are to use a Tele-PrompTer, distribute your eye contact from side to side or from one TelePrompTer to another. Keep a light, pleasant look on your face and a natural smile that you would give to an ordinary speech audience. While you are seeing words through the screen prompters, your audience is only seeing your image. Your facial expression should convey a very professional look.

Display Confidence in Your Voice

Develop a professional sound. Ordinary conversational tones are the best. Keep a consistent volume and rate. Avoid letting your voice drop at the end of sentences. Also avoid displaying anger or high emotion. Maintaining an erect posture and good breath control while talking can help you through the rough spots. Remember, you are the expert.

If you are to use a microphone, ask for a microphone check before you start talking. This will help you determine how loud to talk. If you use a lavalier microphone (one attached to the lapel or tie), avoid coughing, crossing your arms, or slapping your chest. While you do not hear it, your audience will receive a big bang each time such actions occur. Assume that your microphone is always "live," even during cut-aways to commercials.

Post-Interview Evaluation Questions

Following each press or media interview, you should evaluate your performance. The information gathered will prove valuable as you prepare for future interviews. Talk through the following questions alone and with your staff and colleagues. Take careful notes; they will be helpful during the next preparation stage.

1. Prior to the interview, did you take the reporter for granted? If so, what was the result?
2. Did you assume that the reporter understood the issue? Did he or she? If not, what was the impact?
3. Did you anticipate that the reporter might oppose or support your position? Which position did he or she actually take?
4. Before the interview were you prepared to defend your position through a fair and accurate rebuttal?
5. Did you start the interview by presenting your most important news?
6. Did you answer the questions directly and briefly, or did you occasionally get off-track and get into too much depth?
7. Did you allow the reporter to get away from the point of the interview?
8. Did you find yourself answering questions that you knew nothing about?
9. Did you use positive instead of negative words?
10. Were you able to build bridges to your desired answers?

11. Was the reporter overt or covert in nature?
12. Were you familiar with your material?
13. Before the interview did you feel reluctant, enthusiastic, or neutral about meeting the media?
14. Were you bothered by the studio lights, the use of the microphone, the clothing you wore, the heat, or your posture?
15. What specific things do you want to change before your next interview?

Summary

Today every business manager needs to perfect his or her media-management skills. These new and important skills complement what we have described in earlier chapters where we noted the importance of writing letters and reports and of making regular business presentations and public speeches. Increasingly, managers are drawn into writing press releases and must clearly and convincingly give press and media interviews.

The first part of this chapter introduced you to a proactive process of using press releases that invite a working relationship with the media. Ten rules for good press releases were suggested, and numerous examples of actual press releases were displayed. Also discussed was the use of the Internet Web site as an archive for company press releases, and the option of placing releases on video. By building a positive relationship with the media during ordinary business times, your organization can gain image impact and can have a possible safety net in case a crisis develops.

The second section of the chapter turned the attention to applying a developed communication strategy when a crisis hits. The importance of the initial company statement was described, and the necessity to post and update information about the crisis event on the company Web site. This section concluded with the steps to follow in assuring the holding of a proper press conference.

The third section focused on media interviews. At the moment you give an interview, you become "the company." Both your individual credibility and the company image are on the line. With the proper work you can be a star. Your success depends on five important steps: previewing, preparing, practicing, performing, and evaluating the interview. Before you can prepare for the interview you must know why an interview is needed and who will be interviewing you. Check the record and style of the reporter before you respond to an unsolicited call. If a crisis is involved, make sure you are the person who should really address the issue. If there is someone with more authority on or knowledge of the subject, let that individual give the interview. Once you agree to the interview, avoid developing a negative mindset. Maintain a positive picture of how you will convey exciting and useful information. From that moment through the preparation stages you should have a media initiative that will help you discover the correct steps to take.

The preparation stage is more important than the actual interview. First, you should clearly understand both of your audiences: the interviewer and the public. Next, organize the thoughts and ideas you want to convey. With the help of your staff or colleagues anticipate the topics and questions you might be asked, starting with the most difficult. From those questions, develop complete answers. Decide upon the most important news based on your organization's aims and your perception of the public's needs, desires, and wants; then lead with it. Word your message with care, avoiding jargon and employing positive words. Learn to build bridges from the questions that are asked by the interviewer to the statements that you wish to make. Develop a style for handling the tough and tricky questions. More important, learn how to turn negative questions into positive answers.

Before interviews, as before business presentations or public speeches, practice is extremely important. Knowing what you are going to say and saying it are two different things. Media interviews often require that you talk in 30-second statements and respond to tough and tricky questions. This is foreign to the way we usually interact or speak. Spend ample time practicing it with your staff, colleagues, or friends. The results will be well worth it.

After successful preparation and practice, the real performance is less threatening. Dress appropriately for the occasion. Learn to keep your cool during the interview regardless of the circumstances or interviewer's style. Convince your interviewer and the audience of your credibility with a confident voice and effective body language.

After you read this chapter, and before your press or media interview occurs, learn to observe the hundreds of people who are interviewed each day in the media. Be aware of what they do right and wrong. Learn from the worst and copy the best.

Discussion Questions

1. We know it is critical that an organization communicate with the media when a crisis develops—but why and how does a company build relationships and communicate with the media representatives during ordinary times?

2. The chapter opening had ten rules for developing press releases, and it displayed numerous examples of actual press releases from organizations. As you read that material, what tactics did you find that were the most impressive, and which were the least impressive? Of all the examples given, which ones do you believe were actually used by reporters in preparing media stories? Why?

3. Discuss the differences between print and Web releases. How does the Internet, as an interactive medium in which the company controls the flow of information, redefine the use of the release?

4. Video press releases have been popularly used by many organizations. On what occasion and for what purpose would you recommend that

an organization make use of this medium? What are ethical concerns in using VPRs?

5. As soon as a crisis hits, the media representatives become active in searching for information about organizations. What are some of the tactics that they use in gathering information? How can an organization aid the media, yet protect itself?

6. You may have a feeling of nervousness and discomfort when you take a call from a media representative. To help relieve these feelings, what are some of the things you should investigate or do prior to preparing for your interview? Good media interviews rarely occur spontaneously. Most are the result of lots of preparation. What are five things that a person who is waiting to be interviewed should do?

7. Some of the performance techniques for media interviews are basically the same as those you were encouraged to follow while making a business presentation. What are those primary techniques?

Communication in Action

1. You are serving as a volunteer for Like New, a not-for-profit resale store that is affiliated with a local charity. Merchandise is solicited from a very high-income part of town and is sold in the store, and the proceeds are then directed to a shelter for battered women with children. Donations have been down for several months, and the nonprofit organization is cutting its budget. The director knows you are taking a business communication course and asks you to write a press release for the store. The director believes the media will be receptive to a nonprofit's plea and that donations could be impacted.

   Your Assignment: Write the press release, stressing the following points:

   • All donations are used to fund a very worthy cause.
   • When last year's donations were sold it allowed $55,000 to be given to the women's shelter. With six months left on this year's budget, proceeds to the shelter have been only $16,000.
   • The funds that are given to the shelter help women buy medicine and groceries for themselves and their children.
   • Like New can use furniture, appliances, clothing, and toys.
   • Pickup of the items is available.
   • A tax-donation letter will be given to all donors.
   • Any items not sold within six weeks are donated to other local charities helping women and children.

2. Collect two business-related newspaper clippings from your local newspaper. Try to choose clippings that appear to be written by publicists or as press

releases. Often these articles appear in the weekend business news section. Sometimes they even look like articles but carry the label of advertisement.

Your Assignment: Analyze the clippings and write a critique about them. Focus on the news in the articles. Why is it news? Where did it come from; that is, does it appear to be news-generated from a press release or created as a sales piece? Is there any angle that the reporter has not covered in detail that a manager could use as an opening to generate another story? Are there any negative twists to the story?

3. Search the news media coverage for a recent crisis event. This situation could have been large or small, public or potentially public in nature, and occurring in any organization. Most events will be local and minor in nature, compared to product recalls or company bankruptcies. Once you find an event, go to several news-source archives. Use local newspapers, or national newspapers such as *USA Today* and *The Wall Street Journal.* Search magazines like *Business Week, Fortune,* or *Forbes.* Also search radio and television outlets such as National Public Radio (NPR), CNN, or MSNBC.

Your Assignment: Using the crisis event that you have selected, critically evaluate the media coverage of it. Try to find press releases and transcripts of media interviews. Write a short analysis of the crisis event. Start with the pre-crisis period and then the actual event(s) that revealed the nature of the crisis. What were five specific things that the organization did right in managing the crisis? What were five specific things that it did wrong? What do you speculate were five or more issues or situations that, if known by the press, could have made the entire process even more explosive? What was the impact of this event on the public/professional image of the organization?

4. Videotape an investigatory news program like *20/20, 60 minutes,* or *Dateline.* If you have a hard time videotaping such a program, use an Internet search engine. Type in the name of the person being interviewed, along with the words *media interview.* Try to select a segment during which the reporter is playing an antagonistic role. Compare the reporter's questions and the interviewee's answers to those on pages 390–394. How do the questions compare? Would you have answered the same questions differently? How? Be specific.

@ Internet

5. Your instructor has designated a class session to talk in detail about press releases, press conferences, and media interviews. She has assigned the current chapter, but wants each class member to contribute something from the public relations domain. She gives two Web sites that have hundreds of stories on all three areas: **http://www.press-release-writing.com/ newsletters/** and **http://www.e911.com/eaindex.html**.

Your Assignment: Go to the Web sites and select one article from each of the three areas: press releases, press conferences, and media interviews.

Write a maximum one-page summary for each article. The summary should cover the what, where, when, how, and why an organization would use that aspect of media management.

InfoTrac

6. Your instructor wants some examples of how organizations managed the media during a crisis. The Exxon Valdez case is a classic example of how not to manage a crisis or to work with the media. You decide to take that example to class. But along the way you find another example of how Exxon also managed the media well. You decide to report on both of the Exxon cases in your classroom. You can find the stories at: "A Case Study: Framing the Media's Agenda During a Crisis," by Sonya Forte Duhe and Lynn M. Zoch, in *Public Relations Quarterly*, Winter 1994, Article No. A16762591; "The Two Faces of the Exxon Disaster," by Stephanie Pain, in *New Scientist*, May 22, 1993, Article No. A14231429; and "The Alaskan Oil Spill: Lessons in Crisis Management," by Martha H. Peak, in *Management Review*, April 1990, Article No. A8925131.

   Your Assignment: Review the articles and prepare an outline that you can use in reporting the cases to your class.

Notes

1. What the people want from the press (p. 1). (1977, September). Center for Media and Public Affairs. Retrieved October 5, 2002, from **http://www.cmpa.com/ archive/wdtpwftp.htm**
2. McKenzie, S. (1998, November 19). Public relations: Panic situations. *Marketing Week*, p. 39.
3. DiCostanzo, F. (1986, Winter). What the press thinks of press releases. *Public Relations Quarterly*, pp. 22–23.
4. Marr, M. (2001, February). Release me. *Kinko's Impress,* p. 18.
5. Beard, C. K. & Dalton, H. J., Jr.. (1991, January). The power of positive press. *Sales & Marketing Management*, p. 38.
6. Elfenbein, D. (1986, Summer). Business journalists say if it's not local, it's trashed. *Public Relations Quarterly*, p. 17.
7. Marr, p. 19.
8. Helping physicians master the 'de-jargonizing' process. (1998, July 9). *Healthcare PR & Marketing News*. Retrieved June 10, 2002, from **http://www.prandmarketing .com/search/prnews_advanced.htm**
9. Solutions contest. (n.d.). *BuzzWhack*. Retrieved May 17, 2002, from **http://www .buzzwhack.com/**
10. Tips, techniques, and points to consider. (n.d.). *Internet Info Scavenger*. Retrieved May 16, 2002, from **http://www.infoscavenger.com/prtips3.htm**
11. Extend the mileage of your press release with search engine optimization. (n.d.). PRW. Retrieved February 20, 2002, from **http://www.press-release-writing.com/ seo.htm**
12. Lammers, T. (1991, August). The press-release primer. *Inc*, p. 36.

13. Lammers, pp. 34–36.
14. Shell, A. (1990, November). Reaching out to the TV generation. *Public Relations Journal*, pp. 28–32.
15. Rothenberg, R. (1989, September 11). Promotional news: Videos gain support. *The New York Times*, p. D12, col. 3.
16. Berry, S. (1999, April 1). We have a problem . . . call the press! *Public Management*, p. 16.
17. *Ibid.*
18. Key roles and responsibilities of the media guide in a crisis (p. 1). (n.d.). Barry McLoughlin Associates. Retrieved October 31, 2001, from **http://www.mclomedia .com/cc8.htm/**
19. Managing the crisis. (n.d.). CommunEcom. Retrieved February 5, 2001, from **http:// www.communecom.com/CrisisPlan/managing.htm**
20. Rudden, K. (2001, June 26). Creating an e-PR culture. International Association of Business Communicators, New York.
21. How organizational web sites *could, should,* or *do* communicate well. LeFile: Online Crisis Communications. Retrieved April 17, 2002, from **http://www. lefile.com/**
22. Lutnick, H. (n. d.). Chairman of Cantor Fitzgerald and eSpeed. Comment on world trade center tragedy. Cantor, Tradespark, eSpeed Family Information Center. Retrieved: April 19, 2002, from **http://www.cantorusa.com**
23. Harris, J. (1986, September). Get the most out of a news conference. *Public Relations Journal*, 1986, p. 33.
24. Hoffer, H. (1983, September). You're on the air. *Association Management*, p. 93.
25. Dilensschneider, R. L., & Hyde, R. C. (1985, January/February). Crisis communication: Planning for the unplanned. *Business Horizons*, p. 36.
26. Talburt, L. (1975, April). How to be effective in a TV interview. *Association Management*, p. 31.
27. Andrew, G. G. (1990, April). When a reporter calls. *Business Marketing*, p. 71.
28. Beard & Dalton, The power of positive press, p. 40.
29. Talburt, How to be effective, p. 34.
30. *Ibid.*
31. Munter, M. (1983, Summer). Managing public affairs: How to conduct a successful media interview. *California Management Review*, p. 145.
32. Young, L. (1981, November 19). What business media expect from corporations and public relations people. Speech to National Conference of the Public Relations Society of America, Atlanta, GA.
33. Poe, R. (1981, December). Showtime for the CEO. *Across the Board*, p. 47.
34. Byrne, J. M., Mureika, J. M., & Newton, J. H. (1996, January 31). Working with the media: A guide for psychologists (pp. 2–3). Canadian Psychological Association. Retrieved: April 19, 2002, from **http://www.cpa.ca/media.html**
35. Gage, D. (1992, October 19). Media interviews: Follow the scout's motto and be prepared. *San Diego Business Journal*, p. 16.
36. Sherborne, P. (1999, October 4). Communication in crisis. *Amusement Business*, p. 33.
37. Burger, C. (1975, July-August). How to meet the press. *Harvard Business Review*, pp. 62–70.
38. "Demystifying" the interview: Media, training teaches control tactics. (1999, January 4). *PR News*, p. 3.
39. Poe, Showtime for the CEO, p. 39.
40. Sigband, N. B. (1985, Winter). Coping successfully with the media. *Advanced Management Journal*.
41. Migdal, D. (1991, September). Managing the media. *Meetings and Conventions*, p. 49.

42. Sonnenfeld, S. (1994, July-August). Media policy: What media policy? *Harvard Business Review*, p. 28.

43. Penrose, J. M. (1986). The manager as spokesperson for the corporation: Handling the press. In L. DiGaetani (Ed.), *The handbook of executive communication* (p. 69). Homewood, IL: Dow Jones–Irwin.

44. Peterson, D. (1990, October). No comment? No way! Tips for successful press interviews, *Bank Marketing*, p. 69.

45. Levy, R. (1983, August). Crisis public relations. *Duns Business Month*, p. 50.

46. Talburt, How to be effective, p. 33.

47. *Ibid.*, p. 30.

48. James, G. (1999, December 1). Stupid CEO tricks. *MC Technology Marketing Intelligence*, p. 54.

49. Poe, Showtime for the CEO, p. 47.

50. Byrne, Mureika, & Newton, Working with the media: A guide for psychologists, p. 6.

51. *Ibid*, p. 6.

Part Five

Reporting Case Analyses

CHAPTER - 15

Analyzing a Case and
Writing a Case Report

The first fourteen chapters of this book have presented information designed to help you survive and succeed in your professional life once you complete your undergraduate studies or leave the graduate program. Chapters 15 and 16 will help you survive an important part of your advanced program: the case course. The chapters focus on the real-world importance of learning to quickly and accurately analyze problems and arrive at solutions via the case-analysis method. They also help you develop an understanding of how to use the case-analysis process to survive in upper-level and graduate program case courses.

The case method of teaching is popular in graduate business programs throughout the United States. Although schools of law have long used it and the Harvard Graduate School of Business made it a central instrument of its program in the 1920s, many upper-class undergraduates and MBAs find the case method to be a new and anxiety-producing experience. As students move into the analysis process, that anxiety is lessened when they can apply firsthand job experience and the wide array of managerial tools and techniques they learn in their business school classes.

In this chapter, you will learn the proper way to analyze and write a case report for any of the three different types of cases: the formal case, the case story, and the critical incident. To fully understand the case you are assigned, and to effectively analyze it requires mastering a different learning style, overcoming the fear of writing and speaking, and developing your own personal system of analysis.

If you are new to the case method, there is a proper four-step way to read a case. First, preview by looking at the basic outline of the case. Second, skim to identify the key issues. Third, read and reread the case to develop strategic notes. Fourth, scan the case again prior to the class discussion.

As you read a case, you should consider the four approaches to case analysis. You can use a **system** approach and examine the entire organization. Maybe a **behavioral** perspective, which examines people within the organization, would work better. Could a **decision-making** approach be employed? Would you be better off using a **strategy** process?

As you start your case analysis, you should use the six-step problem-solving model: (1) consider the relevant information; (2) define the problem; (3) analyze your facts and underlying assumptions; (4) list all possible solutions; (5) select a solution and prepare to defend it; and (6) determine the correct way to carry out the solution.

This chapter will show you how to communicate your findings by way of a written report. Three organizational formats for the written report are examined: the suspense mode, the news-first mode, and the strategic-issues format.

Understanding the Classroom Case Method of Learning

What Is the Case Method?

The case method applies the ancient Socratic technique of teaching people how to think and how to ask questions. It develops skills in diagnosing situations, defining problems, analyzing the sources and constraints of problems, developing alternative courses of action, and deciding on particular courses of action. The premise of the case method is that you are more likely to retain and use concepts learned through a guided discovery than you would through lectures and note-taking. Learning best occurs when we teach ourselves through our own struggle—especially when we are limited by facts, time, and personal differences.

Skill development distinguishes the case method from other teaching styles. Case courses pull together a broad array of the latest theories, concepts, or techniques of finance, accounting, management, or marketing. Cases present a general and useful way of thinking about, analyzing, and solving actual business problems. Many instructors use this approach as they analyze financial-, marketing-, and operations-type problems in a classroom setting, even though they may not employ formal cases. Along the way, you will discover your strengths and weaknesses in thinking and decision-making, and you will refine your ability to take risks when faced with unknown outcomes.

The case method helps you develop the skills necessary for becoming an effective manager.

Cases also present common pressures and constraints that managers daily confront in the organizational world. "Cases center around an array of partially ordered, ambiguous, seemingly contradictory, and reasonably unstructured facts, opinions, inferences, and bits of information, data, and incidents out of which you must provide order by selectively choosing which bits to use and which to ignore."[1]

Different Types of Cases

You will probably find at least three types of cases being used in your classes: the formal case, the case story, and the critical incident.

The Formal Case
A formal case describes a simulated or real-life situation faced by management. It may deal with a specific problem experienced by one company or by an industry as a whole. Problems and events in the simulated situation are not identified as good and bad; the cases often involve complex financial data and can cover 15 or 20 pages. A single-best solution may or may not exist, although you may apply some theories you have learned and arrive at what you consider to be the best answer.

The case might focus on issues such as: Should a franchise fast-food chain add a new food product? Should a company move from one location to another? Should a company diversify, merge, or acquire a competitor? What marketing strategy should a real estate firm use when the sales are down?

The Case Story

The second type of case presentation, the case story, differs from the formal case in several ways. It is usually written, much like a news story, as a chronological history of a decision made by management. The outcome and an analysis of the decision are presented and little excess information is given. In this form of case presentation, management's answer may not be the best answer.

This type of case can be two or three pages long and usually follows the form of a good magazine or newspaper article that has a one-or two-point thesis and lots of narrative to describe actions taken by individuals or the company. This type of case focuses on issues such as: marketing processes, sales methods, company events, product failures, and human behavior.

The Critical Incident

The third type of case gives little background information and usually presents a scenario in which the impact is greater on the interpersonal relationships than on the organization itself. While the formal case often involves long-term, strategic decisions, the critical incident asks, "What should we do now?" and involves more immediate issues.

The opening paragraph of this type of case often throws you into the middle of a dilemma. For instance, a critical-incident case might begin by saying, "A chemical manufacturing company has had an explosion at a local plant." The case, while short (two or three pages), gives many of the possible solutions that can be developed. This type of case was used as exercises in Chapter 13, on Crisis Management. They can also be developed quickly by managers and used in company training programs.

Overcoming the Difficulties of the Case Method

While the case method is often used in business schools, some people experience difficulties in learning a new style of both studying and responding. The following ideas should help you overcome any anxieties you may experience in learning by the case method.

Conquering a Different Learning Style

The case method is well suited for individuals who like to deal with real-life situations. It is not as well suited for people who find it difficult to operate in an environment of ambiguity and uncertainty or who must have a final or correct solution to a problem.

If you find the case method uncomfortable, strive to transfer from the traditional learning process of teacher-to-student, to a student-to-student mode. As your colleagues share their ideas and analyses, listen to them carefully and add up their thoughts in order to develop your own critical analytical abilities.

The case approach demands that you do extensive preparation outside the classroom. This preparation includes reading, note-taking, conducting library research on data not given in the case or textbook, and organizing your thoughts into writing.

Overcoming the Fear of Writing and Speaking

If you are timid about your ability to present your problem statements or solutions either on paper or orally, take heart: The remainder of this chapter will help you develop a method for reading and analyzing a case and then writing a case analysis. Chapter 16 will present ideas on how to effectively present an oral case analysis. Chapters 2 through 9 should be reviewed for ideas on writing improvement.

Developing Your Personal System of Case Analysis

As you read the following pages and begin the process of case analysis, work on developing your personal system of thinking and decision-making. You will soon be enjoying the new method of learning and will use it in all your classes. You will also find that learning how to think and analyze information in a systematic way will carry over into an effective personal analytical process that you will use long after you leave school.

Reading a Case Properly

Every manager desires solutions to his or her business problems; but solutions can be found only through properly analyzing the problem. With the case method, a proper analysis can be conducted only after careful reading. Your main objectives in reading should be, as efficiently as possible, to cover the material thoroughly and glean the most significant points. Proper analysis generally requires at least two readings of each case. If you are unfamiliar with the case-study method and anxious about how to properly analyze a case, you should probably count on several additional readings. Always assume that your instructor is an expert on each case and can respond to any questions or statements you may have.

There are four basic steps to properly reading a case: previewing, skimming, reading, and reviewing. The first three should be done prior to writing your analysis or making an oral presentation in class. The last, reviewing, should be done as you prepare to discuss the case in class. The early preparation pays off in allowing you to better remember the information and to feel confident of your ability to discuss it.

Previewing

Previewing a case serves the same purpose as previewing a magazine article or a book. Your goal is to learn as much about the case as possible before actually reading it. Look at the title and subtitle. Does this information tell you anything about the focus you should have as you read the case? Examine the title and name of the author. Has your professor, another academician, or a practitioner in the business community authored the case? Size up the case by looking at each page and familiarizing yourself with the main headings and subheadings. Review the organizational pattern around which the information has been developed.

Most cases are divided into two parts: text and supporting exhibits. As you look through the text, highlight key names of individuals and businesses and any proper nouns that will give you valuable information needed to understand the case. As you look at the illustrations and exhibits, carefully note their context and the relevance of their information. In the previewing stage resist the temptation to mark any items on the case. At this stage you are merely sizing up the case to determine how you are going to read and dissect it.

Skimming

Skimming involves previewing in greater detail. Avoid the desire to read each word and especially to underline or mark items in the text. As you skim, look for major ideas, issues, problems, and potential solutions—anything that will help you analyze the case. Your chief objective in the skimming phase is to determine the thesis or key problems or issues in the case. Often, this information is found at the beginning of the case. If it is not, search until you find it.

Reading

Now you are ready for your first reading of the case. Read at a comfortable pace and look for answers to questions, specific facts, or details that you will need in deciding solutions. Resist underlining on the first reading because it is time-consuming and generally indicates you do not understand the information. You can save underlining for a second reading. In this way, you are less likely to highlight unimportant information. If absolutely necessary, make brief, penciled notations to yourself. Later, erase the notes or make them bolder with ink. Some find the use of stick-on flags effective in marking observations made during the reading.

During your second reading, dissect and analyze the case from the standpoint of problems, major issues, and potential solutions. A case story or critical incident usually gives you only facts. Formal cases, on the other hand, contain extensive background material, but much of it provides no real clues to the solutions. While you may find the background information interesting, look for the key information that will benefit you in your analysis.

Reviewing

After you have absorbed the main points in the case, reviewing the highlights and your attached notes should be sufficient to refresh the information in your mind. Reviewing allows you to remember names and facts that are pertinent to the case. A quick scan of the highlights and your attached notes should be sufficient to refresh the information in your mind.

As you read the case, look for the common elements that everyone examines, but also look for unexpected items that might give you an edge on cracking the case. These items might be actions of individuals, methods of recording financial data, or ways inventories are ordered or recorded. If you make a habit of looking for the unexpected, you may find the most significant elements that will improve your analysis of the case. Work on understanding the flow of information from beginning to end, the technical nature of elements as they are described, what characters say and do, and any discrepancies in their actions. Constantly ask yourself, "What is not being said here?"

Be sure to look for issues your instructor may have mentioned when assigning the case. How does the case fit in the flow of the subject matter of any other cases discussed thus far in the class? What comments or inferences did your instructor make about the company or major characters? Was his or her attitude critical or praiseworthy? You may have to make inferences about your instructor at first, but as you work through cases during the semester, you will pick up on his or her philosophy. Finally, look at all aspects of the case. While you will probably separate marketing considerations from accounting, finance, or management issues as you read the case, pull them all together at the end. If you have done an adequate job of reading, the task of analyzing the case will be much simpler.

Case Analysis Approaches

Cases require you to examine issues from the as-is world of reality, rather than the should-be world of theory. Yet as you move through the analysis process you will join both worlds together and make to-be recommendations that will bring optimal closure to the case.

General Analytical Approaches

After reading the case, but before you begin your analysis, determine the specific analytical approach you want to take. The approach you select will be the result of the type of case you are encountering, and the support for your position that you will be able to offer. Four general approaches are often used.[2]

The Systems Approach

In this approach an organization is viewed as a system that converts inputs into outputs. As you examine the problems, opportunities, and actions, try to get information on all the components of the system and the way they interact with each other. This approach works with cases related to marketing, production, finance, and the aspects of management like planning, organizing, and controlling systems. In a manufacturing organization, for example, raw goods are purchased and converted into products that are sold to distributors and, ultimately, to consumers. Manufacturing, as a process, makes more sense from this systems view than from a view that sees it as merely an assembly-line procedure.

A good analysis would start by viewing an organization from the top down and seeking some of the following information: What business is it in? What markets does it serve? What technologies does it use? What is its financial condition? or What is the organizational structure?

The Behavioral Approach

This approach focuses on the behavior of people within an organization. Because an organization is an artificial entity, created by law, it cannot think or act. People in the organization are the real agents of behavioral action. A good analysis will examine behavior both internal and external to an organization. Managerial leadership is a typical focus of such an analysis. Individual traits, behavioral styles, values, and acts committed by responsible people within the organization yield valuable information.

The impact of social structures upon individuals is also something that fits the behavioral approach. Information about corporate culture, organizational change, human resource management practices, and even executive-selection procedures fit the behavioral approach.

The Decision Approach

This third approach makes use of one or more decision-making models or tools that help identify and evaluate alternatives. Table 15.1 gives an extensive list of these tools, along with formulas and descriptions of conclusions resulting from their use. Most of these ratios require financial and numerical data. While you may be familiar with these models, you need to develop a competency in using them quickly to identify and evaluate alternatives. As Rand suggests, you need to be able

Table 15.1	Decision-Making Tools	
Ratio	**Calculated**	**Measures**
Profitability Ratios		
1. Gross profit margin	Sales − Cost of goods sold ÷ Sales	The total margin available to cover operating expenses and to yield a profit.
2. Net profit margin, or Net return on sales	Profits after taxes ÷ Sales	Shows after-tax profits per dollar of sales.
3. Operating profit margin, or Return on sales	Profits before taxes and before interest ÷ Sales	The firm's profitability from current operations.
4. Return on total assets	Profits after taxes ÷ Total assets, or Profits after taxes ÷ Total assets	Net return on total investment of the company or the return on both creditor's and shareholder's investments.
5. Return on stockholder's equity, or Return on net worth	Profits after taxes ÷ Total Stockholder's equity	Rate of return on stockholder's investment in firm.
6. Return on common equity	Profits after taxes − Preferred stock dividends ÷ Total stockholder's equity − Par value of preferred stock	The net return to common stockholders on the investment.
7. Earnings per share	Profits after taxes − Preferred stock dividends ÷ Number of shares of common stock outstanding	Stockholder earnings per share of common stock.
Liquidity Ratios		
1. Current ratio	Current assets ÷ Current liabilities	Firm's ability to pay its current financial liabilities.
2. Quick ratio, or Acid-test ratio	Current assets − Inventory ÷ Current liabilities	Firm's ability to pay short-term obligations without relying on the sale of its inventories.
3. Inventory to net working capital	Inventory ÷ Current assets − Current liabilities	Extent of firm's working capital invested in inventory.

continued

Ratio	Calculated	Measures
Leverage Ratios		
1. Debt-to-assets ratio	Total debt ÷ Total assets	Extent to which total borrowed funds are used as a percentage of assets.
2. Debt-to-equity ratio	Total debt ÷ Total stockholders' equity	A measure of borrowed funds versus funds provided by shareholders.
3. Long-term debt-to-equity ratio	Long-term debt ÷ Total stockholder's equity	The balance between firm's debt and equity.
4. Times-interest-earned, or Coverage ratio	Profits before interest and taxes ÷ Total interest charges	The company's ability to pay all interest payments.
5. Fixed-charge coverage	Profits before taxes and interest + Lease obligations ÷ Total interest charges + Lease obligations	Firm's ability to meet all fixed-charge obligations.
Activity Ratios		
1. Inventory turnover	Sales ÷ Inventory of finished goods	Indication of firm's excessive or inadequate inventory.
2. Fixed assets turnover	Sales ÷ Fixed assets	The sales productivity and utilization of firm's plant and equipment.
3. Total assets turnover	Sales ÷ Total assets	The firm's effectiveness in using total assets.
4. Accounts receivable turnover	Annual credit sales ÷ Accounts receivable	The average length of time to collect credit sales.
5. Average collection period	Accounts receivable ÷ Average daily sales	Average length of time firm waits to receive payment after a sale.
Shareholder's Return Ratios		
1. Dividend yield on common stock	Annual dividends per share ÷ Current market price per share	Owner's return in form of dividends.
2. Price-earnings ratio (PE)	Current market price per share ÷ After-tax earnings per share	The market perception of a firm. Faster-growing firms have higher PE than slower-growing or more risky firms.
3. Dividend payout ratio	Annual dividends per share ÷ After-tax earnings per share	The percentage of profits paid out as dividends.
4. Cash flow per share	After-tax profits + Depreciation ÷ Number of common shares outstanding	Total cash, after expenses, available for firm's use.

Source: Adapted from *Appendix II: Financial Analysis in Case Studies.* (n.d.) (pp. 1–3). Retrieved March 26, 2002, from **http://www.swcollege.com/management/hitt/hitt_student/appendix_2.html**.

to answer questions like: "How are these alternatives related? What events must occur before an alternative can be realized? Are certain events dependent on other events occurring? What is the likelihood they will occur? What is the net cash flow in contribution dollars of a given alternative adjusted for the probability it will occur? Which costs are relevant or irrelevant? Which costs are variable versus fixed? What then is the cash break-even? What will the pro forma P&L and Balance Sheet look like if we follow this alternative?" Asking the right questions is critical.[3]

The Strategy Approach

This final approach is most often used with longer, formal cases and typically in business school policy courses. The learning objective of such courses is to help managers develop strategic thinking abilities, especially as they prepare business and marketing plans. Using the strategy approach, a manager analyzes a strategic fit between the goals and objectives of an organization, the general external environment, the specific internal environment of the organization, and the resources needed to carry out the described strategy.

Such an environmental approach is a good place to ask questions like:

- What do we know and not know about this organization?
- What are the objectives?
- What do the customers want?
- How can services be improved?

Such questions can be asked about a specific department, an entire company, or even an industry.

From the questions come answers regarding the organization's present and future *internal environmental strengths and weaknesses,* and *external environmental opportunities and threats.* The acronym SWOT is used to refer to this form of analysis. SWOT is an analytical tool that is often referred to as a "situational analysis" and an "environmental scan."

To identify internal strengths and weaknesses you can assess resources (inputs), present strategy (process), and performance (outputs). Usually your case will have information on inputs such as salaries, supplier, the physical plant, and full-time equivalent personnel. Unfortunately, cases often do not give a clear idea of the organization's philosophy, core values, distinctive competencies, and culture.

You conduct a SWOT analysis by examining each of the parts. *Strengths* are advantages like resources, market position, new products, professional staff, unique and creative aspects, and leadership expertise, upon which the organization can capitalize. Organizations always desire to build upon their strengths. *Weaknesses* are disadvantages that can hinder performance and goal achievement. For an organization it is often difficult to honestly identify weaknesses. At the same time strengths are often exaggerated. In reality strengths and weaknesses are often similar and can mirror one another. An organization's greatest strength can also be its greatest weakness. In the Valdez accident, Exxon's safety record turned out to be a weakness.

Opportunities are developments in an organization's external environment that focus on the future. They are advantages that the organization should use wisely. Items that often surface here are: technology, experienced personnel who can be hired, or new manufacturing techniques that can be adopted. *Threats* are future events or happenings that can prevent success and cause difficulty. A good list here will allow you to minimize danger. Sometimes threats appear to be current weaknesses projected into the future, such as competition, political action groups, or government regulations. Threats can be met and turned into opportunities.

Table 15.2 presents a checklist of case ideas that you can look for as you conduct a SWOT analysis. Keep in mind that this list is generic in nature and each item does not apply to every organization. Also remember that "what is a strength/ opportunity for one company might be a weakness/threat for another."[4]

Now that you have a better understanding of the case method, realize the importance of a proper reading process, and recognize several case analysis approaches, the job of analyzing a case will be easier.

Table 15.2 **SWOT Analysis**

Internal Assessment	External Assessment
Major Strengths	*Major Strengths*
• skilled workforce	• largest U.S. corporation
• $40-billion capital investment	• market position
• employee layoffs	• popular image
• market position	
• employee comfort	
Major Weaknesses	*Major Weaknesses*
• too many employees	• outdated facilities
• low sales	• distance from suppliers
• production cutbacks	
Major Opportunities	*Major Opportunities*
• state-of-art plant	• move closer to suppliers
• just-in-time inventory	• Poletown site
• reduce jobs	
• tax incentive	
Major Threats	*Major Threats*
• loss of creative employees	• government regulations
• difficulty in learning new tasks	• foreign competition
• strikes	• pressure from Detroit
• poor relationship with unions	• increased unemployment
	• tarnished image
	• displacement of residents
	• public paying for tax incentives

Applying the Six-Step Case Analysis Process

Before you can write a case report, you must first analyze the case. Proper case analysis requires good decision-making skills, which usually follow a six-step process. Most of the cases in your management, marketing, finance, policy, and accounting courses will follow this six-step process:

Step 1. Consider the relevant information.
Step 2. Define the case problem and write a problem statement.
Step 3. Analyze the facts and underlying assumptions.
Step 4. List possible alternative solutions.
Step 5. Select a solution and prepare to defend it.
Step 6. Decide how to carry out the solution.

Before you attempt an analysis of a "formal" case, like those that you will find in many of your classes, we encourage you to use the following primer. The EK&G case story is a short, fictitious, even humorous case. But it will allow you to easily generate answers to the six steps above. Read it and write your own answers to each of the six steps.

EK&G Case[5]

Founded in 1980 as a medical technology firm, EK&G Products spent its early years searching for "the right product" to manufacture. The two owners, Fred Eghart and Irving Kleptow, were engineers from the medical technology field who believed that starting up their own firm could eventually fill a void in the market left by the larger manufacturers.

In early 1982 the Pulsomatic was developed and tested on a limited basis. The Pulsomatic was a small box affixed to a stand, much like a gumball machine. After inserting a quarter in the machine, a customer would lace his thumb in a small hole in the front of the unit. In 45 seconds, a small slip of paper would come out that would indicate the customer's pulse rate and also tell a fortune.

Eghart and Kleptow believed that a large market existed for this product. Supermarkets, restaurants, bars, and nursing homes would be ideal spots for the Pulsomatic. A marketing manager could be used to help distribute the product.

As production began, the costs of the Pulsomatic began to rise. Initial cost estimates had been around $175 per unit. But the fortune-telling logic unit (FTLU) was a specialty item that soon began to rise in price. Because the only manufacturers of FTLUs were in China, there was no way to insulate against price rises or currency fluctuations.

As the manufacturing costs exceeded $250 per unit, Eghart and Kleptow began to wonder if sufficient quantities of the unit could be produced in order to achieve economies in production. Production estimates showed that average costs per unit could be reduced to $200 if more than 1,000 units were produced each year. Because orders of the product totaled 1,000 after three months of marketing, it became apparent that the idea of hiring a marketing manager was well founded.

After screening a number of qualified MBA graduates, Eghart and Kleptow hired Hal Sigoin. Mr. Sigoin promptly increased the number of orders to 2,500 and production resumed.

Delivery began in June 1985, with ten units going out. The revenues from sales of the machine were split as follows: 25 percent to the business where each machine was located, and 75 percent to EK&G. Original estimates showed that revenues would average $150 per machine per month. This would mean that EK&G would recoup its costs in about two and one-half to three months. Over that same time, the host business would receive revenues of more than $100.

On the evening of August 1, 1985, Eghart and Kleptow poured champagne at their victory celebration. It looked as if the product would be a success, and they wanted to share this success with their staff of five dedicated employees.

To complete your analysis of this case, develop answers to steps 1 through 6. After that, check your answers to the ones found in Figure 15A.1 in the appendix at the end of the chapter.

Now we will look at a more "formal" case. This case typifies many formal cases that you will find in your classes. Assume that you are in a decision-making position at General Motors. What would you encourage the company to do, and why?

The New GM Assembly Plant[6]

In early 1980, General Motors (GM) was the largest industrial corporation in the United States. Their sales from the previous year were $66 million and they had over 850,000 employees. But GM, along with the other automakers, faced trouble. Trends toward tighter government regulations and foreign auto competition had produced low sales, production cutbacks, and widespread layoffs. GM's change strategy for staying competitive involved a $40-billion five-year capital investment program that would begin in that same year.

One phase of the program required that two existing Detroit manufacturing facilities, Cadillac Assembly and Fisher Body Fleetwood Plant, would be demolished and one state-of-the-art facility be constructed. GM did not care where the new plant was built (they were examining sites in both Detroit and in Midwestern states within the Sunbelt). The new plant had several needs, however. It had to be close to suppliers to utilize the new just-in-time inventory methods, it required about 500 acres to allow for a new robotics system, and it had to be completed by mid-1981. GM estimated the cost of constructing the facility would be at $500 million.

Immediately Detroit Mayor Coleman Young started applying pressure for GM to remain in the greater Detroit area. Detroit had experienced many years of economic difficulties. Large firms had moved many to the suburbs and others out of the state. Unemployment at the time was 18 percent and the closing of the two plants would create a loss of 6,000 auto assembly jobs, and thousands of other jobs in design, manufacturing, and sales. Because of business closings the structures in the inner city were decaying. The tax burden was high and the base was low. The inner city was 63 percent minority and high in elderly, disadvantaged, and poor.

As GM examined the Detroit area only one site became a possibility. There were 300 acres in Poletown and an adjoining 165 acres in Hamtramck. The latter property presented no acquisition problems; Poletown was another story. The resident base consisted of first- and second-generation Polish descendants, mostly elderly and retired. They considered their homes to be their most valued asset.

General Motors agreed to the site in concept but threw the resident problem back to the city of Detroit because it was applying pressure on GM to remain in the area. The Detroit City Council, without consulting the Poletown residents, decided to use its power of eminent domain. When residents learned of the plot they formed the Poletown Neighborhood Council that immediately brought a lawsuit against the city of Detroit. They asserted that the eminent domain legislation was designed for public usage. They argued that the new plant constituted "private use" and not public. Further, the use of the law in such a way violated the Michigan State Constitution and destroyed both the cultural and social environment of a community. The court voted 5–2 against Poletown.

While the suit cleared the way for General Motors, it left other problems. Poletown had 3,438 persons that would be displaced, and 1,176 homes that would be demolished. GM estimated the following costs: $62 million to the Poletown residents for their property, $28 million for their relocation, $35 million for the home demolition, and $82 million for site preparation. The total cost would be $207 million.

Knowing that the Sunbelt states had offered large tax incentives, the City of Detroit made its proposal. It would find a way to cover the $207 million and would give a 50-percent tax abatement for 12 years, or $13.35 million per year. When capitalized at 12-percent interest that would amount to $83 million. Altogether Detroit's offer would be the best.

The GM case is a short financial and plant-location case story. The case analysis approaches used as examples for this case story combine the decision and strategy approaches. We will now work through the case by using the six-step analysis process.

Analyzing the GM Case

You have read the case and made an initial determination of the analytical approaches that you could possibly use. Now you should enter the decision-making process. Most of the cases in your management, marketing, finance, policy, and accounting courses will follow this six-step process.

Step 1: Consider the Relevant Information

Your first task is to gain a familiarity with the basic details of the case. As you sort these out recognize the degree of certainty (facts) and uncertainty (inferences) that exist. You will seek to determine the who, what, when, where, and how, or general background facts in the case. In detail identify the people, organizations, activities, and contexts of the situation.[7]

What can you learn about the *company*?

- What business is it in?
- What are its products or services?
- What are its characteristics?
- What is its strategy? Goals?
- What is its growth history?
- How is it structured?
- Does it have any critical systems or policies?

What can you learn about the *industry* or *market*?

- Who are the competitors?
- What is the basis of competition?
- Who are the major players?
- What barriers to entry exist?
- What are the market trends?
- What is the company's market share?

What can you learn about the *players*?

- Describe the major players both internal and external to the company.
- What are their characteristics and style?
- Who has to take action? What action?
- Who is influencing the decision maker?
- What pressures are the players under?
- What is the financial position of each principal? (assets and liabilities)

What can you learn about the *products* or *services*?

- What are the products and services?
- What are the product life cycles?

- Are there competitive advantages or risks?
- Are there technological advantages or risks?
- What major factors enhance and threaten distribution or positioning?
- What impact does the sales force exert?

As you remember these basic facts move to condense your information into a process that will guide your analysis. Consider the following four areas:

Environmental and Industry Analysis. An organization must determine what effect marketing dynamics, competitive factors, foreign competition, government regulations, product portfolio, and so forth will have on it. These factors should be stated in terms that affect the strategic options available to the firm.

Organizational Analysis. Organizational factors are crucial in determining an organization's ability to carry out proposed strategies and achieve effective performance. Approaches to alternative organization structures and functional integration are often key determinants of success. The effect of mergers on the culture and leadership of an organization are also important considerations.

Internal Operations. Operations form the basis for carrying out strategies that have been formulated. Greater emphasis is placed on the organization's ability to achieve high quality, high performance, and strategic control. Issues such as robotics, just-in-time manufacturing, computer applications, motivation, culture, and human resource management increasingly determine the competitive advantage of an organization.

Resources. Resources are the lifeblood of an organization. Many consider investments, capacity, facilities, cash flow, return on investments (ROI), and the budgeting of strategic funds to be the bottom line of strategy formulation. Financial analysis, revenue forecasts, and resource allocation, especially for R&D, are important aspects of analyzing cases to determine feasible strategies.

Scan the case again to determine the significant facts and events. List these as statements. After you finish, review your list and outline the facts and events. In the GM case, several significant items can be listed.

1. GM was the largest industrial corporation in the United States, and was profitable until 1980.
2. GM, like the other auto manufacturers, faced pressures from increased government regulations and foreign competition.
3. A capital campaign called for two existing plants in the Detroit area to be demolished and a new plant built either in Detroit or another location.
4. The new plant would be designed around state-of-the-art techniques.
5. The city of Detroit was in economic difficulty, it did not want to lose the GM plant, and it applied pressure to GM to rebuild in the city.
6. One site in the greater Detroit area suited GM. Part of the site consisted of mostly retired and elderly Polish residents.
7. While the residents did not want to move, Detroit gave GM the power to receive the Poletown land through eminent domain.

8. While the cost of purchasing and preparing the Poletown property was more expensive than purchasing property in a Sunbelt location, the city of Detroit offered to cover the cost, and through tax incentives would even contribute more to GM than all the other communities.

Step 2: Define the Case Problem and Write a Problem Statement

The philosopher John Dewey once stated that a problem well defined is half solved. Defining a problem is not simple, but once done, the definition logically leads the person doing an analysis toward the possible solutions.

List the various problems, and symptoms of the problems, that you have identified. What are the facts for each? Is the problem an individual, group, or situation? For instance, does a gap exist between actual performance and desired performance? For whom is it a problem? Why? Are standards being violated? What is the ideal outcome that is desired?

Problems are barriers that threaten to block an organization or person from achieving important goals. The problems could be a competitor introducing a new product or operational procedure. It could be a downturn in the economy, new legal steps to make markets more competitive, or consumer concerns within the social environment.

As you glean problems from the case, separate them as items to solve—but avoid stating problems in such a general way as:

- The company owner has weak management experience.
- The product promotion plan is inadequate.
- The company has a bad credit history.

Such statements blur the case information, make understanding difficult, and create barriers to finding solutions. It is hard to immediately know how to solve a bad credit history. Instead, phrase the problem as a descriptive statement:

- The company owner has never interviewed or hired a sales manager; yet she must immediately replace the current sales manager who abruptly resigned.
- The schedule for the product promotion plan cannot be accomplished in one fiscal quarter because the advertising material will take longer to produce and the plan is inadequately funded.
- Citicorp has refused to extend further credit to the firm until it pays the outstanding loan balance of $100,000 within the 30-day grace period.

A good problem statement should be descriptive, zeroing in on the key issue that must be addressed. It should not rehearse the case in detail. Don't confuse symptoms with causes. Differentiate between fact and inference. Also, be sure that you avoid suggesting a solution at this point.

Start the GM case by listing the different problems or issues that you observe. Next, narrow the issues into a written problem statement. If you find that the statement is too vague as you proceed with the analysis, rewrite it.

Four significant problems are apparent in the GM case:

1. There is pressure from Detroit and the GM stakeholders (union, employees) to remain in the area.

2. Rebuilding in the Detroit area will initially be more costly than in going to the Sunbelt, although the city and other groups will find a way to cover all of those costs.

3. There will be a high toll in human pain and the loss of ethnic identity associated with having to use the eminent domain law to remove the Poletown residents.

4. GM and Detroit may sustain a tarnished image because of treatment of Poletown residents.

After narrowing these issues, we recognize that the most significant problems in the GM case are pressure from Detroit and the local stakeholders to build on the Poletown site, and the pain and harm to be imposed on the Poletown residents. In fact, a dilemma is present because GM is being pressured from both sides. Whatever its decision, one side will be unhappy.

Step 3: Analyze the Facts and Underlying Assumptions

At this point you must decide which theories will be most useful. Choose the analysis methods that are most appropriate to the problem you identified. Run your numbers and analyze the results.

Consider the underlying assumptions in the case. Are your assumptions reasonable and realistic? Do your assumptions relate to decisions the company or key decision makers in the case are making as a result of their control? Or, are the decisions related to uncertainty factors—factors that the company or managers do not control? Can you support the assumptions with information and facts found in the case? Make sure you distinguish among facts, inferences, and opinions. Discuss stakeholder assumptions.

In searching for assumptions, also distinguish between causes and effects, which are often related. For example, a retail organization is losing money (effect). One reason (cause) is that customers are no longer buying the company's product (effect). Careful examination shows that the product is of poor quality (cause). Yet the poor quality of the product (effect) is a direct result of management not spending research development dollars on updating the product (cause). Further searching shows that top management made a decision several months earlier to cut the R&D budget (effect) because of cost-cutting measures (cause).

What you will end up with at this point are the key criteria you will use to design and solve the case problem. What are the constraints that are being faced? At the very minimum a solution must be affordable, legal, and ethical. Are there other constraints that become apparent in your analysis? The final act in this step is listing any key criteria that you will use in making your recommendation.

In examining the GM case we can pull out several assumptions:

1. GM assumes no other site is available around Detroit.

2. Detroit assumes that keeping GM is critical to its economic well-being.

3. Detroit assumes current GM employees would be used in the new plant. GM may make the same assumption, but in reality new employees might be easier to train in new technologies.

4. Detroit assumes the tax dollars it will lose from the tax incentive package will be recouped from GM personnel and their spending.

5. GM and Detroit assume from the start that the Poletown residents are against selling their homes. In reality they may be for the idea if they were allowed to participate in the decision-making process.

6. Detroit and GM assume that the best problem-solving method in this case is the cost-benefit analysis.

It is evident that the list of assumptions is by no means exhaustive. Instead, it points to a seemingly endless string of questions that can be developed from a simple case. If other subject matters were considered, such as accounting, finance, and management, the list would grow even longer. Remember as you are analyzing material to list it in a readily accessible form. Availability facilitates your writing of an analysis.

At this point you can also do a SWOT analysis of the case. Go back to Table 15.2 on page 415 and review the parts.

Step 4: List Possible Alternative Solutions

For every problem there are at least three solutions, one of which is to do nothing. This approach, like recommending additional research, is usually not an acceptable solution. Step 4 is your opportunity to be creative and to think "outside the box." Do not be limited to minimal alternatives, which seem to easily arise from the facts of the case. Alternative solutions for GM are:

1. It can agree to build its new plant on the Poletown site.
2. It can conduct a more extensive survey of the Detroit area to see if a comparable or more suitable site exists.
3. It can allow the Poletown residents to have an active voice in the decision-making process.
4. It can put its human and social responsibilities ahead of its profit-maximization responsibilities. (Does it have a social responsibility to create jobs in Detroit? Does it have a social responsibility not to dislocate Poletown residents? How do these two responsibilities conflict?)
5. GM can move to a Sunbelt location.

As you identify solutions, consider the criteria that must be met in order to accomplish each solution. List advantages and disadvantages to each. Do not predetermine the best solution at this point; it may cause you to ignore important contradictory information and will detract from your analysis. Also consider the pros and cons of each alternative solution. Weighing these against each other often logically guides you to the best solution. Other critical questions to ask and answer could be:

- How do the alternatives fit the company goals?
- Can the behavior of individuals be changed?
- Are there major constraints on elements like time, money, or traditions?
- Do available resources exist?
- Do the decision makers have real sources of power to make necessary changes?
- Should others be involved in the solution (solving and implementation)?

Step 5: Select a Solution and Prepare to Defend It

After analyzing the case in depth, you should be able to select the best solution. If you have analyzed the case carefully, you should know the likelihood of being able to achieve the selected option and what will be needed for implementation. The recommendations of your solution should always address the problems that you isolated in Step 2.

> **Problem:** The company owner has a responsibility to hire the best sales manager.

> **Recommendation:** Ms. Bhappu would be wise to promote the current brand manager, Shandra Johannson, into the sales manager position. Shandra understands the promotion plan for all brands, is well liked, and has the respect of everyone in the marketing department, and her brand has been the top revenue producer for the past five years.[8]

In stating your solution show how the solution will correct the problem. The points and recommendations should be made short and concise. Use the logic and reasoning from the case analysis to defend your selection. You may desire to list the advantages and disadvantages, and costs and benefits, of your solution. In many instances your various alternatives will build one upon another until one is obviously better than all the others. The financial analysis that you rendered often helps this occur. Your solution should clearly address the critical aspect of the case problem. Consider the probability of success, the many risks, and what will happen if failure should occur.

As you examined the GM case, you probably arrived at your preferred solution. You may have felt the best solution was to agree to build the new plant on the Poletown site. You can state that solution in the following way:

> I recommend that GM build the new plant in the Detroit area. Because the total financial allowances Detroit proposes will equal or exceed those of any other location, Detroit makes economic sense. Because GM feels a responsible obligation to the city of Detroit and the GM employees, that obligation would also be covered. The process of allowing the land to be taken by eminent domain, without involving the Poletown people in the deliberations, will create a truly bad image problem. GM would be smart to have the Poletown Neighborhood Council participate in the problem-solving process.

Step 6: Decide How to Carry Out the Solution

At this stage you will develop an action plan for carrying out the solution. Your plan should spell out the specific steps required, along with performance benchmarks. What are the essential changes that are needed? Who will be the change agent? Does he or she have the power, skills, and knowledge to carry out the solution? What is the time element? What are the needed resources? Who will need to be involved? What will be the impact on the organizational structure? Finally, what contingency plan will need to be in place if success does not occur?

A recommendation for an "action plan solution" for the GM case could be: "Because the plant needs to be built by mid-1981, GM should move as quickly as possible to contact the Poletown Neighborhood Council, get them involved in the problem-solving process, and determine the overall impact the new plant will have on GM, GM employees, the city of Detroit, and the Poletown residents."

After completing the six steps of case analysis, you are ready to communicate your findings. In most advanced business programs, three settings exist: written case analysis, class discussion, and group presentation. We will examine only the first setting in this chapter; Chapter 16 covers the latter two. In almost every instance, your instructor will determine which method you and your classmates will follow.

The Written Report

While there is no one correct way to prepare a written case analysis, most include certain specific items and follow one of a few generally accepted formats. The majority of your study time will probably be devoted to analyzing the case, but leave sufficient time to prepare the written report. When you are under a time constraint, it is tempting to consider the completion of your analysis as the end of your assignment. However, your career potential is based on the written report, so you should devote ample time to writing and developing your ideas. This section presents four different formats for a written case analysis. (At this point you may find it helpful to review the overall writing sequence discussed in Chapters 4, 9, and 10. The material on the inductive and deductive writing styles is especially important. Many of the ideas and techniques discussed there can apply here.)

Even though you will have spent many hours analyzing the case, your instructor will usually spend only 20 to 30 minutes grading each written report. It is therefore important that you write clearly enough so that he or she can understand the main points that you want to communicate. You may be tempted to write your report in the same six-step process that you used for analysis. However, your instructor already knows the case, and does not wish to read a restatement of the facts, although he or she may want to see your logic. Organize your material in a succinct and direct manner. There are three schools of thought on the written analysis format: the suspense format, the news-first format, and the strategic-issues format. Ask your instructor which he or she prefers.

The Suspense Format

The suspense, or inductive, format report follows a three-step progression: (1) identify the strategic issues and problems, (2) analyze and evaluate the possible solutions to these issues, and (3) make recommendations. Kerin and Peterson encourage this approach. They believe that:

> The first heading should contain a focused paragraph that defines the problem and specifies the constraints and options available to the organization. Material under the second heading should provide a carefully developed assessment of the industry, market and buyer behavior, the organization, and the alternative courses of action. *Analysis and evaluation should represent the bulk of the written report.* This section should not contain a restatement of case information. It should contain an assessment of the facts, quantitative data, and management views. The last heading should contain a set of recommendations. These recommenda-

tions should be documented from the previous section and should be *operational* given the case situation. By all means, commit to a decision![9]

You can refer to Chapter 9, on report-writing, to review the inductive writing style.

The News-First Format

In the news-first, or deductive format, you: (1) present your recommended solution first, (2) support your recommendation, (3) list the other alternatives and why you did not select them, and (4) provide evidence supporting your observation and recommendations.

The Strategic-Issues Format

Use the strategic-issues format in writing reports on strategy cases. The length of such a report is short, normally one to two pages. To produce such a report in an adequate manner requires careful and thorough analysis. In this written format, you cite: (1) the crucial strategic issues, (2) the assumptions you made about those issues, (3) the strategies you recommend for dealing with the issues, (4) the justification for your recommendations, (5) the plan of action for implementation, and (6) the expected results.

Another approach follows the example used in Chapter 8, "Proposal Writing." Figure 8.2 presents a brief proposal that provides an excellent format for a case analysis: Summary, The Current Situation, The Problem, The Analysis, and The Solution. Many students have found that format to be very helpful.

Exhibits and Typing

Many written reports use case exhibits. Remember that the data in any exhibit should help to support the positions you have taken in your text. If your exhibitions are short, place them strategically in your text to help explain your conclusions. Otherwise, present long exhibits in an appendix at the end of your report. Designate each exhibit by a clear title that describes its purpose; the reader should be able to understand the material contained in the exhibit without referring back to the text. Whenever you refer to an exhibit in the case, make sure that you give an explanation for the exhibit.

Your final typed report should follow the rules of good writing that are discussed in this text. To give you an idea of what a sample written report looks like, we include a case, "Accounting Procedures at Champion Marketing," and a student's written report of the case in Appendices A and B, respectively, on pages 457–460 and 461–464 at the end of the book. The case is a critical incident, and the analysis follows the suspense format. You should read and analyze the case in Appendix A, following the guidelines provided in this chapter, before reading the student analysis in Appendix B.

Some Do's and Don'ts for Case Preparation

Do's of Case Analysis

1. Accept the fact that much of the material in the case is useless to your investigation. This is a valuable lesson. As a future manager, you must learn to slice through the fluff and make decisions based on relevant information.

2. Realize that different professors, in different classes and disciplines, want you to conduct different types of analyses. Just as there is no one managerial style that is perfect for all, there is no one case analysis style. Learn early in the class to identify personality and behavioral characteristics of your professors that will indicate how they want the cases analyzed. Often, the professor gives his or her pet analysis outline at the introduction to the course. Be looking for it.

3. Follow a logical, clear, and consistent path through the case analysis. The conclusion should always flow out of your recommendations, and your recommendations should clearly be supported by your analysis. If this does not occur, your problem statement may be faulty.

4. Recognize the difference between facts and inferences or suppositions. Much case material is clearly presented, but you are often required to make subjective interpretations. Learn to distinguish clearly between the two and refer to inferences as such in your analysis. The more suppositions you make, the weaker your analysis becomes; strive to base your analysis on facts whenever possible.

5. Take a stand in your analysis and support it. Many students try to hedge and take a "let's wait and see what others will say" approach. Instructors recognize this and your peers see it. Learn to trust your judgment, take a stand, and build the necessary support for it. Recognize also that your peers will constantly take shots at your stance. The stronger and better-supported your stand, the better you will look.

6. Recognize that a good written product really is produced in the rewriting. Give yourself time to reread and edit your analysis, even a second and third time.

Don'ts of Case Analysis

1. Don't expect a right conclusion to be available following the study of a case. Many case instructors will not give the correct answer even if they know it. Case information is often based on a specific event or a short period of time. Often, the actual businesses or individuals within the case never know what would have really happened if an alternative decision were made and followed. Your job is to learn to analyze problems and arrive at good solutions.

2. Don't tell the instructor that you need more information before arriving at a decision. Lack of information is common to all cases. Working with incomplete information is good practice because, as a manager, you often will not have all the needed information. Since gathering all the information takes time, and managers must make quick decisions, learn to make proper assumptions based on the information that is available.

3. Don't expect cases to cover a single discipline or to lend themselves to a solution by a given theory or concept. Situations are complicated, and even though you may be in a marketing position, the financial, managerial, and strategic-planning areas of the business can impact your work. The broad view is especially true in policy courses, where an objective is to relate material you have covered to a variety of courses.

4. Don't expect your instructor to give you clear instructions on what he or she expects from your analysis. One professor at a major university tells his students on the first assigned analysis, "I cannot tell you what an excellent analysis will look like, but I will know it when I see it." Although everyone has the same case, the professor expects a multitude of different methods from students as they seek a solution. Most instructors will encourage you to develop your best analysis by not telling you precisely what they want.

5. Don't be so short-sighted that you decide on a conclusion early in the analysis and become locked into that conclusion. The person who develops several solutions will have the advantage and will learn more. This person wisely selects a hypothesis and works through to the conclusion.

6. Don't feel that you have to solve all the problems in the case. This is impossible in case studies. Instead, confront only the major problems. Develop alternative solutions to one problem at a time and then move on to other problems. Businesses have hundreds of minor problems; it is the major ones that are life threatening. Practice quickly identifying the major problems and finding solutions for them.

Summary

The case method is a common style of teaching in advanced business programs. The learning potential of this approach has been demonstrated numerous times. If you learn an effective procedure for analyzing a case and writing an effective report, you will be rewarded both in the classroom and later in your career.

In this chapter, we examined the correct way to analyze a case and write a case report. There are three different types of cases: the formal case, the case story, and the critical incident. There is a proper way to read a case, too. The first step is to preview by looking at the basic outline of the case. The second stage is skimming, where you identify the key issues. The third stage is to read and reread the case, making strategic notes to yourself. The fourth stage is scanning prior to class discussion. Proper reading of a case helps you in the case analysis process.

There are four case analysis approaches. First, consider the organization as a system. Second, look at people within the organization and approach the analysis from a behavioral perspective. Third, use a decision-making approach by employing theories or models to help you arrive at decisions about the information in the case. Fourth, use the strategy approach by conducting a SWOT analysis in light of the organization's goals and objectives. You might also consider combining approaches.

As you analyze the case, follow six important steps: (1) consider the relevant information, (2) define the case problem, (3) analyze the facts and underlying assumptions, (4) list possible solutions to the problem, (5) select a solution and prepare to defend it, and (6) decide how to implement the solution.

Communicate your results in one of three ways: through a written report, class discussion, or group presentation. In this chapter, we concentrated on the written report. While there is no one correct way to prepare a report, three specific organizational formats were given. The first style is the suspense or inductive mode, which identifies the problem first, analyzes and evaluates possible solutions, and makes the recommendation. The second style is the news-first, or deductive mode. Here you present your recommendation first, support why you chose one solution over another, list the alternatives you did not select and the reasons for not choosing them, and finally, give evidence that supports your observation and recommendations. The third style is the strategic-issues format, which summarizes the key points in a one- or two-page memo format.

Discussion Questions

1. What types of cases have you encountered in your academic life? As you read this chapter you probably thought about the case stories and critical incidents you have read in the textbooks for other courses, and any formal cases required in other classes. How do you differentiate among the three types, and how do you prepare differently for studying and discussing them?

2. For many people the use of formal cases in the classroom is an anxiety-producing experience. Describe your level of anxiety with the use of formal cases, and how you have developed a personal system to use in analyzing cases. If you have never before participated in a formal case analysis and discussion, hypothesize how you believe you will feel and deal with it.

3. On the opening day of your business school program one of your instructors was extolling the benefits of the case study method. Since then you have grown confused on the real value of such a classroom learning experience. Your instructor senses this and gives a short assignment designed to show the class how many executives perceive the process as being truly valuable.

Your Assignment: Your instructor assigns the following article found in InfoTrac: "A Crash Course for CEOs: Harvard Business School Tailors a Program to Entrepreneurs," by Lawrence Curran. The article is taken from *Electronics*, June 1991, vol. 64, no. 6, pp. 13–16, Article A10923240.

Read the article and outline several practical benefits that executives at the Harvard Business School have gained from using the case study approach. Develop five or six talking points from the outline. Take your findings to class where they will be discussed.

4. Select a major headline-making event in the business community. A recent crisis situation would be ideal. Collect several newspaper, magazine, radio, television, and Internet stories about the event. Using the four case-analysis approaches describe how the event can be discussed differently using each approach.

5. A SWOT analysis is regularly used when considering strategic plans. Briefly apply it to your own personal career path and describe your strengths and weaknesses, and the external opportunities and threats that you will face when looking for a job.

6. The six-step process presented for analyzing cases is typical to standard decision-making and problem-solving models. Consider each step of the process and describe how you might apply this approach to analyzing problem issues and events in your business classes.

7. Review the section on written report analyses. As you listen to media reports regarding critical business events, discuss which format is used most often. Which is intuitively easier for you and which is the most difficult? If you cannot find suitable media examples, you can also make use of Figures 8.2, 9.4, 9.5, and the sample reports found in this textbook.

Communication in Action

@ Internet

1. Writing your first case analysis is always an anxiety-producing event, especially when you are unsure of how to analyze the material. To help you get started your instructor has decided to use a "What do you leave out?" assignment. Go to **http://www.agric.wa.gov.au/programs/** and click on "New Industries." There you will find a "New Industries Strategic Plan" for the department of Agriculture in Western Australia. This extensive strategic plan is designed in outline form and describes the directions this government department plans to take over a five-year period.

Your Assignment: Read through the "New Industries Strategic Plan." Write a one- or two-page report on this plan. Use the strategic-issues format and cite the crucial strategic issues the department plans to take, the assumptions they have made about those issues, the strategies they recommend for dealing with the issues, the justification for their recommendations, their plan of action, and the expected results.

2. Along with your assignment to read this case chapter, your instructor has assigned the reading of an Internet case. The purpose is to parallel the material in the chapter with material in actual cases. To do this look up an Internet case at **http://www.lib.sfu.ca/researchhelp/subjectguides/bus/ casestud.htm**. Click on "Netscape Communications Corporation." The case is a detailed study of Netscape's early years. Although the details are dated, it serves as a good example of a Web-based case study and as an easily designed case for analysis.

   Your Assignment: Examine the case. You will find it is divided into four areas: the company, the market, the business environment, and technologies. After you have read through the case prepare a memo comparing and contrasting the Web case to the "analyzing a case" material in the chapter. How did the reading compare? Did you find it easy to preview, skim, and then read? Were you able to comprehend the information in the Web case in the same way as when you read a case in the textbook? Which of the four general case analytical approaches does the Netscape case fit? What tools did the presenter use to help the reader analyze the Netscape case? For instance, how easily does the business environment section lend itself to the SWOT analysis?

3. As this chapter suggests, students in case courses often do not know the instructor's case process style when they enter a class. Learning that style, how to prepare for classroom discussions, and how to write case analyses are critical requirements for all case students. The notes of Fred R. David, a professor at Francis Marion University, provide great insight into the case-analysis approaches and how to use them in analyzing a case.

   Your Assignment: Look up David's notes at **http://mars.wnec.edu/ ~achelte/howto.html**. "Ponderosa Inc.– 1988" is a short, strategic-management case about a hostile takeover of the Ponderosa chain of steak houses. As you read the case and notes, determine which tools David would recommend for doing a clear analysis of this case. After reading this material use those tools to write a short analysis of the Ponderosa case.

4. Assume that you have accepted a summer internship with a local health clinic. The clinic is publicly funded and serves a community of several thousand. The clinic's director knows that your knowledge of community health care systems is limited. The first day on the job is orientation. That afternoon your director places you in front of a computer and gives you an Internet site, **http://erc.msh.org/**. She tells you the site is rich in managerial information about health care. She asks you to spend the afternoon reading cases related to the work that she wants you to do.

   Your Assignment: Opening the site you find the home page has a variety of links. The center of the page houses the "Content: tools and information resources grouped by topic" section. When you click on any of the listed subjects you will be given an outline for that subject. Go to the center section that says "content" location and click on "The Manager." That section will list text by "management topic." When you click on that location you will be given a "Topical List of Management Issues." Read through the list and select a topic of interest. Click on that topic and you will find a case scenario, case discussion questions, and a case analysis.

Survey three or four topics. Read the case and answer the questions. You can check your answers by reading the analysis. When you are finished prepare a short memo for the clinic director. In the memo describe what you learned about health management.

InfoTrac

5. Part of the value of good strategic planning is establishing goals that work to your advantage when accomplished. To get to the goal stage requires accurate facts and a discerning analysis of what to do with those facts. Some researchers believe another element is also required: anticipating change. In their article "Anticipatory Management: Tools for Better Decision Making" William C. Ashley and James L. Morrison discuss this concept. Look it up on InfoTrac. After you have read it, write a short memo to your instructor describing how the concept can be used in conjunction with the decision-making material in the textbook. The article was printed in *The Futurist*, September-October 1997, vol. 31, no. 5, p. 47(4), Article A20227223.

Notes

1. Wertheim, E. G. (n.d.). *A model for case analysis and problem solving* (p. 2). Retrieved March 14, 2002, from **http://web.cba.neu.edu/~ewertheim/introd/cases.htm**
2. Ronstadt, R. (1980). *The art of case analysis: A guide to the diagnosis of business situations* 2nd ed. (pp. 18–20). Dover, MA: Lord.
3. Rand, G. E. (1996, December 16). *A manual to help your thinking about various issues in a Capstone case course in business* (p. 22). Retrieved March 26, 2002, from **http://www.imt.net/~grand/manual.htm**
4. *Topics: SWOT analysis* (p. 2). Retrieved April 2, 2002, from **http://www.fibre2fashion.com/topics/swot2.htm**
5. Rasberry, R. W. (1984). EK&G products. Dallas, TX: A Cox School of Business case, Southern Methodist University. Prepared with the aid of David Rudman.
6. Rasberry, R. W. (1992). The new GM assembly plant. Dallas, TX: A Cox School of Business case, Southern Methodist University. Material for this case was adapted from: Joseph Auerbach, "The Poletown Dilemma," *Harvard Business Review* (May-June 1985), pp. 93–99; and "The Poletown Dilemma," *Harvard Business School Case* (1988), 14 pp.
7. *Sales management: BUSI 4413X2* (2001, Winter). (pp. 2–3). Retrieved: March 14, 2002, from **http://plato.acadiau.ca/courses/busi/marketing/SalesManagement/B4413case.html**

8. Wilson, L. (n.d.). "Writing a formal report based upon the BCAP." *In Broadening the prospective: BCAP* (pp. 1–6). Retrieved March 26, 2002, from **http://www.captus.com/bcap/Finalreport.html**
9. Kerin, R. A. & Peterson, R. A. (1987). *Strategic marketing problems: cases and comments*, 4th ed. (p. 51). Boston: Allyn & Bacon.

Appendix

Sample Case Analysis

This chapter concludes with a sample student analysis of the EK&G Products case. As you read the analysis, compare the notes that you made earlier to those presented here.

EK&G Case Analysis

Step 1: Consider Relevant Information

In the EK&G Products case, several significant items can be listed. In this particular case, a chronological listing works well.

1. EK&G was formed in 1980 as a medical technology firm.
2. Pulsomatic was developed and tested in 1981.
3. The company believed that a large market existed and geared up for production of the Pulsomatic.
4. Early estimates of production costs were around $175.
5. Only 1,000 units were first ordered.
6. With a small number of sales the unit cost soared to over $250.
7. Hal Sigoin was hired as marketing manager.
8. Delivery began in June 1984.
9. Between June and August 1984, 2,500 units were ordered.
10. The owners celebrated their "success" on August 1, 1984.

Step 2: Define the Case Problem and Write a Problem Statement

First, list the different problems or issues that you observe. Second, narrow the issues into a written problem statement.

Four significant problems are apparent in the EK&G Products case:

1. a lack of proper market research or market "feel"
2. a lack of a substantial number of orders
3. very high overhead and fixed costs
4. no firm marketing plans or distribution system

The most significant problems in the EK&G Products case are low sales and high per-unit costs, resulting in low profits.

Step 3: Analyze the Facts and Underlying Assumptions

In looking at the EK&G Products case, we can pull out several critical issues.

1. A target market is not clearly defined.
2. Sufficient demand does not currently exist. (Can it be created?)
3. The break-even quantity is not determined.
4. In order to sell the Pulsomatic, a marketing representative may need to be hired in addition to Hal Sigoin. (How will this hiring affect break-even costs?)
5. The actual costs of each unit must be determined, including whether or not the unit cost will increase or decrease.
6. Eghart and Kleptow seem to assume that no similar product currently exists. They must discover if this is indeed the case.
7. The partners are assuming that the product and the revenue proposition are attractive to merchants.

Step 4: List Possible Solutions to the Problem

What are the possible solutions to the major problem you have identified? Alternative solutions for EK&G are:

1. Close down the business.
2. Examine the viability of the entire Pulsomatic venture to determine the likelihood of success. If it is deemed worthwhile,
   a. find a way to market the Pulsomatic broadly to many stores and public locations, or
   b. find a small segment of retail stores or food service locations that are customer intensive and market to that segment.

Step 5: Select a Solution and Prepare to Defend It

A possible solution to this case might be:

"I recommend that EK&G Products examine the viability of the entire Pulsomatic venture to determine the likelihood of success. If the Pulsomatic is determined to be a feasible product, a strategic business plan must then be developed. The plan should include considerations of how to achieve increased sales in one or two markets."

Step 6: Decide How to Implement the Solution

A recommendation for implementation of a solution to EK&G could be:

"Restaurants and bars throughout the state and adjoining states are places of customer intensiveness. Mr. Sigoin should aggressively pursue sales to these businesses either by himself or with the help of commissioned salesmen. This or some other measure should be taken in order to stimulate sales, and therefore increase production, in order to reduce the per-unit cost."

Source: Rasberry, R. W. (1984). EK&G products. Dallas, TX: A Cox School of Business case, Southern Methodist University. Prepared with the aid of David Rudman.

CHAPTER - 16

Discussing and Presenting
a Case Study

Chapter 15 described how most advanced business programs employ some form of case study. Often the teaching methodology of an entire school revolves around the case approach; such is true of the Harvard Business School. You will use the case analysis process in a general way to analyze real-life business problems. For these reasons, it is academically important that all business students learn to adapt to the case method. Your process of analyzing cases—and how you discuss and present your analyses—will affect your grade in the course and will determine your success in your business life.

There is rationale for individuals making oral case presentations and discussing cases in class. More information can be exchanged quickly as a result of a large group discussion; thus, knowledge can be gained more readily. Because class discussion is democratic, everyone has a fair chance to learn and grow. Finally, a positive result of the discussion is the immediate feedback received by individuals as their peers evaluate their ideas and make additional suggestions. Better solutions are selected this way and individual confidence and professionalism are gained.

While Chapter 15 described a process of written analysis, Chapter 16 takes the analysis process one step further and shows how to prepare and present case analyses orally. The overall objective of Chapters 15 and 16 is to help you analyze cases. Our specific emphasis in this chapter will be on class discussions. But because this method is also important for practical business situations, some techniques for group and individual presentations will also be given. To gain additional information about oral presentations in business, refer to Chapters 11 and 12. A review of Chapter 3, on visual devices, will also be useful.

Assuming that you have mastered the case analysis process presented in Chapter 15, you should now learn to prepare, present, and review the oral case analysis.

Preparation Steps for the Oral
Case Presentation

Ask yourself the questions in the following sections as you prepare for your oral case presentation, regardless of whether it is during a class discussion, a group presentation, or individual presentation.

What Type of Discussion Strategy Should You Adopt?

The strategy that you pick for presenting a case should depend on several factors. First, consider your knowledge about different parts of the particular discipline (for example, finance, accounting, marketing). Work experience that you may have from previous jobs or your exposure to an industry or profession will add to your knowledge. Your skills at both analyzing a problem and communicating your ideas will also influence your strategy choice. Finally, consider your confidence level for the particular discipline; that is, how you see yourself and how you desire to appear and communicate within the classroom.

How Visible Do You Desire to Be?

Visibility relates to how active you want to be in the classroom. If your desire is to be conspicuous, you probably will take a very active role in discussing the material. If you desire to have a major impact and perhaps be an authority type, you may desire a more moderately visible seat, because you plan to talk anyway. If, however, you are fearful and desire not to talk at all, you will probably find yourself seeking a hideout position. While nervousness may drive you to such a place, your grade will probably reflect your passiveness and lack of participation.

What Role Do You Want to Play?

The strategy you take in class generally relates to the discussion role you desire to play. Ronstadt describes eight possible discussion roles that we normally see in case courses:

1. *Expert Witness.* This role is played by the individual who has insider information or in-depth knowledge about the case or the case's relationship to other cases.

2. *Bail 'em Out.* This individual usually has a very clear understanding of the case and generally understands an appropriate solution. He or she often waits until the class gets stuck and then comes to its aid.

3. *Assume a Personality.* The strategy here requires assuming the particular role of an individual within the organization being discussed. During a discussion, questions often are directed to the person who likes to assume a particular personality.

4. *Get the Facts.* The student using this strategy desires a minimum amount of participation. He or she usually throws out facts, which can be easily drawn from the case, in a quick and unimportant manner. Such a person, despite talking, has low visibility because others quickly add further information, and the discussion moves on rapidly. If you choose this strategy, avoid one-line statements. Construct your statements with clarity and substance so that it is evident to the instructor that you fully understand the facts of the case.

5. *Industry Expert.* This person is an authority because he or she has analyzed the industry in question and can offer trends and clarification on the case.

6. *I've Got Experience.* This role is generally played by someone who has had work experience in business and who desires that others know he or she has been in situations of the type under discussion. Often the impact of their information-sharing is minimal. If the information is good, however, this person probably becomes the expert witness and is sought out for specific reasons.

7. *Questioner.* The questioner is not someone who merely speaks in class in order to make a statement. Instead, this person generally directs crucial questions toward participants who have made statements regarding analysis, purpose, solutions, and so forth. This role is an important one because it shows an overall understanding of the case and it helps control the direction of the discussion. It also helps to clarify questions that more-silent participants may have but are afraid to ask.

8. *Wrap-It-Up.* The person who plays this role has listened carefully throughout the discussion and is capable of taking all the major issues and boiling them together into a coherent line of thought. This individual goes beyond merely repeating what has been said and helps to leave participants with a clearer understanding of the entire case and discussion.[1]

During your first case course, you may find that you adopt a particular case strategy in the middle of the semester and will either stay with it or change it periodically. Learn from that first experience and adapt a strategy prior to the first class meeting in later semesters. Besides developing a professional approach to problem solving, you may improve your grade considerably.

One of your objectives during the discussion is to be seen by the instructor as a major contributor to the problem-solving process. Instructors determine contributions in a variety of ways:

1. Significant information that leads toward a solution
2. A statement encouraging movement from one part of the case to another
3. A new alternative
4. A statement about key assumptions
5. An insightful generalization
6. Input from use of a key analytical tool
7. A suggested plan of action
8. Clarification of financial statements or quantitative data
9. A quality summary
10. The ability to relate one case to another

Who Is Your Competition?

The case methodology requires a give-and-take movement, flowing from an analysis of problems to a discussion of solutions, in order that a natural collaboration will develop among participants. Even though a grade is given for participation, try not to think of in-class competition as a win-lose situation. Instead, seek to establish the win-win position where you and your fellow classmates will be cooperating together. You will be competing in a puzzle process, trying to arrive quickly and accurately at workable solutions.

During the first few classes, observe which classmates talk the most. Determine whether their comments are accurate. Who plays which of the roles outlined above? How can you work with these different individuals and their strategies so that true collaboration occurs? Likewise, who is less visible? How can you help draw out these individuals so that they, too, will be contributors?

How Well Do You Listen?

As we mentioned in Chapter 1, listening is one of the most important communication skills that a manager can develop. Perfecting the skill will have terrific pay-offs in the business world, and will make the job of discussing cases in the classroom much easier. Most of us admit that we are not good listeners. See how many of the following behavioral patterns you identify with.

1. *The Pretender* looks a speaker in the eye and uses all the right nonverbal moves and gestures, yet mentally is not tuned-in. When you drift to this position, stir yourself to quickly get on track. You never know when the instructor will call on you and you don't want to respond with "I don't know," or worse, "I wasn't listening." Clearing your mind is a vital step toward good participation. It is crucial that you listen to the person who leads the discussion. Avoid the temptation to shuffle your papers and order your thoughts. Listen instead and allow your mind to follow the discussion flow. Be ready to go wherever the discussion goes. As the discussion is taking place, try to keep in mind which phase of the analysis process the participants are talking about. Watch and listen carefully.

2. *I'm-next* listening is performed by a stage hog who can't wait to talk. Case classes are often full of participants with raised hands who are eager to answer the next questions. While the motivation is good, if you are mentally rehearsing what you will say, you might be embarrassed to respond and suddenly realize your answer did not present a sufficient response. True listening allows for real understanding.

3. *Broken-record* listening is performed by people who love to hear themselves talk, and they cannot shut up. The remedy for this is to have a short outline in your mind, then say your answer simply yet logically, and then shut up and wait for the next response.

4. *My-answer-is-better* is the feeling one gets when a responder has tried to one-up a colleague. If your answer is truly better, that's great. But an instructor who was unimpressed with the ego behind an I've-done-one-better answer has embarrassed many students.

5. *Rapid-writing note-taking* is the technique used by someone who wants to remember everything. The problem is that while you are writing the verbatim answers, you are also missing important points that the speaker or others are making. Taking thorough notes is important. Yet do not let the note-taking become the objective. Learn to record just enough to help you stay mentally focused and able to respond. Write key words, dates, and ideas in outline form. Keep in mind a mental outline of the overall analysis, the points made thus far, and the key ideas expressed under each point. Mentally extend your own analysis by building on comments made by

your colleagues. You can even offer these ideas orally, which may help the instructor stay within the prepared format.

6. *Asking questions* often embarrasses a nervous student. But in the flow of a case discussion one often gets the feeling that one seemingly profound statement after another is made. However, it is usually a well-thought-out question that really pulls the discussion back to the desired track. Learn how to actively listen by asking good questions. You can then follow up by making an excellent response of your own.

In the classroom we can become better listeners by doing some of the following: Prepare physically by clearing your mind of everything except the subjects to be discussed. Looking over your case analysis notes will help you focus. Also pick a location in the classroom where you feel comfortable, can see, and from which you can best respond to the instructor and your colleagues. Mentally share responsibility for the dialogue that is about to take place. Develop a "partnership" among yourself and the others in the room. Keep an open mind and avoid developing stereotypes of colleagues and characters in the case. Allow the information that you hear to expand your impression of those around you and the case content. Realize that listening does not mean problem solving or having to provide an answer. Often the best responses are those that advance the entire analysis process. As you listen, hear what is being said, how it is said, and what is not being said. Learn to pick up on things that are left out. Learn to cope with the element of personal risk. If you truly wish to be a "partner" you need to risk responding, even when emotionally you may be anxious to do so.

What Is the Instructor's Style?

In order to prepare adequately, you must also understand your instructor's teaching style. If you have never had the instructor for a previous course, ask questions of your colleagues and try to find out as much as possible about his or her style prior to the first class. During the first class, listen carefully to what the instructor says. Watch, too, for how the instructor communicates and is attracted to communicators. Does the instructor prime participants for discussion? Is he or she attracted to the most vocal participant? Is the instructor active (energetically following an agenda), or passive (letting the group determine the direction and flow of the discussion)? Does the instructor often digress and add personal comments about the case? If digression does occur, are the comments important or distracting?

Ronstadt cites five instructor discussion styles most often used in the case classroom. Some instructors adopt one style and stick with it, whereas others shift styles from case to case or even within a single case. Learn your instructor's style and prepare for the type of discussion that will take place in the classroom:

1. *The Cross-Examiner.* The cross-examiner thoroughly questions each statement made by a student. The goal is to pull out additional information and to develop the logic of a student's position. While the tone may sound adversarial, the instructor is not using the process to harass the individual but merely to advance the discussion.

2. *Devil's Advocate.* The devil's advocate questions students in relation to positions taken. Often, the instructor's line of questioning assumes an opposing

position or role; through the discussion process, the instructor has the class either support or refute the opposing position. The point of such a discussion is to see if other possibilities are indeed tenable.

3. *The Hypothetical Position.* Instead of questioning a position or statement, the instructor may pose a hypothetical situation that is an extreme example of the position. He or she then pushes the student to consider the example in terms of the student's previous recommendations. This style is used to uncover and display the strength of a discussion's logic.

4. *Role-Playing.* The instructor may divide the class into various personalities represented within the case. Each student will assume a personality and the discussion will revolve around how each would make decisions if he or she were the actual person.

5. *The Silent Style.* Often in the course of discussion, the instructor will adopt a silent stance. When this happens, the instructor makes little or no input and allows the discussion to continue so that someone in the class will exert leadership and offer suggestions that will move the class forward or that will turn the course of the discussion. It is important during this time to realize that big points can be gained if you are the one who offers carefully constructed comments that move the class forward.[2]

As you read the case you should get a sense of the exciting problems and personalities involved. The instructor will then peel back layers of the case to reveal its depth to students. If you saw "X" in your reading of the case, the instructor will help you see "2X" through the discussion. Listening is a key to making this happen. Your instructor will listen carefully and will guide you to a successful end.[3]

How Will You Handle the Instructor's Questions?

After previewing possible instructor styles, it is important to consider how you will handle questions posed in the classroom. Because the class operates within a time constraint, coordination between instructor and students is important. Good case teachers use several questioning techniques. First, they ask directive questions that do not invite memorized statements: "What do you project the sales to be for the next quarter, and why?" By asking such a question they are looking for ideas on controversial issues and on how the case material relates to the course theories.

While certain questions may be directed to particular students, the instructor really desires that the entire class answer the question in their own minds. The instructor is interested in the entire class participating in the orchestration process of the discussion. For this reason, instructors usually do not repeat their questions; they expect you to listen carefully and to realize that a question, and its answer, must be incorporated into the orchestrated process. Likewise, instructors do not repeat participant's answers unless they incorporate the answer into part of the next question or by summarizing what has been said.

Your ability to handle a lead-off question is particularly important. The lead-off question is crucial because it stimulates further discussion. Answers often reflect who is best prepared to discuss the case. If for some reason you are not ready to discuss the case or participate in class, tell the instructor. While this may create a negative image in the instructor's mind about your participation, it will save you the embarrassment of being called on and being unable to answer the question in class. Usually, however, you can use this out only one time. If you are perpetually unprepared, your grade will be adversely affected. If you beg out one class period, you should give an excellent performance during the following class.

An effective instructor will ask you what information you need and how you will use it. If you are asked a question that you do not understand, try to direct the question and your answer into an area of the case where you feel confident. Also, do not use the excuse "there's not enough information"; too much information will tell you the complete story of the case and therefore will make discussion unimportant.

Remember that your instructor, in asking questions, realizes that each class member has a different opinion. Such a difference is healthy and students are encouraged not only to have their own opinions but to learn to support their opinions carefully. The freedom of expression of different ideas is key to the decision-making process of the case approach. In asking questions, the instructor will take generalizations and will try to help students channel these into constructive facts that are related to the course. The discussion is most productive when the theories of the course are highlighted and facts from the case are used to further develop the theory.

How Will You Ask Questions?

As part of a case discussion, you will find yourself both answering and asking questions. Several ideas can guide you to ask effective questions. First, minimize the direct questions you pose to the instructor during class discussion that do not relate specifically to the case discussion statement—avoid such questions as "Isn't this just another example of a poorly managed organization?" Instructors are busy working the class through the case and are interested in your input, not your questions. The exceptions to this rule are when you ask clarifying questions or move the discussion with a question, which is really addressed to the entire class—such as saying, "This situation reminds me of the McGuire case that we examined two weeks ago. Isn't the main problem here the weakness of the manager and consequently a poorly managed organization?" Such questions should relate to the logical sequence of the discussion. Avoid a question that asks for premature information; for example, if the class is discussing the analysis of facts, you should not pose a question about a solution to the case.

Second, when you ask a question, make sure it is logical and self-explanatory. A case discussion is not the place for many of the normal questions of why, how, when, and so forth, that passive listeners and talkers insert into normal interpersonal conversations. During class discussion, each participant should strive to make statements and questions simple, clear, and meaningful.

How Should You Prepare Your Discussion Notes?

Before you can prepare your notes, you must adequately analyze the case. In Chapter 15, we discussed a six-step analysis process:

1. Consider the relevant information and underlying assumptions.
2. Define the case problem and write a problem statement.
3. Analyze your facts.

4. List the possible solutions to the problem.
5. Select a solution and prepare to defend it.
6. Decide how to implement the solution.

Many students do excellent, time-consuming analyses, only to be unable to discuss their analyses and findings in class. It is important that you combine the analytical and communicative process into your presentation.

Rescript Your Notes

Rescripting your original analysis notes, or revising them so that they will better serve you in the discussion, is important. During your analysis, remember that certain information and analytical tools will always be a part of class discussion. As you analyze the overall case, remember the various financial statements found in the exhibits. Although you may be tempted to breeze over them quickly, ask yourself instead, "What is the financial stability of the organization?" In your rescripting, make notations regarding questions you can ask or responses you can make about the financial statements. If you learn to do this task well in the classroom, you will find it an invaluable tool in future business meetings.

Refer to the Analytical Tools

As you further analyze the case, you will undoubtedly use many of the analytical tools listed in Table 15.1 (pages 412–413). Whether these tools are profitability measures, projections of financial statements, or cost-revenue analysis formulas, you should be prepared to discuss the case using the tools that will provide the most information. Be careful to make sure your solution encompasses both qualitative reasons and quantitative facts; avoid the tendency to focus on just one or the other.

Make Key-Word Notes

After you have analyzed the case, make notes that can be used as quick references in class discussion or as you deliver your presentation. Such notes generally require larger lettering, key words instead of complete sentences, and facts or statistics organized in a readily usable manner. The key is to design material so it is easily accessible to prevent you from shuffling through piles of paper.

Use the Instructor's Note Pattern

One excellent method of note organization is to design your notes in the same pattern as the one your instructor uses on the chalkboard. Watch as your instructor diagrams cases. Does he or she use an ordering process? Does the instructor chronologically list facts, list alternatives with their pros and cons, put problems with solutions, or arrange a sequence of ideas and information? Is the analysis on the left and the recommendations on the right? Some instructors even use different colors of chalk or markers. By ordering your ideas into the patterns your instructor uses, you can easily follow the class discussion and contribute your own ideas.

Should You Join a Study Group?

Some instructors require that class members participate in study groups prior to class discussion. If your instructor does not have such a requirement, you should still consider developing a study group for the following reasons. First, study groups improve case learning since they require you to practice the development and support of logical positions. They are useful as well because they employ creative brainstorming, which is a by-product of class discussion. Also, small groups are much easier to talk in than large classes of 60 to 80 participants. By practicing in a study group, your confidence for speaking in the classroom should be increased. Finally, while they may not be called *study groups*, you will find that your time will be spent in numerous work groups of one sort or another once you are in the business world. The learning from your case study group will carry over into that environment.

There are several things to consider in organizing a study group. First, you should be acquainted with the other members of the group. Know how they perform in class. Are they shy or assertive? Are they outspoken or knowledgeable? Are they motivated to work? A group should pick individuals who contribute equally to the overall effort. This means that all members agree to meet at the same time, to be fully prepared to discuss each case, and to be committed to helping the entire group effort. Do not join a group if you feel intimidated by any other group participant.

Just as in business, it is often helpful to combine different types of participant knowledge. For example, a study group can use persons with backgrounds in accounting, finance, marketing, and communication. When your group first meets, establish ground rules by which you will operate. Ground rules might include what style of leadership the group will follow, time limits, who will take the notes, how you will handle digressions in discussion, and, finally, how you will ensure that each member is fully prepared for each session. Preparation should include a thorough reading and understanding of the case and a full analysis of the case by each individual.

Presentation of the Oral Case Analysis

In making an oral case presentation, three methods can be used: class discussion, group presentation, and individual presentation. The material that follows on class discussion and group presentations relates to the material on meeting management found in Chapter 12. The material for individual presentations is related to Chapter 11.

Class Discussions

As you participate in class discussion, remember that such a discussion process usually follows an abbreviated form of case analysis: identifying and analyzing the case situation, analyzing key solutions, and choosing a particular solution with recommendations for specific action. While the discussion generally revolves around these three areas, you should be aware that the process is often altered depending on the nature of the case and the opening statements made by both the instructor and the students.

When Should You Talk?
Your first decision is whether you will talk immediately or sit quietly. The strategy you selected during your preparation has prepared you for the discussion. If you talk first, you make yourself vulnerable, but you also set the pace for the remaining

class discussion. Such an assertive position takes courage—you may be wrong, but at least you have started talking.

If you decide to be quiet at the outset, however, you can determine the direction of the class discussion and you can contribute to the direction and flow of the process. Here you run the risk, if you are nervous, of eventually not talking at all. For this reason, you must develop your strategy during the preparatory stages and follow that strategy once the class discussion has started. If everyone starts talking at first, tailor your comments to those made by your colleagues.

While class discussions of cases require risk on your part, they are akin to business decisions in management situations, which also involve risk. Through proper analysis you try to minimize the risk. While speaking out in class is often one of the most risky aspects, it is far worse to sit day after day and never say a word. Your boss on the job would never allow this to happen, and neither will a good case instructor. Because most case-oriented classes include participation as a major portion of the grade, it is important that you talk. The instructor often takes little responsibility for getting you involved or for limiting the input of class members who monopolize discussion. The instructor usually feels this is part of the group participation problem that must be handled by the group itself. Ronstadt summarizes this process of talking versus not talking.

> [I]f you are an active participant, you cannot realistically expect to be right all the time. After all, good learning comes partly from making mistakes. And you can expect to make errors of analysis or reasoning. If your classmates or your professor reveal an error, do not defend it to the death. Defending a defenseless position is foolhardy and the mark of a poor manager who cannot recognize plain facts because of an emotional need to always be right. Remember, people do not do poorly in case courses for being honestly wrong. They do poorly for not doing.[4]

Practice Your Improved Listening

Use the listening techniques mentioned earlier to enhance your learning and to advance the discussion. Keep in mind that listening is not the end result of the exercise. As Harvard professor Charles Gragg states, "It can be said flatly that the mere act of listening to wise statements and sound advice does little for anyone. In the process of learning, the learner's dynamic cooperation is required." If you are listening with the overall idea in mind, you can help the class minimize digressions and wandering. Digressions usually occur because of confusion regarding the process of decision making. Help direct the discussion back toward the key unresolved issues with your comments. The solution will then be easier to see. "The desired result of student participation is achieved by the opening of free channels of communication between students and students, and between students and teachers."[5]

Follow the Instructor's Pace within the Discussion

The role of the instructor during class discussion is to keep the process moving in an orderly and productive manner. He or she will ask questions that invite responses. The strategy you choose should determine the role that you will play in responding. Observe the instructor's verbal and nonverbal communication. How does he or she signal the class to shift gears and focus on new and different material? By observing the instructor's style, you will be better able to participate in the discussion, to move the class toward an excellent solution, and to improve your own grades. A sample class plan is listed in Table 16.1. Refer to this for a general idea of how a case class could be conducted. Realize, however, that individual instructors design and carry out class discussion in their own unique way.

Look for a Place to Insert Good Qualitative Statements

Regardless of whether or not you are a whiz at numbers, many of the most useful statements in a case discussion are phrased from a qualitative, not a quantitative, standpoint. To the financial expert, the bottom line may say it all. If numbers are not your strong suit, however, do not spend all your time looking for answers as you run the numbers. Instead, consider the more difficult questions. For example,

Table 16.1	A Sample Class Plan Outline	

Time (minutes)	Sequence	Activity
	1.	People to call on during this class if they do not volunteer (six or eight names).
0–10	2.	General class announcements.
	3.	Comments about the next class and its assignment.
10–15	4.	Review of the theory readings assigned: a. Any questions or comments? b. Specific questions to be raised if students do not discuss on their own initiative.
15–25	5.	Case introduction. An anecdote about the industry. A tie-back to previous class discussions, etc.
	6.	Who will start? Will I ask or will I wait for a volunteer?
	7.	Key questions I may want to ask.
25–40	8.	Important points to cover: a. *Diagnosis:* What is the problem and why is it occurring? b. *Alternatives:* What are they? How to evaluate them? c. *Action:* What is the decision? What are short-term actions? What are long-term actions?
5–15	9.	Conclusion, if any: a. Questions to ask: Is this problem similar to one in other courses? How different/similar was this case from previous cases? b. Variations that might exist, relevant current news items, relative importance with course content, and further related readings.

Source: Adapted from James A. Erskine, Michiel R. Leenders, and Louise A. Mauffeette-Leenders, *Teaching with Cases*, Research and Publications Division, School of Business Administration, University of Western Ontario, London, Ontario, 1981, p. 126. Reprinted by permission.

a manufacturing firm may have to choose between two parts. By purchasing one, the ROI (return on investment) may be higher than by using the more costly part, but the difficult questions that you should ask may revolve around the implications for product quality.

Give Effective Summaries

Many students expect the instructor to summarize the discussion that has taken place within the classroom. Most instructors prefer that a member of the class not only summarize what has taken place, but also relate the case and discussion to the overall context of the theories being studied within the course. At the same time, they realize that this is a difficult thing to ask of most students. If you really want to impress your instructor, giving effective summaries is one way you can probably do it.

Do Not Expect a Correct Answer to the Case Problem

Few instructors provide their solutions to the case or describe what the organization actually did. Most prefer that the alternatives developed by the class be the ones used in relating the course theory. They believe that disclosing what actually happened is risky and discourages students from carefully providing their own alternatives to cases. They know that in the business world there will always be several available alternatives for solving problems.

Group Presentation

If the instructor assigns a group presentation, start by forming your group if the group composition has not already been assigned. If you have a choice in picking your colleagues, remember that groups are best formed on the basis of complementary skills, not friendships. Skills should represent the analysis process, expertise in the fields of discipline, and so forth. Form the group, like the study group, with members who are committed and dependable and who will work hard to deliver a professional presentation.

Before your group meets, each member should analyze the case and arrive at a solution. Make extensive notes and arrange the notes in a manner that will make it easy to discuss what you have found. Together, meet to discuss the analysis, and then arrive at your group's solution to the problem. After your discussion, divide the parts of the presentation for ease of preparation and presentation. Division may be made by expertise, knowledge, or communicative skills. One method of dividing the group calls for one member to make the introduction and conclusion, another member to provide background information, a third member to present the problem analysis, a fourth member to cover possible solutions, and the final member to give the group's selected solution.

Decide how your group needs to use visual aids. Review Chapter 3 at this point and consider the use of a software graphics package. Various packages exist and are probably available at your school on the local network. Some of the easiest to use are: Microsoft PowerPoint, Lotus Freelance Graphics, and Harvard Graphics.

After the aids are assembled, your group should meet for a practice session. As you practice, look over all handouts and aids to make sure that they are error-free, will be easy to use, and will facilitate retention.

Arrive early on the day of the presentation. Dress appropriately. If you and your group are to be in front of the class, consider wearing appropriate business attire. Arrange the seats in a way that will create a professional image and will aid you in making your presentation. Stick to the time limit. Speak in a professional manner and bridge together the individual contributions through well-thought-out and rehearsed transitions. As each person speaks before the class, support each other with both words and actions (eye contact and facial expressions). Let the class see that the project is a unified effort, not the work of one or two individuals. Talk to the class and not to the overhead machine, computer monitor, or screen. Never disagree with members of your group in front of the class, unless you have previously decided to do so in order to make a point during the case.

When you are finished with the presentation, be prepared to answer any questions from the audience.

The Individual Case Presentation

If you are given the assignment to make an individual case presentation in class, take the assignment seriously. This presentation is your opportunity to shine and score points for yourself. Be aware that there are the three areas that you must adequately cover: preparation, practice, and presentation. This is also a good place to reread Chapter 11 on business presentations.

Preparation

Start your preparation just as you would for a class discussion. Analyze the case carefully and make notes of your analysis. Rescript the notes in a form that will allow you to easily follow while you make your presentation.

As you organize your thoughts, be careful not to repeat a lot of the preliminary information and facts that everyone in the class already knows. If there are major analytical tools that you have employed in the analysis, mention them and outline the information gleaned from them. The outline that you will use is crucial. Reduce your notes to just a few pages. Work from key categories, columns, breakdowns that trigger in your mind the information that is on your page. The more easily you can interpret your notes, the more easily you will be able to communicate to your audience.

While rescripting your notes, consider whether you will use visual aids. (Refer to Chapter 3 at this point.) Three aids that are easy for students to use in individual case presentations are the chalkboard, transparencies, and handouts. If your classroom is equipped with a personal computer and projection system, there are several graphics packages that you might consider using.

Practice

After you have organized and prepared your presentation, go through several practice sessions. First, look over your notes mentally at least once. Second, read through your notes out loud and emphasize the major points you want your audience to remember. Third, talk out loud about your notes and refer to them only occasionally. Practice in this manner at least three or four times. If you do not have time for numerous out-loud sessions, at least practice major blocks of the presentation. Remember, practicing the delivery of the analysis makes for an excellent presentation.

It is to your advantage to memorize two parts: the introduction and the conclusion. If these are clear in your mind, you will have no problem getting into and out of your presentation, and the rest of the material will make more sense to the listeners. Do not try to memorize the entire analysis. Such a task is not time effective, and if you lose your place you will probably freeze. Also, an entirely memorized presentation looks passive and canned, not professional. Rely on your notes during practice and, after several run-throughs, you will have little difficulty getting through the talk.

If you are going to use visual aids, such as PowerPoint slides or an overhead projector with transparencies, make sure you practice with these aids until your presentation is smooth.

Presentation

On the day of your presentation, arrive early to set up the room. If possible, stand during your presentation, but avoid standing locked behind a podium. Look at your audience. Speak to them. Try to establish a dialogue whereby you seem to be carrying on a conversation together. Do not talk to the screen if you are using the overhead projector. Be sure to observe the time limit and save room for questions and answers at the end.

Some rules to follow in the question-and-answer session are:

1. Repeat all questions before answering them.
2. Recognize the questions in the order given.
3. Relate the questions to the logic of your presentation.
4. Avoid digressing and getting into individual conversations with classmates.
5. Make your answers brief.
6. Be courteous.
7. Do not be afraid to say "I don't know" if you do not have an answer. Do not use the phrase as a cop-out, however.

Reviewing the Oral Case Analysis

During class discussion, you should be listening, watching, and talking instead of writing. But as soon as class is over, the wise student summarizes what happened in class. A format such as questions/issues/specific facts/comments is helpful. Within your summary, list the key ideas and any overall generalizations. Be sure to note how this case relates to cases previously covered in the course. Compare and contrast the issues and cases. Also list any analytical tools that were employed to explain the case. A thorough review, written out immediately after the discussion, will help you in your overall understanding of the course theories and will save you time in studying for the final test. An example of just such a review list is found in Table 16.2. Ronstadt uses the acronym *FIG* to guide the summarization notes. The letters stand for *facts, ideas,* and *generalizations.*

Table 16.2	A FIG Review List

Session No. 1

Fact 1: More than half of all retail businesses fail within the first two years of operation.

Fact 2: The average business life span is six years.

Fact 3: You cannot buy time when running a business operation, and there is no such thing as a sure deal.

Fact 4: There are 2,575,000 dry-cleaning businesses in the United States.

Fact 5: There are 4,150,000 grocery stores in the United States.

Idea 1: The concept of "interstice theory" applies to large corporations that are too small for large companies to get involved with and too large for small business ventures. An example would be producing wooden spools for large cable and wire manufacturers.

Generalization 1: You need three primary resources to start a business: people, capital, and an idea.

Generalization 2: A marginal business will return a lower profit than the salary realized if one had decided to work for someone else.

Generalization 3: The entrepreneur's basic goal is to maintain a level of survival.

Source: Adapted from Robert Ronstadt, *The Art of Case Analysis: A Guide to the Diagnosis of Business Situations,* 2nd ed., Lord, Dover, Massachusetts, 1980, p. 38. Reprinted by permission.

Summary

While Chapter 15 helped you develop the tools for analyzing a case and writing a case report, this chapter gave you an understanding of how to discuss and present a case analysis in the classroom.

As you prepare for the oral case presentation, there are nine important questions that you should ask. First, what type of discussion strategy should you adopt? The answer to this question depends on how conspicuous and vulnerable you wish to become. Second, how visible do you desire to be? If you desire to take an active role in the discussion, you will have a highly visible profile in the class. Third, what role do you want to play? The strategy you take in class relates to one of eight possible roles: expert witness, bail 'em out, assume a personality, get the facts out, industry expert, I've got experience, questioner, or wrap-it-up. The fourth question to ask is, who is your competition? Knowing something about your classmates' styles will help you in planning your role. Fifth, what is your instructor's style? This is a vital question; the answer determines how you will strategically prepare for the discussion. Instructors have one of five styles: the cross-examiner, the devil's advocate, the hypothetical position, the role-player, or the silent style. Sixth, how will you handle the instructor's questions? This determines not only the strategy you will take in the discussion but also how you will prepare for the process. Seventh, how will you ask questions? As a student your role is generally one of providing answers, but there are important ways to ask questions. Eighth, how should you prepare your discussion notes? Proper note preparation requires rescripting your notes, making references to the analytical tools, making key-word notes, and using the instructor's note pattern. Finally, should you prepare for class discussion by joining a study group?

Preparation pays off during the final presentation that generally takes the form of class discussions, group presentations, or individual presentations. Points that are important for the class discussion are knowing when to talk, learning to actively listen, following the pace the instructor sets within the discussion, looking for a place to insert good qualitative statements within the discussion, learning to give effective summaries, and learning not to expect a correct answer for the overall case. Group presentations closely follow Chapter 12 on meeting management. An effective group presentation requires a great deal of coordination between members before, during, and after the actual presentation. Individual presentations follow the points made in Chapter 11 on business presentations. Preparation is vital and so is learning the correct visual aids to use.

Finally, the wise student reviews the case analysis immediately following a class. A useful analysis summary focuses on three aspects: facts, ideas, and generalizations.

Discussion Questions

1. As you prepare for your first case discussion, remember the preparation steps that were presented at the start of this chapter. Go back to those questions on pages 437–444 and develop a short response to each. As you think about the questions and your answers, commit to using that as a strategy for your first case discussion.

2. One of the key preparation steps asked the question, "How well do you listen?" Think back over other courses that you have taken, especially those that required a great amount of active participation. What were your listening strengths and weaknesses in that and other courses? How do you plan to better prepare yourself as a listener in your current case course?

3. Study groups are often recommended and even required in case courses. What do you consider to be the advantages and disadvantages of a case-study group? For every disadvantage, describe how you and others in the group can possibly turn it into an advantage.

4. Making reference notes on a case to use during the in-class discussion is always an important decision. How will you reconcile what you think you need, and what you actually will use? Think through the case, the abundant information, and your general ability to listen, look at notes, and respond to an instructor's facilitation. How do you plan to design your note cards?

5. After your first case discussion revisit the chapter to revise your discussion strategy. Look at the sample class-plan outline on page 446. How well did the instructor's facilitation fit with the generic timetable? What can you determine about the instructor's style as a result?

6. Anticipating that your instructor will assign individual or small-group presentations of a case, reread the material on pages 447–449. Also revisit Chapters 3 and 11, and the discussion on visuals and presentation-making. Describe what you need to use from that material to ensure that your case presentation will be exceptional.

Communication in Action

1. As you prepare for your next case discussion in the classroom, decide which role to play. Take a sheet of paper and write down the eight possible roles described in this chapter. List under each role type the pros and cons of playing each role, given the composition of your class. Next, list several techniques that you could use in employing each technique. Finally, take your list with you to class and try to use at least two or three of the techniques during the next case analysis.

2. This assignment asks you to team with six of your classmates, and to conduct a simulated discussion on the case "What Could Have Saved John Worthy." It involves a man who recently changed health insurance plans to a managed care plan. The case examines the business of managed health care, and the ethics of making critical health decisions. You can find the case at: "What Could Have Saved John Worthy," *The Hastings Center Report*, July-August 1998, vol. 28, no. 14, p. 81(17), Article A21195468. Printing out the case, and determining your individual role, makes it easier to read and discuss.

    Your Assignment: You and your student colleagues should examine the case and read the first five pages. After reading the case each person should choose one of the following roles:

    1. Fran Davis, Family Doctor
    2. Edward R. Post, Emergency Department Physician
    3. Connie S. Rodgers, Customer Service Representative
    4. Michael Depp, Medical Director, GoodCare
    5. Peter Ferrell, President, Factory Inc.
    6. Jane Worthy, Patient's Wife and GoodCare Member
    7. Collective Agency in the Design of Managed Care

    After everyone has picked a role, read the description of each role. After having read all of your material, assemble as a group and discuss the case. Try to use the six-step analysis process presented in Chapter 15:

    1. Consider the relevant information and underlying assumptions.
    2. Define the case problem and write a problem statement.
    3. Analyze your facts.
    4. List the possible solutions to the problem.
    5. Select a solution and prepare to defend it.
    6. Decide how to implement the solution.

@ Internet

3. Good classroom discussions revolve around asking and answering questions. In preparation for your in-class case discussions your instructor has asked you to look at two short cases and respond to the questions asked by the author. The cases are housed on an Internet site created by Donald Clark.

The site address is: **http://www.nwlink.com/~donclark/hrd/learn2
.html**. When you open the learning activities page you will see the link for
two cases: *Wholesome Food* and *The Fall of Quest*. Pay particular attention as
you read the material that prefaces the cases, which is quite good and helps
you understand the concept of the cases.

Your Assignment: Open the Internet page and read the two cases. When
you finish each case create answers to the questions that are asked. Clark's
own answers are then posted for your comparison.

InfoTrac

4. Entering the in-class discussion process for a formal case usually requires a
trial-and-error method. The process does not seem so overwhelming if you
have the opportunity to interact with some of your classmates prior to the
first big discussion.

The exercise involves reading an InfoTrac article and discussing the
questions to two cases presented. You will get a general understanding of
the discussion process, and will also be introduced to several multicultural
issues.

Your Assignment: In InfoTrac find, "Challenging Students to Respond
to Multicultural Issues: The Case-Study Approach," by Helen M. Sharp,
Business Communication Quarterly, June 1995, vol. 58, no. 2, p. 28(4),
Article A17190262. With two of your classmates read the article and each
case that is presented. At the end of each case you will find five discussion
questions. Discuss the questions as a group. At the end of your discussions
talk as a group about what you have learned from the exercise and how
you will apply it to your course.

Notes

1. Ronstadt, R. (1980). *The art of case analysis: A guide to the diagnosis of business situations*, 2nd ed. (pp. 33–35). Dover, MA: Lord.
2. *Ibid*, pp. 30–32.
3. Talking with Professor John Quelch. In *Teaching materials*. (1998, Fall). (p. 2). Boston, MA: Harvard Business School Press.
4. Ronstadt, R. *The art of case analysis*, p. 36.
5. Leading classroom discussion: learning vs. listening, *Teaching materials* (1998, Spring). (p. 1). Boston, MA: Harvard Business School Press.

Appendices

Appendix A
A Formal Case

Appendix B
A Written Analysis of a Formal Case

APPENDIX - A

A Formal Case

The following case and the evaluation of it in Appendix B serve as an example of an effectively written analysis. The case describes an ethical quandary being faced by a managerial accountant at Venture Sports, a division of Champion Marketing, Inc.

Work through the case using the steps presented in the chapter on case studies. Take the time to list the significant events and facts, the major problems, the possible solutions, and your recommendations. Do all of this before reading the student analysis of the case in Appendix B.

Case: Accounting Procedures at Champion Marketing, Inc.

Introduction

In the late afternoon of Friday, May 9, 2002, Cathy Rodgers walked slowly to her car. As she climbed inside, the warmth from the afternoon sun suddenly felt soothing. She had just completed a two-day continuing education program for CPAs. Throughout the sessions, she had been troubled about a recurring problem at work. It all started as the seminar leader led the participants through a discussion of the ethical behavior of accountants. The objective was to raise the sensitivity of the men and women attending, and to help them see clearly the many ethical pitfalls they could possibly encounter as CPAs. But for Rodgers, the message was more immediate. For the past six months Rodgers had bounced between solutions regarding an ethical problem at her company—Champion Marketing. As she put the key into the ignition of her car, she knew that she had to resolve the problem and that she had to do it quickly.

Champion Marketing, Inc.

Champion Marketing, Inc., is headquartered in Lansing, Michigan, with four sales offices located in different regions. It is a large specialty marketing firm that has traditionally sold promotional items to sales representatives. Their products include mainstream items like calendars, pens, pencils, coffee mugs, and watches, and a variety of other items that carry a company logo or salesperson's name, address, and telephone number. For the last five years, Champion has been the most profitable company among the four major specialty marketing firms in the United States.

Venture Sports Products

In January 2002 Champion began an acquisition program. One of the first companies that it purchased was Venture Sports Products. Venture was a financially successful operation responsible for selling most of the giveaway items distributed to fans at collegiate and professional sports events across the nation. The items are purchased by large corporate sponsors who advertise regularly at sporting events. These sponsors are firms who make and sell alcoholic beverages, soft drinks, sporting goods, fast-food items, and automotive products. A typical giveaway item might be a full-color poster of the team's players or a T-shirt with the team's name embossed across the front. The sponsoring firm would place its name in a significant location such as the back of the T-shirt.

Mike McMann founded Venture Sports Products in 1982 in Detroit. Mike had played college football at Michigan State University in Lansing and graduated in 1976. For four years he was a linebacker for the New Orleans Saints, before a serious injury ended his professional career in 1981. Drawing upon his numerous contacts in the collegiate and professional ranks, McMann formed Venture so he could return to his hometown, create a firm with real growth potential, and remain close to the sports world he loved.

From the beginning Venture was successful. As sales grew McMann added more employees. Soon he found himself constantly on the road servicing old customers, discussing promotional items with manufacturers in Japan and Hong Kong, and selling new people on the merits of specialty advertising.

In late 2001 Cecil Osburn, president of Champion Marketing, approached Mike about the possibility of selling his company. He was willing to pay a premium for the company, and he asked McMann to remain as an employee of Champion. When McMann agreed to the sale, he became vice president of Champion Marketing, heading the Venture Sports Product Division.

Cathy Rodgers

Cathy joined the accounting staff at Champion in 1999, following her graduation from Michigan State University. At MSU she had majored in accounting and was a member of the Beta Alpha Psi accounting fraternity. In the summer she worked as a relief teller in a hometown bank. During tax season she worked at a Lansing branch of Quick Tax. The faculty sponsor of the fraternity helped Rodgers land the job in the accounting department at Champion. Rodgers seemed to fit in from the very start. She started in general accounting and was quickly promoted to the managerial accounting level.

In early January 2001, Cecil Osburn called Rodgers into his office. For the next hour he told her about the board of directors' plans to expand the company. A few days later that expansion started with the acquisition of Venture Sports Products. Venture Sports became a new division of Champion, and Rodgers became the management accountant responsible for the new area, reporting to Mike McMann. She was elated. She received a promotion, a sizable pay increase, and the promise that she would become a regional office assistant vice president within three to five years.

The Ethical Quandary

For the first two months Rodgers was exuberant, but the feeling soon faded when Mike McMann arrived on the scene. After just a few weeks she became concerned about McMann's honesty.

The first event occurred when McMann turned in an expense account for a ten-day sales trip to California. Included were the customary receipts for travel, lodging, meals with drinks at expensive restaurants, and sporting events. But Rodgers became troubled when she saw that receipts for a weekend stay for two at a resort in Phoenix were attached to those of the sales trip.

After reviewing the expense report, Rodgers asked McMann about the charges. He became defensive and told her he had worked so hard while in California that he needed the downtime with his wife before starting the sales calls the following week. When pressed further he told her, "The California trip was very productive, as was the trip to the Midwest the following week. The time in Phoenix was my charge-up for the days to follow. It was part of the expense of doing business." Rodgers did not argue further with him because the expense form had the signature of Cecil Osburn, to whom McMann directly reported.

From mid-March until the seminar, McMann seemed to stretch his spending past the limit. He purchased a camera, a cell phone, a VCR, cases of wine, and a variety of other items that clearly seemed to not be a part of ordinary sales expenses. Cecil Osburn had signed each of the expense reports that Rodgers reviewed. In April she again confronted him. This time she was told, "Cecil brought me on board to make this division financially successful. I am doing that and our sales are higher than ever. Besides, he signs off on all my expenses. Seems to me that you would realize I know what is right and wrong, and I'm not about to turn in an expenditure that does not qualify for reimbursement. I'm going to make this division the most profitable in the entire company. I like you, Cathy, and I hope you are on my team and not against me."

Rodgers left that meeting shaken. As the division accountant, she had to enforce the policies and procedures regarding expense reports, review the expense reports, record the expenses, and, in case of discrepancies, check all questionable expenditures to make sure that policies were accurately enforced.

Rodgers's Deliberation

As Rodgers tried to resolve the quandary, she considered several possible factors. Was Cecil Osburn testing her, or did he just not look at the types of expenses on McMann's forms when he approved them? Did McMann really have a special deal established with Osburn? Could he be entering the items after Osburn signed off on the reports? Rodgers felt the real bind of not only having to post the expenses, but also approving them—but she questioned whether they should be approved.

She was hesitant to share her problem with others. Whom should she tell? Jerry Parr, vice president of accounting, chaired a review board of which she and the other divisional accountants were members. This board customarily heard discrepancy issues of this nature. If she talked to one or more of her colleagues she could jeopardize her case if she had to eventually send the issue to the board of review. She knew she could go directly to Osburn and find out if McMann had a special deal or if he was merely overlooking the items listed on the reports.

The Seminar's Impact

The seminar that Rodgers attended was sponsored by the American Institute of Certified Public Accountants (AICPA), of which she was a member. During a session on ethical behavior, the facilitator talked about how an AICPA member had to assume an obligation of self-discipline above and beyond the requirements of laws and regulations. According to the AICPA Principles of the Code of Professional Conduct, Rodgers has a responsibility to her employer and her colleagues to display ethical behavior, even at the sacrifice of personal advantage. There are lots of risks for her. She knows that she could lose not only her future promotion but also her job. Monday morning will arrive too soon. Rodgers has the weekend to decide what she will do.

APPENDIX - B

A Written Analysis of a Formal Case

The following sample represents an effective case analysis. The suspense format is used to determine the actions that Cathy Rodgers should take regarding expense report discrepancies. Before you read this analysis, you should read the case in Appendix A.

Case: Accounting Procedures at Champion Marketing, Inc.

Strategic Issues and Problems

Cathy Rodgers faces a perplexing moral quandary. As the accountant for Venture Sports Division, she is in a position to review expense reports submitted by her boss, Mike McMann. McMann has repeatedly presented expense reports with unreasonable expenses. In addition he has requested reimbursement for items that are clearly against company policy. Rodgers confronted him on the policy discrepancies and left with the impression that her job could be in jeopardy if she pursued the issue further. To make matters more difficult, she believes that McMann's boss, Cecil Osburn, automatically approves the expense reports and expects her to check them. She is not absolutely sure that McMann does not have some kind of special arrangement with Osburn. Because Venture is a new acquisition of Champion and the transition between cultures is still under way, his actions may be anticipated by the president.

It is evident that management has not made it clear to Rodgers how she should proceed when faced with apparent violations of company policy within this new division. She has been left to decide for herself what procedures to follow. Rodgers has to decide her true role. Is it to adjust the accounting practices of a division in order to accommodate the individual wishes of employees, or is it to serve as a professional expert who interprets the activities of the division in an unbiased manner? As a managerial accountant she cannot afford to become the middle person, caught between presenting facts accurately and honestly and pleasing a superior who wants data presented in the most favorable light. Her duty as a professional is to uphold the standards of accounting, and this should help her make decisions concerning her actions.

As a result of attending the seminar, Rodgers is motivated to resolve the quandary. She wishes to maintain her integrity, fulfill her responsibility to the company, and not damage her career.

Analysis and Evaluation

Typically in a corporate environment the board of directors and the CEO endorse a philosophy related to various business practices. The philosophy is then supported with policy statements, which are distributed throughout the organization for all employees to know and follow. These policy statements include what reimbursable expenses are approved. As an accountant Rodgers obviously knows these policies and has applied them in her work. It seems safe to assume that McMann is also familiar with the policies, especially as she has discussed them with him. It is logical that, if McMann had received special approval from Osburn regarding particular expenditures, Osburn would have told Rodgers.

Is McMann wrong to request reimbursement on the expenses? After all, he is an executive with Champion and is helping the company make a profit. The answer to this question is determined at the level at which particular policy is made. If McMann is given authority to establish policy, he is also given authority to change it. The policies in question would be within his authority to change. In this case, however, he is claiming authority not given to him. To the extent that this results in personal gain for McMann, he is in every legal sense stealing from Champion, Inc.

Osburn's role in this situation is critical. He must sign McMann's expense report. This indicates that the company requires a higher-level approval for cash reimbursements. The reason for this policy is to ensure that cash is reimbursed strictly for authorized company expenses. By rubber-stamping McMann's reports, Osburn is an unknowing participant to the deception.

Rodgers has been placed in a delicate situation. Generally it is not the accounting department's responsibility to make judgment calls concerning reimbursement expenses. But because Osburn has not stopped reimbursables that violate corporate policy, she believes she has to double-check the items. Because she is emotionally stressed over this issue, we can assume that she wants to act in an ethical way and to continue working at Champion.

Rodgers's Alternatives

Rodgers has four alternative courses of action for resolving the problem. First, she can do nothing. This will mean going along with McMann and making no issue of the policy violations. This will avoid further confrontations with him that could end her career. However, she will allow a double standard to exist for enforcement of company policy. She will also be ignoring her obligation to the company and to Osburn regarding the safeguarding of company assets. If McMann continues to purchase more disallowed items, she could even be labeled as an accomplice. Rodgers also runs a risk that the expense discrepancies would be discovered later by someone else in the organization. At a minimum her reputation for integrity would be tarnished; at a maximum her job could be in jeopardy. There is even an outside possibility that McMann is getting Osburn to sign the reports and then adding the expensive items to it before submitting it to accounting, thus leaving Osburn unaware of the fraud.

The second alternative is to approach the audit review board and let them hear the case. Taking this action will result not only in identifying McMann's violations of company policy, but also in focusing attention on Osburn for approving expenses contrary to the company policy. While this step would allow Rodgers to fulfill her obligation to the company and maintain her integrity, it could also be very detrimental to her career at Champion. This procedure does not follow the organizational chain of command; it bypasses Osburn, who will probably become upset when his managerial actions are questioned. It is also possible that McMann does have some special arrangement regarding expenses or that Osburn has other reasons for approving Mike's reports. Going around Osburn would result in embarrassment for everyone involved and would not win Rodgers the future support and confidence of him or of those on the review board. Rodgers simply does not have enough information to follow this alternative, and she would be foolish to escalate the matter into a board audit before learning the facts.

The third alternative is to go directly to Osburn and, using McMann's expense report as an example, ask for clarification of company policy. At least three possibilities could result: Osburn could clarify that McMann did have special arrangements for expense claims; he could realize that McMann is using company assets for his personal benefit and that changes are in order; or he could become aware that McMann was following habits from his old company and that new guidelines needed to be issued. While this alternative does follow the chain of command it still places Rodgers in a precarious position if McMann, in fact, does have a special arrangement with Osburn.

The last alternative focuses on policy instead of personality. Without mentioning McMann, Rodgers can ask Osburn if he expects her to rubber stamp all expense reports that he approves or whether he is relying upon her to surface irregularities. If Osburn desires that she approve all reports, she can then request that he send a memo to that effect to everyone in the division. This step would enhance her position without her having to denounce McMann to Osburn. If he expects automatic acceptance of his approvals, she could ask Jerry Parr, vice president of accounting at headquarters, if there are printed guidelines for the proper way to handle a questionable expense that has been approved by management. If guidelines do exist, she should then ask that they be distributed to every division in the company. If guidelines do not exist, she should request that they be established and then distributed to all divisions.

Plan of Action

Rodgers's best alternative is to take the policy approach. This allows her to avoid personalities and to focus on the policy regarding reimbursable expenses. If guidelines do exist, she should ask Parr to distribute those to every division as quickly as possible, along with a memo encouraging employees to refamiliarize themselves with the policy. If guidelines are not available, she could be the catalyst for clarifying necessary policy at Champion. She could even volunteer to serve on a committee to draft the policy statement.

This alternative addresses the policy of reimbursable expenses and will allow all employees in the future to know what is and is not allowed. It will give management and accounting the sufficient data to be able to make conclusions and recommendations that will allow them to uphold accounting principles and resolve future issues correctly. Employees will see that top management has set the tone for the company regarding approved expenditures and the rules of accounting. Sent from top management, this helps establish the attitude of cooperation and professionalism throughout the organization. It should tell all parties that accounting serves an integral role at Champion Marketing, and it is not there to constantly question each expense and raise unnecessary flags.

This procedure will also help Rodgers in future communication with McMann. While he will not appreciate the distribution of the policy, he will have the written statement to refer to when submitting future reports. She can use the statement to justify nonpayment of any items from the recent past. If McMann questions the policy, he should be directed to Parr in the headquarters office for further clarification. Parr, in turn, can direct Rodgers to Osburn for answers to additional questions. With this plan of action, Rodgers's integrity is intact and her job security is maintained.

Index